CELLULOID ADVENTURES

GOOD MOVIES
BAD TIMING

CELLULOID ADVENTURES

Good Movies Bad Timing

Nicholas Anez

Midnight Marquee Press, Inc.
Baltimore, MD 21234

Cover and Interior Design: Susan Svehla

Copyright © 2006, Nicholas Anez

Without limiting the rights under copyright reserved above, no part of this publication may be reproduced, stored in or introduced into a retrieval system, or transmitted, in any form, or by any means (electronic, mechanical, photocopying, recording, or otherwise), without the prior written permission of the copyright owners or the publishers of the book.

ISBN 978-1-887664-71-4
Library of Congress Catalog Card Number 2006937718
Manufactured in the United States of America

First Printing by Midnight Marquee Press, Inc., November 2006

Acknowledgments: Linda J. Walter

For Margaret

Table of Contents

8	Introduction
12	Tarzan and the Lost Classic
62	Bond...James Bond
125	Wyatt Earp on Film
184	Twelve "A" Westerns of the 1950s
214	Twelve "B" Westerns of the 1950s
249	Two Hammer Horror Classics: Dracula Meets the Werewolf
279	Afterword

Introduction

In the summer of 1959, a classic adventure film began its engagement at the Stadium Theater in Woonsocket, Rhode Island. For the opening day's show, there were perhaps a couple of dozen people in the audience. By the third day, there were seven people in the theater for the evening show. The film's engagement ended that evening.

The movie was *Tarzan's Greatest Adventure* and its poor performance was representative of the movie's reception by the public all over the country. At the end of the year, its total North American theatrical rentals amounted to approximately $750,000.

The movie's qualities were, and remain, indisputable. It was conceived as a different kind of Tarzan movie, not one with stampeding elephants, rampaging warriors and battles with man-eating lions. This movie was designed to be a more intimate film, a duel of wits and strength between two powerful antagonists amidst the background of a wild, untamed land. It emerged as a superb movie, filled with suspense, atmosphere, thrills and excitement.

However, for the most part, it was seen as just another Tarzan movie. And this was due primarily to the period in which it was released, a time in which it had virtually little chance of being judged on its own merits. If the movie had been released 15 years earlier, when the series had a large adult following, or 15 years later, when the character was no longer represented by an annual juvenile entry, it would have had a far better chance of receiving the acclaim it deserved.

But it was not. The timing was wrong. It could be called a film out of time, for it was released during the worst possible period for a movie of its kind and quickly relegated to the dustbin of forgotten films.

This general rule applies to all of the films that are the focus of this book. Because of the time in which they were released, they were often critically savaged and were either commercial failures or disappointments, despite their high quality. These movies perhaps would have been judged more fairly and would probably have been more profitable if not for the period in which they were released.

On Her Majesty's Secret Service is another example. When the sixth James Bond movie was released in 1969, it was greeted with derision and ridicule by most critics and, within a few years, it became known as a mistake or an aberration in the series. Judged on its own terms, the movie is the best film of the entire series but, in 1969, it did not attract the huge audiences of the previous Bond films. A decade or more later, when the public had become less resistant to change, not only of the lead actor but also of the style of the films, the movie would have had a far better chance to succeed.

Since the relative failures of the Bond and Tarzan films in question are related to how they were perceived within the entire series, it is important to provide within their respective chapters a history of both series. The relative successes of the films preceding or following the ones that I focus upon have a relationship to those particular films and may also give an indication of why they failed. The failure of the best Tarzan movie cannot be fully analyzed without explaining the success of, for instance, *Tarzan the Ape Man* and *Tarzan and his Mate*. Similarly, the relative failure of the best Bond movie is directly related to the success of the classic Bond movies like *From Russia with Love* and *Goldfinger*. By comparing the concepts of the films and the periods in which they were released, some explanations can be suggested or theorized.

The same year that the best Tarzan film was released, a classic Western was also released. *Warlock* was also a major disappointment at the box office for its studio that had lavished a large amount of money on its production and had signed major talents on both sides of the camera to bring the novel to cinematic life. By the time *Warlock* reached the Park Theater in Woonsocket, it was part of a double feature with another 20th Century Fox commercial failure, *The Sound and the Fury*. *Warlock* was a complex Western that would have been more appreciated if it had not been released during a period in which an unprecedented number of adult Westerns appeared in theaters and on television

Originally, *Warlock* was going to be the subject of an entire chapter, but I found that the film could only be fully understood within the context of how it relates to movies and books about Wyatt Earp, as well as to Earp's actual life. This was helpful in attempting to present as complete a picture as possible on each of the films that are discussed. Including all of the relevant factors pertaining to the more significant films will hopefully provide a better understanding of their reception by critics and the public.

Thus, a summary of Wyatt Earp's life is followed by a brief analysis of major books about him because the images presented in those books have directly influenced the screen images, which have been subject to the prevailing winds of one time period or another. It was also necessary to give a description of all of the films in which that real-life character was featured in order to provide an overview of how he has been depicted in different periods. This will lead to other films within the category of "Wyatt Earp movies" which were also victims of wrong timing (*Hour of the Gun*, *Wyatt Earp*, etc.). But the fates of these films cannot be explained without discussing the films that were successful (*My Darling Clementine*, *Gunfight at the O.K. Corral*, *Tombstone*, etc.).

Similarly, the reception by the public and the critics to *Horror of Dracula* and *The Curse of the Werewolf* can only be fully understood by providing an account of other films that dealt with the subjects and the differences in the environment in which they were

produced. It is only by providing such an overview that the box office performances of the films in question can be explained. *Horror of Dracula* is a far superior motion picture to *Bram Stoker's Dracula* and yet received neither the critical attention nor the public reception of the latter film. *The Curse of the Werewolf* is a classic horror movie but it wasn't even reviewed in most major publications. A few decades later an overblown and pretentious movie like *Wolf* featuring a top director and big name star would be treated with respect and acclaim, yet it is a markedly inferior motion picture.

Concerning the two chapters on the Westerns of the 1950s, the entire decade itself is the important factor so I have attempted to give an overview of the motion picture marketplace at that time by listing representative samples of other Westerns released during the particular year. In the fifties, the major studios churned out Westerns at the rate of several each month. Noting which Westerns attracted audiences may shed some light on why others did not. A brief overview of the history of Westerns is also relevant because the movies that are identified as fifties Westerns were the result of trends of other decades and naturally didn't begin or end with a calendar year.

The degree of recognition and acclaim given to Westerns has always been affected to some degree by the political climate within the film industry. The Westerns of John Ford and Howard Hawks contain far more artistry and intelligence than the overblown anti-Westerns of the nineties that reaped so many awards, and yet Hawks never won an Academy Award and Ford never was awarded one for a Western. In the fifties, the qualities of Westerns made by such directors as Anthony Mann, Delmer Daves and John Sturges were practically taken for granted, but even their lesser films, such as those discussed herein, contain more creativity than the entire body of work of Clint Eastwood. Numerous other less renowned but memorable fifties Westerns, such as *Man Without a Star* and *The Bravados*, appeared in theaters, played their relatively brief engagements and then disappeared into their respective studio's vaults. Hopefully the chapter on A Westerns of the fifties will shine some light on them.

Though B Westerns in the fifties were usually treated like nonentities, many deserved more respect. *No Name on the Bullet* is more stimulating and satisfying than the entire genre of Italian Westerns, with which it has in common a central character that is seemingly immoral and mercenary. *Decision at Sundown* didn't even receive reviews in major publications but is a faultless and haunting depiction of adult frailties and relationships. And even the flawed and uneven *Hannah Lee*, about the conflicts between large ranchers and small homesteaders, is more rewarding than the exorbitantly expensive *Heaven's Gate*, which is about the same subject. These B movies could only have been made in the fifties when the genre was undergoing a transformation. The quality of many of these B Westerns should have received more notice but, because of their status as bottom-of-the-bill features, they received none. The chapter on B Westerns provides some recognition and, in some cases, the acclaim they never received.

In discussing all these relevant movies, I have found that it is helpful to provide not only a summary of the particular film's plot but, when appropriate, some information on its development and production. The often unique and different circumstances that created the particular movie are naturally significant factors relating to the final product. Thus, when a movie is based upon a novel, a summary of the novel itself is also provided since it may be informative to compare the two art forms if only to see what kinds of changes were made during the adaptation process and how these changes may have affected the film's reception.

Providing details of each film's box office performance, as reported in the trade newspaper, *Variety*, will hopefully present a better understanding of the extent of the film's acceptance, or lack of it, by the public. By giving details on its financial earnings and comparing those earnings to more successful films of the year, I have tried to provide a comprehensive overview of the atmosphere in which the movie was released. Showing what types of films were popular during the period in question will hopefully give an idea of the flavor of the period and how movie-going tastes at the time may have impacted upon a particular film's box office performance.

Also included, when appropriate, are samples of critical reviews at the time of the particular film's release, especially when those reviews may have had an impact upon the film's commercial fate. Such criticism will hopefully contribute to a comprehensive understanding of still another factor that contributed to the reception of the films.

However, the factors that were relevant upon a film's release are no longer relevant today. With the passage of time, separated from the period in which it was released, a movie's qualities can be more fully appreciated. Today, years after their release, all of the particular films have to stand on their own. They no longer have the burden of having to open big at the box office, to make huge profits and to please critics. Now they can be judged as movies, pure and simple. Judged now, not by the time in which they were released, each film has a far better chance to entertain, to please and to delight audiences.

In essence, all of these movies have something in common besides being commercial disappointments if not outright box office failures. They are underrated and unappreciated motion pictures. Many of these are good movies, some are great and a few are classics.

These movies may be films released at the wrong place and time, but they are also timeless.

Tarzan and the Lost Classic

In October 1912, the cover of the monthly magazine *The All Story* pictured a half-naked man astride a lion with his arm raised ready to plunge a dagger into the raging beast. On the cover were the words, *Tarzan of the Apes*, and below in smaller letters were the words, *A Romance of the Jungle*.

This was the first appearance of one of the most popular and highly recognizable fictional heroes of all time, Tarzan of the Apes, Lord of the African Jungle, as well as of Greystoke Manor in England. The name of the author, Edgar Rice Burroughs, was unknown since his only previous work, a science fiction story, had been published under a pen name. Under his real name, millions of copies of his books would be sold and Tarzan would be translated into more languages than any other fictional creation. Throughout his career, he would also write numerous science fiction novels as well as Westerns, detective stories and even a few romances. However, Burroughs will always be famous as the creator of Tarzan.

Tarzan of the Apes was an immediate success and, two years later, when it was published in book form, became a literary phenomenon all over the world. The tale of a human raised by animals was not original, since Kipling's *Jungle Book* was very popular and the story of Romulus and Remus was known by almost every school child.

However, the adventures of the infant adopted into a tribe of ferocious apes fascinated readers in an unprecedented manner. The story contained every angle, including adventure, excitement, romance, suspense and just the right amount of enchantment.

In 1888, following a mutiny aboard ship, John and Alice Clayton, Lord and Lady Greystoke of England, are put ashore on the African coast and desperately try to survive. Alice gives birth to their son but later dies and John is subsequently killed by Kerchak, the brutal leader of the tribe of apes. The human baby is saved from Kerchak's wrath by Kala, a female ape who has lost her own baby. The boy, named Tarzan because of his white skin, develops physical prowess and excels in various feats due to his agility and skill.

Upon discovering his parents' cabin, the young Tarzan is able detect the first signs of his humanity, which awakens his noble heritage. Due to his innate curiosity, he slowly teaches himself to read and write from picture books. Though he gradually becomes aware of his human superiority, he also tragically learns that humans are the only animals that kill for pleasure. But he utilizes human weapons and strategy in a battle to the death with Kerchak, which results in his ascendancy to kingship of the apes.

Tarzan is still unable to speak when he comes into contact with a party of castaways, which includes Professor Porter, his daughter Jane, and Tarzan's cousin, Cecil Clayton, who hopes to inherit the title of Lord Greystoke. Tarzan becomes the protector of the party and saves Jane from a predatory ape. Though they cannot communicate, Tarzan and Jane fall in love. The castaways are rescued by men from a French ship but one of the officers, Lieutenant D'Arnot, is left behind. After Tarzan rescues the officer from cannibals, D'Arnot discovers Tarzan's true identity and teaches him to speak. He encourages Tarzan to accompany him to civilization to claim his birthright, but Tarzan's primary interest is finding Jane. After a series of adventures which take him from the jungles of Africa to the forests of Wisconsin, he chooses to return to the place of his birth. This decision, by which he rejects human society, is accomplished through an act of nobility and self-sacrifice that affirms his essential humanity.

Twenty-three more Tarzan books followed, plus two others written expressly for children, and although Burroughs tended to become increasingly repetitious toward the end of the series, the first several are well-written adventure novels. Contrary to popular belief, they are not children's stories. *The All Story* magazine and other magazines that the Tarzan novels initially appeared in (*New Story*, *Blue Book*, etc.) were published for adult consumption and the novels were reviewed in adult sections of newspapers.

Underlying the adventurous narratives of the novels are commentaries on various philosophical subjects that elevate the author and his body of work to a level of respectability that is generally denied him. The mere mention of the name Tarzan practically invites derision and patronization from some academicians, in part because the character first appeared in pulp magazines and later became a popular comic strip. Numerous movies aimed toward juveniles have reinforced this attitude. Ethnic and racial stereotypes in some of the novels have also harmed the author's reputation.

Some indications show evidence that this image is gradually changing. Richard Lupoff's *Edgar Rice Burroughs: Master of Adventure* (Canaveral Press; 1965) was the first serious study of the author's literary output and presents a convincing case for reevaluation of his work. *Tarzan and Tradition: Classical Myth in Popular Society* by Erling Holtsmark (Greenwood Press; 1981) is an invaluable reference work that explores the various philosophical themes that permeate the novels and establishes Tarzan's position as a genuine descendant of the great mythical heroes of classical literature. Also informative are *The Burroughs Cyclopaedia* by Clark Brady (McFarland; 1996), which illustrates the volume and complexity of ideas contained in the author's works and *The Tarzan Novels of Edgar Rice Burroughs* by David Ullery (McFarland; 2001), which gives an indication of the adult themes of the early novels in particular.

The Tarzan films, of which there have been 50 to date, are still generally considered not worthy of serious attention, except for a few, and even these few are treated with condescension because of how the character of Tarzan is depicted. There have been two excellent books about the films, *Tarzan of the Movies* by Gabe Essoe (Citadel;

1968) and *Kings of the Jungle* by David Fury (McFarland; 2001), but these are usually considered by mainstream critics to be works by fans for a select audience.

This condescension is an egregious oversight since, in the midst of some of the most forgettable films in the series, a genuine classic was released. Unrecognized at the time, it remains forgotten and neglected. Although noticed by several discerning critics and a small but enthusiastic audience, the movie didn't have a chance, being sabotaged by an indifferent studio's poor distribution and by a public that had been conditioned through years of juvenile films to expect mediocrity from any movie with the name Tarzan in the title. The fact that this film occurred at that particular time was amazing in view of the steady deterioration in quality that had plagued the series for so many years, a regrettable situation in view of the Ape Man's celebrated film history.

The first Tarzan film, *Tarzan of the Apes*, was released in 1918 by National Film Corporation of America and is an official adaptation of the novel. The original version of the film was over two hours long but only half of the film survives today. It stars Gordon Griffith as the young Tarzan and Elmo Lincoln as the adult Ape Man with Enid Markey as Jane. Although it follows the novel fairly closely for the first half, it creates its own story for the second half. It was a critical and commercial success, being one of the first silent films to gross over a million dollars. During the last year of World War I, known then as The Great War, audiences rushed to see the movie which was perfect escapist fare from a war-ravaged world. Lincoln is a quite impressive Tarzan and is very convincing in the action sequences. The scene in which he places his foot upon the carcass of a lion he has just killed and beats his chest in the victory cry of the bull ape brought cheers from audiences. Even though the cry naturally cannot be heard, it can be vividly imagined because of the realistic ferocity Lincoln displays.

A sequel with Lincoln and Markey, *The Romance of Tarzan*, was hastily produced by National Film Corporation and followed later in the year. Officially based upon the last part of the novel, it made a profit but did not approach the success of the first film because reviews alerted the public to the fact that most of the story takes the Ape Man out of the jungle. Believing Tarzan to have been killed, Jane returns to California. Tarzan follows Jane and subsequently becomes involved with a seductive woman and a duplicitous Greystoke relative. Dressed in evening clothes, Lincoln was not as imposing as he had been in the first film and the broadness of his acting is more evident. However, two years later, *Tarzan of the Apes* and *The Romance of Tarzan* were rereleased on a double bill and again attracted huge audiences.

Burroughs refused to attend the premiere of the first film because he did not approve of the script which implied a happy ending for Tarzan and Jane. And he was incensed over the sequel because he had not realized that two films could be made from his novel. Thorough details on the author's reaction to the first two Tarzan movies and subsequent ones, as well as the complex legal difficulties between the author and film producers, can be found in the biographies, *Edgar Rice Burroughs: The Man Who Created Tarzan* by Irwin Porges (Brigham Young University Press; 1975) and *Tarzan Forever* by John Taliaferro (Scribner; 1999).

Edgar Rice Burroughs

Burroughs also disapproved of Lincoln, who was a muscular man with huge chest and arms. This did not fit the author's description of Tarzan, whom he describes as having a "straight and perfect figure, muscled as the best of the ancient Roman gladiators." In later correspondence, reprinted in the Porges biography, he stated that Tarzan as a movie character "must be the epitome of grace (and) built more like a panther than an elephant," cautioning film producers not to get an actor with over-developed muscles. Of course, he had no idea that, four decades later, another muscular actor would become the ultimate screen Tarzan.

The Revenge of Tarzan (1920) starred a less brawny former fireman, Gene Pollar, in the title role. Produced by Numa Pictures Corporation, which was formed for the express purpose of making a Tarzan movie, this was another source of displeasure for Burroughs. Though officially based upon the second novel *The Return of Tarzan*, the movie had only superficial similarities to its source. Audiences again were not enthusiastic for the story that took Tarzan out of the jungle for long periods, and Pollar's inexperience as an actor is apparent. Karla Schramm plays Jane in this film, which was a moderate commercial success on the strength of the Tarzan name.

Also in 1920, National Film Corporation released *The Son of Tarzan* with P. Dempsey Tabler as the Ape Man and Karla Schramm as Jane. This was the first Tarzan serial and was a pleasant experience for the author since he supervised the development of the script. As a result, the film follows the author's fourth Tarzan novel fairly closely. Actually, Tarzan and Jane are supporting characters since Kamuela Searle plays their son, Korak, whose adventures are the subject of the film. (Contrary to popular belief, Searle did not suffer fatal injuries during production; for full details, see Taliaferro's biography.) The serial was a huge hit at the box office.

Elmo Lincoln returned in the serial, *The Adventures of Tarzan* (1921), released by Numa Pictures and which was loosely based upon the last chapters of the second novel. The story continues from *The Revenge of Tarzan* and avoids the mistake of that film and of *The Romance of Tarzan* by setting most of the story in the jungle and putting Lincoln back in a breechcloth. Sixteen-year-old Louise Lorraine is the youngest actress to play Jane, though she looks older than her years. Burroughs fans were also pleased to see one of the most intriguing characters from the novels, Queen La of the lost city of Opar, on screen for the first time. The scenes in which Tarzan fights a succession of lions are particularly exciting and even impressed Burroughs. Regardless of the author's opinion of Lincoln, audiences identified him with Tarzan and his return to the role made the serial a phenomenal success. This would be Lincoln's last portrayal of the Ape Man.

In general, Burroughs' experiences with Hollywood had left him dissatisfied. He dreamed of seeing his original conception of Tarzan brought faithfully to the screen and he believed that his public shared this dream, particularly since his concurrent novel, *Tarzan the Terrible*, the eighth in the series, was a worldwide best-seller. Of the five Tarzan films made thus far, the only one that merited his approval was *The Son of Tarzan* and, in 1923, he personally edited it into a feature film, though a theatrical release was not reported.

Burroughs had a peripheral hand in the Film Booking Offices production of *Tarzan and the Golden Lion* (1927) and chose former college football star James Pierce for the title role, publicly claiming that Pierce was the closest visualization of his character. He was also pleased with the selection of Dorothy Dunbar to play Jane. The author hoped that his literary Tarzan would be faithfully brought to the screen in this adaptation of his ninth Tarzan novel but, upon viewing the finished film, he was dissatisfied with the results. The action scenes seemed unrealistic and Pierce, though convincing as Lord Greystoke, was not credible as the Ape Man. Though not a commercial failure, grosses were below expectations.

Universal released the next Tarzan film, a serial with Frank Merrill as the Ape Man entitled *Tarzan the Mighty* (1928). This film is technically based upon Burroughs' sixth Tarzan book, *Jungle Tales of Tarzan*, but since that book is a collection of stories about the young Tarzan, there is little if any relation between book and serial. Burroughs was particularly unhappy over the fact that Jane was replaced by another character as the Ape Man's romantic interest. Merrill's physique, however, approximated that of the literary Tarzan and he displayed an athletic agility and authority in the title role that impressed fans of the novels, with his vine-swinging being particularly impressive. The serial was still another commercial hit for the Ape Man.

Frank Merrill returned in a second Universal serial in 1929 called *Tarzan the Tiger*. Based upon Burroughs' fifth novel, *Tarzan and the Jewels of Opar*, this serial at least has some relationship to the novel. The studio apparently heeded the author's complaint since Natalie Kingston, who had played a different love interest in the first film, plays Jane in this one. Also involved in the plot is Queen La, who has her own designs on Tarzan. A good argument could be made for Merrill as the best silent Tarzan. Since his films were released on the eve of the sound breakthrough, his acting is not as expansive as many silent stars and his action scenes are very impressive. Historically, he deserves mention because, since the film was released with limited sound effects, his victory cry is the first time Tarzan's yell is heard.

Despite the varying quality of the silent Tarzan films, they were all financially successful to some degree, particularly in foreign markets where the character was extremely popular. The Ape Man's popularity was also increased by his first appearance in a comic strip in 1929, initially appearing in daily newspapers and later in Sunday newspapers. Unlike most other comic strips, the Tarzan strips were adventurous narratives, which would continue from one day or week to the next. Also unique at the time was the replacement of the usual speech bubble above each character's head with written narratives and dialogue underneath the strip. Hal Foster's version of the Ape Man was particularly pleasing to Burroughs, who felt that it approximated his visualization of his character more than any of the film actors to date. Tarzan's continued popularity in films, books and comic strips ensured that the series would continue into the sound

era. Indeed, the first all-sound adaptation would be the most financially and critically successful Tarzan film to date.

Tarzan the Ape Man, released in 1932, was the first sound Tarzan movie and a major production from MGM. It introduced Olympic swimming champion Johnny Weissmuller in the title role as an inarticulate and illiterate king of the jungle. Burroughs didn't object to this departure from the character's literary origin because his contract with the studio had stipulated that the film could use his characters but not duplicate the plot elements of his novels. Thus, in the film, there is no explanation of Tarzan's birth and Jane Porter of Baltimore, Maryland becomes Jane Parker of London, England. Of less significance, Tarzan's chimpanzee, Nkima, becomes Cheetah. The story about a search for the elephant's graveyard by a safari which includes Jane and her father is basically an original one. Jane, as played by Maureen O'Sullivan, is saved by Tarzan and the romance that follows is charged with erotic tension.

Tarzan the Ape Man was a box office sensation. It was perfect escapist entertainment for Depression-weary audiences who forgot their misery and stood in long lines outside theaters all over the world. The movie still stands today as a great adventure film with action scenes that remain unparalleled. Tarzan's fight with a giant gorilla alone is worth the price of admission, but equally thrilling scenes remain breathtaking. Particularly impressive is the rescue of Tarzan and the safari by the herd of elephants that stampedes through the village of pygmies that has captured Jane and her party. And the scenes of Tarzan swinging through the trees, doubled for Weissmuller by a famous trapeze aerialist, set the standard for all the films that would follow.

Weissmuller's swimming achievements had made him famous and he already had a huge following prior to his first film appearance. Though he had no acting experience, his streamlined athlete's figure projected total credibility as half-savage, half Greek god. Not overly muscular but lean and supple, he presented an appearance of strength and sensitivity. O'Sullivan also endeared herself to the public as Jane, projecting both innocence and sensuality in the role. And Tarzan's yell became one of the most famous sounds in the history of motion pictures. Contrary to reports at the time, the yell was Weissmuller's voice alone and was not mixed with other sounds.

The success of the film resulted in increased popularity of the character of Tarzan and, perhaps because of this, Burroughs publicly expressed his endorsement of Weissmuller and O'Sullivan. Of course, he had no idea at that time that the MGM-Weissmuller conception of Tarzan would prevail for almost three decades. Interestingly, Burroughs by this time had become friendly with Elmo Lincoln, who expressed his disapproval to the author of Weissmuller's interpretation, feeling that it lacked dignity.

The popularity of the movie also gave impetus to the Tarzan radio series, which began in September 1932. Burroughs personally reviewed all of the scripts for the show and cast James Pierce, who was married to his daughter, Joan, in the role of the Ape Man and his daughter as Jane. The premiere of the radio show was held in Hollywood and was attended by Burroughs, James and Joan Pierce and Johnny Weissmuller. The radio show was an instant hit with the public. This had to be gratifying to Burroughs, especially since his recent novels were lacking the originality of his earlier ones and were not selling as well. In fact, the concurrent Burroughs novel, *Tarzan Triumphant*, seemed particularly self-plagiaristic.

Producer Sol Lesser had obtained the rights to make a Tarzan movie from a producer with whom Burroughs had signed a contract several years earlier. To avoid a conflict with MGM, he agreed to postpone his film. After the success of the MGM film, Lesser signed another Olympic swimming champion, Buster Crabbe, to star in *Tarzan the Fearless*, released by Principal Distributing Corporation in 1933. Crabbe portrays Tarzan in a manner similar to Weissmuller's inarticulate Ape Man, though in an infantile and annoying manner. The movie also suffers from inferior production qualities as well as Lesser's decision to release the film as a feature, which would be followed by 10 chapters to complete the story. The unfinished resolution of the feature confused audiences and the film was not particularly successful in the United States though, once again, the Tarzan name attracted audiences in other countries.

Incidentally, while on a European trip publicizing his film, Lesser discovered that a New York company was distributing a new version of the 1920 silent film, *The Son of Tarzan*, which had been converted into a sound film with dubbed dialogue, sound effects and music. He immediately notified Burroughs, who used his legal resources to stop the distribution.

At this time, Lesser may have seemed like a spoiler but he would not always be one.

Johnny Weissmuller and Maureen O'Sullivan in a studio publicity shot to promote the 1932 *Tarzan the Ape Man*.

A behind-the-scenes shot of O'Sullivan and Weissmuller in *Tarzan and His Mate*.

Indeed, his career would be closely linked with Tarzan for almost a quarter of a century and he would be responsible two decades later for choosing an unknown lifeguard to play the Ape Man. This choice would make many Tarzan fans eternally grateful to Lesser.

In 1934, Weissmuller and O'Sullivan returned in MGM's sequel, *Tarzan and His Mate*, another superb adventure movie. In this film, ivory hunters again are in search of the elephant's graveyard and one of them almost succeeds in killing Tarzan. The film alternates between scenes of incredible action and scenes of tender romance with Tarzan and Jane. Among the memorable action scenes are Tarzan's fight with a giant crocodile, Tarzan's riding on the back of a murderous rhinoceros and the entire climactic sequence involving man-eating lions and rampaging elephants. On the romantic side, the underwater swimming scene of Tarzan and Jane cleverly combines sensuality and purity. Only one sour note exists in the movie and that is when Jane issues her own female version of Tarzan's yell. Somehow, it seems more humorous than dramatic. The movie was another worldwide success and solidified in the public's mind the image of Weissmuller and O'Sullivan as Tarzan and Jane.

Extensive details on the production of the first two MGM Tarzan movies can be found in the article "Tarzan: Hollywood's Greatest Jungle Hero" by Rudy Behlmer in the January 1987 issue of *American Cinematographer.*

While Burroughs derived satisfaction from the success of the MGM movies, he still hoped to see his original conception of Tarzan realized on the screen and formed Burroughs-Tarzan Enterprises to produce his own film. The result was released in 1935

as *The New Adventures of Tarzan*, which was available to exhibitors as either a complete feature or a serial. Olympic decathlon champion Herman Brix plays a literate and educated Tarzan who is introduced in a tuxedo. The movie was filmed in Guatemala, the setting of the original story by Burroughs, which provides exotic locations for the story. However, the completed film disappointed the author. By this time, the MGM movies had become the standard by which others were measured and this movie lacks the professionalism of the Weissmuller films. Further, although Brix possessed the physical requirements to make an impressive Ape Man, his inexperience as an actor is frequently evident. The movie did not do well commercially, in part because MGM pressured exhibitors not to show it, though foreign audiences again made it profitable.

The third MGM Tarzan movie to be released was technically the fourth. Originally, Weissmuller and O'Sullivan returned for *The Capture of Tarzan*, which continued the adult approach of the first two films. In this entry, greedy relatives of Jane attempt to swindle her out of her inheritance while an unscrupulous hunter plans to cage Tarzan and exhibit him as a circus attraction. Like the first two films, this one was reportedly filled with incredible action scenes as well as an erotic subtext in which Jane's cousin is attracted to Tarzan who appears to reciprocate, inciting Jane's jealousy. Unfortunately, preview audiences were shocked at some of the film's more terrifying scenes including vampire bats, giant lizards and a brutal ritual prepared for the captured safari members by native warriors.

The official reasons given by studio executives for their dissatisfaction with the movie was that it was devoid of a central plot menace, but this was simply a pretext. The first two movies had been immensely popular because of the exhilarating action

TARZAN ESCAPES   Johnny WEISSMULLER
                  Maureen O'SULLIVAN

scenes as well as the romance between Tarzan and Jane; the villains were almost secondary. MGM was undoubtedly afraid of the newly formed Production Code and various censorious groups which had complained about the sensuality of the first two films. As a result, the studio made the drastic decision to film practically a new movie from a revised script and with a different director, despite the official statement that the existing film would simply be modified.

Tarzan Escapes, released in 1936, contains scenes from the first version, scenes from the previous two films and entirely new scenes. The rewritten script ennobles Jane's relatives, eliminates the sexual triangle as well as the more horrific scenes of the first version filmed and expands the clothing worn by Tarzan and Jane. It also provides an elaborate new treehouse which looks like it was built by an army of architects. In addition, Cheetah's antics are more intrusive and the climactic rescue by the elephant herd, which was excitingly original in the first films, now looks like a cliché. Even Tarzan's yell has lost its freshness due to overuse. The movie is entertaining but lacks the adult appeal of the first two films. But it was very successful financially, the title perhaps being appropriate for audiences looking for escapist fare in the midst of a Depression that seemed to have no end in sight.

In this present age of restored films, a search of MGM vaults might produce an original version of *The Capture of Tarzan*. Unfortunately, since the once-great studio is practically nonexistent at this time and, in view of the numerous changes in management and ownership over the past few decades, such a miracle seems unlikely. Comprehensive information on the production of both versions as well as the next three films in the series

Sequences such as the vampire bat and the new Production Code regulations forced MGM to revise the script and replace the director for the original *The Capture of Tarzan*.

can be found in the second part of Rudy Behlmer's article entitled "Tarzan and MGM: The Rest of the Story" in the February 1987 issue of *American Cinematographer*.

In 1938, Sol Lesser produced *Tarzan's Revenge* with Olympic decathlon champion Glenn Morris in the title role. Released by Principal Distributing Corporation, this is another inferior effort from Lesser with an unconvincing lead actor whose minimal screen time and dialogue practically make his Ape Man a supporting character. The flimsy plot involves a group of big game hunters menaced by a sheik and is cheaply produced and looks like a second-rate programmer. Jane is not in this story, though another romantic interest for the Ape Man is available. The movie was a financial failure.

Also in 1938, Burroughs-Tarzan Enterprises released a second feature, which was edited from the last chapters of their 1935 serial with Herman Brix. Entitled *Tarzan and the Green Goddess*, this film both continues and reworks the story from the first feature version. Burroughs-Tarzan Enterprises produced no additional films after this release. Of some note is the fact that in the Brix films, Tarzan's chimp is called Nkima, as in the novels. Nevertheless, neither this film nor Lesser's second effort had any impact upon the MGM series.

The domesticating of Tarzan continued in 1939 with the release of MGM's *Tarzan Finds a Son!* with Weissmuller and O'Sullivan. In this entry, Tarzan and Jane adopt the son of parents who have been killed in a plane crash. The exclamation point in the title is apparently included to convey to audiences the excitement of the discovery. Eight-year-old John Sheffield plays the son, who is called simply Boy, and the movie is targeted at

a family audience. Sheffield proved to be a likeable screen personality and has always been an underrated child star who probably would have received more recognition if he had played additional roles. He was also an excellent swimmer and his scenes with Weissmuller in and under water are thrilling to watch. In other scenes together, they project genuine warmth which audiences found endearing. He even gives his own juvenile version of Tarzan's yell, which unfortunately further reduced its uniqueness.

Incidentally, O'Sullivan was tiring of her role and, as a result, Jane was supposed to die in this film after receiving a spear in the back while helping Boy to escape from warriors who have captured them. However, as word of the plot twist leaked out, fans all over the country loudly expressed their disapproval. Even Burroughs publicly voiced his objection to having Jane killed. Eventually the studio executives realized that they had underestimated the attachment of millions of fans to the couple and hastily filmed new scenes ensuring Jane's survival. Ironically, almost two decades earlier, Burroughs had also attempted to kill Jane in his seventh novel in the series, *Tarzan the Untamed*, but objections from his editors persuaded him to resurrect her in the concluding pages.

Tarzan's Secret Treasure, released in 1941, proved to be the weakest of the MGM series and indicated that the studio was losing interest in the character. The plot, which involved still more white hunters in search of gold on Tarzan's land, incorporates plot elements as well as extensive familiar footage from the previous films. Sheffield is again on hand as Boy and is even more assured in the role, but his scenes with a native boy whom he befriends place the film further into the juvenile mold. Cheetah is given more screen time and once again the elephants come to the rescue at the end. While the previous film had been aimed at families, this one seemed to target youngsters. Also, the movie was released just after the attack on Pearl Harbor and adult audiences, preoccupied with other matters, did not patronize the film in large numbers.

Tarzan's New York Adventure (1942) took the Ape Man and Jane to New York in search of a kidnapped Boy and the plot seems more of a gimmick than a genuine dramatic device. Weissmuller in a suit and the scenes of Tarzan and Jane arguing in court for custody of Boy are simply not what is expected in a Tarzan movie. Even in the big city, elephants come to the rescue at the end in response to Tarzan's now familiar yell, breaking their chains at the circus owned by Boy's kidnappers. However, the movie has some well-staged action sequences and also includes a memorable romantic embrace between Tarzan and Jane, which is appropriate since this would be O'Sullivan's last appearance in the series. And, of course, the always-present Cheetah was on hand for her share of predictable antics in the big city. Also included in the cast in a small role is Elmo Lincoln, who reportedly was still unhappy with Weissmuller's portrayal of the Ape Man.

While the change of setting may have been publicized as a new challenge for Tarzan, it actually indicated that MGM was running out of ideas for the Ape Man. Furthermore, by the time this movie was released, the United States was at war and grosses for this film as well as the previous film reflected the loss of the foreign markets. As a result of these two factors, MGM ended the series.

Weissmuller and Johnny Sheffield in *Tarzan Finds a Son!*

However, Sol Lesser's fondness for the character had never diminished and he took over the franchise and brought it to RKO along with Weissmuller and Sheffield, who would now be billed as *Johnny* Sheffield. Despite the diminished grosses of the last MGM films, Lesser believed that the character of Tarzan could still be profitable with a fresh approach. In general, the RKO films would be solid, well-produced adventures for the entire family but with enough elements to keep adults entertained. Since the expenses of the films would be lowered to reflect the move to the less prestigious studio, the spectacle of the MGM films would be replaced by the more intimate but hard-hitting action for which RKO was noted. And as an additional cost-saving measure, instead of a herd of elephants racing to save Tarzan, Cheetah would become the rescuer.

Tarzan Triumphs was released in 1943, less than a year after the last MGM film, and is an entertaining, fast-paced adventure that is an improvement over the preceding films in the series. Lesser realized that wartime audiences might respond to a Tarzan who was also at war and commissioned a script which would take the Ape Man into the conflict. As a result, Tarzan is pitted against the Nazis, who have made the mistake of assuming that his isolationism is a sign of weakness. Jane's absence is explained by having her visiting relatives in England, but Boy and Cheetah are around to help in the fight. Fortunately, the action scenes are so plentiful that Cheetah's presence for the children can be tolerated. And the plot element of a lost city in the jungle is straight out of Burroughs. The movie was a big hit at the box office.

Tarzan's Desert Mystery followed later in the year but betrays signs of hasty production and, though it again has Tarzan fighting the Nazis, is less successful. The

Tarzan, Jane, Boy and Cheetah take a bite out of the Big Apple in *Tarzan's New York Adventure*.

plot involves a request from Jane, still in London and now nursing wounded soldiers, asking Tarzan for a malaria serum extracted from a jungle plant. The Ape Man's quest leads him and Boy across the Sahara into a Nazi plot involving a sheik, a wild stallion, a chorus girl and unconvincing battles with giant monsters spliced in from other movies. The script makes the mistake of taking Tarzan out of the jungle and involving him with uninteresting characters, quite unlike the previous film. As a result, the movie's brief running time of 70 minutes seems much longer.

Tarzan and the Amazons, released in 1944, is more successful. Jane returns in this film and is portrayed by Brenda Joyce, who blends into the family without any trouble and who would play the role in five movies. The plot concerns another lost civilization in the jungle, this one ruled by women. While archaeologists want to find the city for its scientific value, an unscrupulous trader plans to plunder it for gold. Tarzan refuses to disclose the location of the city, which leads to tension with both Jane and Boy. However, he doesn't realize that Boy had followed him when he brought a wounded Amazon back to her home. When Boy leads the expedition to the city, Tarzan must again come to the rescue. Atypically, though there are many good action scenes, some of the more memorable scenes are the quiet ones in which the relationship of Tarzan and Boy is strained. The movie was another box office success.

Tarzan and the Leopard Woman followed in 1945 and continued the winning streak of the Ape Man. The story involves a secret cult of leopard-worshippers led by a priestess and a native doctor. The movie is filled with thrilling action sequences, particularly when Tarzan rescues four women who have been captured by the leopard men. Equally involving are the encounters between Tarzan and the priestess, played exotically by Aquanetta. Also creating quite a bit of suspense is the subplot of the priestess' young brother who ingratiates himself with Jane for the purpose of quite literally stealing her heart. The fight between Boy and the brother allows Sheffield to show that he can be just as much a protector of Jane as Tarzan. There isn't a dull moment in this rousing movie.

Tarzan and the Huntress, released in 1947, is a disappointing entry in the series. The storyline about an expeditionary party of trappers who capture animals for zoos seems imitative as does the friction between members of a tribe's royal family. The use of stock footage of animals and the rescue by the herd of elephants at the end also make the movie appear overly derivative, particularly to adults who wanted more dramatic substance in their films after the conflagration of World War II. Johnny Sheffield was now almost 16 years old and made his last appearance as Boy in this movie, having

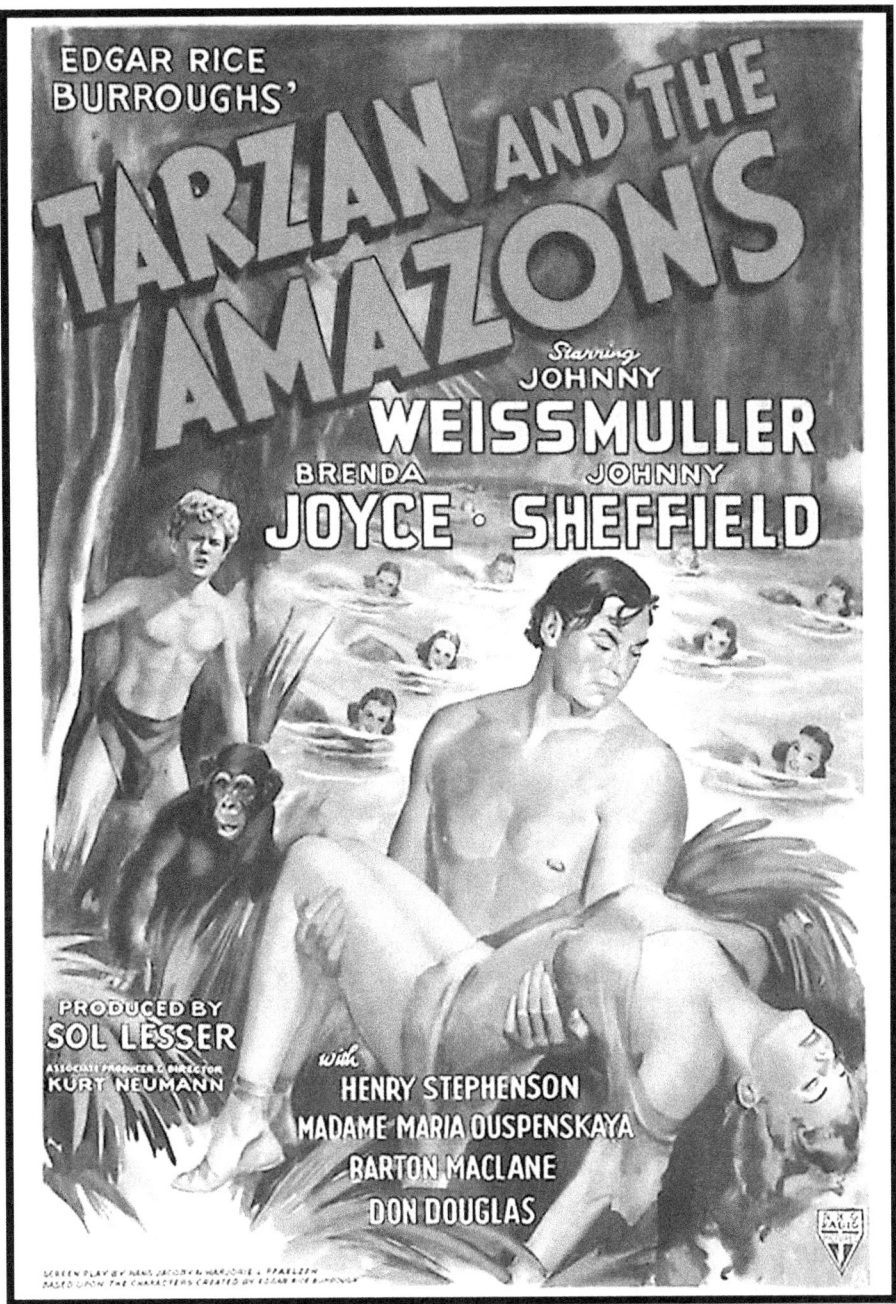

outgrown the role. The sincerity he projected in his role for eight years was a definite asset to the series, something future juvenile actors would not be able to achieve.

Tarzan and the Mermaids, released in 1948, was filmed in Acapulco which, doubles as an island off the coast of Africa. In this entry, Tarzan helps a native girl who is being forced to marry an evil trader. Boy's absence is explained by having him away in

school in England. This is another movie that lacks any appeal for adults, despite an overabundance of music and the lush Acapulco setting, which gives a surreal effect to the film since many of the natives look decidedly Mexican. However, it is important because it would be the last appearance of Weissmuller in the series. After 16 years and 12 films, the screen's most popular Ape Man bade farewell to the role with which he would always be identified.

Weissmuller quickly segued into the role of Jungle Jim in a series of low-budget programmers. After leaving the role in 1955, he was typecast and found that his acting career was over. He then apparently had varying degrees of success in private business ventures. Sadly, his last years were tragic ones. According to his son, Johnny Weissmuller, Jr., as reported in his book, *Tarzan My Father* (ECW Press; 2002), the last of his six wives exploited him and his name, particularly when he was too ill to know what was happening. He died in 1984, but his last years do not take away his glory as an Olympic swimmer or his fame as the screen's most popular Tarzan.

Weissmuller's departure from the Tarzan series would have an impact upon the direction the series would take. The Olympic champion had many adult fans who had aged with him and had continued to see his Tarzan movies because of his presence. Simultaneously, the perception existed that the character of Tarzan was becoming stale. By the late forties, Tarzan already had screen longevity far longer than virtually all other fictional heroes. As a result, the target age of the films had been slowly lowering and the adult content of the RKO movies had already been decreasing in Weissmuller's last two films. And in 1948, the Tarzan comic book became a regular monthly issue and was aimed toward children, lacking the major artists and adult storylines of the newspaper comic strips. In view of these factors, the subsequent actor for the role would, through no fault of his own, star in films that would be aimed toward a lower age group.

After an exhaustive search, Lex Barker was chosen by Lesser to be the new Tarzan. A descendant of Roger Williams, founder of Providence, Rhode Island, Barker had also distinguished himself during World War II, rising to the rank of major and being discharged after being wounded. He had been cast in small roles in several movies but was generally unknown as an actor prior to his casting as Tarzan.

Barker's first film, *Tarzan's Magic Fountain*, was released in 1949. Barker plays the role essentially as Weissmuller had, per Lesser's approach, with Cheetah practically co-starring to make up for the loss of Boy. The tired story, involving a missing aviatrix and a secret fountain of youth, doesn't realize the adult potential of the

Lex Barker

intriguing premise and simply uses it as a fantastic lure for younger audiences. Barker easily assumes the role and proves to be a very athletic and graceful Ape Man. But the juvenile approach of the movie limited the audience to youngsters, who made it a commercial success. Brenda Joyce plays Jane for the last time in this entry and would be replaced by different actresses for the next four films. Though Joyce never received the praise given to O'Sullivan, she brought earnestness to the role and was always an appealing Jane. Elmo Lincoln, incidentally, has a bit part in this movie; this would be his last association with the Ape Man for the screen's first adult Tarzan.

Tarzan and the Slave Girl followed in 1950 and is a slight improvement. But though it has quite a bit of action in it, the plot about Jane and a nurse being kidnapped by a lost tribe is hackneyed. The scenes involving the pit filled with lions are too obviously spliced in from another movie, with Barker doing his best to pretend he is actually facing the animals. Vanessa Brown plays an energetic Jane, who has her own bow and arrow to match Tarzan's. During production of this movie, Edgar Rice Burroughs visited the set and posed for photographs with Barker. By this time, he was probably resigned to the cinematic conception of Tarzan. He could not have known that, within a decade, the literary character that he created so many years earlier would be brilliantly brought to the screen. In March 1950, the author of Tarzan died.

Barker was now accepted as Tarzan by younger fans, with photographs of the actor even appearing on the covers of the Tarzan comic books. However, despite Barker's sincerity in the role, his first two movies had the distinct appearance of rehashed programmers with uninspired direction and tired scripts.

However, Sol Lesser was not ready to give up on the Ape Man and the next film in the series, *Tarzan's Peril* (also known as *Tarzan and the Jungle Queen* in the United

Kingdom), would prove to be Barker's best. Released in 1951, this movie features a good villain, played by George Macready, and a plot which features some adult elements. Macready plays a vicious gunrunner who also nurses a hatred for Tarzan and is not above using Jane, played by Virginia Huston, as a shield to kill his foe. Both direction and script indicate improvement over the previous two films while the acting also reveals more commitment to the roles. The movie would be even better if Cheetah could have been away visiting relatives. This was supposed to be the first Tarzan movie filmed in Africa and in color, but weather problems and other difficulties caused the feature to be filmed in black and white in Hollywood. However, the location photography was used and added some authenticity to the film.

Tarzan's Savage Fury followed in 1952. This film also had potential since the Ape Man's heritage as Lord Greystoke is part of the plot, though the circumstances of his early years are different than the legend. When Tarzan's cousin is murdered, his identity is used by villains as part of a scheme to steal diamonds. The chief villain is given a Russian name, Rokov, probably because of the Cold War between the United States and Russia, or perhaps in response to the House Un-American Activities Committee. A less interesting plot device is the discovery by Tarzan of a white boy whose parents were killed by lions. The character lacks credibility and interferes with the main storyline, but he is obviously included to appeal to juveniles. While Dorothy Hart makes an impression in her sole appearance as Jane, the frequent change of actress for the role didn't seem to have any impact upon youngsters, who were interested in Tarzan and merely tolerated his mate. Lower production qualities are evident in this movie, which reflected RKO's unstable financial state as well as the decreased profits of the previous two films.

This perhaps reflected the unstable state of the film industry in the early fifties. Due to television, movie attendance was at an all-time low and theaters were closing all over the country. The major studios were in financial trouble and were hoping to get audiences back into theaters with adult themes and new technical developments, such as Cinerama, Cinemascope and Three Dimensional movies. RKO was having additional problems due to mismanagement and a dearth of box-office winners. As a result, the studio was attempting to produce movies that would have commercial potential among adults and no longer had interest in a juvenile franchise that seemed outdated, particularly since children were becoming increasingly glued to their television sets.

The Ape Man faced other problems. Despite Lesser's attempts to increase the adult appeal of the last two movies, the Tarzan movies were still perceived as juvenile entertainment. Also, his franchise was contractually bound to a studio that was sinking fast.

Furthermore, the genre of science fiction was attracting many younger audiences who were beginning to view Tarzan as out of date in the new modern age of space ships and invasions from other worlds.

As a result, the budget for *Tarzan and the She-Devil* (1953) was lowered even further and such reduction is evident. In this feeble effort, Tarzan faces off against some greedy ivory hunters who are working for the woman of the title.

The uninspired script foolishly keeps Tarzan a prisoner for a long period while Cheetah runs around looking like even she is bored. The elephant stampede at the end of the movie is so obviously taken from another movie that even juveniles weren't fooled by the grainy footage. Joyce Mackenzie is as competent in her sole effort as Jane as the three previous actresses. This was the first Tarzan film to be released as the lower half of a double bill, a sign that perhaps the series was coming to an end. Barker could certainly detect the poverty look of the production and, for the sake of his career, had no alternative but to leave the role.

Barker starred in numerous non-Tarzan films but nothing of distinction. Frustrated with the course of his career, he went to Europe and achieved enormous success. Being fluent in five languages, he appeared in films all over the world. In Germany, he was especially popular, starring in a series of Westerns and being voted Best Foreign Actor in 1966. He eventually returned to the United States and appeared in various television episodes before dying of a heart attack in 1973.

In the summer of 1953, the deterioration of the series was particularly evident even to youngsters when RKO rereleased nationally a double bill of *Tarzan and the Leopard Woman* and *Tarzan and the Amazons*. The double-feature made a healthy profit for RKO (though not as healthy as the reissue of *King Kong* the year before) and was evidence that the character of Tarzan could still result in strong box office, particularly if there was no production cost. Audiences viewing the double bill could easily detect the differences in quality between the two older movies and the more recent ones. But RKO was in no financial position to pour additional money into the next Tarzan film.

Sol Lesser nevertheless pursued his quest for a new Tarzan and, in a stroke of genius that would not be immediately realized, settled on a former army drill instructor, military policeman, fireman, cowboy and current Las Vegas lifeguard named Gordon Werschkull, who would be renamed Gordon Scott. By this time, public interest in the character was at an all-time low and the series was considered within the film community to be insignificant children's entertainment, not worthy of even the slightest critical consideration. In view of this, the casting of a new Tarzan was barely noticed by anyone other than die-hard fans of the series. No one had any indication that Scott would turn out to be the preeminent screen Tarzan.

Gordon Scott

Scott's first film, *Tarzan's Hidden Jungle*, released in 1955, is even worse than Barker's last film and again played as a supporting feature. Scott's appearance as the Ape Man, played in the Weissmuller-Barker tradition, was greeted with indifference and even youngsters found the movie to be boring with its cheap sets and stock jungle footage. The shabby story, involving unscrupulous hunters invading sacred territory, includes little dramatic substance and less action. The attempt to contemporize Tarzan by involving him with United Nations medical workers who are trying to find cures for native diseases simply doesn't work. Jane is absent from this movie but Cheetah is still present, failing to amuse anyone but the smallest children. The movie quickly disappeared and made no impact at all. It was an embarrassing debut for Scott.

By this time, RKO had not been able to recover from its financial problems and its last days as a studio were already in sight, particularly after its sale in 1955 to the General Teleradio Corporation. Since the studio was facing an uncertain future, it had neither time nor money to spend upon an unprofitable series. Lesser, however, was able to interest MGM in taking another chance on the Ape Man and even investing in a trip to Africa for the first Tarzan movie in color. *Tarzan and the Lost Safari* was released in 1957 as the top half of a double bill and, thanks once again to the studio's publicity machine, was a mild financial success. However, though the plot involving a group of people who survive a plane crash includes some attempts to appeal to adults, the movie is basically children's fare.

Apparently, profits were not large enough to justify another trip to Africa because the next film, *Tarzan's Fight for Life* (1958), was produced by MGM on the studio back lot, though African photography shot for the previous film is utilized. The story involves Tarzan's battle with an evil witch doctor and a search for a serum. After being absent for two movies, Jane returns in this film and is played by Eve Brent. Introduced is a new son for Tarzan called Tantu, played by Ricky Sorensen, whose inclusion signaled the scarcity of ideas for the series. The movie played most dates as a supporting feature and failed commercially. In both this movie and the preceding one, Scott acquits himself competently but, in general, is as bland as the films.

At this time, Lesser attempted to interest network executives in a television series and filmed three half-hour pilots featuring Scott along with Brent and Sorensen from the previous movie. The episodes, dull and unimaginative, failed to interest any potential sponsors and this must have been a factor, along with the failure of the last film and the inability to arrange distribution deals with any studio, in Lesser's decision to sell the rights to Tarzan to producer Sy Weintraub. Unable to draw audiences into theaters and unable to even get on television, Tarzan appeared to be an anachronism, a product of an earlier age, a hero for previous generations. The Tarzan novels could not even find a paperback publisher and only two were available in edited children's editions. Even the Tarzan comic strips had reached a low point with the introduction of speech bubbles. The future indeed looked bleak for the Ape Man. However, under Weintraub's vision, the stage was set for the best Tarzan film of all time.

In a 1965 interview printed in the *London Sunday Times*, Weintraub stated, "In our first movie, we took Tarzan out of the grunt and groan stage and made him literate." However, he modestly oversimplifies the changes in the character of Tarzan, for much more was accomplished than improving his diction.

Weintraub must have realized that Tarzan's potential as a screen hero could be enormous if Burroughs' original conception could be captured on film. An analysis of previous films reveals that Tarzan had not only been stripped of his bestiality but he had also been stripped of his culture as well. The increased emphasis on his domesticity as husband, father and owner of a cute pet had emasculated him. Furthermore, he had become indistinguishable from numerous other jungle heroes, all of whom were imitators of the Ape Man.

Tarzan and Jungle Jim, whom Johnny Weissmuller played in 16 films from 1948 to 1956, as well as in a television series in the mid-fifties, differed only in the amount of clothing they wore. Tarzan, King of the Jungle, and Sheena, Queen of the Jungle, another television series of the fifties, differed only in sex. The Ape Man and Bomba, the Jungle Boy, whom Johnny Sheffield played in 12 movies from 1949 to 1955, were separated only by age. And all of these film series and television episodes seemed to use the same stock jungle footage of giraffes running, crocodiles swimming, rhinos yawning, lions roaring, etc.

In order to return Tarzan films to their former prominence, inferior productions with hackneyed plots made for children could no longer be tolerated. To raise Tarzan to the stature he deserved, his uniqueness had to be emphasized. In essence, Tarzan is a man who lives on the thin edge between civilization and savagery. He lives in the jungle because he prefers the company of beasts to that of humans. He lives by his code of the jungle and, although that code has been modified by his exposure to civilization, it remains his irrevocable law. He has learned the ways of civilization but has rejected them. He is feared and respected by humans and by beasts and rules over all who venture into his domain.

Such a characterization would require the elimination of Tarzan's family. Although Jane had been an important ingredient in the most successful films in the series, marriage had tamed the Ape Man and had become an impediment in later films. Boy or any child substitute would also be excluded, for there was no room in the jungle for an adolescent with growing pains. Being indigenous to the jungle, Cheetah would still be present, not as a comic relief but as a pet and one with limited screen time.

Having established the foundation for a new kind of Tarzan film, Weintraub and his production partner Harvey Hayutin were also intent on hiring actors who would approach their roles with professionalism and sincerity and without any condescension. The principal role of Tarzan was already determined, since Gordon Scott's contract had been acquired along with the rights to the character. While this might have caused some concern to the producers in view of Scott's previous unremarkable performances, the decision to film in Africa with British actors and technicians must have helped to offset any concern. The presence of top-grade personnel who had never before worked on a Tarzan movie would help enormously in creating a new image for the Ape Man.

Signed to play Tarzan's arch-enemy, Slade, was one of England's most respected actors, Anthony Quayle, whose distinguished list of credits included Laurence Olivier's *Hamlet* (1948) and Alfred Hitchcock's *The Wrong Man* (1957). As important a role as Tarzan, Slade is the equal of the Ape Man in cunning and in strength as well as in the force of his hatred for his antagonist. Such a role would require an actor of considerable stature and talent, both of which Quayle possessed in abundance.

Another highly respected actor, Niall MacGinnis, was signed to play Slade's devious henchman Kruger. MacGinnis had distinguished himself for over two decades with notable performances in such films as Olivier's *Henry V* (1945) and Vincente Minnelli's *Lust for Life* (1955). Al Mulock, a fine Canadian character actor, was cast as Dino, a killer whose pensive expression masks a horrible past. A young Scotsman named Sean Connery, whose credits included small roles in unmemorable movies and larger roles in *Another Time, Another Place* (1958) and the still-unreleased Disney film, *Darby O'Gill and the Little People*, was cast as the slow-witted O'Bannion. And Scilla Gabel, who had appeared in several Italian movies, would make her British film debut as Slade's sultry mistress Toni.

Sara Shane, from Hollywood, was signed to play Angie, the female lead. Shane had started her film career with small roles in *Magnificent Obsession* (1954) and *Daddy Long Legs* (1955). Her most important previous role had been a supporting one in *The King and Four Queens* (1956) with Clark Gable. She had not yet achieved public recognition when she was cast as Angie, the hedonistic playgirl whose aerial taunting of the Ape Man plunges her into a totally different and much more deadly game.

To complement the actors, personnel behind the cameras would have the formidable task of creating a cinematic world which would not only have to erase previous screen incarnations from the collective minds of audiences, but would also have to make such a radically new screen conception acceptable and believable. Such a task would require gifted technicians and artists.

John Guillermin, who had started his film career as a writer and who had directed several small British films which had attracted attention, was signed to direct. Guillermin would also co-write the screenplay, based on an original story by Les Crutchfield, with Berne Giler. It was a formidable task, for the script would have to achieve all of Weintraub's intentions for the character of Tarzan and would also have to be an exciting adventure story that could stand on its own. Director of Photography would be Ted Scaife, noted for his excellent work on Carol Reed's *Outcast of the Islands* (1951) and Reed's *A Kid for Two Farthings* (1955). Other production personnel would also be chosen from the highest ranks of their professions.

Once the screenplay was completed, the film crew departed for Africa with little fanfare and no publicity. No one in Hollywood or the British film industry paid much attention to the start of production of another Tarzan movie. Coincidentally, MGM's huge publicity machine was able to obtain notices for its pending remake of *Tarzan the Ape Man*. Since the studio owned the original film, they had the legal right to remake it. While this caused Weintraub and Hayutin some concern, they were powerless to do anything about it. They just remained intent on making a good movie.

When it was released a year later in June 1959, *Tarzan's Greatest Adventure* proved to be exactly what the title promised. Beautifully photographed in stunning

African locations, the film is nonstop excitement, drama, suspense and even includes a hint of romance. Not a moment is wasted as the film begins with a pre-credits raid by Slade and his gang upon a peaceful settlement. The object of the raid is to steal dynamite to be used in a deserted diamond mine, but villagers are alerted and several people are killed. The gripping and fast-moving sequence is just the first indication of the superb screenplay that is tight and compact and includes nothing superfluous.

Following the credits, the Ape Man is introduced simply and dramatically in a manner that immediately alerts the audience that this is a different Tarzan. As the Slade gang travels downstream, Slade looks ahead and suddenly cautions his crew to be quiet, ordering that the engine be turned off. A moment later, his face fills with hatred as a treehouse near the bank of the river comes into view. The boat moves silently by, no one making a sound, the eyes of each gang member upon the tree house. The scene then cuts to the interior of the treehouse as Tarzan, alerted perhaps by the sudden silence or by his own instincts, suddenly awakens and sits up. He rushes out but it is too late to see anything for the boat has rounded the bend. This is without doubt the best introduction to Tarzan in any film. He speaks no dialogue and performs no heroic feat but it is apparent that this Tarzan is a man to fear, a man to respect, a man who has sensed an invasion of his domain and is instantly ready to deal with the intruders.

Gordon Scott and Sara Shane

Upon hearing of the raid from jungle drums, Tarzan hurries to the settlement where he is given details by the police inspector. This Ape Man is in total command of the English language. Angie then arrives, having earlier landed her plane, which is owned by a man for whom Tarzan has no use. Angie appears amused at the sight of Tarzan and unconcerned over the loss of several lives. She likes fun and games and Tarzan doesn't hide his disgust for her. But she does provide important information. On the radio in her plane, she heard the last gasp of a dying man who had recognized his killer. "Slade," she tells the men. Tarzan's expression alters almost imperceptibly as his eyes narrow and his lips tighten. It is obvious that he knows Slade and that he despises him.

If by this time audiences needed any further indication of the fact that this was a new kind of Tarzan movie, they are now completely reassured by the next scene in which Tarzan dismisses Cheetah. Though the chimp had accompanied Tarzan to the settlement, her presence had been almost negligible. Now, Tarzan simply leaves her behind and she will not be seen again.

And thus the manhunt begins. The story unfolds at a breathtaking pace with a startling degree of realism. The film is concise and compact, the dialogue sophisticated and adult. Every scene and every line add to the story and to the characterizations. Not a moment's release exists from the action and tension that builds to a series of brutal confrontations until the final duel between two men whose hatred of one another takes precedence over everything else. Though the famous Tarzan yell had become meaningless through repetition in previous films, it signals in this movie both a prelude to the battle and, more significantly, a victory cry that is probably the most emotionally satisfying moment in the history of Tarzan movies.

The new characterization of Tarzan is ideally conceived. Though Tarzan speaks perfect English, he is a man of few words. He does not initiate conversation but, if asked, will say what he feels, without regard to how his words might affect others. He doesn't conceal his feelings toward others, whether respect or scorn. He is a man who understands humor but does not laugh. He may smile and enjoy taunting a rhino but only to show other denizens of his jungle that he is in control. He does not invite affection or offer it. He needs no one but himself. He is content to stay apart from humans and all of their foibles. The only response he gives to a beautiful playgirl's flirtatiousness is impatience bordering on contempt. He has no time for a frivolous female, though he can later recognize her conversion and respond with respect and perhaps something more.

John Guillermin's fluid direction is perfectly paced and superbly staged. He displays a genuine feeling for action scenes and doesn't waste a moment on extraneous

dialogue or needless devices that unnecessarily prolong the story. The suspense never flags and the film is taut and tight, yet the scenes of intimacy are handled with equal skill. Throughout the film, Guillermin frequently parallels Tarzan and Slade through the use of dissolves and quick cuts that highlight their similarities as well as their differences. This helps immensely to build up the suspense and the anticipation of the battle between the two men that will eventually occur.

The film benefits immensely from the photography of Ted Scaife that magnificently captures the visual grandeur as well as the hidden dangers of Africa. Another asset is the editing of Bert Rule, which keeps the story moving at a rapid pace. Also adding to the feeling of authenticity that pervades the film is the sound recording by Charles Knott and Bob Jones and the art direction of Michael Stringer. There is an excellent score by Douglas Gamley that is completely different from the usual nondescript jungle music associated with most of the previous films.

All of the characters are brought to life by exemplary performances. Anthony Quayle is perfect as the ingenious leader of the killers, his voice projecting assurance and command as he exercises control over his subordinates, his lips tightening at the sight of Tarzan. Slade is a man whose motives initially appear obscure. At one moment, he appears interested only in diamonds but later seems to have little interest in wealth. At one point, he seemingly has little affection for his mistress but later is painfully affected by her loss. There is, however, consistency in his characterization. It soon becomes obvious that he is a man of greed and a man of passion, but he is mostly a man of hatred and it is this hatred that overpowers all other emotions and propels him forward. All facets of this complex man are contained in Quayle's flawless performance.

Sean Connery as O'Bannion

Niall MacGinnis is suitably sneaky and treacherous as Kruger, fright and terror exuding from his eyes as clearly as the sweat on his brow as he anxiously waits for the right moment to betray the man whose anger he fears the most. When that moment arrives, greed gives him the courage he would otherwise lack but the child-like exultation that follows is soon replaced by horror and panic. MacGinnis captures all of these emotions in every detail.

Sean Connery is a cruelly mischievous O'Bannion, displaying dense shock when he realizes that he has misjudged his colleague and later when he fatally underestimates his enemy. Al Mulock's Dino is seemingly emotionless, his face an empty cavern, until he explodes with rage. As Toni, Scilla Gabel projects just the right amount of earthiness that would attract a man like Slade.

In the important role of Angie, Sara Shane gradually and believably changes from a self-indulgent woman to a courageous ally of the Ape Man, willing to risk her life to save his. Shane convincingly portrays growth and maturity with an underlying trace of sadness and regret that is increasingly evident in her expression and tone as the story progresses. It is a very good performance that captures all of the nuances of the character's development.

However, it is the title role that is the most important, the one that would have to hold the entire film together. And Gordon Scott more than rises to the occasion. Whether he is inspired by the immensity of the talent surrounding him or whether his own potential had just been waiting for the right project in which to express itself, Scott realistically and powerfully becomes the Lord of the Jungle. Intelligent and literate, yet brutal and ferocious, Scott brings a degree of conviction and intensity to the role that no other actor had ever attempted, much less realized. Whether he is reacting to the news that his nemesis has "broken man's law" with a subtle expression of combined animosity and satisfaction or whether washing his face in a pool after his kill and gazing with pleasure upon his reflection as proof of his triumph and survival, Scott is totally convincing. It is a superb performance, one that would prove to be the standard by which past and future ones would be judged. It is a Tarzan that can be clearly traced back to his literary origins but one that is modernized by an actor in total command of his craft and with complete understanding of the character he is playing.

Weintraub and Hayutin must have been proud of the results of their first effort. Their vision had been realized with care and integrity. Their investment had paid off, at least creatively and artistically. Now it was time to present the new Tarzan to the critics and the public.

Tarzan's Greatest Adventure was released by Paramount, a studio that had never before produced or distributed a Tarzan movie. It quickly became obvious that studio executives had no idea of the quality of their own film and, considering the manner in which it was released, it is doubtful that they even bothered to view it. In June 1959, Tarzan's Greatest Adventure was released without any publicity to alert the public of the new screen conception of the familiar character. Furthermore, it was released somewhat disgracefully as a supporting feature to a Jerry Lewis movie, Don't Give Up the Ship in the New York City area and as half of a double feature with a horror movie, The Man Who Could Cheat Death, in other cities.

After all of their hard work, Weintraub and Hayutin had to be disappointed by the release of their movie at the bottom of a double bill, placing it in the same category as a cheap B movie. To add insult to injury, the type of movie it supported indicated vast ignorance on the part of Paramount executives. The average Jerry Lewis fan, entering the theater in anticipation of slapstick humor, would not be in the mood for the serious merits of the Tarzan film, nor would the filmgoer attracted by a movie advertised as an exploitation shocker. Studio executives foolishly decided that audiences in search of easy laughs and easy thrills would probably enjoy what they perceived as a juvenile jungle movie about an out-of-date pulp hero.

In New York City, *Tarzan's Greatest Adventure* was given very little space on opening day in advertisements that highlighted the Lewis film. The double bill played for one week at the Paramount Theater before opening wide in neighborhood theaters with the same neglect given to the Tarzan movie. In some advertisements, only the title of the film was listed in small letters below a large picture of Lewis in the midst of a pratfall.

The trade paper, *Variety*, gave the film a generally favorable review, though mostly for the wrong reasons. Evaluating it from a commercial point of view, the reviewer named Ron calls the movie "a knock-'em-down, drag-'em-out jungle yarn which Tarzan fans will eat up." Ignoring the fact that the film could be appreciated by non-Tarzan fans, Ron places too much emphasis on alleged "wholesale violence," condescendingly believing that fans will be satisfied by "exploitable gore." The reviewer also displays a lack of knowledge of the literary Tarzan by writing that the character "is more conversational than Burroughs pictured him." Ron gives deserved praise to the technicians behind the camera, the authentic locales and Quayle and MacGinnis, but he misses the subtlety of Scott's performance by saying that the actor "puts little emotion" into the portrayal.

Reviewing from a more artistic viewpoint, Howard Thompson in *The New York Times* writes that, "They've finally spruced up a Tarzan picture and be rejoicing (that) with a competent cast clustered around the brawny Gordon Scott, here is one entry in a ragged series that moves fast, makes a little sense, and looks more Africa than Paramount." Thompson was obviously astute enough to discern the merits of the film, particularly compared to the main feature, and reviewed it ahead of the Lewis movie, to which he gave a brief negative review.

However, the most perceptive review came from Philip K. Scheuer in *The Los Angeles Times* who was unhesitant in his praise for the movie. "A unique adult tale," Mr. Scheuer writes, adding that "I would single it out for its impact, even brilliance, as cinema-making."

The reviews had no effect on Paramount, which continued to treat the film as an unwanted child, using it as support for more prestigious features or at best something to give to exhibitors until more important films were released. Nevertheless, the movie attracted attention. Tarzan fans loved it, overjoyed at last to see their hero given the respect he deserved. Parents who took their children to see it, or the main feature, were pleasantly surprised. Lovers of good movies, alerted by the excellent reviews, tracked it down and knew something special when they saw it. Word of mouth was beginning to spread, but it was too late. These fans were too few in number and the movie just wasn't around long enough. In most cities, it disappeared after a week.

If Paramount had been even slightly motivated to reward the efforts put into the making of the movie, they could have recognized their mistake and given it another chance in the market. In New York, the movie could have been placed in an uptown theater and given a new ad campaign highlighting some of the glowing reviews. It is quite possible that audiences previously unaware of the movie would then have had an opportunity to see it. In Los Angeles, the Scheuer review alone could have been used to propel a new release in a prestigious location, one perhaps accustomed to playing art films. If only given the respect and attention it deserved, the movie could well have been a commercial success or, at the very least, would have been seen by a much larger and more appreciative audience. But Paramount had neither the interest nor the incentive.

The studio viewed the character of Tarzan as being irrelevant to the current culture. He was a character who may have been popular with a prior generation but was irrelevant in 1959. Studio executives didn't realize, or didn't want to realize, that Weintraub and Company had brought Tarzan back to the mainstream with its new conception and with a film that was sophisticated and modern. Due to the studio's lack of faith and interest, *Tarzan's Greatest Adventure* was a movie dead on arrival.

To add further insult to injury, MGM's remake of *Tarzan the Ape Man* with Dennis Miller in the title role was released several weeks later. Infantile to the point of senselessness, the movie is an offense to the 1932 original and to unwary audiences. It was filmed cheaply on obvious soundstages and incredibly interpolates footage from the original, tinted to approximate the color of the remake, and doesn't even conceal Johnny Weissmuller's face in the crocodile-fight scene from *Tarzan and His Mate*. It also has principal characters wear

Dennis Miller

clothing similar to that worn by the actors in 1950's *King Solomon's Mines,* which allowed scenes from that film to also be used. This pathetic excuse for a movie damaged Weintraub's efforts to bring respectability back to Tarzan.

In *Variety*'s annual Top Films chart for 1959, 82 movies are listed as having achieved a minimum of $1 million in theatrical rentals in the United States and Canada. (Theatrical rentals were the amount of money returned to the studio from exhibitors and were approximately 40% of the domestic gross.) *Tarzan's Greatest Adventure* is an extremely disappointing No. 80, just barely making the list with actual rentals of $750,000 and anticipated rentals of an even million. This is not surprising considering the shoddy distribution it received from Paramount. By comparison, *Ben-Hur*, released at the end of the year, would earn $36 million. Other top grossers were *Some Like It Hot* and *Pillow Talk* at $8 million. *Don't Give Up the Ship*, despite poor reviews, is 17th on the list and is credited with $3.5 million. At least *Tarzan the Ape Man* didn't make the list.

In 1963 *The Los Angeles Times* stated that Weintraub's payment of $3 million for the Tarzan rights would be earned back "within 18 months, out of the green grosses of Tarzan's trip to Africa." In view of the poor U.S. showing, it must be presumed that this profit accrued from foreign grosses, particularly since Tarzan had maintained continued popularity all over the world. This must have been gratifying to Weintraub and perhaps, along with the reviews, encouraged him to try again with the same formula.

The following year, the efforts of Weintraub and Hayutin were rewarded a second time when their next production, *Tarzan the Magnificent*, was released. Following the same tone and style of the first film, this movie was also filmed in Africa and proved to be an excellent follow-up with many of the same ingredients that made the first film so successful. Directed by Robert Day from an astute screenplay by the underrated Berne Giler and Day, this is another adult tale filled with action, thrills and suspense. And the guiding hand of Weintraub is more than evident in the completed film, which emerges as a perfect companion piece to the first effort.

In this entry, Tarzan is pitted against the Bantons, a criminal family whose ruthless murders of two policemen are the latest atrocities in a reign of terror that has all of the territories, inhabitants living in fear. When Tarzan captures the eldest son Coy, the rest of the family is determined to obtain his release and another manhunt ensues, this time with the Ape Man the quarry along with five civilians.

Once more, Tarzan is introduced in a superbly dramatic manner. A police inspector, Coy Banton in tow, is on his way back to the outpost when he is shot to pieces by the family. Seemingly triumphant, Coy and the Bantons race together to reunite in victory but an arrow, appearing out of nowhere, plunges into the chest of one of the brothers. Other arrows strike the trees and the ground, causing the Bantons to flee from their unseen enemy before they can untie Coy. As Coy hastily tries to free himself, a large shadow suddenly looms over him. He looks up. It is Tarzan, and Coy Banton is now a prisoner that his family, minus one, will not again find so easy to free.

Robert Day had started his film career as a cinematographer and eventually started directing television films. His first theatrical film, *The Green Man* (1957), earned him some acclaim as a director of distinction. Competent programmers such as *The Haunted Strangler* and *First Man into Space* followed, but it was with this film that he first made his mark. Action, tension, suspense and characterizations are all perfectly balanced while the narrative moves along briskly and efficiently. As in Guillermin's film, Day uses his camera to frame Tarzan and his adversary in similar positions that highlight their relationship to one another, which heightens the expectancy of the final duel.

Like the first film, this one benefits immensely from the exquisite photography of Ted Scaife and the tight, crisp editing of Bert Rule. Art direction, this time by Ray Sims, and sound reproductions by Buster Ambler and Bob Jones are of superior quality and once more create a sense of naturalism and authenticity. Another terrific score, this time by Ken Jones, perfectly complements the action.

Gordon Scott is once again excellent and commands the screen with his presence. Now completely owning the role, Scott projects magnetism and charisma as well as the extraordinary ability to make viewers believe not only that he is Tarzan but that such a person could actually exist. Of the many fine examples of how Scott perfectly realizes his characterization of the Ape Man, as well as that of the film-

makers and of Burroughs, one scene deserves mention. As Tarzan and Johnny Banton fight violently, Johnny is definitely losing and grabs his rifle. The two men struggle for the weapon with the barrel wavering between them until it fires into Johnny's face, hurling him backward. Tarzan stares down at the body for a moment, an expression of abhorrence on his face, then looks at the rifle and disgustedly throws it away. This Tarzan is accustomed to killing and death but considers human weapons of destruction repugnant. Scott flawlessly conveys these passions.

In the role of Coy Banton, Jock Mahoney might initially seem like an odd choice to inherit the equivalent of Anthony Quayle's role, that of an enemy the equal in strength and ruthlessness as the Lord of the Jungle. Mahoney, one of Hollywood's all-time great stuntmen, had graduated to leading roles in B Westerns. In the early fifties, he was known to children as television's *The Range Rider*, one of Gene Autry's stable of juvenile heroes and, later in the decade, starred in *Yancey Derringer*, a less successful adult series. However, Mahoney makes an excellent foil for Scott as the favorite son of the criminal clan. He is very chilling as the cold killer who has enough charm to coax a frustrated wife into helping him escape and more than enough depravity to leave her to the jaws of a hungry lioness once he no longer has any use for her. By the time of the final duel, he has earned his status as a worthy antagonist for the Ape Man.

As the paternal head of the clan, John Carradine exudes amorality in a finely tuned performance that is bereft of the hamminess of some of his other roles of the period. Despite self-parodies in inferior horror films, Carradine was an actor of considerable skill and was a favorite of John Ford, appearing in nine of the famed director's films. His performance as the sadistically evil Abel Banton in this film restored him to his

legitimate position as one of the screen's great character actors. Returning from the previous film, Al Mulock again is effective in a totally different characterization as Martin Banton, whose increasing disgust with his family leads to an unexpected development. Gary Cockrell, formerly a dancer, is introduced in this film and is equally impressive as Johnny Banton, the youngest son.

Of the members of the group who accompany Tarzan on the dangerous trek, Lionel Jeffries stands out as Ames, a former Army officer whose lies about his service shield his cowardice. As Ames' interior is gradually exposed, Jeffries provides a painfully veracious portrait of a man whose façade is publicly crumbling under the stress of the journey. Betta St. John, who had a supporting role in *Tarzan and the Lost Safari*, is also very good as Fay Ames, whose desperation reaches unbearable proportions during the course of the journey. Earl Cameron as Tate, Alexandra Stewart as Laurie and Charles Tingwell as Conway capably complete the team of civilians and bring depth and sincerity to their roles, thus contributing to the overall impact of the film.

Only some script deficiencies prevent this film from achieving the classic status of its predecessor. The reasons for which the civilians accompany Tarzan over hazardous jungle terrain are somewhat contrived. The manner in which the fallen doctor redeems himself and the resulting romantic implications are a bit trite. Also, the character of Tarzan is slightly softened from the previous film and his savagery is not as pronounced, one result being the absence of the Ape Man's victory cry. On the plus side, Cheetah is nowhere to be seen and is not missed. Despite the few faults, *Tarzan the Magnificent* deserves status as the second-best Tarzan film and is a worthy successor to *Tarzan's Greatest Adventure*.

Paramount, obviously having learned nothing from its previous mistake or perhaps out of pure disinterest, again dumped the film on the market, this time as a supporting feature to another Jerry Lewis film, *The Bellboy*, in some markets and *Under Ten Flags* with Van Heflin as a German naval officer in other markets. Once again, advertising for the film was practically nonexistent with the top feature getting most of the space and attention. As a result, the movie didn't have a chance to gain an audience.

The *Variety* review by Tube was strangely negative. Oddly calling the film "rather glum, unexciting and slow-moving," Tube must have wandered into the wrong screening room. It is also difficult to explain Tube's contention that the producers "have taken the charm and vigor out of the character." Tube apparently didn't realize that Tarzan was never meant to be charming and he seems equally unaware of the character's literary origins when he laments the loss of "the dear departed spirit of Burroughs' character." With such ignorance of the character, it is unsurprising that he is equally unappreciative of Scott's performance, writing that the actor "seems uncomfortable in the role and brings it little more than ample physique."

Other critics were more objective and artistically oriented. Since it was not the main feature, it received only a brief review in *The New York Times* but Eugene Archer stated that the movie "is equally remote (as the Jerry Lewis film) but much more enjoyable. It presents its loin-clothed hero with expert diction, a broad vocabulary and without sign of wife, son or even chimpanzee," adding somewhat patronizingly "it is filmed with juvenile zest." Critic Maurice Gardner, however, was much more perceptive, calling the movie "one of the best Tarzan films to date (and) let's hope that still more films of this exceptionally high calibre are forthcoming."

In *Variety*'s Top Films chart of 1960, 74 films are listed. *Tarzan the Magnificent* is not on the list, failing to achieve minimum theatrical rentals of $1 million. *The Bellboy* is 16th on the list with $3.7 million and *Under Ten Flags* is Number 73 with an even $1 million. Worldwide figures for *Tarzan the Magnificent* are unknown but hopefully foreign grosses helped to justify the film's distinction. Unfortunately, the commercial failure doomed any chances for additional films of such high quality. The artistic peak reached by the two movies would never be attained again.

Sy Weintraub ended his partnership with Harvey Hayutin and took several steps backward for the next Tarzan movie, thereby starting the series on another inevitable decline. Gordon Scott, despite having brought the cinematic Ape Man to stature never before equaled, was replaced as Tarzan by Jock Mahoney, who had just finished desperately trying to kill the character he would now be playing. However, it would be the same character in name only. The new Tarzan would still be articulate and civilized but his bestial side would once again be absent. Mahoney would play a globe-hopping savior, traveling the world to do good deeds, helping innocent victims of shallow villains. Inevitably, one of the victims would be a young boy and if that wasn't a clear enough sign of which familiar direction the Ape Man was headed, then Cheetah would also be back as a supporting star.

Making Tarzan a world-traveler may have sounded good in 1962, the year of the first James Bond film, but it would prove to be as ultimately damaging to him as taming his savagery. The unexplored and uncivilized jungles of the Dark Continent are as much Tarzan's symbolic domain as his geographical home. He is a part of that jungle just as the jungle is part of him. Leaving that home and forsaking his territoriality to be a knight in shining loincloth violates the spirit of the character and damages his very essence.

Commercially, however, Weintraub's decision proved to be a wise one. The producer returned the Ape Man to MGM, which heavily advertised and promoted *Tarzan Goes to India*, released in 1962 as the main feature of a double bill. The plot involves Tarzan being summoned to India to help save a herd of elephants from engineers who are building a dam. Also concerned for the elephants is a boy whom Tarzan befriends. The movie has little appeal for adults, though it earned $1.1 million from younger audiences. *Tarzan's Three Challenges* followed in 1963 and followed the same formula. The Ape Man travels to Thailand to help still another boy, the heir to a kingdom, but the formula apparently was already a bit thin since the film was less successful at the box office, earning an even $1 million. As a result, MGM dropped plans for more Tarzan movies.

Ironically, in addition to Weintraub, many of the personnel responsible for the two superior Scott films were involved with the two Mahoney films. John Guillermin and Robert Day directed, respectively, the two movies while Guillermin co-authored the first one and Day and Berne Giler reteamed to write the script for the second one. This perhaps serves as an illustration of how artistry is often sacrificed for commercialism. This is not to criticize Guillermin, Day or Giler, for they deserve credit for the Scott films. However, the fact remains that the Mahoney films are distinctly juvenile entertainment. While there are attempts to make the villains realistic, the tone of the films invalidates any appeal to adults.

In bookstores, at least, Tarzan was enjoying renewed success. In 1963, Ballantine started reprinting all of the Tarzan novels in paperback and the series soon became a publishing phenomenon. An entire new generation was being introduced to the Tarzan created by Burroughs.

Mahoney, probably due to his age of 44, left the series after his second film. In his two performances as Tarzan, Mahoney is required to be a conventional hero for young audiences. He is as competent as the juvenile hero but is nowhere near as memorable as he was as Coy Banton.

Former professional football player Mike Henry was chosen to be the next Tarzan. By this time, the mid-1960s, secret agents were the rage and Weintraub decided to present a Tarzan that is more Ian Fleming than Burroughs. Arriving in a foreign airport in his tailored suit ready for his next assignment, this ultra-modern Tarzan is as far removed from Burroughs' conception as Weissmuller's portrayal, though in a different direction. As an example of just how hip this Tarzan is, in the 1965 *London Times* interview, Weintraub cites a passage from an upcoming script in which the Jungle Lord is swinging on a vine with a woman in his arms and tells her, "We may be swinging together quite a while." Weintraub also states that this Tarzan "is equally at home in a posh nightclub as in the densest jungle." Furthermore, this Ape Man finds nothing loathsome about human firearms and handles a machine gun and other modern weapons with more than sufficient aptitude.

Such an image, fashionable though it may be, is incongruous for a man who has been raised by apes and has spent his formative years in a jungle without any human contact. Tarzan of the Apes, cultured and refined though he may be as Lord Greystoke, has rejected that society for his jungle domain. Though he may be willing to adjust to civilization as overseer of the Greystoke Estate, he has no desire to become a part of the Swinging Sixties. He has no use for posh nightclubs and doesn't use language for bad puns and double entendres.

Such misguided changes obliterated Tarzan's uniqueness, ironically the same uniqueness that Weintraub and Scott had restored only a few years earlier. These changes placed Tarzan into the same category as numerous other clones of James Bond that were crowding theater and television screens. The Ape Man would once again become indistinguishable from other heroes, only this time, he was the imitator and not the one imitated.

Tarzan and the Valley of Gold, released in 1966, is the only Tarzan film released by American-International, a minor studio that produced movies for teenagers. In this film, Tarzan is summoned to Mexico by an old friend to do battle with an international criminal who has a penchant for explosive devices. The plot also includes a kidnapped boy, played by Manuel Padilla, as well as a pet chimp for Tarzan. Though these elements are obviously included for youngsters, the film also features graphic violence

and sadistic villains designed to appeal to adults. Weintraub was obviously attempting to get away from the juvenile approach of the Mahoney films, but still includes elements that would appeal to children. It is an uneasy combination that doesn't work in this film and wouldn't work in the next two Henry films. The movie didn't make any impression at the box office.

Tarzan and the Great River followed in 1967 and takes the Ape Man to Brazil. The plot is about a tribe of leopard-worshippers who terrorize the jungle. Padilla is around again, though he plays a different character, and Cheetah is back for some silly antics. There is a brutal fight at the end between Tarzan and the native leader, obviously patterned after the climactic fights in the two Scott films, but it seems gratuitous. *Tarzan and the Jungle Boy*, released in 1968, involves the Ape Man's search for the lost boy of the title and a battle between two native warriors. Although filmed in Brazil, the setting is supposed to be Africa, but returning Tarzan to his home didn't bring any freshness to the series. Both of these movies were ironically released by Paramount as main features, which was more respect than the studio had shown the Scott films. Despite the fact that the first two Henry films were directed by Robert Day, all three lack originality and, though designed to appeal to adults as well as children, appealed to no one.

Henry quit the series after three films. Though he had the physical requirements to make a good Tarzan, he couldn't make an impact because his screen conception was similar to other screen heroes of the sixties, except that he wore less clothing. But it wasn't just the Bond films that were being imitated. In one sequence of the second film, the Ape Man initiates an attack upon a group of villains and brutally kills them with a gasoline bomb. The scene doesn't work, not necessarily because Tarzan characteristically only kills men in self-defense, but because it is included in the movie only to emulate the amorality of the anti-heroes of Italian Westerns which were also popular during this time. The Henry movies fail not necessarily because of the change of character of Tarzan, since other screen conceptions including Weissmuller's had also changed his character, but because Tarzan is forced into the mold of other fictional heroes.

Ironically, Edgar Rice Burroughs similarly violated his own code for Tarzan in one of his last novels, *Tarzan and the Foreign Legion*. In that novel, written during World War II but published afterward, Tarzan callously stalks and kills an entire squad of Japanese soldiers. The sequence stands out in the Burroughs canon because the motivation for the action is not within the novel but outside of it due to animosity toward the Japanese during the war. Whether in print or on film, the motivation for Tarzan's killings must be intrinsic to the plot as well as faithful to his distinctive character.

Even before the last two Henry films were released, however, Tarzan was already swinging through living rooms. Wientraub had succeeded where Lesser had failed a decade earlier and, in September 1966, brought Tarzan to the small screen as a prime-time series with Ron Ely in the title role. Incidentally, as publicity for the debut of the series, the NBC network arranged for Johnny Weissmuller, Jock Mahoney and James Pierce to pose with Ely and the resulting photographs received national exposure.

The first several episodes of the series were filmed in Brazil until Weintraub found a permanent location in Mexico. Unfortunately, having been refined to fit the standards of network executives, this Tarzan can no longer be called an Ape Man. Accompanied by Cheetah and Jai, his ever-present young ward played by Manuel Padilla from two of the Henry films, this television Tarzan is so cleansed of his literary and bestial origins that he is practically immaculate. Ely's Tarzan is polite, considerate, uses colloquialisms, preaches sermons, smiles often and laughs voluminously.

Ely, incidentally, continued the tradition begun by Scott and Weintraub of having Tarzan be articulate and eloquent. But the diction and manner of speaking of Ely, Henry and Mahoney, as well as successive actors, betray the origins of the actors and identify them as born in the United States. Linguists can determine with no difficulty what part of the country they are from. Scott, on the other hand, speaks the King's English perfectly, as though he had learned it later in life or as a

Ron Ely, as Tarzan, would swing into living rooms via television.

second language and with no hint of the actor's origins. This is just one more example of why Scott's interpretation of Tarzan has never been equaled.

The series was moderately successful and survived for two seasons on NBC with a summer of repeats on CBS. Incidentally, while the series was on the air, the second and third Henry films were released to theaters. Since Henry was originally set to star in the series, it would have been interesting to see the same actor simultaneously playing a violent version of the character on theater screens and a family-friendly version on small screens. However, Henry had become increasingly dissatisfied with the role and refused to star in the series.

Before the series ended, Weintraub was no longer the owner of the character. In 1967, he sold his production company and the rights to Tarzan to National General Corporation, though he remained as executive vice president. In 1970, NGC released to theaters two features compiled from two-part episodes of the television series. The films, one of which featured Jock Mahoney as the villain, received limited distribution in second-run theaters. Tarzan would not appear in theaters again for over a decade.

Despite his absence from theater screens, however, the year 1972 was a big one for Tarzan. *Tarzan Alive* by Philip Jose Farmer was published by Doubleday. Subtitled *A Definitive Biography of Lord Greystoke*, the book postulates, seriously though facetiously, that Tarzan was a real person and that facts were changed by Burroughs to protect his actual identity. The book is grand fun and a must for all Tarzan fans. In the same year, Watson Guptill published a new full-color hardcover pictorial version of *Tarzan of the Apes*, as drawn by the world-renowned artist, Burne Hogarth, who had replaced Hal Foster in 1936 in the newspaper comic strips. Watson Guptill published a sequel, *Jungle Tales of Tarzan*, in 1976, though in paperback and black and white. And in 1977, Chelsea House published a monumental volume entitled *Burne Hogarth's The Golden Age of Tarzan*, which reprinted Hogarth's original strips as they appeared in the Sunday newspapers. The book sold for $100 and is now a collector's item. Also in 1972, D.C. Comics acquired the rights to Tarzan and started a new series of comic books, which was more polished than the previous series, a trend which would be continued by Marvel Comics in 1977.

The Ape Man did make another appearance of sorts on the small screen, though adults were probably unaware of it. *Tarzan, Lord of the Jungle* was the title of an animated series that was televised on Saturday mornings, beginning in 1976 and, after merging with other heroes, lasted for four seasons. The series featured inferior animation and was naturally oriented toward children. At least it introduced the character to a new generation, who hopefully developed enough interest to trace his origins.

In 1981, Tarzan returned to theaters rather ignominiously. MGM's second remake of *Tarzan the Ape Man* is so incredibly inept that it makes the first remake look good by comparison. This is undoubtedly the worst film in the series, not only because it is shallow and boring but because it wastes the character of Tarzan to showcase the very limited talents of Bo Derek as Jane, who seems to think that giggling, whining and taking her clothes off are acting. Myles O'Keefe as a semblance of Tarzan simply struts around in this mishmash. Since this was produced in the eighties, it pretended to be sexually frank but emerged only as substandard exploitation for substandard audiences. This pathetic excuse for a movie is also a sad testament to the depths to which the once-great studio of MGM had fallen. Fortunately, the Ape Man's dignity was restored only three years later.

In 1984, Warner Bros. released the most ambitious and expensive film in the series entitled *Greystoke: The Legend of Tarzan, Lord of the Apes*. This British production was the first since the 1918 version to be based upon the Burroughs novel and to tell the story of the origin of the Ape Man. Ironically, like the silent version, this film would also follow the book fairly closely for the first half and then deviate in its own direction for the second half, completely changing characterizations and situations.

The son of Lord and Lady Greystoke, John and Alice Clayton, is born in a crude cabin erected after his parents are shipwrecked off the African coast. After his mother dies and his father is killed by the leader of a tribe of apes, the infant is adopted by a female ape who has lost her baby. Raised among the apes, the human child develops proficiency which eventually enables him to become the leader of the tribe of apes. His first contact with other human beings results in the death of his ape-mother and a vicious revenge. When he saves the life of a Belgian explorer, Captain D'Arnot, he learns to speak English and becomes aware of his heritage. Encouraged by D'Arnot, Tarzan accompanies the explorer back to his ancestral home, which in this version is Scotland, where he is lovingly welcomed by his grandfather and meets Jane Porter, a ward of the Greystokes. But the cruelties of civilized society and a tragic reunion with his ape-father result in his rejection of civilization for his return to the jungle.

Christopher Lambert as Tarzan

In this film, Tarzan is more animalistic than human even in civilized society and does not develop his cultural side to any degree. His growth among the apes and his transition from a child who is ostracized because of his different appearance to an adolescent who is slowly developing his ingenuity is developed believably. By the time he becomes an adult, the stage is set for his emergence as leader. But there is a deliberate attempt to downplay any heroics. The action scenes are brief with the killing of his nemesis, the ape-leader, taking place mostly offscreen. This fight to the death should have been shown in all of its graphic detail, particularly since it is followed by a terrific scene in which Tarzan is raised by the apes above their heads as their king.

Andie MacDowell as Jane in *Greystoke*

Once he meets D'Arnot, who becomes his mentor, Tarzan functions as a passive character, reacting to events in a sullen manner. His eventual decision to leave the jungle is due more to separation from D'Arnot than to any desire to discover his human roots. Furthermore, he needs his friend's assistance to accomplish this and is almost helpless once D'Arnot leaves him. He is unable to assimilate into civilized society and is an object of derision or amusement from everyone except his grandfather, who assumes the role of protector vacated by D'Arnot's departure. Indeed, by making Jane a few years older than he is, she becomes another protector. It seems unlikely that this Tarzan who has become king of the apes would be reduced to a figure of awkward dependency. As a result, Tarzan never ascends to a position of dominance which would enable him to tower over the story, thus weakening the character and the film's overall impact.

Greystoke is both a different interpretation as well as a radical revision of the novel. It cleverly contrasts the naturalism of ape society with the hypocrisies of Victorian society and provides distinct portraits of individual apes as well as individual humans. It also captures the author's message of the cruelty of humans who kill for pleasure as opposed to the animals who kill only for food. But it reverses the novel's theme of heredity triumphing over environment by illustrating Tarzan's inability to overcome his bestiality and adjust to human society. The fact that civilization is illustrated as being more barbaric than the jungle is secondary to Tarzan's inability to accept the brutality of humanity, as represented by the British Museum, along with the good, as represented by D'Arnot, his grandfather and Jane.

The movie features excellent performances, including that of Christopher Lambert, who provides an incisive portrayal of a complex man with unique emotional and psychological problems. Andie MacDowell as Jane competently does what is required of her character. The pace of the film is deliberately slow to allow the title character to be more than just a cipher. The script is interesting for its revision of the familiar story, but secondary plot elements, such as the viciousness of the men at the African outpost and the relationship of Tarzan to the apparently mentally handicapped stable hand, are not fully developed. This perhaps is the result of the fact that the director's original three-hour version was cut down to slightly over two hours. The photography is beautiful and the period recreation is credible. There is also an excellent musical score by John Scott.

As a movie, *Greystoke* succeeds as a study of an emotionally tortured man who is helplessly torn between two cultures. As a Tarzan movie, it falls short of expectations not necessarily because it is a different interpretation of the Ape Man but because that interpretation lacks any semblance of heroic or mythic stature. Nevertheless, Edgar Rice Burroughs might have approved simply because the movie succeeds in bringing a degree of artistic respectability to his creation that was denied him during his lifetime. The movie was surprisingly successful at the box office. The fact that a film about a sensitive and vulnerable hero whose conflicts are mostly internal would attract audiences in an era dominated by science fiction spectacles and other epics overburdened with special effects is testament to the enduring power of Tarzan.

Greystoke and *Tarzan's Greatest Adventure* are totally different films in concept, style, story and execution but the fact that they share the same literary origin and feature the same central character invites brief comparison. Lambert's Tarzan is unable to adjust to civilized society and returns to the jungle broken-hearted. Scott's Tarzan, though never venturing out of his jungle domain, makes it clear through his relationships with others that he can adjust anywhere but has no use for the society that Lambert tries desperately to embrace. At the end of *Greystoke*, Lambert's face is masked with sorrow, having lost his human grandfather, his ape-father and the woman he loves. At the end of *Tarzan's Greatest Adventure*, Scott's face is filled with satisfaction, having rid the jungle of his enemy. Lambert returns to the jungle to escape from the emotional pain inflicted upon him by a society he does not understand. Scott has suffered physical pain inflicted upon him by humans but prevails over it. Lambert cannot have the woman or her society and sees no way out of his dilemma but to run away. Scott can have the woman and everything she represents but prefers the wilderness unspoiled by humanity. Lambert, his expression one of defeat, is a small figure who is virtually enveloped by the surrounding foliage of the jungle. Scott, looking down from his high perspective with an expression of triumph on his face, walks back into the jungle—*his* jungle.

In 1989, the Ape Man appeared in his first made-for-television movie entitled *Tarzan in Manhattan,* with Joe Lara in the title role. The story has Tarzan traveling to New York to avenge

Joe Lara, Jan Michael Vincent, Kim Crosby and Tony Curtis in *Tarzan in Manhattan*

the killing of his ape-mother and to rescue a kidnapped Cheetah. Upon his arrival, he meets a wise-cracking taxi driver by the name of Jane Porter, which is only the first indication of the silliness of the movie. The telefilm, which is oriented toward adolescents, contains some lines of dialogue that indicate the screenwriters went back to the source for their characterization of Tarzan. But the characterizations of Jane and her father, who is a private detective, are ill-conceived and the concept is absurd. Having Tarzan decide to stay in New York, presumably as an assistant to the detective, is simply ridiculous. This telefilm was a pilot for a series that thankfully never materialized.

Regrettably, the producers of the telefilm persevered and eventually brought a series entitled *Tarzan* to the small screen. In 1991, Wolf Larsen starred as the Ape Man in this syndicated series which was filmed in Mexico though set in Africa. Like the previous series, this one also sanitized its hero to the point of unrecognition. This Tarzan is a politically correct environmentalist and animal-rights activist who battles villains while befriending a zoologist by the name of Jane who speaks with a French accent. In one episode of this forgettable series, Ron Ely played a villain. The series lasted for one season in the United States and three seasons in foreign markets.

In 1996, the jungle king was the star of his third television series, this one entitled *Tarzan: the Epic Adventures*, with Joe Lara returning in the role of the Ape Man. Jane was absent from this syndicated series though Tarzan was given a faithful sidekick. While Lara was a more convincing Ape Man here than he was in Manhattan, there was little else to recommend it. The series did attempt to please Burroughs fans by featuring characters, including Queen La of Opar, from the novels. But it also included an abundance of fantasy in a misguided attempt by the producers to imitate the success of a series about the mythical Greek hero Hercules. As had already been proven in the '60s, Tarzan is too unique to be an imitation of anyone and the series lasted only one season.

After being absent from theater screens for 14 years, the Ape Man returned in the 1998 Warner Bros. release of *Tarzan and the Lost City*, but perhaps he shouldn't have. In England, Tarzan is about to marry Jane Porter when he is summoned back to Africa by a witch doctor and informed that treasure hunters are spreading mayhem in an effort to find the lost city of Opar. Jane follows him and this leads to tepid action scenes involving a one-dimensional villain and unconvincing men in ape-suits. The dreary plot includes the shaman's inexplicable magical powers and a total absence of logic. Particularly disappointing is Opar, which seems to consist of one deserted pyramid and no sign of Queen La. Casper Van Dien and Jane March are completely uninspired as

Tarzan and Jane in this movie, which disappeared from theaters quickly

In 1999, Disney's animated film entitled *Tarzan* was released. Technically, this is the third film to be officially based upon the novel, following the 1918 silent version and *Greystoke*. Though the more adult elements of the novel are expunged, the film contains mature themes designed to appeal to adults. The infant Tarzan is raised by gorillas and grows up to become leader of the tribe after killing the leopard that killed his parents. His discovery of his parents' treehouse and subsequent contact with other humans, including Jane Porter and her father, leads to his agonizing inner battle to discover his true identity. Since this version of the story is naturally designed to entertain children, it contains many humorous characters and scenes, yet the script's development of the romance and, more specifically, Tarzan's gradual discovery of his human nature maintain interest for adults.

Tarzan uses the novel as an inspiration for still another revision that changes characterizations and themes. Kala survives but endures maternal pain of raising an outsider. Kerchak is transformed from the killer of Lord Greystoke into an initially suspicious but eventually loving ape-father. Tarzan's yell is not a victory cry but a symbol of his coming of age and acceptance of his differences. Jane is given a British accent, which may be homage to the MGM-Weissmuller films. Strangely, the villain is named Jack Clayton, which in the novel is the name of Tarzan's father, the noble and tragic Lord Greystoke, as well as Tarzan's real name. The basic theme of Tarzan's internal conflict between his humanity and his bestiality remains intact, though the resolution is different from the novel. While Burroughs celebrated the superiority of human intelligence over bestiality, the movie dismisses the higher wisdom and superiority of humans in favor of interspecies assimilation and observes the familiar Disney theme of peaceful animals menaced by predatory humans.

Nevertheless, the movie remains a grand adventure that illustrates how the complexities of ideas in the original novel can be interpreted in still another manner. The story is brought vividly to life by the animation, which is filled with lush backdrops and a three-dimensional effect, which makes the film a visual treat. Though this is a Disney animated film, it is not a musical since the songs function mostly as background music. The film was a huge commercial success in a period in which conventional animation was being replaced by computerized animation, thus proving again the continuing attraction of Burroughs' creation.

Disney followed the film with an animated children's television series entitled *Disney's Legend of Tarzan* in 2001. This led to a direct-to-video sequel to the movie entitled *Tarzan and Jane* in 2002, but adults who praised the original movie were disappointed in the video, which contained three episodes from the series held together by Jane's reminiscing about her life with Tarzan on their first anniversary.

In 2003, Tarzan returned to television screens with a fourth ridiculous series, this one again simply titled *Tarzan*. Telecast in prime-time on the WB network, this series certainly had the most ridiculous premise of all the series. It featured former model Travis Fimmel as a youthful Tarzan who is kidnapped from his jungle home and taken to New York by his ruthless billionaire uncle who is also the head of Greystoke Industries. After he escapes from captivity, he comes into contact with a police detective whose name is Jane Porter. In view of this bizarre storyline, it is surprising that the series survived as long as it did, which was about six weeks.

In 2005, Disney released a second direct-to-video animated feature entitled *Tarzan II*, which is a prequel to the 1999 film. As Tarzan enters his childhood, he realizes that he is different than his ape-friends and begins a search for his true identity. Like the previous home video, this is primarily children's entertainment and lacks the themes and sophisticated animation of the movie, but at least is more satisfying than the slapdash *Tarzan and Jane*.

However, Disney is not relegating Tarzan to children's fare. As evidence of the character's enduring appeal to adults as well as children, Disney's adaptation of its theatrical film as a Broadway musical opened in May 2006 to mixed reviews but

Tarzan's Greatest Adventure, French poster

sold-out shows and massive advance ticket sales. Also, Warner Bros. is currently in preproduction on a major Tarzan motion picture to be released in 2007, with advance publicity heralding a return of the character to Edgar Rice Burroughs' original conception. Almost a full century after his debut, Tarzan of the Apes remains extraordinarily popular, which is an achievement of almost unprecedented proportions.

However, the most artistic and exceptional appearance of the Ape Man is generally unknown. Almost a half-century after its release, *Tarzan's Greatest Adventure* remains a lost classic. Prior to the emergence of cable television, when movies from the major studios were telecast on the three networks in prime time, the movie and its companion *Tarzan the Magnificent* were never telecast, though other Paramount movies from the same years often received such exposure. When they did finally appear on television, the films were usually shown on local stations on Saturday afternoons in children's slots, brutally edited and interrupted by numerous commercials. The first positive sign came in the nineties, when the cable network American Movie Classics (before it became the generic and commercial-plagued AMC) telecast the movies several times, often in prime time. More recently, Cinemax presented both movies, though the pay cable network didn't give them prime-time exposure. Nevertheless, such uncut and uninterrupted presentations have earned new fans for both films. To date, regrettably, neither film is available on home video.

However, regardless of the unjust fate of the films, the creative people responsible for them have earned the pride of their achievements. Sy Weintraub and Harvey Hayutin deserve the credit for bringing the Ape Man back to the forefront of modern cinematic heroes where he belongs. Although he later took the Ape Man in different directions, Weintraub will forever be deserving of the gratitude of Tarzan fans and lovers of good movies for his vision, which he brought to fruition despite innumerable obstacles. If not for Weintraub's determination, it is possible that Tarzan would never have reached such cinematic heights.

John Guillermin eventually traveled to Hollywood and enjoyed success with big budget films such as *The Blue Max* (1966), the underrated *The Bridge at Remagen* (1969), *The Towering Inferno* (1974) and *Death On the Nile* (1978). He also directed the abysmal *King Kong* in 1976 and returned to Africa for the equally dreadful *Sheena* in 1984. Robert Day continued his career with such films as the Hammer remake of *She* in 1965 and also emigrated to Hollywood, subsequently working mostly in television.

As for Gordon Scott, his contributions to the films and his commendable talents remain generally unacknowledged, except by discerning genre authors and film enthusiasts. Gabe Essoe refers to Scott as "the best screen Tarzan." Essoe further states that the success of the two films is due "greatly to Weintraub's vision but in no lesser way to Scott's excellent characterization." Jeff Rovin in *The Fabulous Fantasy Films* (A.S. Barnes; 1977) calls Scott "the finest of all screen Tarzans." In *Lost Films of the Fifties* (Citadel; 1988), Douglas Brode acknowledges Scott's talents and calls *Tarzan's Greatest Adventure* "not so much a superior series entry as a remarkably well paced and stunningly atmospheric suspense story."

Following his exit as Tarzan, Scott starred in many European sword-and-sandal movies, playing such heroes as Maciste, Goliath and Samson. He played Remus opposite Steve Reeves' Romulus in *Duel of the Titans* in 1962. (This dubbed Italian pseudo-epic was released by Paramount and, when it played the San Diego area, the studio rereleased *Tarzan the Magnificent* as the supporting feature. During a Saturday evening showing, after grimly sitting through the main feature which looked like numerous other muscleman movies, the appreciative and surprised audience actually applauded at the end of the Tarzan movie. This was a clear indication of the success the two Scott films could have achieved if they had been given the care they deserved.) Scott also played the title role in *Buffalo Bill, Hero of the Far West* (1964), one of the first European Westerns to receive international distribution. In 1965, he starred as Hercules in a one-hour television pilot shown on ABC-TV, but interest in the Greek hero had waned and a series did not develop. In 1966, he starred with Joseph Cotton in *The Tramplers*, a Western filmed in Argentina. Jeff Rovin writes that Scott "gave his portrayals class (and) watching him, one is aware of the actor's desire to do more than show off his build."

In 1984, when *Greystoke* was released, Gordon Scott appeared in Los Angeles with Jock Mahoney and Dennis Miller as members of the PTA or Past Tarzans Association. As the three reminisced, Scott humbly did not mention his accomplishments and only expressed praise for the new film and its star. He has since appeared in the Hollywood Collectors Show conventions and has been an extremely popular attraction, signing autographs and repeatedly displaying characteristic modesty.

Undoubtedly, fans all over the world who recognize Scott as the definitive screen Tarzan will always be aware of his achievements. To all of them, Gordon Scott is the most magnificent Tarzan and *Tarzan's Greatest Adventure* is Tarzan's greatest film.

Tarzan's Greatest Adventure [Paramount/1959]
CREDITS: Presentation: Sy Weintraub and Harvey Hayutin; Producer: Sy Weintraub; Director: John Guillermin; Assistant Director: Peter Bolton; Screenplay: John Guillerman and Berne Giler, based upon an original story by Les Crutchfield; Director of Photography: Ted Scaife; Additional Photography: Skeets Kelly; Editor: Bert Rule; Art Director: Michael Stringer; Sound Recording: Charles Knott and Bob Jones; Music: Douglas Gamley.
CAST: Gordon Scott (Tarzan); Anthony Quayle (Slade); Sara Shane (Angie); Niall MacGinnis (Kruger); Sean Connery (O'Bannion); Al Mulock (Dino); Scilla Gabel (Toni)

Tarzan the Magnificent [Paramount/1960]
CREDITS: Presentation: Sy Weintraub and Harvey Hayutin; Producer: Sy Weintraub; Director: Robert Day; Assistant Director: Clive Reed; Screenplay: Robert Day and Berne Giler; Director of Photography: Ted Scaife; Additional Photography: Jack Mills; Editor: Bert Rule; Art Director: Ray Simm; Sound Recording: Buster Amuil and Bob Jones; Music: Ken Jones
CAST: Gordon Scott (Tarzan); Jock Mahoney (Coy Banton); Betta St. John (Fay Ames); John Carradine (Abel Banton); Lionel Jeffries (Ames); Alexandra Stewart (Laurie); Earl Cameron (Tate); Charles Tingwell (Conway); Al Mulock (Martin Banton); Gary Cockrell (Johnny Banton); John Sullivan (Inspector Winters); Ron MacDonnell (Ethan Banton); Harry Baird (Warrior Leader); Christopher Carlos (Native Chief); Ewen Solon (Dexter); Jacqueline Evans (Mrs. Dexter); Thomas Duggan (Frye); Peter Howell (Dr. Blake); John Harrison (N'Gome); George Taylor (Capt. Hayes)

The Tarzan Films and Their Actors

1) *Tarzan of the Apes* (1918) Elmo Lincoln
2) *The Romance of Tarzan* (1918) Elmo Lincoln
3) *The Revenge of Tarzan* (1920) Gene Pollar
4) *The Son of Tarzan* (1920) P. Dempsey Tabler (Serial)
5) *The Adventures of Tarzan* (1921) Elmo Lincoln (Serial)
6) *Tarzan and the Golden Lion* (1927) James Pierce
7) *Tarzan the Mighty* (1928) Frank Merrill (Serial)
8) *Tarzan the Tiger* (1929) Frank Merrill (Serial)
9) *Tarzan the Ape Man* (1932) Johnny Weissmuller
10) *Tarzan the Fearless* (1933) Buster Crabbe (Feature and Serial)
11) *Tarzan and His Mate* (1934) Johnny Weissmuller
12) *The New Adventures of Tarzan* (1935) Herman Brix (Feature and Serial)
13) *Tarzan Escapes* (1936) Johnny Weissmuller
14) *Tarzan's Revenge* (1938) Glenn Morris
15) *Tarzan and the Green Goddess* (1938) Herman Brix (2nd feature from 1936 Serial)
16) *Tarzan Finds a Son!* (1939) Johnny Weissmuller
17) *Tarzan's Secret Treasure* (1941) Johnny Weissmuller
18) *Tarzan's New York Adventure* (1942) Johnny Weissmuller
19) *Tarzan Triumphs* (1943) Johnny Weissmuller
20) *Tarzan's Desert Mystery* (1943) Johnny Weissmuller
21) *Tarzan and the Amazons* (1944) Johnny Weissmuller
22) *Tarzan and the Leopard Woman* (1945) Johnny Weissmuller
23) *Tarzan and the Huntress* (1947) Johnny Weissmuller
24) *Tarzan and the Mermaids* (1948) Johnny Weissmuller
25) *Tarzan's Magic Fountain* (1949) Lex Barker
26) *Tarzan and the Slave Girl* (1950) Lex Barker
27) *Tarzan's Peril* (1951) Lex Barker
28) *Tarzan's Savage Fury* (1952) Lex Barker
29) *Tarzan and the She-Devil* (1953) Lex Barker

30) *Tarzan's Hidden Jungle* (1955) Gordon Scott
31) *Tarzan and the Lost Safari* (1957) Gordon Scott
32) *Tarzan's Fight for Life* (1958) Gordon Scott
33) *Tarzan and the Trappers* (1958) Gordon Scott (Originally three television pilots; not shown in theaters)
34) *Tarzan's Greatest Adventure* (1959) Gordon Scott
35) *Tarzan the Ape Man* (1959) Dennis Miller
36) *Tarzan the Magnificent* (1960) Gordon Scott
37) *Tarzan Goes to India* (1962) Jock Mahoney
38) *Tarzan's Three Challenges* (1963) Jock Mahoney
39) *Tarzan and the Valley of Gold* (1966) Mike Henry
40) *Tarzan and the Great River* (1967) Mike Henry
41) *Tarzan and the Jungle Boy* (1968) Mike Henry
42) *Tarzan's Deadly Silence* (1970) Ron Ely (Originally two television episodes from 1966)
43) *Tarzan's Jungle Rebellion* (1970) Ron Ely (Originally two television episodes from 1967)
44) *Tarzan the Ape Man* (1981) Myles O'Keefe
45) *Greystoke: the Legend of Tarzan, Lord of the Apes* (1984) Christopher Lambert
46) *Tarzan in Manhattan* (1989) Joe Lara (Television movie)
47) *Tarzan and the Lost City* (1998) Casper Van Dien
48) *Tarzan* (1999) (Animated)
49) *Tarzan and Jane* (2002) (Animated; direct to home video)
50) *Tarzan II* (2005) (Animated; direct to home video)

The Tarzan Novels by Edgar Rice Burroughs

1) *Tarzan of the Apes* (1914)
2) *The Return of Tarzan* (1915)
3) *The Beasts of Tarzan* (1916)
4) *The Son of Tarzan* (1917)
5) *Tarzan and the Jewels of Opar* (1918)
6) *Jungle Tales of Tarzan* (1919)
7) *Tarzan the Untamed* (1920)
8) *Tarzan the Terrible* (1921)
9) *Tarzan and the Golden Lion* (1923)
10) *Tarzan and the Ant Men* (1924)
11) *The Tarzan Twins* (1927; Children's book)
12) *Tarzan, Lord of the Jungle* (1928)
13) *Tarzan and the Lost Empire* (1929)
14) *Tarzan at the Earth's Core* (1930)
15) *Tarzan the Invincible* (1931)
16) *Tarzan Triumphant* (1932)
17) *Tarzan and the City of Gold* (1933)
18) *Tarzan and the Lion Man* (1934)
19) *Tarzan and the Leopard Men* (1935)
20) *Tarzan and the Tarzan Twins* with Jad-Bal-Ja, the Golden Lion (1936; Children's book)
21) *Tarzan's Quest* (1936)
22) *Tarzan and the Forbidden City* (1938)
23) *Tarzan the Magnificent* (1939)
24) *Tarzan and the Foreign Legion* (Written in 1944; published in 1947)
25) *Tarzan and the Madman* (Written in 1940; published in 1964)
26) *Tarzan and the Castaways* (Three stories originally published in magazines in 1940 and 1941; published as a book in 1964)
27) *Tarzan the Lost Adventure* (Unfinished novel; completed by Joe R. Lansdale and published in 1996)

Bond...James Bond

James Bond of the British Secret Service, also known as 007, is undoubtedly one of the most popular characters in the history of motion pictures. To date, the film series which began in 1962 includes 20 official films as well as two nonofficial ones. It is the most successful film franchise of all time and has grossed over $3 billion dollars worldwide. However, while the quality of the films has varied, five genuine classics resulted and, of those five, one stands out even among that select group.

Ian Fleming

The James Bond movies have presented a fantasy hero who is able to surmount overwhelming obstacles, defeat villains, seduce women and do it all with panache. The five classics accomplish this in a style that is consistently entertaining, occasionally shocking, quite exciting and thoroughly enjoyable. But as in the novels upon which they are based, brutal realism often unexpectedly pierces the thin shell of the fantasy. Bond may survive his perilous adventures but others, including those who are close to him, are not always so fortunate. The filmgoer learns, as the reader does, that it is unwise to live in a fantasy, for too often the dream turns into a nightmare.

The origin of the films is the series of novels written by Ian Fleming, which are primarily escapist adventures. Fleming's James Bond is the perfect fantasy hero, not only because he succeeds where most would fail, but because he is both larger than life yet still quite believable. The novels have always been underrated by many critics who put them in the same category as pulp novels. In fact, the novels are extremely well-written and can be quite different in tone and style. Some are crisp thrillers, while others are fantastic adventures and at least one is a romantic tragedy. Though the balance between reality and fantasy is maintained through the series, different novels have different proportions of each. And as the plots become more fantastic, Bond becomes more human. The cold and ruthless Bond of the first novel gradually becomes more vulnerable until emotional suffering cripples and almost destroys him.

Bond's tragic odyssey throughout the series places his status above the level of heroes of other series with which he was originally compared, such as Mickey Spillane's Mike Hammer of the United States or H.C. McNeile's Bulldog Drummond of Britain. Bond is best placed alongside more prestigious heroes such as Raymond Chandler's Philip Marlowe and Ross Macdonald's Lew Archer. Beneath the exciting adventures, Fleming suggests that Bond is more complex and more neurotic than most genre heroes. As the series progresses, the fantasy of James Bond cannot escape the darker realities of the actual world. Through his daring adventures, James Bond rises from anonymity to public celebrity upon his assumed death, but in actuality Bond is trapped within the depths of private despair, his mind traumatized and his will to live extinguished.

The pompous attitude of the anti-Fleming critics has since been punctured by insightful studies of the novels. *007 James Bond: A Report* by O.F. Snelling (Signet; 1964) was one of the first and is still enlightening. *The James Bond Dossier* by Kingsley Amis (Jonathan Cape; 1965) remains a very perceptive analysis of the talent behind the novels. *The James Bond Bedside Companion* by Raymond Benson (Dodd, Mead and Company; 1984) provides an excellent overview of the character of Bond, the author, the novels and the films. The two best

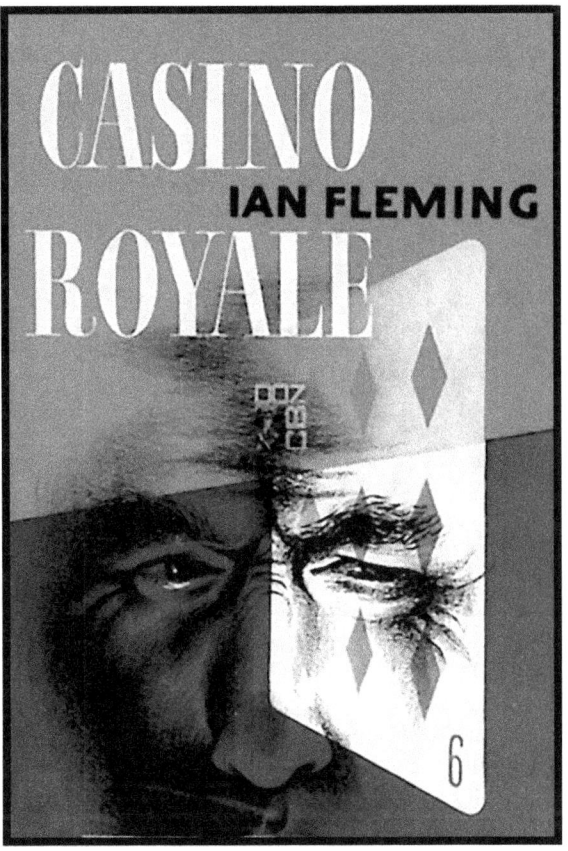

Casino Royale, U.S. First Edition

biographies of the author are *The Life of Ian Fleming* by John Pearson (Jonathan Cape; 1966) and *Ian Fleming: The Man Behind James Bond* by Andrew Lycett (Weidenfeld & Nicholson; 1995).

A detailed examination of the first seven Bond films can be found in *James Bond in the Cinema* by John Brosnan (Tantivy Press; 1972) with a second edition published in 1981 covering the films made up until that date. *The James Bond Films* by Steven Jay Rubin (Arlington House; 1981) is another fine history of the making of the first 12 movies. *License to Thrill* subtitled *A Cultural History of the James Bond Films* by James Chapman (Columbia University Press; 2000) is an excellent analytical study of the films and their reflection of, as well their impact upon, entertainment and world culture.

Also definitely worthy of mention is *James Bond: The Authorized Biography of 007* by John Pearson (William Morrow & Company; 1973). This entertaining book postulates that Bond was a real person whose adventures were fictionalized by Fleming. (Edgar Rice Burroughs' Tarzan had been the subject of a similar "biography" by Philip Jose Farmer the previous year.)

The journey to bring Bond to the screen was not an easy one. Fleming wrote 12 James Bond novels and two collections of short stories. The first novel, *Casino*

Barry Nelson and Linda Christian in *Climax Mystery Theater* version of *Casino Royale*

Royale, was published in 1953 and introduced the character of Bond to the world. The novel was very successful in Britain but barely made a ripple in the States, despite a title change and a lurid cover in its paperback publication to make it appear to be a Spillane-type potboiler. *Climax Mystery Theater* broadcast an adaptation of *Casino Royale* in 1954 on CBS-TV. The first actor to play Bond was Barry Nelson in the 50-minute episode, which is an average thriller, hampered by the limitations of time constraint and live television. Its major interest today is due to the fact that it is the first dramatization of Bond and would be forgotten if not for this fact.

The future looked more promising for Bond when Fleming sold the rights to the novel to producer Gregory Ratoff in 1955, but attempts to make a film version were unsuccessful and Ratoff eventually sold the rights to Charles K. Feldman. Further attempts to bring Bond to the screen over the next several years were beset with delays and difficulties, despite the continued successes of additional Bond novels. In 1958, another attempt to bring Bond to the screen seemed more promising when Fleming, producer-director Kevin McClory and writer Jack Whittingham collaborated on an original story, which would serve as the basis for a James Bond movie, but, once again, delays occurred. This story was later adapted by Fleming as the novel *Thunderball*, which would lead to a legal dispute between the author and McClory.

Then, in 1960, Fleming met producer Harry Saltzman who secured an option on all of the Bond novels, except for *Casino Royale* and *Thunderball*. Equally significant, in 1961, President John F. Kennedy listed a Bond novel, *From Russia with Love,* as one of his favorite books. Sales of the series dramatically rose in the United States after this revelation. That same year, Saltzman formed a partnership with Albert R. Broccoli and formed Eon Productions and the two men shortly thereafter signed a six-picture deal with United Artists. James Bond was finally set to appear on the big screen.

Eon's first production, *Dr. No*, was based upon Fleming's sixth novel, which had been published in 1958. This decision by Eon to begin the film series out of sequence is understandable. Since they didn't own *Casino Royale*, they couldn't film the first Bond novel. And the sixth novel is an exciting, action-filled story with a great villain. Since the continuation of the series would depend upon the success of the first film, Eon had to pick a novel that would have a good chance of being a commercial hit. Also, while references would often be made to previous novels, the stories up until the sixth were independent of one another. In view of this, Eon's decision was probably a wise one, particularly since the second novel, *Live and Let Die*, with its racial angle, might be a touchy subject for the early 1960s.

Dr. No was filmed on a relatively small budget and premiered in England in October 1962 but didn't open in the States until May 1963. Although the movie was successful in Britain, United Artists didn't seem to have too much faith in the movie's potential in the States. In the San Diego area, it did not rate a prestige theater but instead opened in a downtown house as the top half of a double bill. The film's advertisements invited audiences to "meet the most extraordinary gentleman spy in all fiction" adding that this was "the first James Bond film adventure." The name James Bond probably meant little to most of the patrons since readers of the novels still numbered only a small segment of the film-going public.

For the first evening show, the theater was about one-third full and a dismal co-feature put the audience in a foul mood. When the main feature began, the disgruntled patrons exuded little enthusiasm. On the screen, a series of circles darted across the screen until one circle was left, and as it grew larger, the audience seemed to be looking down a gun barrel at a man who was walking quite purposefully and, then suddenly, he pulled a gun and fired directly at the screen, causing a wave of red liquid to wash down the screen. It was an effective way to grab the attention of the audience. Less noise was heard in the theater as the title of the movie appeared.

The odd-sounding title was followed by the unfamiliar name of the lead actor, someone named Sean Connery. In England, Connery was fairly well known due to his television work and several low-budget films, but in America, his name did not ring any bells. A few years earlier, he had received a big break with a major role in a Lana Turner movie, *Another Time, Another Place*, but the movie had bombed. In 1959, in

Sean Connery in *Dr. No*

addition to playing a villain in *Tarzan's Greatest Adventure*, he had starred in Disney's *Darby O'Gill and the Little People,* but this also proved also to be a commercial disappointment. In view of these setbacks, Connery's name simply had no power at the box office.

More unrecognizable names followed, except possibly for co-star Jack Lord who had just finished a year on television in the unsuccessful series, *Stony Burke*. If there were any film buffs in the audience, they may have recognized the name of the lead writer, Richard Maibaum, who started writing screenplays in 1936 and whose career included the scripts of such fine films as *The Big Clock* (1948), *Ransom* (1956) and *Bigger Than Life* (1956).

Dr. No opens in Jamaica with the brutal murders of a British agent and his secretary. Though not explicit, especially by later standards, the scenes contain a sudden violence that demands the attention of the audience. The film then shifts to a London casino where a man, his face not shown, plays at a table. When his name is asked, his face is revealed and he replies, "Bond. James Bond," the words accompanied by an arresting musical theme. In that downtown San Diego audience, it is highly unlikely that anyone had the slightest inkling that the name, the theme and the actor would within a year and a half achieve almost unprecedented popularity.

However, it was apparent from that moment who the star of the movie was. The ruggedly handsome actor with the Scottish accent seemed to radiate screen charisma and the road to superstardom began for Sean Connery when he spoke those three words. In addition to exuding charm and sexuality, his face also suggested a trace of cruelty which, it would soon become clear, was essential to the character.

After displaying his charms to an attractive woman, Bond is summoned to the office of his chief, who is known as M, and he is referred to as "Double-0-Seven." Once again, no one in the audience could have known that the designation would eventually become known to moviegoers everywhere. The story moves along very quickly as Bond is given his assignment to find out what happened to the missing agent. Once he arrives in Jamaica, a series of confrontations make it quite clear that 007 has superior capabilities and that the doctor of the title is of equal stature. And mentioned briefly is the fact that Dr. No works for the international criminal organization known as SPECTRE.

Though the plot of the film follows the novel fairly closely, SPECTRE, which is The Special Executive for Counter-Intelligence, Terrorism, Revenge and Extortion, is not a part of the novel and was only created by Fleming with McClory and Whittingham for *Thunderball*. In the novel, Dr. No is employed by the Russians. Interjecting the organization into the first film seemed to indicate the intent of the producers to create a recurring criminal organization to be the hero's adversary.

The plot, involving Dr. No's development of a missile-deflector and his plan to blackmail the U.S. government, borders on science fiction. But there is little time to consider the incredibility of the events as scenes of action, suspense, intrigue and spice quickly follow one another, along with a trace of dry wit, particularly in Bond's clever one-liners. And the characters and situations are so modern that the fantastic elements of the story become believable. Memorable moments in the movie include the tarantula scene, the introduction of Honey Rider, Bond's dalliance with the deadly Miss Taro and a series of exciting confrontations beginning with Dr. No's capture of Bond.

And let's not forget the controversial scene in which Bond executes the treacherous Professor Dent. As the audience has learned, the "Double-0" status gives him the license to kill and he exercises that privilege against the man who was responsible for the deaths of at least two people. Furthermore, Dent has just emptied his gun into what he presumed was Bond's body and, after divulging certain information, reaches for his discarded gun and fires once again at Bond, but the weapon is empty. Bond then calmly raises his gun and shoots Dent, once in the chest and a second time in the back. He then lowers his eyes for a second, indicating a trace of regret, not that he had to kill the man but that he knew it was necessary. Some critics attacked the alleged immorality of the scene, apparently believing that perhaps Dent could have been rehabilitated. But audiences deserved satisfaction from seeing a murderer get his just penalty. In the downtown San Diego theater, the audience was hooked after that scene.

The end of the movie was greeted with applause from the surprised audience. *Dr. No* had proven to be unexpectedly entertaining and quite different from the usual action movie. Many reasons exist for the film's success, not the least of which is its faithfulness to its source, despite alterations in the storyline. The screenplay by Maibaum, with Johanna Harwood and Berkeley Mather, is solid and doesn't waste a single line. Maibaum actually tightens Fleming's storyline and the scenes with Professor Dent and Miss Taro, not in the novel, are among the movie's most memorable moments.

Jack Lord as CIA agent Felix Leiter gets the drop on Bond in *Dr. No*.

The crisp and tight direction is by Terence Young, who had been directing since 1946. His previous movies were mostly action programmers, including some co-produced by Albert Broccoli (*Paratrooper* in 1953 and *Safari* in 1956) which probably led to his assignment on the first Bond picture. Another of his films was *Action of the Tiger* in 1957 and in which Sean Connery had a small part. Peter Hunt's editing aided Young's direction and the film doesn't include a single dull moment.

The performances are all fine, with Joseph Wiseman standing out as Dr. No and Ursula Andress making a memorable Honey, the series' first "Bond girl." Bernard Lee as M and Lois Maxwell as his secretary, Miss Moneypenny, who seems to have a persistent crush on Bond, would become regulars in the series. Also notable is the constantly underrated Anthony Dawson as Dent, while Jack Lord as CIA agent Felix Leiter and John Kitzmiller as Quarrel make fine colleagues for Bond. (This was when the CIA was falsely believed to be a laudable agency.)

However, it is Connery's portrayal of Bond that dominates the movie from his classic introduction to the fade-out. Smooth, confident, brutal and charming, Connery proved to be the perfect choice for 007. It was a performance that was largely unappreciated due to the seemingly effortless manner with which he approached the role. Anyone who, at the time, doubted Connery's abilities should have viewed some of his previous roles, from the singing farmer in the Disney film to the slow-witted killer in the Tarzan movie but, most significantly, to his portrayal of the washed-up fighter in the British television production of Rod Serling's *Requiem for a Heavyweight*.

Music would be an integral part of the best James Bond films and the score by Monty Norman, while mostly reflecting the Jamaican setting, is notable for introducing the memorable *James Bond Theme*, which would be used in almost all of the future films. According to Danny Biederman in his liner notes for the 1992 double-disc CD, *The Best of James Bond 30th Anniversary Limited Edition*, John Barry arranged and orchestrated Norman's theme while borrowing from one of his own compositions. The result was the famous instrumental sound that would soon become instantly recognizable around the world. And Barry would become an indispensable member of the Eon team.

Also of significance to the distinct look of the film are the main titles by Maurice Binder, which would become increasingly characteristic and identifiable for the gun barrel introduction as well for the gymnastics of the scantily clad girls that accompany the titles. He would not work on the next two films but would return for the fourth and remain as part of the Eon team for a total of 14 films. Equally distinctive is the production design by Ken Adam, whose embellished sets create a futuristic appearance that was just slightly unnatural but not to the extent of being overly fantastic. He would work on seven films in the series.

Most of the reviews for the film in the United States were not favorable. Stanley Kauffman in *The New Republic* expressed an aversion to the Fleming novels and didn't like Connery or the movie, which he felt "never decides whether it is suspense or suspense-spoof." The reviewer for *Time* was equally disapproving, referring to Bond as a snob who "doesn't mind if he shoots the wrong bloke as long as it is with the right gun." The reviewer for *Newsweek* called Bond "an exquisite thug (with whom) cultivated sado-masochists" could identify. Only Bosley Crowther in *The New York Times* seemed to understand the movie and called it "a wildly exaggerated adventure, pure escapist bunk, contagious, silly and entertaining."

Though the movie was a commercial success in England, it did not make much of an impact in the States, despite the favorable reaction of audiences who did see it. In the San Diego area, it only played one week. A few weeks later, it reappeared in downtown theaters as a supporting feature to a United Artists programmer. (In the 1960s, when B movies were slowly dying out, the studios would use previous releases that had failed at the box office to support current features in neighborhood theaters.)

Spanish *Dr. No* poster

In *Variety's* annual chart of Top-Rental Films for the United States and Canada, *Dr. No* achieved disappointing theatrical rentals (the amount of money returned to the studio from theaters, which was approximately 40% of the domestic gross) of $2 million and ranked 44th on the list, just below such movies as *Flipper* and *Captain Sinbad*. In comparison, the top films of the year, *Lawrence of Arabia*, *How the West Was Won* and *The Longest Day*, in which Connery had a small role, earned within the $15 to $17 million range in rentals. Worldwide revenues were higher, particularly in Britain, and considering its modest cost of approximately one million dollars, it earned a healthy profit, thus justifying a second movie with a larger budget.

From Russia, With Love **French poster**

Eon's second film in the series was *From Russia with Love*, which was based upon the fifth novel. It premiered in October 1963 in England but again the U.S. opening was delayed until April 1964. In the Los Angeles area, the film received a citywide opening, since the film was not important enough to be granted an exclusive engagement in a first-run theater, despite its success in England. However, it was treated with more respect than the first movie, due possibly to its increased cost as well as larger profits already earned abroad. Also, it was a straight espionage story without the borderline science fiction trappings of its predecessor. The downtown Los Angeles theater was about half full for its first evening showing. The marketable title attracted a fair amount of curious patrons in addition to those few who may have remembered *Dr. No*.

The plot involves a Russian spy, Tatiana Romanova, who offers a decoding machine to Britain upon condition that James Bond is sent to receive it and help her defect. The fact that Tatiana has supposedly become enamored of Bond by simply seeing his photograph is accepted by the British government in a tongue-in-cheek style that doesn't subtract from the intrigue, though the conceit is offset by the suspicion of both Bond and M that the ploy is a trap. And it is a trap, for unknown to Tatiana, the decoding machine is actually the bait to lure Bond into a compromising situation and eventually to his death at the hands of expert assassin, Red Grant. Also unknown to Tatiana, who is loyal to her homeland and its government, is that fact that her immediate superior, Rosa Klebb, is working not for Russia but for SPECTRE.

Once again, integral to the film's success is the fact that Bond is pitted against opponents who are extremely capable and create a genuine challenge for him. Bond's climactic fight with Rosa Klebb is thrilling enough and might well have proved fatal to Bond if not for Tatiana's intervention. However, nothing can quite top the fight to the death between Bond and Grant in a small compartment aboard the Orient Express. Incidentally, Ernst Stavro Blofeld, the head of SPECTRE, makes his first partial appearance in this film, although he is referred to only as "Number One." Though his ominous voice is heard as he affectionately strokes his white cat, his face remains hidden, creating an image of supreme evil as he plots the death of his arch-enemy, James Bond. Also of note is the fact that this film begins with a pre-credits sequence that is quite suspenseful with a twist ending.

The pre-credits sequence would become the norm for the series, though in this film, it is actually related to the main story.

The movie isn't all action and includes many fine dramatic scenes, such as Bond's confrontation with Tatiana following the death of his friend, Kerim Bey. Kerim is such a likeable and warm character that his death is genuinely affecting. The pained expression on the face of Kerim's son when Bond abruptly tells him of his father's death is peripheral to the main plot, yet the sequence is quite poignant. Rosa Klebb's initial meeting with Tatiana is filled with an underlying tension and Klebb's acceptance of Red Grant for her assignment is both humorous and sadistic. And the manner in which Grant stalks Bond and then impersonates a colleague carefully builds suspense and tension.

All of the characters are realistic and this helps to make the story very plausible. Unlike Dr. No who appeared at times to be almost alien, both Klebb and Grant are firmly entrenched in the real world of espionage, which makes them both quite believably dangerous. The gadgets that would eventually be identified with Bond films are introduced in this movie but they are also quite plausible and don't interfere with the story. Suspense, drama, action and satire all are perfectly blended to create an excellent film adventure for 007 and a superb espionage tale by any standards.

The firm hand of director Terence Young is apparent in his second Bond movie. A tougher edge exists to this film, as befitting the more realistic situations and characters, yet the director still takes time to develop the relationship between Bond and Tatiana. As a result, Bond is able to display more emotion than in the first film. His anger is palpable when it appears that Tatiana has betrayed him, and his sorrow upon Kerim's death is apparent from a gentle touch of the dead man's arm. The fantasy element of the first film is largely absent from the second film and, as a result, while Young's emphasis was on action in *Dr. No*, he emphasizes gritty reality in *From Russia with Love*, which perhaps accounts for the absence of Ken Adams as production designer. Young is also aided again by the superb editing of Peter Hunt.

The score is by John Barry, his first of many for the series, and includes another theme for Bond entitled simply *007*, that would reappear in some future films. More than any other composer, Barry would display both the talent and an affinity for Bond that would produce the finest scores for his film adventures. Also featured is a lush title tune composed by Lionel Bart and sung by Matt Monroe.

Screenwriter Richard Maibaum also encores with Johanna Harwood on this film to create a faithful translation of Fleming's novel. Since Harwood's only other screen credit is a Bob Hope comedy, Maibaum probably deserves most of the praise for the taut, realistic script. Some minor changes occur from the novel. Once again, the Russians are replaced as the enemy by SPECTRE. Most significantly, while Bond escapes Klebb's poisoned shoe blade in the film, he is not so lucky in the novel and falls to the floor unconscious, his fate unknown. (In the next novel, *Dr. No*, it is revealed that he almost died but recuperated after months of hospitalization and convalescence.)

The movie is extremely well cast. Daniela Bianchi is touching as Tatiana while Pedro Armendariz exudes warmth as Kerim. Also notable is Vladek Sheybal as Kronsteen, whose expertise at chess is matched by his proficiency at planning a treacherous crime. The movie also introduces Desmond Llewelyn as Major Boothroyd, later to be known simply as Q, and who would join Bernard Lee and Lois Maxwell as series regulars.

Most memorable, however, are Robert Shaw and Lotte Lenya who give standout performances as Red Grant and Rosa Klebb. Shaw makes Grant an extremely dangerous adversary for Bond because he projects the same kind of power and strength that makes Bond seemingly unbeatable. Shaw initially plays Grant almost like a killing machine devoid of human emotions but, after rendering Bond helpless, he displays a personal satisfaction that makes him even more menacing. Equally frightening is Lenya as the hideous and lethal Klebb. She projects authority in the way she moves and speaks and manages to look equally threatening as either a Russian officer or a maid. Her determination to kill Bond at the climax is accompanied by a frenetic energy that makes it quite possible she might succeed just as her novel's counterpart almost does.

Once again, however, it is Sean Connery who captivates audiences as James Bond. In his second outing as Bond, the actor seems more comfortable and secure in the role, quite possibly because the script allows him to display a more fully rounded character. Most moviegoers were probably not aware that he didn't quite fit Fleming's description of 007, but he inhabits the role so perfectly that even readers of the novels found themselves changing their image of Bond to suit Connery.

Reviews were again mixed. Stanley Kauffman in *The New Republic* once more expressed his displeasure, calling Fleming a "hack" and referring to Bond as "the sadistic-suave agent (who) is again played by Sean Connery (who) is not very good at it." Other reviewers seemed reluctant to endorse the movie without reservations, as though

they were ashamed at having enjoyed it. For instance, Hollis Alpert in *The Saturday Review* liked it but wrote that "it was hard to remember anything about the movie an hour later." Bosley Crowther in *The New York Times* was professionally secure enough to praise another Bond movie, writing that "007 is very much with us again and anyone who hasn't yet got to know him is urged to do so right away."

From Russia with Love was extremely popular in Britain but it achieved only modest success in the United States. On *Variety's* annual chart, it was 17th on the list with theatrical rentals of almost $4 million, just below a Disney film, *The Misadventures of Merlin Jones*. By comparison, *The Carpetbaggers*, a trashy potboiler, was at the top of the list with $14 million. Like its predecessor, the movie returned to the Los Angeles area several weeks later as the bottom half of a double bill in support of a second-rate action movie. Connery, however, was achieving acclaim as well as offers to star in other movies, including Alfred Hitchcock's *Marnie*, which premiered in the U.S. two months after the second Bond movie.

Connery's increased popularity and the overseas success of *From Russia with Love* encouraged United Artists to provide an even larger budget for the third movie in the series, *Goldfinger*. This film is based upon the seventh novel in the series and officially began the Bond phenomenon that exploded in the 1960s. Studio publicity, effective marketing and word of mouth all contributed to the movie's extraordinary success all over the world. Sadly, the man who created Bond would not be alive to see the extraordinary popularity of his creation. Ian Fleming died in August 1964.

Goldfinger premiered in London in September 1964 and huge audiences greeted it with enthusiasm. This success in Britain combined with its increased cost convinced United Artists to make the movie its major Christmas release in the U.S. In Los Angeles, *Goldfinger* opened exclusively at Hollywood's most prestigious theater,

Grauman's Chinese, where lines formed for blocks on opening day. This instant and enormous success was duplicated all over the country where many theaters scheduled early morning and late evening showings to accommodate an eager public.

The plot concerns the wealthy egomaniac of the title who has an obsession with gold. With the help of Red China, he plans to raid Fort Knox and contaminate all of its gold, thereby crippling America's economy and making himself the world's richest man. The film begins with a pre-credits sequence that includes a regrettable visual joke in which Bond rises out of harbor waters with a stuffed seagull on his head. This type of humor which borders on slapstick is inappropriate for a Bond movie. Fortunately, this nonsense is followed by a terrific fight and a closing witticism by Bond that is an example of the type of droll humor that distinguishes a Bond movie (and would later be imitated by countless inferior clones of 007).

Auric Goldfinger is one of Bond's most memorable villains. He is certainly the most physically imposing adversary that Bond will face. He is a large, almost rotund man whose initial appearance is one of the many memorable scenes in the film. And if he doesn't convey the physical strength of a Red Grant, then his manservant, the massive and muscular Oddjob, more than compensates as an opponent for 007. Bond's mission involves discovering how Goldfinger is smuggling illegal gold around the world but, before embarking on his assignment, Bond decides to teach Goldfinger a lesson about cheating at cards. This leads to another memorable scene, the discovery by Bond of Jill Masterson's gold-painted body. And this is only the beginning of the movie.

Goldfinger is filled with action, suspense, humor, thrills and innocuous sex. As Bond and Goldfinger play a cat and mouse game from Miami to London, from Switzerland to Kentucky, the roles are reversed as Bond becomes the mouse and is only saved from certain death by his quick wits. Among the film's many memorable scenes are Goldfinger's meeting with the crime chieftains and deciding their fate as well as the pressing engagement of the lone dissenter. Other standout sequences include Bond's distressing encounter with a laser beam, Bond's meeting with Pussy Galore (whose initial immunity to his charms is amusing), the marvelous raid on Fort Knox and Bond's battles with both Oddjob and Goldfinger.

Direction this time is by Guy Hamilton, who had directed his first film in 1952. He received acclaim for an early small film, *An Inspector Calls,* in 1954, and moved on to bigger-budgeted films such as *The Devil's Disciple* in 1959. *Goldfinger* moves swiftly from one sequence to the next with a refined touch. As a result, there appears to be a tendency away from the toughness of the first two films. The brutal side of Bond is muted to some degree and, while this sophistication of 007 perhaps makes the character more engaging to a wider audience, it tends to decrease the tension. However, in view of the outrageous plot, this was perhaps a wise choice and the film emerges as totally entertaining with not a single dull or unnecessary moment. Lighthearted scenes and even a couple of tender ones are often punctuated by violent ones such as the unexpected deaths of not only Jill Masterson but her sister Tilly. Once again, such scenes benefit immensely from the editing of Peter Hunt.

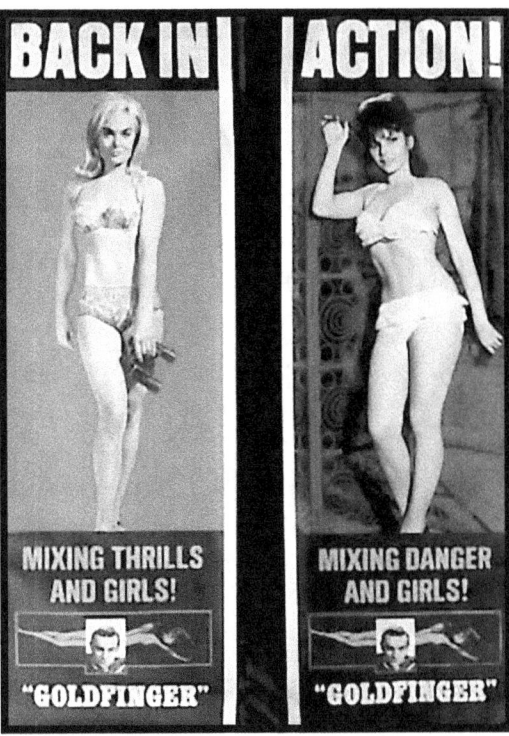

Promotion door panels for *Goldfinger*

The screenplay by Richard Maibaum, this time with Paul Dehn, is clever and concise while capturing the spirit of the novel. It actually improves upon the novel in some respects, particularly regarding the reason that Bond accompanies Goldfinger to Kentucky. Also, the fights with Oddjob and Goldfinger at the end of the film are more satisfying than in the novel. Gadgets have a larger part of this movie, particularly those associated with Bond's famous Aston Martin, but they serve a useful purpose. They are acceptable because they are not intrusive and because Bond initially views the gadgets presented to him by Q with impatience. Incidentally, Bond's political incorrectness and chauvinism are particularly refreshing, particularly in the opening Miami scenes.

Once again, at the core of the movie's success is Sean Connery, whose increasingly confident interpretation of James Bond made him a superstar. To quote Bosley Crowther, the actor portrays 007 "with an almost insultingly cool and commanding air." However, in addition to his charisma, Connery also proves again that he is a fine actor, not only in the dramatic scenes but in the manner in which he speaks his dry witticisms. This may not look difficult, but when his delivery is compared with that of so many actors who would imitate him, his expertise is more than evident.

The supporting cast is again perfect. Gert Frobe as Goldfinger, Honor Blackman as Pussy Galore, Harold Sakata as Oddjob and Shirley Eaton as Jill Masterson are so memorable that they would forever be identified with their roles in this movie. Returning to their regular roles and settling into them quite comfortably are Bernard Lee, Lois Maxwell and Desmond Llewelyn.

Also of enormous value to the movie is the score by John Barry, now the official composer of the series, which adds immensely to the excitement of numerous scenes, especially the raid on Fort Knox. This is the first score for a Bond movie that seems to blend in entirely with the images and the distinct character of 007. It is simply impossible to imagine this score as anything but music for a James Bond film. The score also produced a title song by Shirley Bassey with lyrics by Anthony Newley and Leslie Bricusse, which became a hit on both sides of the Atlantic despite not following any fashionable trends. (The 30th anniversary CD includes a low-key vocal version by Newley that is less effective than Bassey's but still interesting to hear.)

Critics were not as enthusiastic as the public. Bosley Crowther in *The New York Times* expressed some slight disappointment. "007 is slipping or his scriptwriters are," he wrote, adding that "they are involving him more and more with gadgets and less and less with girls." Brendan Gill in *The New Yorker* wrote somewhat strangely that "the secret of Bond's success lies with his constant failures" and calls Bond a bungler. Even more bizarre was the reviewer for *Newsweek* who wrote that the movie "exploits a real problem, the contemporary blurring of male and female roles," adding that "the film is about sexuality; the triumph of good over evil is the triumph of normality over perversion." Though still not liking Connery, Stanley Kaufman in *The New Republic* patronizingly seemed to like the movie, writing that "the acting is too straight to be a satire and the plot too extreme to be a surrogate fulfillment of adult repression," thus concluding that it must be "a pleasant travesty of adolescent daydreams." Kauffmann and the *Newsweek* reviewer probably enrolled in different psychology courses.

The reviews had little effect on the movie's popularity. Only a year and a half earlier, James Bond's film debut in the U.S. had been greeted with little interest but now he was easily conquering America. *Goldfinger* would serve as the prototype for countless imitations from around the world. The movie broke box office records everywhere and was the top grossing film of the year in Britain. In the United States, it was the second highest grosser of the year, earning theatrical rentals of over $22 million, with another Britisher, *Mary Poppins*, beating Bond to the top spot on *Variety*'s annual chart.

At this point, the name of James Bond was familiar all over the world. Merchandising flourished. Articles on the Bond phenomenon and on Connery appeared in newspapers and magazines. Reports appeared on network newscasts. Sales of Fleming's novels skyrocketed. The first two movies were rereleased on a double bill and earned more money than on their first releases. At the first-run Village Theater in Westwood, an expensive suburb of Los Angeles near the U.C.L.A. campus, the double feature packed the house. Only the year before, the Village had declined to show the second Bond film as part of its city-wide engagement, its management perhaps believing that the film would not appeal to its typical audience. Now, the theater was more than eager to show the double bill. Theatrical rentals for *Dr. No* rose to over $6 million and for *From Russia with Love* to almost $10 million.

While Bondmania exploded everywhere, certainly unnoticed in the year 1964 was the arrival in London from Australia of 25-year-old George Lazenby, who would soon become one of the country's top models. He probably saw *Goldfinger* at a local theater but, at that time, could have had no idea that his fate would become entwined with Bond's.

Saltzman and Broccoli wasted no time in producing their next Bond movie, but this one would be co-produced with Kevin McClory. The lawsuit involving the novelization of the story that McClery had developed with Whittingham and Fleming and the film rights to it were settled in McClory's favor. Rather than have a competing film on the market, Eon agreed to the co-production arrangement.

Beginning with this film, no delays occurred between British and U.S. premieres. *Thunderball* opened in both countries in December 1965 and was another blockbuster from the opening day. At the Paramount Theater in New York City, hundreds of people stood in long lines for every show in intensely cold weather.

Audiences around the world were not disappointed. *Thunderball* is extremely entertaining and proof that, unlike most series, each Bond movie seemed to be just a bit better than the one it followed. The plot involves another power-hungry lieutenant of Blofeld's SPECTRE organization, Emilio Largo, who hijacks a nuclear armed aircraft and threatens to blow up two major cities. The movie begins with an excellent pre-credits fight between Bond and a crafty opponent dressed as a woman that concludes with 007's escape by the use of a personalized rocket suit. This bit of high-tech gadgetry is once again not offensive simply because Bond has defeated his

Sean Connery and Claudine Auger in *Thunderball*

enemy through brute strength and uses the gadgetry only to make his escape.

The movie proper begins with the ominous Mr. Largo arriving at SPECTRE headquarters, which is visually quite impressive. Blofeld, or Number One, presides over the meeting, though he is again partially hidden as he strokes his cherished white cat. The hijacking plan is proceeding satisfactorily, according to Largo, and the scene shifts to the actual plan in progress. Through plastic surgery, an imposter will replace the pilot of the nuclear aircraft. Unfortunately, the impersonator is a bit greedy but this is a minor glitch to Largo's chief assassin, Fiona Volpe. A more serious obstacle to the plan is that James Bond is recuperating at the same clinic as the impersonator. Though Bond's suspicions are too late to stop the hijacking, they lead him to Nassau where he meets Domino, who is Largo's mistress and the sister of the murdered pilot. Bond will also be introduced to both Largo and Fiona, who makes it her personal mission to kill 007.

The screenplay for *Thunderball* by Richard Maibaum and John Hopkins, which was based upon the original McClory-Whittingham-Fleming script, is filled with sharp and witty dialogue as well as interesting characterizations. Largo's sinister arrogance, evident from his first appearance, makes him a worthy antagonist for Bond. Their verbal duels are just a few of the film's many highlights. Bond's relationships with Fiona and Domino are also logically developed. Credible motivation exists for Domino's conversion to Bond's side as opposed to the tongue-in-cheek reason in the previous film. Fiona Volpe, who is not in the novel, is a memorable assassin. Her pride in her professional capabilities combined with her self-confidence as a temptress result in her believably furious response to Bond's insult after their tryst. The heated words they exchange indicate the genuine human emotions of both Bond and Fiona and this scene is one of the few in which Bond is shown as a real person and not just a fantasy hero. The dialogue is also just one example of the script's clever awareness of the fantasy the series has created and the self-mockery that co-exists with the more realistic scenes.

Terence Young, directing for the third time, successfully combines the drama and toughness of the first two films with the stylish action and humor of the third film.

With this movie, which would unfortunately be his last Bond film, Young perfected the technique that would prove difficult to duplicate, perfectly blending all of the necessary elements to create an enormously entertaining adventure film. Bond's scenes with Domino are actually quite tender while his scenes with Fiona are suitably tense. The action scenes are particularly exciting and Young manages to keep even the confusing plot twists at the beginning of the film moving quite rapidly. The chase scene through the annual Nassau parade that follows Bond's escape from Fiona's captivity is especially thrilling. The film builds carefully to an exhilarating underwater battle between Largo's army and Navy frogmen which in turn leads to a thrillingly staged hand-to-hand fight between Bond and Largo aboard a super-yacht careening wildly out of control.

The impact of the parade and underwater scenes, which could have been unimaginatively dull due to the necessarily slowed movements, is increased substantially by Peter Hunt's magnificent editing. Hunt may not have realized it at the time, but he was in training to prepare for his directorial Bond debut, his only Bond film as director, and it would be the best of the entire series.

A false performance does not exist in the entire film. Sean Connery is again perfect as Bond, projecting marvelous self-assurance as the ultimate fantasy hero. He is equally believable whether he is saving the world or charming a lovely nurse at the health spa. He is also convincing projecting various down-to-earth emotions such as sympathy for Domino when he must give her bad news, smoldering anger toward the nefarious Count Lippe, and just the right amount of suppressed rage when he sees the dead body of his colleague, Paula.

In support, Adolfo Celi colorfully brings Largo to life with just the right amount of haughtiness and evil. As Fiona Volpe, Luciana Paluzzi combines sensuality and wickedness in a way that virtually all other actresses playing a villainess in future films would be unable to do. She is such an exciting opponent for Bond that her death is regrettable when it occurs long before the climax. Equally striking is Claudine Auger as Domino, who convincingly changes from a pampered woman to an ally. Both of the lead female roles are fully developed and add to the film's enjoyment.

John Barry again contributes a terrific score that begins with a main theme that suggests both mystery and danger. As sung by Tom Jones, the title song becomes even more foreboding through its ominous lyrics by Don Black. However, it is Barry's scoring of the parade scene and the climactic battles underwater that are perfect examples of the merger of film and music. Also of note is the theme, "Mr. Kiss-Kiss Bang-Bang," another melodic work that conveys the character of 007. (Shirley Bassey and Dionne Warwick recorded vocal versions of this tune with lyrics by Leslie Bricusse, but neither version was used in the movie and remained unreleased until the 1992 CD.)

After the huge success of *Goldfinger*, critics were prepared to pounce on *Thunderball* if only because it was considered fashionable to attack any movie that was awaited with as much anticipation as the next Bond film. Some critics complained about the formula of the series that was seemingly apparent in the fourth film, but this type of criticism is ridiculous. Any series has to have a formula and the question is not whether one exists but how originally it is presented. The basic ingredients of a formula can simply be reshuffled to produce superficial changes or they can be modified through creativity and inventiveness. *Thunderball* does just this. But some critics are notoriously subjective.

The reviewer for *Newsweek* wrote that the "very premise of the picture is a bore" and called it a predictable failure. The reviewer for *Time* called the film "spectacular" but condescendingly added that Bond fans won't notice the lack of wit or "nickel's worth of plot." However, Bosley Crowther in *The New York Times* proved his perceptiveness again by naming the movie one of the Ten Best Pictures of the Year. "The image of Bond," Crowther wrote, "as a man who has everything is being cheerfully expanded. He has power over women, skill in perilous maneuvers, knowledge of everything (and) now he has a much better sense of humor and this is the secret ingredient that makes *Thunderball* the best of the lot."

The public agreed with Crowther. *Thunderball* would break many records, even some set by *Goldfinger*. It was the highest grossing film of the year in Britain and numerous other countries. In the United States, it topped *Variety*'s annual chart of Top Rental Films with theatrical rentals of $28 million (though it would eventually be eclipsed by *The Sound of Music*). The movie was an event and, though it was not known at the time, this film would reach the commercial peak of the entire series.

An indication of the film's appeal, and this would probably apply to the first three films as well, was the reception *Thunderball* received when it played in theaters on military posts. At Fort Devens, Massachusetts, the audience was a very difficult one to please, since soldiers were unsure of their future during those tumultuous years. The members of such audiences were known to walk out en masse on some films and shout derisively at others. But *Thunderball* held their rapt attention and was greeted with wholesale approval. At the end of the film, the audience gave it a round of applause, which was extremely rare.

The first four Bond movies are classics. With each movie, the creative film artists sharpened their talents and focused on the objective of bringing 007 to the screen faithfully and imaginatively. Anyone interested in understanding why the Bond phenomenon reached such astronomical heights during the 1960s has only to view these movies. They set the pattern not only for most of the future films of the series but for the spy boom that took over the movie industry. Just about every studio tried to cash in on the bonanza as competitors and rivals flourished in America and abroad. Direct imitators such as Derek Flint with James Coburn and Matt Helm with Dean Martin were minor commercial successes but very pale copies. Serious spy films starring such actors as Richard Burton, Laurence Harvey and Michael Caine achieved some critical acclaim. Stars such as Paul Newman, Frank Sinatra, George Segal, Montgomery Clift and countless others made espionage movies with varying results.

The year 1967 promised to be the biggest year of Bondmania yet with two major films scheduled for release, the official fifth Eon film in the series for United Artists and another rival production from producer Charles Feldman for Columbia. Instead, the year would prove to be the most disappointing one for Bond fans and the first sign of the inevitable decline.

Film rights to Fleming's first novel, *Casino Royale*, had been acquired by Feldman in 1960 and, in view of the success of the Eon films, he was now ready to bring the novel to the screen. After being rejected by Broccoli and Saltzman for a co-production deal, Feldman apparently decided that it would be unwise to compete directly with the Connery films. As a result, he produced a comedy-extravaganza that turned out to be a bloated, over written, over acted and over directed atrocity that is dreary and unfunny.

No plot really exists here and the movie resembles an old vaudevillian show in which various routines are presented in quick succession in hopes of generating some laughter. Five directors, several writers and numerous guest stars conspired to create this muddle, which rarely makes sense. David Niven plays Sir James Bond who is lured out of retirement when M is killed and convinces several other people to impersonate Bond to confuse the enemy. This is the premise for having such comedy actors as Peter Sellers and Woody Allen play variations of Bond and, with such talented persons involved, some funny moments should have existed, but there are none. The various skits fall flat, the comedy actors are lost without humorous material to work with and the more serious actors, such as William Holden and Deborah Kerr, embarrassingly overact.

The decision to exploit the Bond name was unfortunate, particularly since the novel that introduced 007 is a relatively brief but gripping thriller with

great cinematic potential. (In fact, the 1954 television adaptation is more interesting than this cinematic monstrosity, which was made 13 years later.) In the novel, Bond is an intrepid and somewhat callous agent who is assigned to defeat a vicious and sadistic Russian agent by the name of Le Chiffre at baccarat in the French casino of the title. Bond is assigned a partner, Vesper Lynd, whom he initially resents, preferring to work alone. Though he is captured and tortured by Le Chiffre, Bond succeeds in his mission. After he is saved, ironically by Russian agents, Bond and Vesper fall in love and plan to marry but she is actually a Russian agent and commits suicide, leaving Bond bitter and angry.

The novel, besides being an absorbing thriller, is also interesting because it depicts Bond's first serious relationship. His bitter last line in the novel is revealing since it sets the pattern for his future relationships with women. After the pain of this first love affair, he avoids total commitment until the 10th novel when he again falls in love with even more tragic results. If *Casino Royale* had been filmed as written, it could have been a riveting romantic thriller with an emotionally powerful ending. Since its style would have been necessarily different from the Eon films, it would not have been competitive but complementary and would have added to the Bond mystique. Instead, a good spy novel was ruined to produce a wretched waste of time.

Casino Royale earned U.S. theatrical rentals of $10 million and was considered a commercial success but, due to its exorbitant cost, performed below expectations. When it played at the Music Hall Theater in Boston in the summer of 1967, the highlight of the evening was a preview of the official Bond movie, *You Only Live Twice*, which was due to open a few weeks later. To avoid confusion with pretenders to the throne, the preview repeatedly proclaimed that "Sean Connery *is* James Bond."

Unfortunately, several foreboding signs surfaced about this movie and they were evident from the moment the title was announced the previous year as being the next Eon film. Fleming's 11th Bond novel, *You Only Live Twice*, was a direct sequel to the 10th novel, *On Her Majesty's Secret Service*, which had not yet been filmed. Both novels were major highlights of the series and expanded upon the characterization of Bond. In *On Her Majesty's Secret Service*, Bond finally gets to meet his archenemy Blofeld and also falls in love and gets married, only to witness Blofeld's murder of his bride, which leaves him emotionally devastated. *You Only Live Twice* begins with a grief-stricken and alcoholic Bond who is about to be dismissed out of the service by M but, out of pity, is sent on a minor mission to Japan where he finds that his quarry is none other than Blofeld. Bond's quest for vengeance ends when he kills Blofeld and then escapes from the pain of his life via amnesia.

Both novels were bestsellers during the height of Bondmania (they were published, respectively, in 1963 and 1964) and this was evidence enough that the public was enthralled by Fleming's evolution of Bond. Sadly, the author died after the publication of *You Only Live Twice* and his final novel, *The Man with the Golden Gun*, was published posthumously. In this novel, Bond is brainwashed by the Russians and sent back to England to kill M but is rehabilitated. The novel is disappointingly written and plotted and it is suspected that Fleming's illness affected his creativity. For many 007 fans, the 11th novel is really the end of the Bond saga.

(None of the Bond novels authorized by Fleming's estate after his death have been able to duplicate the author's distinctive style. *Colonel Sun* by Robert Markham, a pseudonym for Kingsley Amis, is readable but too graphic regarding violence and sex. The series of novels by John Gardner from 1981 to 1996 is negligible due to the ridiculous updating of Bond as well as plots and characters that are imitative of Fleming's originals. Raymond Benson's current series is closer to Fleming's style but still tries to be too contemporary and lacks the enthralling uniqueness of the original novels. The fact is that only Fleming could write an authentic Bond novel.)

Thus, the decision of Broccoli and Saltzman to film *You Only Live Twice* before the novel from which it continues indicated arrogance and a lack of consideration for fans of the literary series. When the film version was released in June 1967 it appeared that the producers were also ignorant of what had made the first four films so unique. Like the disaster that had preceded it into theaters a few weeks before, *You Only Live Twice* uses only the title and setting of the novel and creates an entirely new story. The result totally misses the Fleming touch and is a terrible movie. Indeed, it is difficult to

believe that it was made by the same company that produced the first four films in the series.

Actually, there were two major new team members to Eon who worked on this film, both unfortunate choices. The screenplay is written by Roald Dahl, who is a master of the macabre short story but apparently knew nothing about James Bond or Ian Fleming. Indeed, he seems to have prepared for the assignment by viewing the previous four films since the script is a patchwork effort with copies of scenes from the previous films thrown together in haphazard fashion. The director is Lewis Gilbert, who had been responsible for some fine small films, including *The Greengage Summer*, but he displays none of the necessary touches perfected by Young and Hamilton.

The plot, involving Blofeld's capture of an American space shuttle to provoke World War III, is totally lacking in credibility with no realistic component to balance the fantasy. The pre-credits sequence, in which Bond is supposedly killed, makes no sense except to provide an excuse for the title. Any child in the audience knows that Bond is not really dead, which makes his supposedly clever rebirth scene predictable. Situations are contrived and the banal characterizations are poorly conceived. No sense of danger exists throughout the film, which is particularly disappointing because for the first time Blofeld is actually a major character. However, in this film, he lacks the evil magnitude indicated in the previous films and doesn't convey the menace of Bond's previous adversaries. His brawny henchman and female assistant are equally uninspired and are merely pallid copies of characters from previous films.

Another major reason for the movie's failure was the decision of the producers to spend millions of dollars on enormous sets and special effects which literally dwarf Bond. As a result, even 007 is depersonalized and converted into a character whose only purpose seems to be to operate the silly gadgets and wander through the lavish sets. The aircraft battle, in which each enemy pilot positions his plane at the exact point which enables Bond to use his mini-plane's appropriate gadget, is totally hackneyed. And the climax in Blofeld's volcano headquarters is as ineffective as the rest of the movie, despite the extravagance of the set, since both Bond and Blofeld are merely ciphers instead of believable characters.

Sean Connery looks understandably bored in this movie and it is sad to see him simply going through the motions. Donald Pleasance is a fine actor but he is miscast as Blofeld, though the role is badly conceived. None of the supporting actors, including Charles Gray as an ally and Karen Dor as a villainess, stands out. One of the few assets of the movie is another fine score by John Barry, which includes appropriately Japanese-flavored melodies and a lush title tune with interesting lyrics by Leslie Bricusse. The choice of Nancy Sinatra to sing the title song may have been Eon's first attempt to directly appeal to a younger audience, since her previous record had been popular with teenagers. Perhaps this movie served one useful purpose since Peter Hunt graduated from editor to second unit director and would take the reins for the very next film.

You Only Live Twice was very successful, earning U.S. rentals of $19 million, about twice as much as its summer rival but down about one-third from *Thunderball*. It was suggested at the time that the lower grosses may have been due to the competition of *Casino Royale* but this is unlikely. The movie simply lacks the creativity, excitement, drama and humor of the previous films. It is not surprising that Connery quit the series after this major disappointment.

It was two and one-half years before the next film in the series was released, the longest period between films since the start of the series. By 1969, indications pointed to the fact that the spy boom was over and that Bondmania was on the wane. Anti-war movies and anti-establishment movies were popular, making a government agent with a license to kill passé to many. Connery's highly publicized departure combined with the poor quality of his last Bond film combined to indicate that there was little hope for the future of the series. Indeed, it seemed almost sacrilegious to many that another actor would even attempt to portray James Bond. And another bad omen, at least for fans of the novels, was indicated by the fact that the new movie was based upon the novel to which the sequel had already been filmed.

In any film series, it is always the second actor to play the lead role that has the most difficulty gaining popular approval. Subsequent actors have it easier since resistance to change lessens with each successive replacement and with the inevitable decrease of interest. In this case, making the situation even more formidable for the second actor was Sean Connery's immense popularity as Bond and as a personality.

As the movie's premiere approached, publicity for the new actor was noticeably deficient. In the advertisements for the film, the name James Bond was prominently displayed but the name of the new actor playing him was not highlighted. Since his arrival in England from Australia, George Lazenby had become a successful model and been chosen from among hundreds of candidates to be the new James Bond. However, during production, problems between Lazenby and the producers as well as with the director occurred. In the midst of filming, Lazenby had informed Broccoli and Saltzman that he would not make another Bond movie. In response, the understandably angry producers perceived no benefits in promoting him in the role. Thus, just before the film's release, all the signs pointed to a major disaster.

However, when *On Her Majesty's Secret Service* premiered in December 1969, it emerged as a perfect movie and the crowning achievement of the series. It is filled with breathtaking action scenes, terrific villains, suspense, intrigue, humor and the added element of romance. It is totally entertaining from start to finish and manages to thrill, jolt, delight, amuse and eventually stun audiences with its unexpectedly tragic ending.

The screenplay by Richard Maibaum is his first solo effort of the series and follows the novel very faithfully. (Ironically, the novel was the first one published after the start of the film series, and author Fleming pays tribute to Sean Connery by mentioning Bond's Scottish ancestry.) James Bond is more human in this film, displaying character change and emotional vulnerability. His increased humanity is also aided by the elimination of gadgets, except for a safe-cracking device, as he must rely totally on his own attributes. The plot involves Blofeld's development of a bacteriological virus with which he plans to contaminate the world's food supply if he is not granted pardon for his past crimes and a respectable title. This demand, instead of asking for his usual millions of dollars, makes Blofeld more human as well, adding immeasurably to his character and to the plot's believability despite the fantastic trappings.

Simultaneous with Bond's pursuit of his archenemy, he meets the emotionally unstable Comtesse Teresa di Vicenzo and saves her from a suicide attempt. Concerned for her safety not only from her own actions but from some shady characters who hover around her, Bond pursues Tracy. After a misunderstanding involving an offer of a bribe to Bond from her father, the relationship between Bond and Tracy develops into romance and eventually love.

Like Bond and Blofeld, Tracy is also a fully developed character. She is perfectly depicted as Fleming's vulnerable "bird with a wing down," just the kind of woman

who would appeal to the emotionally scarred Bond of the novels. Though this aspect of Bond's past is not referred to in the film, his attraction to her is equally credible because of the manner in which the relationship is carefully developed from their first meeting to her father's birthday party. Marc Ange Draco, the head of the Union Corse criminal organization, is Tracy's father and is another well-conceived character whose concern for Tracy makes him far more than just a local criminal. Of all of Maibaum's screenplays for the Bond films, this is certainly the most carefully developed as far as characters and relationships are concerned, but that is only one facet of the script's excellence.

Lazenby is introduced as the new Bond in the pre-credits sequence, though his face is initially in shadow and not shown until after he rescues the self-destructive Tracy from a plunge into the ocean. A well-staged fight ensues with Lazenby displaying his capability as an action hero against two gunmen. As Tracy runs away, Lazenby looks directly at the camera and states with a smile, "This never happened to the other fellow." This is an ideal way to tell audiences that it isn't the end of the world that another actor is portraying James Bond. It reminds moviegoers everywhere that, as Alfred Hitchcock used to say, "It's only a movie."

During the main titles, various clocks and timepieces drift across the screen, the first sign of the time motif that will pervade the entire movie. Tracy feels that her time for living is over until she falls in love with Bond. Blofeld is in a hurry to gain respectability and has no time to waste. Time suspensefully encloses Bond during the safecracking scene. The time bomb that will destroy Blofeld's headquarters ticks away swiftly as Bond races for the exit. And as it turns out, time is quite deceptive because when Bond tells Tracy that they have all the time in the world, neither of them has any premonition that for them, time will soon run out. The titles also contain a connection to the past, at least the cinematic past, as brief scenes from previous movies intermingle with the timepieces.

The movie is divided into a prologue, which is the pre-credits sequence, followed by three acts and an epilogue. During the first act, romance alternates with suspense as Bond gradually falls in love while closing in on Blofeld. Bond's obsession with locating Blofeld and bringing him to justice has worn out M's patience, and the crusty head of the Secret Service orders 007 to drop the case. Furious, Bond threatens to resign but is given a brief vacation which he uses to return to Portugal, where he had been following a lead on Blofeld and where he had met Tracy. The two plots converge when Bond begins a romance with Tracy and obtains information on Blofeld from her father.

In the second act, humor and tension co-exist as Bond poses as a genealogist to infiltrate Blofeld's eyrie in the Swiss Alps and must socialize with girls from all over the world who will unwittingly transmit the deadly virus to their home countries. Irma Bunt, Blofeld's assistant, is introduced and makes an immediate impression as a sinister villain. However, the dramatic highpoint of the entire series is the scene in which Bond finally meets with his long-time antagonist, a meeting that both men have been looking forward to for over seven years. (Fortunately, Maibaum's script ignores their meeting in *You Only Live Twice* and proceeds as if that movie had never been made.) Bond's nighttime dalliance with two of the girls, though done for Queen and Country to learn details of Blofeld's plan, is perhaps an indication that his old habits have not been alleviated by love, but that will happen soon enough when Tracy reappears fortuitously in his life. Such habits also lead to Blofeld's discovery of his identity and his captivity.

The final act of the movie begins with Bond's escape from captivity and leads to a series of increasingly exciting chase scenes, each one more daring than the preceding one. A brief respite from the action scenes provides Bond with an opportunity to propose to Tracy. It is logical that Bond should choose this particular time to not only propose marriage but offer to leave the Secret Service for Tracy because she has just reappeared in Bond's life when he is at his rope's end, trapped and surrounded by Blofeld's men and displaying, for the first time in the series, actual fear. This time, it is Tracy who saves Bond's life and it seems quite reasonable, particularly since the relationship has been carefully developed, that he would want to settle down at this point in his life.

But Blofeld is not about to let the one man who has so often foiled his plans to slip out of his fingers so easily. The extent of his hatred for Bond is indicated by the manner in which he throws his cherished white cat away from him upon being told of Bond's escape. Another exciting mountain pursuit on skis follows and precedes Blofeld's capture of Tracy, a helicopter assault on Blofeld's eyrie and the climactic duel between Bond and Blofeld on speeding bobsleds, which alone must rank as one of the screen's all-time great action sequences. Adding immensely to the incredibly well-executed sequence is the fact that the super-agent and super-villain are finally battling hand-to-hand, their fists slamming into one another's faces as they desperately try to kill one another. The resolution of the battle is extremely satisfying but quite deceptive, since it will be followed by the tragic epilogue.

Maibaum's excellent screenplay is perfectly realized by the direction of Peter Hunt. Though the movie is almost two and one-half hours long, the longest of the entire series, it has a distinct style and passion that separates it from all of the other films in the series. The stunning action sequences flow naturally from the plot and do not stand out

as they did in the previous film because they advance the narrative development of the story. Similarly, the fight sequences are realistically choreographed and are startlingly brutal without being graphic. The development of the romance is also beautifully realized by a montage of scenes showing Bond and Tracy gradually falling in love while accompanied by the film's love song. The fact that this sequence, which could have been a cliché, succeeds in a James Bond movie is testament to Hunt's skill.

With the exception of *You Only Live Twice,* which was devoid of anything resembling Ian Fleming's style, the previous Bond films had all contained the author's themes and characterizations to some degree. However, *On Her Majesty's Secret Service* is perhaps the closest approximation of the novel on which it is based, more so than even *From Russia with Love,* and it is not coincidental that the services of Ken Adams are again not required. Hunt is obviously not only appreciative of Maibaum's screenplay but he also tries and often succeeds in translating many of the more descriptive passages that distinguish the novel, such as the natural beauty of some of the surroundings and the sophistication of some of the more intimate scenes. Hunt deserves more than his share of credit for the film's success because of his knowledge of Fleming and the insight into the character of Bond that he must have learned from the novels as well as the previous movies. It is an extremely impressive directorial film debut.

Also of tremendous value is the quintessential Bond score by John Barry which includes a pulsating main theme, variations of which enhance the action scenes, particularly the pursuit on skis of Bond and Tracy down a mountain by Blofeld and his men. This is a purely instrumental theme, which was a wise decision; though lyrics were written by Leslie Bricusse, they were fortunately not used since the title simply does not lend itself to lyrics. The score also includes a pleasant Christmas song, "Do

You Know How Christmas Trees are Grown?" which is sung by Nina and which serves as an ironic background for the scene in which Bond is ensnared by his foes. However, it is the romantic and haunting ballad, "We Have All the Time in the World," sung by Louis Armstrong, with tenderness and honesty, that lingers in the memory. This beautiful song, with lyrics by Hal David, conveys the optimism of the doomed romance as well as the poignancy of Bond's last line to his murdered bride. Barry's exceptional score perfectly integrates music and visual imagery to enhance the film's impact and achievements.

The two main roles, besides that of Bond, are wonderfully cast. Diana Rigg gives a memorable performance as the doomed Tracy, projecting just the right amount of both independence and vulnerability needed for the role. She displays more passion than any other Bond heroine and it is this trait that makes Bond's change of character so credible. The manner in which she responds to Bond at her father's birthday party suggests just the right of emotional pain that indicates deep-rooted feelings. And her surprised response to his proposal is equally moving and convincing.

As Blofeld, Telly Savalas perfectly captures the spirit and grand malevolence of the character that Fleming created. Though his characterization may lack the mystery and stateliness barely glimpsed in the earlier movies, this is a necessary result of making Blofeld an integral part of the story and not just a symbol of evil. After his many previous attempts to dominate the world had been thwarted by Bond, it is only natural that some humility has seeped into his personality. This Blofeld has been knocked off his evil pedestal by Bond and Savalas superbly projects the necessary hatred and desire for vengeance toward his adversary required by his character.

In support, Gabrielle Ferzetti makes a strong impression as Draco. The sincerity he displays in his concern for Tracy and his willingness to help Bond smash Blofeld makes it quite clear that, while he may be a criminal, he is not evil like Blofeld. Ilse Steppat as Irma Bunt, on the other hand, does suggest the malevolence that would make her a loyal ally of Blofeld. Though she conveys a motherly appearance toward her female charges, her tone and expression convey pure wickedness. She is certainly the most reprehensible female villain of the series since Rosa Klebb, particularly in view of her final act. Bernard Lee's M seems a bit more impatient with Bond than usual in this film but still conveys authority and paternal concern, while Lois Maxwell as Moneypenny has her best moments in the series at Bond's wedding. Desmond Llewellyn doesn't have much to do as Q since gadgets are quickly dismissed from the movie, but his appearance at the wedding shows that he also is not just Bond's colleague but also a friend.

In the pivotal role, it is true that George Lazenby lacks Connery's screen presence but so do most actors, including the four that would follow in the role. However, Lazenby proves to be quite effective in the action scenes and generally gives a very compelling performance. In one respect, he may actually be more appropriate than Connery for this film's 007. Connery's previous interpretation of the irresistibly charming Bond with no hint of the subconscious desire for love and stability might have made his proposal to Tracy difficult to accept. Lazenby, playing Bond for the first time, doesn't have this burden and could be more credible. His relative youth and apparent awkwardness in some scenes also add to the sense of vulnerability necessary for the characterization. And, most commendably, in the final scenes he projects a dramatic range that is quite impressive for a film debut. (In an interview over three decades later, Lazenby related

Lazenby...George Lazenby in *On Her Majesty's Secret Service*

that he originally played the scene with tears on his cheeks but the director preferred the less emotional take that is in the film. This may have been Hunt's only miscalculation.)

In general, considering the fact that his first acting role was the centerpiece of a multimillion dollar production that was continuing the most successful series of all time, Lazenby succeeds quite admirably. Regardless of the talents of the experienced actors and filmmakers surrounding him, he has the major burden of the movie and carries it more than satisfactorily. At the DeMille Theater in New York City, the action scenes were greeted with cheers while the finale caused a silence that was deafening. This type of audience involvement would not have been possible if the lead actor didn't have considerable screen presence.

Nevertheless, many critics had their knives sharpened for Lazenby. And not only was Lazenby the object of unfairly cruel and subjective reviews but in some circles it was also open season on 007 as well. The reviewer for *Newsweek* wrote that "the James Bond craze has ended but James Bond movies live on. (The new movie) carries the slightly faded air of chic coat two years out of style," adding that Lazenby has "an open, characterless face (and) blank eyes reflecting a mind that has never held a thought." Hollis Alpert in *The Saturday Review* called Lazenby "a rank amateur," adding somewhat cruelly that "it's kind of touching watching him attempt to get the necessary insouciance into the delivery of his lines." A.H. Weiler in *The New York Times* wrote more fairly that Lazenby "is, if not a spurious Bond, a merely casual, pleasant and satisfactory replacement." Weiler liked the movie's "breakneck, devastating chases (and) overabundance of continuous action, flip dialogue and characterizations."

Unfortunately, *On Her Majesty's Secret Service* proved to be relatively disappointing at the box office. It earned U.S. theatrical rentals of just over $9 million, approximately half of the previous film's earnings. It was more successful overseas and earned a healthy profit, though not as large as the previous three films. In assessing the blame for the reduced profits, Lazenby was considered a major factor. It was apparently forgotten that the earnings of *You Only Live Twice* had also decreased considerably from *Thunderball,* so it was unfair to blame Lazenby for a decline that had started with Connery's last movie. Lazenby was a convenient target, particularly since Eon and United Artists no longer had an investment in him.

Another detrimental factor was the anti-Bond sentiment that became fashionable in 1970. A typical example was a ludicrous article by A. Marks in *The New York Times* shortly after the release of the Lazenby movie. Marks expressed regret for having liked the previous Bond movies and castigated anyone who might have the temerity to like the new one. The writer confessed that as a result of the Viet Nam war, the killing of Robert Kennedy and other acts of violence, he could no longer be entertained by the Bond movies in which "even the people die beautifully." Marks patronizingly explained that "we have all changed," implying that those who still liked Bond movies were not as socially conscious as he was. As if speaking from a pulpit, Marks wrote that "we are enlightened young men and women (who) aren't buying hate propaganda." Attacking Bond's allegedly fraudulent masculinity, Marks farcically concluded that 007 represents "the sadistic and cruel last-ditch expression of that confounded militant egotism which used to be the trademark of the normal middle class male." After this sentence, it is difficult to believe that the article was not a spoof.

Not only was Marks classically wrong in singling out the Bond movies for their alleged violence and in his interpretation of the character of Bond, but he also apparently never understood that the movies are good-versus-evil morality tales as well as fantasies. Actual events of the 1960s may have clouded the issue of who was right and who was wrong in the real world, but no such confusion exists in the world of 007. Perhaps Marks really believed that villains like Blofeld and Goldfinger were innocent victims of British and American militarism, but in the fantasy world of James Bond the Viet Nam war didn't exist and neither did political assassinations.

It is also difficult to understand the writer's condemnation of the violence in the Bond movie, which isn't at all explicit compared to other films of the era, including such critically acclaimed films as *Bonnie and Clyde* and *The Wild Bunch*. Apparently, "socially meaningful" films by auteurs are not subject to the same criticism as James Bond movies. Bonnie Parker and Clyde Barrow were "in" but 007 was "out." Arthur Penn and Sam Peckinpah were fashionable, but who was Peter Hunt?

Marks had also been blissfully unaware of the fact that the purpose of escapist entertainment is to enable the audience to escape from the real world into a better world. It was not accidental that Bondmania exploded the year after the assassination of President John F. Kennedy. The horror of that act made millions of people want to escape from the real world into a fantasy world.

Nevertheless, however faulty the anti-Bond polemic, it represented an opinion that was considered chic. Time would eventually prove the absurdity of the argument. The allegedly socially conscious audiences of the 1970s would cheerfully applaud movies with increasingly graphic violence that would by comparison validate the Bond films as delightful and innocuous entertainment. For this and so many other reasons, the column by Marks would, in the long run, be of as little account as a sparrow's tears.

But in the film industry profits are the bottom line. It was easy for Eon to blame Lazenby for the movie's lower grosses, but he was simply a scapegoat. However, timing was definitely a factor, not only for the external factors mentioned but for internal ones within the film. Introducing a new James Bond was drastic enough, but presenting him in movie that was different in style and tone may have been too much of a change for some fans of the previous movies. If Lazenby had first made a couple of Connery-type adventures, thus giving audiences the opportunity to acknowledge him in the role, he could have then made *On Her Majesty's Secret Service* and it would have been more acceptable. The timing was simply wrong. It was the wrong film made at the wrong time.

The movie was considered a failure and Lazenby was ostracized. In

addition to Lazenby, another reason for the commercial disappointment of the movie was believed to be the departure from the formula of the previous movies, specifically Bond's marriage and the downbeat ending as well as the absence of gadgets. This perception, misguided as it was, would have a tremendously negative effect upon future films in the series. And Eon, in planning the next film in the series, made all the wrong moves.

One right move would have been for Broccoli and Saltzman to patch up their differences with Lazenby for the sake of the series and for Bond fans to whom they owed loyalty. Another right move would have been to film *You Only Live Twice* as written. Since nothing of substance from the novel had been used in the 1967 movie, it could still have been filmed intact by simply changing the setting from Japan to another exotic location and giving it a different title. If Lazenby and Savalas had repeated their roles, if Richard Maibaum had written the screenplay and if Peter Hunt had directed again, the sequel would have been the necessary companion piece to *On Her Majesty's Secret Service* and the thrilling culmination of the entire series. With the experience of one film behind him, Lazenby would certainly have been even more effective in reprising the role. The movie would not only have been an adventure classic but also a haunting tale of love and death, of vengeance and retribution. It would have been an emotional experience of rare depth and poignancy...the ultimate Bond film. However, such a movie would have departed even further from the formula than *On Her Majesty's Secret Service*, thus being a financial risk and totally unfeasible for Eon.

Thus, Fleming fans could only imagine the pleasures of a Bond movie which begins with a pre-credits sequence that has 007 bungling an assignment that almost gets him killed. They could only envision the movie proper beginning with a grief-stricken Bond about to be cashiered out of the Secret Service. They would never get to see scenes of Bond drinking too much, losing money at the casinos and slowly going to pieces. They would never see a reluctant M relieving Bond of his "Double-0" status and, based upon the advice of a psychiatrist, giving Bond one last chance to salvage his life. Other imaginary delights include the deranged Blofeld's garden of suicide and death, the scene in which Bond realizes that the mysterious Dr. Shatterhand is actually Blofeld or the scene in which Irma Bunt recognizes Bond. One of the greatest unfilmed scenes of all time has to be the one in which Bond and Blofeld meet once again. But even that scene would be secondary to the one in which Bond strangles the life out of his bride's murderer. And one of the most haunting endings in film history would have to be the never-filmed one in which a traumatized and amnesiac Bond, believed dead by his country, is sheltered from civilization by the mother of his unborn child. Living as a simple fisherman, James Bond is a shell of the man he once was.

Such cinematic pleasures were never to be. Fidelity to Fleming and commitment to fans were apparently not to be considered. Eon and United Artists executives probably figured that only a small percentage of Bond's movie fans actually read the novels, so the majority of moviegoers wouldn't know or care about the difference. Thus, while the next Bond movie would begin with 007 searching for Blofeld, no mention would be made of Tracy. If audiences took it as a continuation, that was permissible but it was preferable that they didn't since it would be unwise to remind anyone of the serious nature of the preceding film. Such was the attitude of the travesty that would follow.

Having agreed to play Bond one more time, Sean Connery returned in the 1971 release, *Diamonds Are Forever*, which features all of the wrong ingredients. High-tech gadgets, visual stunts, lavish sets, borderline science fiction and special effects combine to produce another misfire. Guy Hamilton, director of *Goldfinger*, returns for his second Bond movie and the result proves the necessity of a good script. Richard Maibaum cowrote the tired screenplay and it must have been depressing for him to work on this type of material after his previous

solo effort. Also credited with the final screenplay is Tom Mankiewicz, whose previous scripts included *The Sweet Ride*, an adolescent mess about surfers. This choice was perhaps another indication of the direction toward a younger audience that Eon was apparently pursuing.

The title of Fleming's fourth novel and the plot about diamond smuggling are used as the basis of an original screenplay, which replaces Mafia-type criminals with Blofeld as the villain. Blofeld, supposedly killed in the pre-credits sequence, is not really dead but no one cares, since the tone of the entire movie is so lighthearted. The master criminal is reduced to being a comic strip character but, for that matter, so is 007. The plot, which concerns Blofeld's development of a diamond-powered laser that he intends to aim at Washington, contains no plausible events or characters and is played for laughs. There are some well-staged action scenes, including a fight between Bond and an opponent in an elevator, but the film's tone mitigates any serious audience involvement.

The film received a great deal of publicity due to Connery's return to the role of Bond. However, while it is pleasant seeing him once again playing 007, it is also discouraging to find him in a vehicle that was so far below the standards of his first four films. Also, like the film itself, his characterization is very tranquil and lightweight without any trace of the serious side he brought to the role, much less the cruel side. As the "Bond girl," Jill St. John is simply inadequate while Charles Gray is a bland Blofeld. (Gray, incidentally, played a colleague of Bond's in *You Only Live Twice* and when the series played in repertory theaters in the 1980s, the two films in which he appeared were often paired together, causing confusion among audiences.) Only John Barry's flavorful score, including a title song with lyrics by Don Black that was sung by Shirley Bassey, stands out among the film's mediocrity.

The backlash against Bond was no longer stylish and the comedy approach of the film prevented any kind of serious critical reaction. And Connery's return proved to be a big commercial draw. As a result, *Diamonds Are Forever* was very popular worldwide and earned U.S. theatrical rentals of over $19 million, more than twice the amount of the preceding film and about equal to that of *You Only Live Twice*. Thus, the pattern was set for future films, regardless of who would be playing the lead, since Connery was once again saying never again.

Eon received many letters asking for Lazenby's return in another serious Bond film, which would continue the story of his first film, but such a possibility was not even considered. Popular British television star Roger Moore was chosen to be the third James Bond. Moore, a very likeable screen personality, was well-known to U.S. and world audiences. He had appeared in several U.S. films in the late 1950s and early 1960s but had failed to hit the big time. Ironically, like Connery, his biggest role had been opposite Lana Turner in a movie titled *Diane*, which had also bombed. He starred in several television series on both sides of the Atlantic but finally became a star as Simon Templar in the British series *The Saint*. Though he was adept at playing light comedy, he had proven in the little-seen 1971 film *The Man Who Haunted Himself* that he could also manage serious, dramatic roles quite skillfully.

Moore didn't get much of an opportunity to display such skills in *Live and Let Die*, released in 1973. Following the pattern of the preceding movie, Moore's first Bond film is filled with gadgets, high-speed chases and juvenile humor surrounding a thin plot and even thinner characterizations. Moore plays Bond as more sophisticated and less physically imposing than Connery. However, the characterization is secondary to the foolish stunts and gratuitous chases which seem to occur at regular intervals, whether aboard a plane, a speedboat or a double-decker bus. In the previous decade, the idea

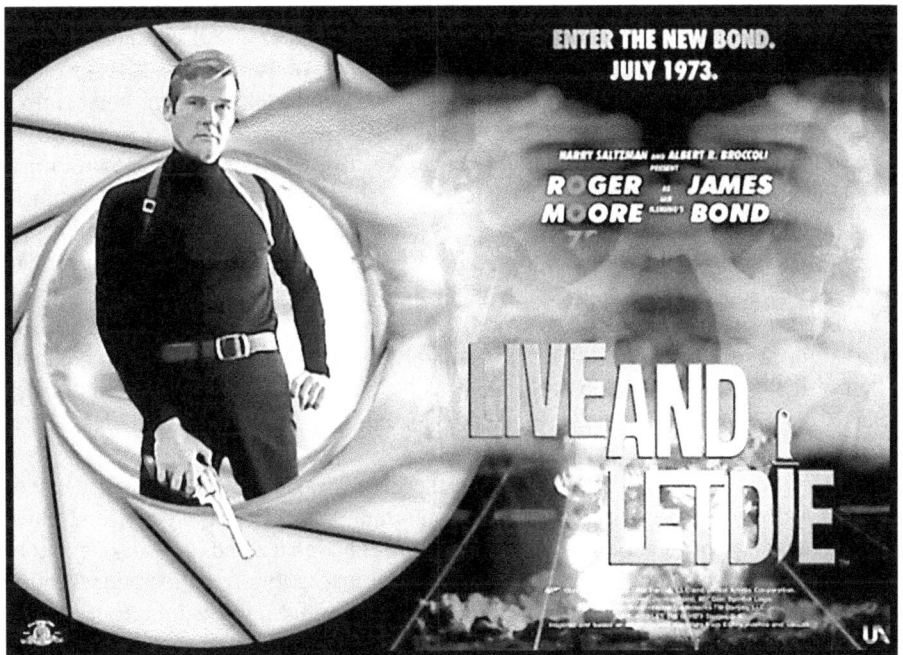

of having Bond escape a dangerous situation by hopping across the backs of alligators would have been unthinkable, but in this mishmash, such a scene clearly indicates the type of audience toward which the film was directed.

Moore isn't even provided with a good introduction as Bond. After a pre-credits sequence in which 007 doesn't even appear, Bond is first seen in bed with a woman using a silly gadget. The scene that follows is equally ridiculous in a different way. Bond is interrupted by M and Miss Moneypenny, who arrive at his apartment to give him his new assignment and a new gadget. Reducing M to the status of an errand boy is both absurd and anti-Fleming. It's all downhill from there. In general, the Bond of this movie just is not the same Bond that Connery, or for that matter, Lazenby played. One scene on a beach tries to give the new Bond a tough veneer but it simply doesn't work due to the tongue-in-cheek approach of the movie.

The flimsy plot involves a villain named Mr. Big who is smuggling heroin into the United States from a Caribbean island. The script is loosely based upon Fleming's second novel but, except for the names of some characters, there is little relationship between novel and film. In fact, the novel is a very violent one with Bond resorting to some brutal action while his friend, Felix Lieter, suffers a gruesome fate. This was all discarded in favor of a rather silly story that takes Bond from New York to Florida to the Caribbean and even resorts to a supernatural subtheme. Perhaps the most regrettable sign of the direction the series was taking is the appearance of the southern redneck Sheriff Pepper as a slapstick foil for Bond. Once this character appears, there really is no hope for the movie.

This approach was certainly due to the absence of Richard Maibaum, whose scripts had proven to be one of the most important elements of the best Bond films. The screenplay for this mess is written by Tom Mankiewicz and is totally devoid of originality. Direction again is by Guy Hamilton and is totally uninspired. Another essential ingredient to the best Bond films that is also missing is a John Barry score. Instead, the undistinguished score is composed by George Martin and the terrible title song is written and sung by Paul McCartney in still another bid by the producers to attract a younger audience. The song is so awful that it brings to memory a line spoken by Bond in *Goldfinger*: "It's like listening to the Beatles without ear muffs."

Moore retains his likeability but seems a bit unsure of himself as Bond. Actually, there is little difference between Moore's Bond and his equally debonair Simon Templar, though this is really due to the shallowness of the script and is not the fault of the actor. Yaphet Kotto has a powerful presence and could have convincingly played the Mr. Big of the novel, but his character in the film is simply not credible. Jane Seymour brings nothing except blandness to her role of Solitaire, the Bond girl. Bernard Lee and Lois Maxwell make their obligatory appearances as M and Moneypenny, but the familiarity of their characters is not enough to make this film look like part of the original series. Maxwell, incidentally, had appeared in several episodes of *The Saint* with Moore.

Live and Let Die was successful at the box office. Its U.S. theatrical rentals were over $15 million, down from Connery's last film but higher than Lazenby's sole effort. This seemed to indicate public approval of Moore as Bond, though it was evident that interest in the character had declined. The release of the movie had not attracted an exorbitant amount of attention, except for the fact that it featured a new Bond. This was a far cry from the days when the opening of a Bond movie was an event.

Moore's next movie, *The Man with the Golden Gun*, was released in 1974 and continued Bond's losing streak. Though this entry uses the title and the title character of Fleming's last and weakest novel, it is once again basically an original story that takes Bond to Hong Kong and Thailand in search of a missing solar energy device and the infamous assassin, Scaramanga. Guy Hamilton is back for his fourth and final Bond movie and, fortunately, his résumé will always include *Goldfinger* to balance the other three duds.

Richard Maibaum is also back and is credited with Tom Mankiewicz for the screenplay which is mediocre at best, since it is too often illogical as well as uninteresting. This is unfortunate, for the idea of super-agent Bond pitted against a super-assassin had the potential to be an excellent film. Based upon Maibaum's track record, he probably could have fashioned a suspenseful, realistic thriller out of this theme but the producers apparently preferred a lighthearted, humorous film that often resembles a travelogue with still more juvenile humor, fantastic stunts and superfluous chase scenes. Without doubt, one of the worst scenes in the entire series has to be the reappearance of Sheriff Pepper as a tourist. Equally absurd is the idea of having M and Moneypenny set up headquarters inside a sunken Queen Elizabeth in the Hong Kong harbor. Even the climactic duel between Bond and Scaramanga is totally uninspired.

Moore seems more relaxed as Bond, though he still gives the impression that he may at any moment glance upward to see Simon Templar's halo above his head. International star Christopher Lee plays Scaramanga and is a very imposing actor who could have made a formidable adversary for Bond but isn't utilized to his potential. Lee is even hampered by the pedestrian characterization. Also returning to the series was John Barry, but his score for this film is below his usual high standards, though even average Barry is superior to the best efforts of Paul McCartney and George Martin.

The Man with the Golden Gun earned approximately $9 million in U.S. theatrical rentals, down from the previous film and about equal to Lazenby's film. But it was still profitable around the world and Moore would not be held responsible for the lower grosses the way that Lazenby was. Different standards would be used to assess the reasons for this movie's relative financial disappointment. Eon and United Artists had a sizeable investment in Moore and was not about to let him take the fall.

Harry Saltzman sold his share of Eon to United Artists, leaving Albert Broccoli as the sole producer. In view of this, Broccoli has to be held responsible for guiding Bond even further from his origins. After two and one-half years, the third Moore Bond film was released in 1977 and it is spurious Bond at best. *The Spy Who Loved Me* uses only the title of Fleming's 10th novel but, unlike previous bastardizations of the novels, Ian Fleming requested this approach. The novel is unique in the series since it is narrated by a woman and is more soap opera than a Bond novel. Fleming had tried to provide a different perspective of Bond but he considered the book a failed experiment and requested that there be no direct film version. Despite the deficient qualities of the novel, it is still more interesting than the movie that would use its title.

The Spy Who Loved Me has a justly famous pre-credits sequence with Bond skiing off a cliff and freefalling until his parachute opens. It is visually

100   Celluloid Adventures

quite impressive, but the problem with such a stunt is that it overshadows everything else in the film and establishes the Bond movies as excuses for spectacular set-pieces. The stunt has nothing to do with the main story and yet it is what most people remember about the film. Actually, little else remains to remember since the entire film seems to revolve around sumptuous sets, slapstick humor and chase scenes, one of which includes Bond's car turning into a submarine, delighting adolescents. The plot is devoid of ingenuity and, like *You Only Live Twice*, takes scenes from all of the previous films and rearranges them with minor variations. The story involves another megalomaniacal villain, a spurious Blofeld, who tries to cause a nuclear war between America and Russia by capturing submarines from each country.

Surprisingly, Richard Maibaum is credited as co-writer of the script but top billing is given to Christopher Wood, a writer of crude sex comedies. The choice of Wood was perhaps another depressing portent of the younger audience to which the film was being targeted. A perfect example of this is the introduction of a character known as Jaws who seems designed to humor anyone under the age of six. Standing over seven feet tall with steel teeth, this character is the worst villain of the series because he is straight out of a comic book and converts the film into a comedy by his mere presence. One good scene in the film exists, when Bond's marriage to Tracy is mentioned. Maibaum must have written the line, but it seems out of place since the rest of the movie is defined by its monstrous sets and exotic locations.

Lewis Gilbert, director of *You Only Live Twice*, returns for this equally ragged and disjointed effort. Roger Moore seems to put his own stamp on the role in this entry, though he is handicapped by the emphasis on spectacle and humor. His reaction when Tracy is mentioned is quite effective. Curt Jurgens is wasted as the poorly conceived villain. Barbara Bach plays a Russian agent who is assigned to work with Bond, but she is basically a young boy's idea of a spy and lacks the maturity and credibility of the best Bond heroines. For instance, in *Goldfinger*, when Honor Blackman throws Bond over her shoulder it is believable, but when Bach tells Bond in this film that she is going to kill him, the sequence is laughable. Bernard Lee, Lois Maxwell and Desmond Llewelyn try not to look bored in their regular roles. An appalling score by Marvin Hamlisch includes something called "Nobody Does It Better," which is a strong candidate for the worst Bond song.

However, *The Spy Who Loved Me* was a huge financial success, earning over $24 million in U.S. theatrical rentals, two and one-half times more than the previous movie, which apparently justified the approach of the movie. Its commercial success paved the way for the next film, *Moonraker*, released in 1979. Completely written by Wood and again directed by Gilbert, this movie is so atrocious that it is painful to watch. The silly script, which seems to have been written by a committee of children, uses the title of Fleming's third novel which is a suspenseful mystery and could have been adapted into a smart thriller. Instead, this expensive fiasco puts Bond in a spacesuit in an obvious attempt to exploit the popularity of the outer space epics that were the rage at the time.

The plot of the movie, concerning the villain's attempts to destroy humanity and rule the earth from a space station, is infantile science fiction and serves as an excuse for even more monstrous sets along with the usual silly gadgets and elaborate special effects. Besides Bond's embarrassingly unfunny one-liners, an example of the film's humor is the childishly vulgar name for the female lead which is typical of the script's smirky attempt at wit. Even more inexcusable is the return of Jaws, much to the delight of the subteens for whom this movie was made. In the midst of this inanity is an unpleasant scene in which a woman is chased and devoured by killer dogs. Particularly pitiable scenes include a slapstick chase scene involving a gondola that turns into a hovercraft and the entire climactic sequence aboard and outside of a space shuttle.

Roger Moore seems to be simply going through the motions in this debacle and there is no blaming him. Michel Lonsdale is another actor who had the potential to be a good villain but is simply a synthetic character. Lois Chiles is an allegedly liberated female lead but her character is also created out of cardboard. Bernard Lee, Lois Maxwell and Desmond Llewelyn are along to collect their paychecks. Even John Barry's score is unremarkable, not surprising since nothing in the film exists to inspire him. This mockery proved to be very popular with young audiences and earned over $33 million in U.S. theatrical rentals. But Ian Fleming must have been twisting in his grave, cursing the day he ever sold film rights to his creation.

Fortunately, after this extravagant monstrosity, James Bond was brought literally and figuratively back to earth in *For Your Eyes Only*. Released in 1981, this film finally gives Moore an opportunity to play an authentic Bond. This is an espionage thriller in which Bond is pitted against a Soviet villain for possession of a missing computerized device used to transmit commands to Polaris missile submarines. During the course of his mission, Bond forms an alliance with Greek smuggler Columbo as well as with Melina Havelock, a woman who is determined to avenge the murders of her parents. The film includes good villains, an interesting heroine and some excellent action scenes. Most significantly, Bond is once again a tough and resourceful agent who has to rely on his physical strength and ingenuity and not gadgets to win battles and prevail over barriers.

The film's serious tone harks back to the great Bond films of the 1960s. The espionage theme is reminiscent of *From Russia with Love,* while the style and even some content establish ties to *On Her Majesty's Secret Service*. It thankfully avoids the futuristic sets and outlandish spectacle of the films of the 1970s. And, for the most part, though not totally, it excludes the visual jokes and slapstick humor that marred the more recent films. However, while the story is a definite improvement over all of the films of the 1970s, it also lacks the sense of grand adventure of the five classic films of the 1960s. And this is due in part to the origin of the film.

The script is by Richard Maibaum and Michael G. Wilson, who is producer Broccoli's stepson. Maibaum's expertise has already been established, so the good parts of the script can be attributed to him as well as to Ian Fleming since the basis of the script is two of the author's short stories, "For Your Eyes Only" and "Risico." (Since the titles of all of Fleming's novels had been used, the titles of his stories remained the only direct connection to the author's works.) Broccoli must be given credit for returning to Fleming as inspiration for the film after so many deviations. The problem, ironically, is that the stories lack the grandeur of the novels. They are well-written and interesting but they are not novels specifically for the reason that Bond's missions are not grand enough to require novelistic length. They lack the grandiose villains and the sense of sweeping adventure that distinguishes Bond's best adventures. As a result, this film is a similarly minor adventure, despite the addition of the missile tracking device

to give the story more substance. The fact is that, while Bond completes his mission successfully, the suspicion exists that any other competent agent could have achieved the same objective.

The pre-credits sequence is deserving of mention not only because of its reference to *On Her Majesty's Secret Service* but because it encapsulates the uneven tone of the movie. The sequence begins with Bond standing over Tracy's grave, looking quite emotional and somber. It is a credit to the filmmakers that the date of Tracy's death on the tombstone is 1969, the year the Lazenby film was released and 12 years before the release of this movie. After paying his respects, Bond is picked up by a Secret Service helicopter but the pilot is quickly killed and the copter careens wildly out of control, apparently being directed from afar. The person responsible is then revealed, though he is only seen from behind, as a baldheaded man in a neck brace and a wheelchair. This is clearly meant to be not only Blofeld but the Blofeld portrayed by Telly Savalas. (He couldn't be identified as Blofeld because the character had been created for *Thunderball* and Eon didn't want to risk infringing on Kevin McClory's property.) The sequence is quite thrilling and suspenseful as Bond perilously regains control of the copter but then it ends in a farce as he uses the copter's landing rod to pick up Blofeld's wheelchair and drop him into a smokestack.

This ambivalent approach seems to indicate the reluctance of the producers to make a completely serious movie without at least one silly visual joke. Equally disappointing is the fact that the sequence has nothing to do with the main story and Tracy is not mentioned again. Slapstick humor is also not discarded completely, as evident from the equally inappropriate last sequence in which the Prime Minister and her husband are depicted. It's an amusing scene, especially for the British, but it doesn't belong in a

Bond movie and destroys the serious mood of the story that has preceded it. Also harmful to the film is the inclusion of the character of a teenage Olympic skater who serves no useful purpose other than to inject comedy moments and perhaps give teenagers in the audience someone with whom to identify.

Nevertheless, *For Your Eyes Only* is a very good adventure film. Action and characterizations predominate in this film, which features Moore's best performance as Bond. He is convincingly tough, particularly in the scene in which he exacts vengeance from an enemy who has just killed a woman. He also displays the proper amount of emotion in the opening sequence. Most interestingly, as it pertains to the entire series, this Bond is clearly meant to be an older 007, which is evident not only from the opening sequence but from the manner in which Bond treats the young nymphet. Moore projects this maturity in subtle ways that distinguishes his portrayal in this film from the preceding ones.

In support, Carole Bouquet is convincing as Melinda, displaying credibility as an independent woman that previous actresses in the Moore films lacked. Topol provides a good performance as Columbo, whose similarity to Karim Bey is probably intentional. As the teenager, Lynn-Holly Johnson not only has the burden of playing an unnecessary character but also she cannot act. Lois Maxwell and Desmond Llewelyn appear but noticeably absent is Bernard Lee, who died just before production. His authoritarian and avuncular presence is missed in this film and would be missed in future films.

Direction is by John Glen, who had functioned as editor or second unit director of three previous Bond films, including *On Her Majesty's Secret Service*, which probably accounts for the influence of that film in his directorial debut. Glen skillfully gives priority to the story and the characters while allowing the realistic action sequences to be part of the narrative and not superfluous set-pieces. The disappointing score is by Bill Conti and is inappropriately modern. John Barry could have added immeasurably to the film's impact.

For Your Eyes Only was successful at the box office, earning $25 million in U.S. theatrical rentals. This was down from *Moonraker* but since it was a less expensive film to make, its profits were considerable. And, though it does not achieve classic status for the reasons mentioned, it is Roger Moore's best Bond movie. It was certainly a welcome step in the right direction for Eon.

Possibly due to the reduced grosses, Eon's next movie would attempt to retain the serious tone of *For Your Eyes Only* but also contain the childish humor and amazing stunts associated with Moore's other films. This would be Eon's next mistake. However, their film would have competition from another Bond, the "original" Bond. The year 1983 would be the second year in which two James Bond movies would be released, a fact which in itself is testimony to the character's durability. And although both films would prove to be disappointing, neither would be as bad as the two 1967 movies.

Eon's production of *Octopussy* was released in the summer of 1983. Since United Artists had merged with MGM with the previous year, this was the first Bond film to be released under the MGM logo. It appears that Broccoli and Company arrived at the wrong conclusion regarding the content and tone of *For Your Eyes Only*. Instead of correctly seeing the two inappropriate intrusions of comedy at the beginning and the end as liabilities, they apparently saw the *lack* of those scenes as the problem. Thus, the next film would contain equal amounts of serious aspects and comedy aspects, a mixture that simply doesn't work.

Octopussy takes Bond to India to investigate the smuggling of jewelry organized by an exiled prince, Kamal Khan, who is allied with a renegade Russian officer whose plan is to explode an atomic bomb on an American military base. Also aligned with Khan is a wealthy woman known as Octopussy whose traveling circus is used to smuggle the jewelry across borders. This film is even more schizophrenic than the previous film, since the relatively serious scenes are regularly interrupted by far too many scenes of juvenile humor, topical in-jokes and broad self-parody. After the obligatory pre-credits sequence and its accompanying spectacular visual stunt, the movie proper begins quite excitingly with a realistic chase involving one of Bond's colleagues who is being pursued by a pair of killers.  There are many other similar scenes throughout the movie, all of which display the expertise that director John Glen showed in his first effort. If the film had maintained the serious, realistic tone of this first sequence, it could have been quite impressive.

Unfortunately, the movie loses all credibility due to scenes of Bond taming a wild beast with a verbal command or, in what is certainly another low point for the series, Bond swinging on a vine accompanied by the famous Tarzan yell. The movie also has its share of silly gadgets and juvenile one-liners, few of which are funny. Though not as outlandish as *Moonraker* or *The Spy Who Loved Me*, this movie tries to please both the fans that welcomed the return of the serious Bond in *For Your Eyes Only* and the younger fans who enjoyed the action-comedies of the 1970s. Since the latter were less demanding than the former, they left theaters amused while the serious fans were once again disappointed.

Roger Moore displays his talent again as a somewhat older Bond, but the broad comedy intrusions destroy the credibility he developed as 007 in the previous film. This is regrettable because in the scenes in which he is required to again be rather harsh, particularly those he shares with Khan, he is very convincing as Fleming's Bond. Louis Jordan is a suave and crafty Khan and would have been a more memorable villain if the tone of the film had matched his portrayal. Maud Adams conveys earnestness as Octopussy, but her character seems more of a symbol of the mandatory female enemy-turned-ally than a real person. As the new M, Robert Brown is adequate but lacks Bernard Lee's crustiness. Lois Maxwell is her usual appealing Moneypenny but, perhaps due to her showing her age along with Moore, she has a younger assistant to share her chores and flirt with 007. Desmond Llewelyn is always welcome but he doesn't belong in the climactic battle scene.

John Glen directs for the second time and it seems obvious that his skill is more suited to the action scenes; it is unfortunate that he was probably obligated to include the inappropriate elements. The script is by Richard Maibaum and Michael Wilson along with George Macdonald Fraser and is once again based upon two of Fleming's stories, "Octopussy" and "The Property of a Lady," but uses less of their content than the previous film. John Barry is back on the team and he provides a nice score, including a melodic theme song entitled "All Time High," which is sung pleasantly by Rita Coolidge. Despite its shortcomings, or perhaps because of them, *Octopussy* was a major commercial success all over the world, earning U.S. theatrical rentals of over $34 million, once again proving Broccoli's decision to have been a correct one, at least from a commercial perspective.

Less than four months after the release of *Octopussy*, Sean Connery returned as James Bond in *Never Say Never Again*, released by Warner Bros. When Kevin McClory was legally awarded film rights to produce *Thunderball* in the early 1960s, he was also awarded the rights to remake the story after a 10-year period. After several false starts, he sold his remake rights to producer Jack Shwartzman and was able to proceed with the film as executive producer, particularly after Connery took back his never again statement and agreed to return to the role that had made him famous.

In *Never Say Never Again*, the filmmakers try not to be too similar to *Thunderball* but still capture the style of the early classics. Once again, Bond is pitted against a fanatical Largo, here given the first name of Francisco, and SPECTRE's scheme to extort millions of dollars from world governments after stealing two nuclear bombs. Since the film thankfully avoids the absurd visual jokes and slapstick humor of the recent Eon films, it is closer to the spirit of Fleming and, in that respect, it is a welcome relief from the juvenile antics of the recent Eon films, excepting *For Your Eyes Only*. And, of course, the presence of Connery as Bond is an extremely welcome sight. But in other respects, the movie fails to achieve its aspirations.

Director Irvin Kershner had previously worked with Connery in 1966 during the height of Bondmania on a relatively small and intimate film, *A Fine Madness*, which featured a very good performance from the star as a nonconformist poet. It is therefore not surprising that the best scenes in their Bond collaboration are the more personal ones focusing on the characterizations and relationships. However, the action scenes lack the flair of those of the Eon films and the fight scenes in particular lack conviction. Also, the world domination game Bond plays with Largo may be symbolically interesting, but playing a computer game doesn't make for very exciting cinema. As a result, the movie is often sluggish, especially in the climactic battle and the fight between Bond and Largo.

However, the major deficiency of the movie is the screenplay, which is credited to Lorenzo Semple, Jr. When the decision to sign Semple was announced, it was disheartening to many Bond fans in view of his disastrous scripts for the remakes of *King Kong* in 1976 and *Flash Gordon* in 1980. Their fears proved justified. Though based upon the original McClory-Whittingham-Fleming script, the revised screenplay lacks originality and wit while the characters lack the flair and appeal of their counterparts. This is particularly disappointing since the characters of Emilio Largo, Domino and Fiona Volpe are some of the most memorable ones of the entire series. In particular, Fatima Blush, who takes the place of Fiona, is undeveloped and her confrontations with Bond lack the erotic tension of the original, despite a sexual encounter which goes a bit too far for a Bond movie and is unwelcome. Furthermore, her demise is predictably telegraphed when she foolishly does something that has no purpose other than to give Bond an excuse to use a silly gadget.

On the plus side, Connery is naturally excellent. He gives the impression that he is the same character he first played over two decades earlier, only perhaps more mellow and with less verve. Like Roger Moore in his two recent films, Connery plays an older Bond, one who is not held in such high esteem by the new M as by his predecessor. But though his reflexes may be slowing down, as apparent from a mistake he makes in a war games prelude, they are just as proficient as ever when called back to duty to save the world. (Unfortunately, the war games scene doesn't really make any sense since the deaths appear so realistic, which wouldn't be the case in an actual training exercise.) It is Connery's performance that really holds the film together, not only for nostalgic reasons, but because of his undeniable charisma as 007.

Other performances are not up to his standards. Klaus Maria Brandauer lacks the appearance of power conveyed by Adolfo Celi. His Largo appears to be a bit psychotic and it makes his character more perverted than dangerous. The intent may have been to emulate the psychopathic Red Grant of *From Russia with Love* but Brandauer lacks the force of Robert Shaw. The two female leads are noticeably deficient compared to their counterparts in the original. As Domino, Kim Basinger lacks the vulnerability of Claudine Auger and her performance is a very transparent one since she seems to try too hard to project her character's emotions. Even more damaging is Barbara Carrera as Fatima. Not only does Carrera lack the mature sensuality and convincing menace of Luciana Paluzzi's Fiona Volpe, she also plays the role like a spoiled debutante and doesn't come near to being an even match for Bond.

It is good to see Blofeld back again and Max Von Sydow is an excellent choice for the role. Though seen only briefly, he conveys the villainous stature required by the character. As M, James Fox seems so snobbish toward Bond that even Bernard Lee would approve if Bond just slapped him. Alec McCowen is humorous as Algernon, the equivalent of Q, while Pamela Salem doesn't have much of an opportunity to make an impression as Miss Moneypenny.

Another major handicap of the movie is a wretched score by Michel Legrand which includes a bland title song that is sung incongruously over the title credits and the simulated violence of the war games. This was the first and only Bond movie that was not accompanied by a soundtrack album in Britain and the United States, although a Japanese pressing was issued.

Never Say Never Again is at best moderately entertaining but disappointing. It might seem better if not for the superiority of *Thunderball*. This was made obvious to millions in the U.S. when ABC-TV broadcast a rerun of *Thunderball* just prior to the release of the remake. McClory might have been more successful if he had had the right to film a completely new Bond story. Nevertheless, Connery's return as Bond was greeted enthusiastically by audiences and the film was successful, though it didn't do as well as *Octopussy* in America, earning theatrical rentals of $28 million. But McClory appeared to be on the right track and fans hoped that he would be producing additional 007 movies, especially since his fondness for the character of Bond was apparent. It was a vain hope and didn't take into consideration the legal potency of Eon.

Roger Moore returned for *A View to a Kill*, released in 1985. This film uses only the title of another Fleming story, or at least most of the title which is actually "From a View to a Kill." The script by Richard Maibaum and Michael Wilson is an original one and concerns a power-hungry industrialist who plans to cause an earthquake in

California to control the microchip traffic. This is one of the most derivative films of the series with only superficial changes in the story and characterizations. The movie has the requisite chase scenes, the requisite villain and his henchman, the requisite good girl and bad girl and all of the other familiar elements which add up to tedium.

John Glen directs his third Bond film and, though the action scenes contain his usual verve, the film fails to hold interest. The film has two interesting actors in the cast but they are both wasted. Christopher Walken can be a very dynamic actor but the script does not allow his character any depth. Patrick Macnee is a very likeable and popular star, thanks to his television series *The Avengers*, and he enlivens his scenes but he isn't given enough to do. Tanya Roberts plays a geologist but she looks like she doesn't know how to spell the word. The alien-looking singer Grace Jones is supposed to play a combination of Oddjob and Rosa Klebb, but she is only capable of playing Grace Jones.

A View to a Kill earned U.S. rentals of $25 million, below both *Octopussy* and *Never Say Never Again*. Roger Moore wisely chose to leave the series after his seventh Bond movie. The film also included Lois Maxwell's last appearance as Moneypenny after 14 films, though Robert Brown and Desmond Llewelyn would stay on as M and Q.

When Timothy Dalton was announced as the fourth James Bond, it was publicized by Eon that the 007 of Ian Fleming's novels would return to the screen. Only the decreased grosses of the previous film could force Eon to make such a radical announcement. In 1987, *The Living Daylights* was released and it does present Dalton as a more serious and ruthless Bond. The movie begins with a good introduction of the new 007 in the pre-credits sequence in which an enemy assassin infiltrates a test of Gibraltar's defense system by the British Secret Service. Initially seen from behind, Dalton's Bond turns quickly to show his face upon hearing the scream of a colleague. The chase and fight that ensue are exciting and realistic.

The screenplay is by Richard Maibaum and Michael Wilson who, with this film, became the co-producer with Broccoli. It uses Fleming's story of the same title as an inspiration for another original script that is more intricate than the usual Bond film. The plot of the film is quite complicated and involves a Russian agent who apparently wants to defect because he is opposed to a KGB plan to murder British agents. But the Russian is another renegade officer who is actually aligned with an American arms dealer in a plan to make millions of dollars through the illegal sale of arms and drugs. The story takes Bond from Vienna to Czechoslovakia to Afghanistan where he joins the rebels in their battle against the Russians.

With such a complex plot, the characters of the duplicitous Russian and the right-wing American should be more developed than they are. Similarly, while attempts are made to define the cellist who functions as Bond's only romantic interest, it is an overly simplistic explanation and she also is undeveloped. The script contains shades of moral gray which are usually associated with more serious espionage novels, such as those of Len Deighton or John LeCarre, and are not really a part of the Fleming fantasy. But they are introduced and then given a back seat to the action scenes. The introduction of the Afghan freedom fighters complicates an already convoluted plot and seems to have been included just to provide an action-packed sequence. But it doesn't work because James Bond, though suitable to an Aston Martin or a Citroen, should not be on horseback.

John Glen directs his fourth Bond film and he seems more comfortable without having to include superfluous scenes of childish comedy. The climactic fight between Bond and a villain in midair swinging on a net from the open cargo door of a plane heading for a crash is quite skillfully staged and, along with the introductory fight, would have been more than sufficient for the film's action requirements.

Timothy Dalton is persuasive as a more dangerous Bond. He is so serious that the droll one-liners he is required to speak seem out of place for his characterization, as does a silly scene in which he escapes down a mountain in a cello case. He is also a more angry 007, directing his rage toward anyone who annoys him and that includes his colleagues and M. It is an interesting debut for Dalton as Bond, but the characterization is marred by the formulaic requirements of the producers. Just as the Bond films of the 1970s followed trends of that decade, this film follows the trends of its own period. Movies featuring such heroes as Rambo and Indiana Jones were huge commercial successes in the 1980s and Eon attempted to turn Bond into a similar hero. But this doesn't fit in with the introspective Bond that Dalton played, and the blend of genres does not mix well.

Maintaining continuity with previous films, Robert Brown and Desmond Llewelyn are back as M and Q while Caroline Bliss is the new Moneypenny. John Barry composed the music and, though it is only adequate, it is better than any of the scores by other composers. It was his 11th Bond score and it would be his last. His brilliant scores were invaluable ingredients for the best films in the series and were definite benefits to the lesser films on which he worked.

The Living Daylights emerges as a fairly good adventure film but it doesn't stand out as a James Bond film because, while it is not derivative of other 007 films, it is derivative of other adventure films. However, it earned U.S. theatrical rentals of over $27 million, slightly more than Moore's last film and was even more successful in worldwide markets. This success seemed to indicate public acceptance of Dalton as Bond. However, while such grosses were considered astronomical in the 1960s, after 20 years of inflation they were only considered average and other action heroes were earning higher profits.

In view of this, the emphasis on action would increase even more in the next movie, *License to Kill*, released in 1989. Like its predecessor, this film is both formulaic and imitative of other action movies. In fact, the influence of other films seems to permeate the entire film, which isn't surprising since Michael Wilson gets billing in the writing credits over Richard Maibaum in this entry. Maibaum was always a distinctly original writer but, when he shared credits with others, his creativity was infected by commercial requirements and production personnel who wrote with one eye on the box office. And since the big box office hits at that time did not fit the Bond formula, then Bond would have to adapt to them, much to the dismay of fans of Fleming's 007.

In *License to Kill*, the villain is a South American drug dealer,

Sanchez, who maims Bond's friend, Felix Leiter, and murders Leiter's bride. Bond then quits the Secret Service and embarks on a personal quest for vengeance. Sanchez lacks the stature to be a worthwhile opponent of James Bond, but such sadistic villains were fashionable at that time in films like *Lethal Weapon*. Thematically, this movie departs from the formula in some ways, most notably the fact that Bond operates independently without an official license to kill. Bond's relationship with M seems based upon mutual contempt instead of mutual respect. The character of Pam, the main female character, is more derivative of other action movies. Her ability to handle a shotgun is an obvious attempt to appeal to the women in the audience who think that shooting men is a sign of independence. Most regrettable is the fact that Bond is not the sophisticated agent of previous films but a hot-blooded vigilante similar to Charles Bronson's character in the *Death Wish* movies.

From a cinematic perspective, the film is also noticeably different primarily due to its disturbing emphasis on graphic violence, including several tasteless scenes. The supposedly witty remark that Sanchez makes after one particularly gruesome killing illustrates the wide gulf between the genuinely witty lines of the early films and the sick humor of this one. Sanchez is also so sadistic that he doesn't belong in a series that was originally designed as escapist entertainment. Violence in the best Bond films was never explicit and this is part of what makes them so entertaining. Nothing funny or entertaining exists about this movie that seems to be trying to attract the teenage audience of the *Friday the 13th* exploitation movies. And then, in the denouement, "Shotgun Pam" uncharacteristically becomes teary-eyed and vulnerable as she and Bond embrace in an improbable scene designed to appeal to women who love romantic endings.

This attempt by the filmmakers to appeal to as wide an audience as possible by imitating commercial trends is chiefly responsible for the film's uninspired look and its failure as a Bond movie. It has little connection to Fleming, despite the fact that Leiter's fate is taken from the novel *Live and Let Die*. Indeed, the only interesting scenes seem inspired by Fleming, such as the one in which Leiter's bride offers Bond her garter and he sadly declines, with Leiter explaining later about Bond's ill-fated marriage. This reference to *On Her Majesty's Secret Service* is probably the only memorable scene in the entire script but it relates to nothing else in the movie. The line is most certainly Maibaum's but if it was intended to indicate a connection between the murder of Bond's bride and the murder of Leiter's bride, this theme is never followed through. Somehow the suspicion exists that Maibaum's artistic creativity was again stifled by the commercialism of the producers.

As the villains, Robert Davi, Anthony Zerbe and Don Stroud are all good actors and are familiar to fans of American crime thrillers, which adds to the film's imitative appearance. Talisa Soto is at least believable in her role as Sanchez' mistress, but Carey Lowell is simply unconvincing as Bond's ally, particularly when handling weaponry. The score by Michael Kamen is unmemorable.

This was John Glen's fifth and last film as Bond director. Also departing from the series would be Robert Brown after four performances as M and Caroline Bliss after just two appearances as Moneypenny, while Desmond Llewelyn was still hanging in as Q. Most significant, Timothy Dalton would also leave the series after just two appearances as James Bond. Dalton displayed considerable talent as an actor but he had the misfortune to be cast in the role when the producers didn't seem to know what to do with the character. Dalton had the potential to be Fleming's Bond but, due to the misconception of his two films, he wasn't allowed to make a lasting impression.

Public response to *License to Kill* at least in the United States was below expectations. Although it was more successful abroad, it achieved U.S. theatrical rentals of only $16 million. This was the lowest figure for a Bond movie in some time, particularly when the inflation factor is considered. While *Batman*, *Lethal Weapon 2* and *Indiana Jones 3*, in which Sean Connery had a co-starring role, were reaping tremendous profits in the summer of 1989, James Bond 18 was struggling to break even. Some industry analysts were predicting the end of the series but Eon was not ready to throw in the towel.

In August 1990, Albert Broccoli announced that he was turning over control of Eon to his daughter, Barbara, and his stepson, Michael Wilson. It was reported in *Variety* that new directors and writers associated with financially successful contemporary heroes would be hired for the next 007 film "to bring Bond into the action-adventure mold of the 1990s." Thus, it appeared that the company planned to take the character further away from his source. James Bond would no longer blaze new trails and serve as a model and inspiration for numerous inferior imitators. He would now be fully converted into an inferior imitator who would follow trends set by other characters. Actually, Eon's decision would be a very wise one, at least commercially. But it would also do what SPECTRE and Blofeld could never do. It would kill 007.

It was it six years before James Bond returned to the screen and, when he did return, it was James Bond in name only. Bond had undergone many changes and variations since first appearing on the screen in 1962, but he had managed to survive all of them. One thing he could not survive was political correctness. Of all the modifications he had been subjected to by Eon, none was more damaging to him than raising his consciousness.

Goldeneye, released in 1995, introduces Pierce Brosnan as the screen's fifth James Bond. The confusing plot involves the hijacking of a Russian satellite weapon

by a crime syndicate run by a former Double-0 colleague and still another renegade Russian officer. The plot is incidental to the familiar stunts, set-pieces, explosions and pyrotechnics. In the scene in which Bond pilots a Russian tank through the streets of St. Petersburg, demolishing buildings like matchsticks, he looks like a fool with his head sticking out of the turret to let viewers know that it really is Brosnan in the tank. The fight scene at the end is clearly patterned after the fight between Bond and Red Grant, but it is an artificial imitation. In fact, the entire movie seems synthetic due to the terrible double-entendres, the numerous product placements and the humdrum action scenes.

Goldeneye is not as much a movie as a calculated attempt to make Bond commercial once again by appealing to currently fashionable tastes. Bond's stature is significantly reduced due to the obvious intent of the producers to prove to skeptical audiences that this Bond is very responsive to past complaints and is not going to offend anyone, particularly feminists. Bond has always been involved with strong women, especially in the five classics, but the women of those films derived their strength from their characterizations and not from a politically correct ideology. This does not apply to *Goldeneye,* in which the female characters are not real persons but symbols. The most obvious example of this is the new female M, and this highly publicized casting was designed to alert the public that Eon was attuned to modern sensibilities.

This new M admonishes Bond by calling him a chauvinistic dinosaur or words to that effect. This reprimand is supposed to be cute because it is delivered by a woman in a tutorial manner to Bond, who smirks like a naughty schoolboy. The line alerts audiences that M is a modern woman who will tolerate Bond's primitive needs but only on her terms. It is supposed to alert men in the audience that Bond is still his same old rascally self, despite his subservience to an authoritative woman. And it alerts women that not only has Bond been put in his place but that subsequent women in the film will also determine the course of their dealings with him. Even Moneypenny merely tolerates his flirtatiousness in a manner that suggests she is bored by his antiquated attitude.

Now, if Sean Connery's Bond had to deal with a female M, he would have patted her on the rear and sent her away, telling her he had to have some "man-talk" with Q or some other male. Even Roger Moore's Bond would probably have said something like, "Now, darling, why don't you be a dear and get me some coffee while I figure out how to save the world." But Brosnan is a male of the 1990s and is extraordinarily sensitive. The irony is that, though Eon's publicity material declared that the women in the new Bond film would no longer be "bimbos" as in the past, nothing could be further from the truth. If the unnamed publicity agent who invented that fallacy ever called Honey Rider a bimbo to her face, he'd quickly find a spider in his bed. Pussy Galore would throw him against a wall and Fiona Volpe would send a motorized rocket crashing into his boot. And Rosa Klebb and Irma Bunt would play football with his head.

Bond's diminishment is furthered in other ways. In the pre-credits sequence, he is sent on a mission with 006. But the Bond of previous films and the novels always acted alone and it was suggested that he was the best agent who was often sent on assignments after other agents had failed. In this film, he is simply one of many.

As promised by Eon, the production personnel of *Goldeneye* are mostly new names. Direction by Martin Campbell is conventional as is the screenplay by Bruce Feirstein. The score by Eric Serra is reminiscent of elevator music. In the cast, the only familiar name is Desmond Llewelyn as Q. Judi Dench tries to look stern as M but doesn't succeed. Samantha Bond (no relation) is the new enlightened Moneypenny. As far as Pierce Brosnan is concerned, he simply isn't the Bond that Ian Fleming created or that previous actors played. The entire film has nothing to do with Fleming, despite the title being taken from the name of the author's Jamaican estate.

However, Eon's strategy worked. Brosnan's debut film was very successful at the box office. By the time of this film's release, a movie's earnings were no longer determined by theatrical rentals but by actual grosses, and *Goldeneye* grossed $121 million domestically and even more in the rest of the world. Commercial success breeds imitation and the next movie, *Tomorrow Never Dies*, released in 1997, is more of the same. Instead of a renegade Russian officer, a renegade Chinese warlord who is aligned

with an evil media mogul attempts to start a war between Britain and China by sinking a British frigate. And the thoroughly modern Bond is aligned with a female Chinese agent who naturally is a martial arts expert. Once again, explosions and chases become mechanical after a while. And obligatory scenes of the Chinese agent chop-socking a dozen bad guys appear, as do the Bondian quips, which now are groaningly awkward. Having a media mogul as the villain is supposed to make the film topical, but the best Bond films were never designed to be topical. They exist in their own fantasy world which this film doesn't recognize.

Roger Spottiswoode directs by the numbers while Bruce Feirstein's script is more confusing than his previous one. David Arnold's score tries to recall the splendor of John Barry but dismally fails. Casting is woefully deficient. Johnathan Pryce looks like a car salesman and simply doesn't come close to being a worthy adversary for the old Bond. Michelle Yeoh, a famous Asian action star, is included to sell tickets at Asian box offices. Samantha Bond is an increasingly progressive Moneypenny who, in collaboration with Judi Dench's M, keeps Bond on a leash like a spayed puppy. Desmond Llewelyn is still around as Q, the only reminder of just how entertaining the films used to be. And Pierce Brosnan's Bond can't be anything but bland in view of the concept of the character. However, the movie was another box office hit, grossing $135 million in the U.S.

The World Is Not Enough, released in 1999, uses the Bond family motto as the title but the film is another derivative exercise in familiarity. The plot has Bond avenging the killing of an industrialist who was M's friend. And when M sends Bond on a mission to protect the industrialist's daughter, she uses a bad double entendre which proves that she can even outwit 007 in verbal repartee. More embarrassing is the fact that even Moneypenny has her share of witless puns.

The movie includes the standard chases, one on high-speed boats, another on flying snowmobiles and so on. The usual stunts appear like Bond dangling over London's Millennium Dome and hanging onto a hot-air balloon. However, though the action scenes are well choreographed, they are modeled on those of other movies, such as the *Die Hard* series. One of the most unintentionally humorous scenes of the entire series occurs when the nuclear physicist is revealed to be a woman who looks like a teenager and is played by Denise Richards, who apparently thinks her title refers to physical education. The casting of the villain is even worse since Robert Carlyle fails to project any menace. As the daughter, Sophie Marceau acts like she is only in the movie for the salary, which will enable her to continue making French art films.

Pierce Brosnan is again only a pseudo-Bond. And although Desmond Llewelyn still appears as Q, he refers to his pending retirement and introduces his assistant, played by John Cleese, who will take over his role. Llewelyn projected a likeable screen presence and made his Q amusing for almost four decades. Cleese can be genuinely hilarious but his humor, always a cross between Monty Python and Basil Fawlty, is incompatible with a Bond movie, which is probably why his antics are not out of place in this feeble effort.

Direction by Michael Apted is suitable to the uninspired screenplay by Bruce Feirstein with Neal Purvis and Robert Wade. Both script and direction seem to indicate the guiding hand of producer Michael Wilson, who is probably responsible for the computerized appearance of all of the films since he first became involved in the series, whether as executive producer, co-writer or producer. This was another box office hit, earning a domestic gross of about $133 million.

Die Another Day, released in 2002, begins with Bond captured by the Koreans and held prisoner for over a year. Scenes showing Bond unshaven and tortured are supposed to make this entry a realistic espionage story but all it does is further diminish the stature of Bond, particularly when remarks are made by allies questioning his worth. (James Bond was captured and tortured on several occasions in the novels and in the early films, but he always escaped and prevailed due to his own ingenuity. Of course it was fantastic, but that's the point.) Once he is released, this metrosexual Bond once again aligns himself with a feisty female operative, who naturally is as tough and daring as he is. From then on, the movie is banal and boring with even the requisite action scenes and spectacular stunts looking merely perfunctory.

The movie also achieves an all-time low for the music of the series by having Madonna sing the terrible title song for which she also shares co-writing blame. And, to add insult to injury, she appears in the film in a brief scene which invites derisive laughter from audiences.

Pierce Brosnan again plays an emasculated hero, despite the seductions, which in keeping with the times are not as innocuous as in the classics but still look as mechanical as the special effects. Halle Berry is simply not credible as the female agent. John Cleese does his John Cleese routine as the new Q while Judi Dench makes another feeble attempt to project authority. Toby Stephens plays another smaller-than-life villain that Blofeld wouldn't have allowed to be even a janitor in his organization.

Direction by Lee Tamahori is strictly by-the-numbers and indicates that the new Bond directors must all attend a training class run by the producers, who probably instruct them on how to adapt their technique to the Bond formula. The script by Neal Purvis and Robert Wade indicates that the new writers also are taught which elements must be included and at which intervals. The classes seem to have the desired results. This movie proved to be more commercially successful than Brosnan's previous entries and grossed $160 at U.S. box offices.

The figures for the Brosnan films are somewhat misleading. Upon the release of *Die Another Day*, the newspaper *USA Today* published a chart which converted the grosses of the entire Eon series into 2001 dollars to adjust for inflation. The chart includes both North American and Worldwide grosses and provides a means of comparison for all of the films in the series.

On the North American chart, Sean Connery's films are in the top positions. *Thunderball* tops the list with $351 million followed by *Goldfinger* with $283 million, *You Only Live Twice* with $225 million and *Diamonds Are Forever* with $193 million. Roger Moore's top-grossing movie, *Moonraker*, is fifth with $164 million. Brosnan's *Die Another Day* with its final gross of $160 million would place it at sixth position. Out of 20 films in the Eon series, incidentally, *On Her Majesty's Secret Service* is Number 14 with $112 million in between two Moore films, *Octopussy* and *For Your Eyes Only*. Dalton's *License to Kill* is last with $50 million.

The Worldwide chart is similar. *Thunderball* again tops the list with an astounding $780 million followed by *Goldfinger* with $695 million and *You Only Live Twice* at $588 million. Moore's top film on this chart is *The Spy Who Loved Me* at Number 4 with $556 million followed by *Live and Let Die* with $552 million. Brosnan's top film is *Die Another Day* with $424 million, placing it at Number 9. *On Her Majesty's Secret*

Service is Number 17 with $318 million while *License to Kill* is again last with a still impressive $225 million. It is apparent that the series peaked in the 1960s.

Identifying the causes of the destruction of James Bond on film isn't too difficult. Quite simply, Eon has traveled too far from the source. James Bond has lost his uniqueness. Eon could begin to restore Bond's former glory by returning to Fleming for inspiration. All of the classic films have been quite faithful to the novels, while the worst movies have been either totally original screenplays or have used only the titles of the novels for scripts that are mostly original. Thus, many Fleming novels have yet to be filmed. Some of them may seem dated and uncommercial, but Eon should stop using commercial potential as a basis for their films. The primary objective should be to bring Ian Fleming's James Bond to the screen as faithfully as possible.

As of this writing, some indications surfaced that Eon may be attempting to do this. Eon, 21st Bond movie, currently in post-production, is a remake of *Casino Royale* with Daniel Craig as 007. Publicity releases from Eon state that the movie will be a faithful adaptation that will depict James Bond's first romance and its effects upon his character. If this is true, then Eon can begin to atone for its egregious mistakes of the past. However, true Bond fans have little hope, considering Eon's track record. Current previews emphasize action scenes and spectacular stunts, which are not ingredients of Fleming's first novel. Time will tell.

Many Fleming fans hope that Kevin McClory will someday be able to produce another Bond movie. In 1986, McClory took out a full-page advertisement in *Variety* to announce that his Paradise Film Productions III would make "a series of James Bond productions commencing with *SPECTRE*." Apparently, legal problems with Eon postponed this project. In 1989, it was reported in newspapers that McClory would indeed produce another Bond movie entitled *Warhead*. Once again, it seems that Eon sent its legal powerhouse to prevent the film and apparently succeeded.

McClory persevered and, in 1996, he again announced plans to make the film, now called *Warhead 2000 A.D.* The following year, Sony Pictures announced that the studio was embarking on a James Bond series in partnership with McClory based upon the stories McClory had originally developed with Ian Fleming and Jack Whittingham. MGM-UA immediately filed suit, claiming that McClory only had the rights to *Thunderball*. Sony countersued MGM-UA but, in 1999, Sony gave up the fight. As part of the agreement, Sony gave $5 million to MGM-UA for damages and MGM-UA paid Sony $10 million for exclusive rights to James Bond and for ownership of *Casino*

Royale, which Sony had owned since its acquisition of Columbia Pictures. Ironically, in April 2005, Sony acquired MGM-UA and will be the new distributor for the Eon series, beginning with the remake of *Casino Royale*, leaving McClory out in the cold.

This is unfortunate since McClory appears to have a clear understanding of the character of James Bond. Even if Eon follows through with its promise to faithfully bring *Casino Royale* to the screen, there is room in the marketplace for another Bond, particularly from the man who helped to create Blofeld and SPECTRE. Competition is healthy and would most likely be an incentive for both parties to create a better Bond. But Eon and Sony now appear to have a stranglehold on the character of James Bond and McClory may not have much of a chance, much to the dismay of Fleming fans. Hopefully, he or his heirs will prevail in the future.

Regardless of what the future holds for James Bond, the original films remain available on home video and are frequently shown on cable television stations. Bond remains popular with each new generation and the superiority of the early films, especially the five classics, is evident to anyone who watches the entire series. Regarding the directors, the writer and the stars responsible for the classics, their subsequent careers have had different results.

After directing the last of his three Bond films, Terence Young had commercial successes with *Wait Until Dark* in 1967 and *The Valachi Papers* in 1972. He also directed several other big budget films such as *Red Sun* in 1972 with an international cast that reunited him with Ursula Andress, an expensive turkey called *Inchon* in 1981, and many foreign movies but nothing of distinction. Before Young died in 1994, he had witnessed the release of the remake of *Thunderball* that paled next to his original. He has the distinction of having directed three of the Bond classics and the most commercially successful Bond of all.

Terence Young

Guy Hamilton, in between his four Bonds, directed two films for Harry Saltzman, *Funeral in Berlin* in 1966 and *The Battle of Britain* in 1969, a notable commercial failure. After leaving the Bond franchise, he had a busy career with such films as *The Mirror Crack'd* in 1980 and *Evil Under the Sun* in 1982. In 1985, he directed *Remo Williams: The Adventure Begins*, another attempt to establish a lucrative series in the spirit of 007, but the adventure ended before it began. Hamilton has the satisfaction of knowing that *Goldfinger* has served as the inspiration for innumerable copies and imitations, some within the franchise itself, and none of which has approached its level of pure escapist entertainment.

Peter Hunt, after his notable directorial film debut with *On Her Majesty's Secret Service*, directed a couple of episodes of the television series, *The Persuaders*, with future Bond Roger Moore. He then directed several adventure films, including two with

Roger Moore (*Gold* in 1974 and *Shout at the Devil* in 1976). However, he never had a major commercial success, despite having been responsible for a superior adventure classic with his first effort. When he died in 2002, he hopefully was aware of the fact that his only Bond movie was considered by many to be the pinnacle of the entire series.

Richard Maibaum's immense skill as a screenwriter is a major reason for the success of the initial films in the series. He co-wrote the four Connery classics while he alone wrote the Lazenby gem. Of all the writers who have worked on the Bond films, only Maibaum had the ability to combine drama, fantasy and genuine wit with the spirit of Ian Fleming. His value to the series would be apparent after his departure. None of the subsequent films would equal the early ones and it became increasingly apparent that his creativity was stifled by having to work with less talented writers or by having his scripts rewritten by others. Maibaum died in 1991, his last screen credit being *License to Kill*.

Guy Hamilton

Sean Connery went on to a long and distinguished film career. In the midst of the Bond films, he had opportunities to display his skill as an actor in films such as *The Hill* in 1965. In *The Offense*, released in 1973, he gives an exceptionally powerful performance as a police officer who cannot control his rage. He went on to star in numerous movies, retaining his popularity all over the world. However, despite playing roles ranging from Robin Hood (*Robin and Marian* in 1976) to King Arthur (*First Knight* in 1995), he will always be remembered as the first and most popular James Bond.

George Lazenby, after refusing to play Bond a second time, soon regretted his decision. He has since admitted responsibility for his own actions during the making of *On Her Majesty's Secret Service*, stating that he shouldn't have listened to bad advice. But once he realized this, it was too late. Eon was not about to give him a second chance and he was unable to obtain work, at least not in major films. For the next several years, the only work he could find was in Hong Kong martial arts movies, exploitation films and independent movies, none of which received wide distribution.

In 1979, Lazenby had a supporting role in a major film, *Saint Jack*. During the next several years, he appeared in episodes of several U.S. television shows, including *Hawaii Five-0* and *Hotel*, and appeared briefly as a regular on the soap opera *General Hospital*. When his former co-star Telly Savalas became a star in 1973 in the television series, *Kojak*, he called Savalas several times to inquire about guest starring in an episode but Savalas never returned his calls. Savalas was apparently not above rubbing salt in Lazenby's wounds. In an episode telecast in 1974 entitled, "A Very Deadly Game," as Kojak runs out of his office he recites the line, "I feel like James Bond."

Though his primary interest for several years was racing motorcycles, Lazenby acted occasionally in independent movies. In 1983, he appeared in the television movie, *The Return of the Man from U.N.C.L.E.*, which was based on the hit series of the 1960s

that was part of the Bond craze during that decade. In the movie, Napoleon Solo, the hero of the series, is trying to escape from the villains by racing through the streets of Las Vegas when he receives some assistance from Lazenby, whose unnamed character is driving a car with the letters JB on the license plate. Other roles followed but none of distinction. In 1999, he had a recurring role as the hero's father in a television series, *The Pretender*, and has since had small roles in several direct-to-video films.

Lazenby's only Bond film was initially subjected to the same disgraceful treatment as its star. In 1976, when it was initially telecast on ABC-TV, it was destroyed by the network. Although the Connery films had received prominent showings on Sunday evenings, the Lazenby movie was separated into two weekly parts and then presented on two consecutive Monday nights from 8:30 to 10:00 before the evening soap opera, *Rich Man, Poor Man*. Furthermore, during the first part, clips of action scenes from the second half were interjected at various intervals as though to repeatedly assure viewers that the movie wasn't a total waste of time. Narration by an unidentified voice was also added to the telecast, further impairing it.

However, the movie was slowly but steadily winning new fans not only from its television showings but its reappearances in movie theaters. Before the video-cassette explosion ruined the market for revival houses, *On Her Majesty's Secret Service* was frequently shown in repertory theaters along with the other 007 films and it often turned out to be the surprise hit of the series. Throughout the 1970s and 1980s, it was presented at various revival houses in the Boston area where it invariably thrilled new audiences. On separate occasions, at the Coolidge Corner Moviehouse and the Kenmore Square Theater respectively, it was enthusiastically received and returned for a second engagement by popular demand at both theaters.

With each passing year, the movie attracts more fans and becomes more renowned. The Bond series is always in demand seems to make the rounds from one cable station to another. Such exposure is particularly rewarding because the films are not cut or edited as they were on the broadcast networks. In the early years of the 21st century, four decades after the series began, the film received wide exposure on the TBS Superstation network and, in 2004, was the highlight of the year on the Starz network. Whenever *On Her Majesty's Secret Service* is telecast, its acclaim increases and Lazenby becomes more appreciated.

George Lazenby often appears at film conventions and is a very popular attraction. Gracious and friendly, he harbors no bitterness over the direction his career took or for his mistakes, for which he takes full responsibility. At least, he has the satisfaction of knowing that his one and only Bond movie is held in high esteem by innumerable Bond fans and that his performance is now held in equally high regard. Indeed, he has to be proud of the fact that he starred in the best James Bond movie ever made.

Dr. No [United Artists/1962]
CREDITS: Producers: Harry Saltzman, Albert R. Broccoli; Director: Terence Young; Screenplay: Richard Maibaum, Johanna Harwood, Berkely Mather, based upon the novel by Ian Fleming; Editor: Peter Hunt; Music: Monty Norman
CAST: Sean Connery (James Bond); Ursula Andress (Honey Rider); Joseph Wiseman (Dr. No); Jack Lord (Felix Leiter); Bernard Lee (M); Lois Maxwell (Miss Moneypenny); Anthony Dawson (Professor Dent); John Kitzmiller (Quarrel); Zena Marshall (Miss Taro); Eunice Gayson (Sylvia Trench); Peter Burton (Major Boothroyd); Yvonne Shima (Sister Lily); Michele Mok (Sister Rose); Marguerite Lewars (Girl Photographer)

From Russia with Love [United Artists/1963]
CREDITS: Producers: Harry Saltzman, Albert R. Broccoli; Director: Terence Young; Screenplay: Richard Maibaum, Johanna Harwood, based upon the novel by Ian Fleming; Editor: Peter Hunt; Music: John Barry; Title Song: Lionel Bart
CAST: Sean Connery (James Bond); Daniela Bianchi (Tatiana); Pedro Armendariz (Kerim Bey); Robert Shaw (Red Grant); Lotte Lenya (Rosa Klebb); Bernard Lee (M); Lois Maxwell (Miss Moneypenny); Eunice Gayson (Sylvia Trench); Vladek Sheybal (Kronsteen); Walter Gotell (Morzeny); Francis de Wolff (Vavra); Martine Beswick (Zora); Desmond Llewelyn (Major Boothroyd–Q); Francis de Wolff (Vavra)

Goldfinger [United Artists/1964]
CREDITS: Producers: Harry Saltzman, Albert R. Broccoli; Director: Guy Hamilton; Screenplay: Richard Maibaum, Paul Dehn, based upon the novel by Ian Fleming; Editor: Peter Hunt; Music: John Barry; Title Song lyrics: Anthony Newley, Leslie Bricusse
CAST: Sean Connery (James Bond): Gert Frobe (Goldfinger); Honor Blackman (Pussy Galore); Shirley Eaton (Jill Masterson); Tania Mallet (Tilly Masterson); Harold Sakata (Oddjob); Bernard Lee (M); Lois Maxwell (Miss Moneypenny); Martin Benson (Solo); Cec Linder (Felix Leiter); Austin Willis (Simmons); Bert Kwouk (Mr. Ling); Desmond Llewelyn (Q); Richard Vernon (Colonel Smithers); Bill Nagy (Midnight)

Thunderball [United Artists/1965]
CREDITS: Producer: Kevin McClory; Executive Producers: Albert R. Broccoli, Harry Saltzman; Director: Terence Young; Screenplay: Richard Maibaum, John Hopkins, based upon an original screenplay by Kevin McClory, Jack Whittingham, Ian Fleming; Editor: Peter Hunt; Music: John Barry; Title Song lyrics: Hal David
CAST: Sean Connery (James Bond); Claudine Auger (Domino); Adolfo Celi (Largo); Luciana Paluzzi (Fiona Volpe); Bernard Lee (M); Lois Maxwell (Miss Moneypenny); Rik Van Nutter (Felix Leiter); Martine Beswick (Paula); Guy Doleman (Count Lippe); Molly Peters (Patricia); Philip Locke (Vargas); Desmond Llewelyn (Q); Roland Culver (Home Secretary); Earl Cameron (Pinder); Paul Stassino (Palazzi)

On Her Majesty's Secret Service [United Artists/1969]
CREDITS: Producers: Harry Saltzman, Albert R. Broccoli; Director: Peter Hunt; Screenplay: Richard Maibaum, based upon the novel by Ian Fleming; Editor: John Glen; Music John Barry; Lyrics: Hal David
CAST: George Lazenby (James Bond); Diana Rigg (Tracy); Telly Savalas (Blofeld); Ilse Steppat (Irma Bunt); Gabriele Ferzetti (Marc Ange Draco); Bernard Lee (M): Lois Maxwell (Miss Moneypenny); Desmond Llewelyn (Q); Yuri Borienko (Grunther); Virginia North (Olympe); Geoffrey Cheshire (Toussaint); Irvin Allen (Che Che); George Baker (Sir Hilary Bray); Angela Scoular (Ruby); Catherine Von Schell (Nancy); Bernard Horsfall (Campbell); Dani Sheridan (American Girl); Joanna Lumley (English Girl); Ingrid Black (German Girl); Julie Ege (Scandinavian Girl); Jenna Hanley (Italian Girl); Zara (Indian Girl); Sylvana Henriques (Jamaican Girl)

The James Bond Films and Actors

1) *Dr. No* (1962) Sean Connery
2) *From Russia with Love* (1963) Sean Connery
3) *Goldfinger* (1964) Sean Connery
4) *Thunderball* (1965) Sean Connery
5) *Casino Royale* (1967) David Niven
6) *You Only Live Twice* (1967) Sean Connery
7) *On Her Majesty's Secret Service* (1969) George Lazenby
8) *Diamonds Are Forever* (1971) Sean Connery
9) *Live and Let Die* (1973) Roger Moore
10) *The Man with the Golden Gun* (1974) Roger Moore
11) *The Spy Who Loved Me* (1977) Roger Moore
12) *Moonraker* (1979) Roger Moore
13) *For Your Eyes Only* (1981) Roger Moore
14) *Octopussy* (1983) Roger Moore
15) *Never Say Never Again* (1983) Sean Connery
16) *A View to a Kill* (1985) Roger Moore
17) *The Living Daylights* (1987) Timothy Dalton
18) *License to Kill* (1989) Timothy Dalton
19) *Goldeneye* (1995) Pierce Brosnan
20) *Tomorrow Never Dies* (1997) Pierce Brosnan
21) *The World Is Not Enough* (1999) Pierce Brosnan
22) *Die Another Day* (2002) Pierce Brosnan
23) *Casino Royale* (2006) Daniel Craig

The James Bond Novels by Ian Fleming

1) *Casino Royale* (1953)
2) *Live and Let Die* (1954)
3) *Moonraker* (1955)
4) *Diamonds Are Forever* (1956)
5) *From Russia with Love* (1957)
6) *Dr. No* (1958)
7) *Goldfinger* (1959)
8) *For Your Eyes Only* (1960 – story collection)
9) *Thunderball* (1961, based upon a screen treatment by Kevin McClory, Jack Whittingham and Ian Fleming)
10) *The Spy Who Loved Me* (1962)
11) *On Her Majesty's Secret Service* (1963)
12) *You Only Live Twice* (1964)
13) *The Man with the Golden Gun* (1965)
14) *Octopussy* (1966 – story collection)

Wyatt Earp on Film

In the history of the American West, one of the most legendary and controversial figures to emerge from that era is Wyatt Earp. Although less than six of his 80 years were spent in law enforcement, his exploits during that period have been discussed, disputed, distorted and dissected ever since.

Wyatt Berry Stapp Earp was born in 1848 in Monmouth, Illinois and during the course of his life was a farmer, buffalo hunter, saloonkeeper, mine owner, prospector, sportsman and businessman. And, of course, he was a lawman. He learned his trade in Wichita, built his reputation in Dodge City and became a legend in Tombstone. He held such positions as City Marshal, Deputy Sheriff, Deputy United States Marshal and was also occasionally employed as a Wells Fargo detective. Despite attempts by detractors to denigrate his achievements, historical evidence proves that he served with distinction and was considered a man of integrity and courage who avoided gunplay whenever possible. Indeed, to prevent gunplay, he perfected the art of buffaloing troublemakers, or clubbing them over the head with his gun. Prior to Tombstone, he was only forced to kill one man in Dodge City and this was a cowboy who fired at him first.

The deadly conflagration known as the Gunfight at the O.K. Corral is the most celebrated event in Wyatt Earp's life. On the afternoon of October 26, 1881, two groups of men faced each other in a vacant lot about 30 yards west of the corral in Tombstone, Arizona. In one group were five men known as "the Cowboys." They consisted of Ike and Billy Clanton, Frank and Tom McLaury and Billy Clairborne. Opposing them were U.S. Marshal Virgil Earp, his brothers and deputies Wyatt and Morgan, and John "Doc" Holliday. Almost immediately after Virgil Earp ordered the cowboys to surrender their arms, guns were drawn and over two dozen shots were fired.. Approximately 30 seconds later, Billy Clanton and the McLaury brothers were dead and Virgil, Morgan and Doc were wounded. Since then, what actually happened during that minute has been shrouded in confusion, contradictory testimony, prejudicial accounts and outright lies.

The gunfight, known as the Streetfight in Tombstone, was quite notorious in its day and was reported in newspapers across the country. Despite what revisionists may claim, the Earps and Doc were enforcing the law against anarchistic outlaws, who were breaking the law by being armed. The Clantons and McLaurys, along with their cohorts, had made repeated threats against the Earps and Doc. Incredibly, as the Earp party made their famous march toward the corral, Frank McLaury refused to disarm unless the lawmen also disarmed. And objective eyewitness testimony indicates that the gunfight began when

Wyatt Earp

The main street of Tombstone, Arizona in 1881

Frank McLaury and Billy Clanton reached for their guns and Tom McLaury reached for his Winchester rifle. Wyatt and his party responded to this concerted action of the outlaws by drawing their guns and firing.

A number of factors led up to that bloody day. Since the discovery of silver in1877, Tombstone had become a prosperous mining town with a population of over twelve thousand. The booming metropolis had attracted investors, merchants, settlers and, inevitably, outlaws who found the proximity of Mexico, the lack of established law and the shortage of beef conducive to criminality. The Clantons, who had a ranch near the San Pedro River, were rustlers and killers and the McLaurys were long-time allies. Other cronies of the Clantons included noted outlaws and killers Johnny Ringo and Curly Bill Brocius. They were all on a friendly basis with Cochise County Sheriff John Behan.

Political factors were relevant. The Earps were Republicans while the Clantons and McLaurys were aligned with the Democrats, one of which was Behan. Economic factors were also important. The Earps had mining, property and gambling interests and were investing heavily in the town. The Clantons didn't want any group, particularly one associated with law enforcement, usurping their lucrative positions of power. Based upon his exploits in Dodge City, Wyatt already had a reputation before arriving in Tombstone as a tough lawman who believed in rigidly enforcing the law. Though neither he nor his brothers came to Tombstone with the intention of wearing a badge, circumstances would change dramatically during the course of their residence in the lawless town.

Wyatt's personal life was also a factor. When Wyatt was 18 years old, he was married for the first time but his wife, Urilla, died within a year and he rarely spoke about her afterward. Though Celia Ann Blaylock, known as Mattie, lived with him in Tombstone as his second wife, they were never actually married. Wyatt eventually left her for Josephine Marcus, and Mattie's suicide the following year is frequently used to discredit his personal character, though details of the personal relationships are cloudy. Significant is the fact of Josephine's prior romance with Behan. When he lost Josephine to Wyatt, Behan's animosity toward Wyatt increased considerably.

Ironically, both factions would make a similar mistake in sizing up their enemies. The outlaws would assume that Wyatt Earp, like other lawmen, would either bend or break in the face of their overwhelming odds. And Wyatt would not realize until it was too late that he was facing a new kind of organized criminality, quite unlike any of the outlaws he had dealt with in other towns, criminals more powerful and brutal than any he had previously encountered.

After the gunfight, Ike Clanton charged the Earps and Holliday with murder but overwhelming evidence convinced Judge Wells Spicer, a jurist known for his honesty, to find the cowboys were killed in a fair fight by peace officers in the line of duty. Charges that the deceased were unarmed were proven false by witnesses as well as by the wounds suffered by Morgan and Virgil Earp. The accusation that the Earps wanted to kill Ike Clanton was dismissed since none of the defendants had fired at Ike, who apparently had disarmed himself once the shooting started and was told by Wyatt to leave the scene in the midst of the battle. The repeated threats made against the Earps by the cowboys prior to the gunfight were also considered relevant. The unsavory reputations of the Clanton gang members were also important in assessing the truth.

Virgil Earp

Detractors of the so-called "Wyatt Earp myth" tend to forget two important pieces of evidence used as part of Wyatt's defense. One was a written statement from Dodge City signed by over 60 highly respected citizens attesting to his honorable character and courageous performance while Marshal in that city. A second statement from Wichita signed by over a dozen people confirmed his integrity and bravery while on the police force of that town.

Morgan Earp

Other supporters of Wyatt Earp were of equally high caliber. John Clum had a reputation for integrity not only as Mayor of Tombstone but as a former Indian agent of the San Carlos Apache Reservation. As founder and editor of the crusading newspaper, *The Tombstone Epitaph*, he championed the Earps and remained Wyatt's lifelong friend. Future Los Angeles businessman George Parsons, whose honesty was never questioned, kept a nonpartisan journal which remains an excellent source of what actually happened. Clara Brown, visiting correspondent of the *San Diego Union*, filed numerous reports which are excellent examples of journalistic objectivity. William Barclay "Bat" Masterson might well have been a participant in the gunfight if he hadn't been summoned away from Tombstone to help his own brother. Bat had frequently served as lawman with Wyatt and always defended his friend's reputation, even after he had become a respected New York journalist.

After the acquittal, the killings continued. Morgan Earp was murdered and Virgil Earp was shot and permanently crippled. If further proof is needed of the criminal nature of the Cowboys, Morgan was shot in the back and Virgil was ambushed from a dark alley. Wyatt's subsequent actions are as controversial as the O.K. Corral gunfight, but he was a deputy U.S. marshal with legal warrants. A warrant was issued for Earp, the basis of which was the corrupt local law of Tombstone. The Vendetta Ride by Wyatt Earp and his posse was reported in newspapers across the country. Readers followed each new report with both excitement and shock as Wyatt tracked and killed at least three men responsible for his brother's murder. And regardless of his personal motivation, his actions effectively destroyed the criminal organization that had reigned throughout the territory so ruthlessly that the governor of Arizona and the President of the United States had threatened martial law.

Doc Holliday's participation in these events has often been used to discredit Wyatt. Born in Georgia in 1850 and educated as a dentist, Holliday left his family's home for reasons that have never been clearly determined. One theory involves a romance with his cousin Melanie, whose Catholic religion prevented their marriage due to his family's disapproval. Another theory involves a shooting incident, while still another refers to the beginnings of his disease. Only the first theory would perhaps account for the bitterness and anger he carried for the rest of his life.

Contracting tuberculosis, called consumption at that time, apparently caused Doc to give up his dental practice and become a gambler, gunfighter and deadly killer. Crippled by his disease and frequent coughing, Doc didn't seem to care whether he lived or died, much to the dismay of his occasional traveling companion, Kate Fisher. He is described as being a mean-tempered and spiteful man with no friends until he met Wyatt Earp, who became his only friend. Despite advice from relatives, Wyatt remained loyal to Doc and ignored attacks upon his own integrity as a result of the friendship.

Doc remained equally loyal to Wyatt. He walked with Wyatt and his brothers toward the O.K. Corral on that fateful October day and he rode with Wyatt on the Vendetta Ride. Doc died of his disease in Glenwood Springs, Colorado in 1886 shortly after Wyatt visited him for the last time. It was an emotional farewell for the two friends. Prior to his death, he had only corresponded with one other person. That person was his cousin Melanie, who had entered a convent.

Following the Vendetta Ride, some historians allege that Wyatt continued to secretly track down other members of the Cowboys and enforced his own brand of justice upon them, but details are sketchy and will probably never be known. What is known is that he pursued various business interests, including prospecting, gambling and horse-racing. The rest of his public life was generally uneventful, except for one major episode.

In 1896, Wyatt refereed the Sharkey-Fitzsimmons heavyweight championship fight in San Francisco. In the eighth round, Sharkey fell to the canvas, clutching his groin and screaming in agony. Wyatt called a foul and ruled in Sharkey's favor. His decision was supported by many witnesses but disputed by just as many others. In retrospect, the prevailing opinion is that Wyatt either correctly made the decision or was duped by Sharkey's team. The charge that he was bribed to throw the fight is neither credible nor supported by any facts, but the accusations brought him emotional pain and humiliation.

Another incident has also been the subject of debate. In 1900, youngest brother Warren was murdered. Some historians believe that this was part of the legacy of the Tombstone Vendetta and that Wyatt secretly exacted justice once again. All that is known for certain is that Wyatt once more suffered intense grief.

Despite his attempts to lead a quiet life in the 20th century, controversy always followed him and articles on the events in Tombstone appeared regularly in whatever city he happened to be living. Some would praise him while others would attack him. To set the record straight, Bat Masterson wrote an article in 1907 on Wyatt, praising his honesty and courage. However, the controversies continued and reached new heights in the late 1920s with the publication of two books about him and his era.

Wilcox gravesite of Warren Earp

Tombstone: An Iliad of the Southwest by Walter Noble Burns (Doubleday; 1927) painted a heroic portrait of Wyatt, whom the author calls "The Lion of Tombstone." Burns based his account on interviews and research that was available to him. One year later, *Helldorado* by William Breakenridge (Houghton Mifflin; 1928) painted a less than flattering image of Wyatt. However, the author's objectivity was questionable since he had been a deputy for Johnny Behan and had always envied and disliked Wyatt Earp. Wyatt's annoyance with the Breakenridge book gave him the incentive to cooperate with a writer to pen his own autobiography, but Wyatt's refusal to disclose secretive details and the writer's florid style doomed the book's chances for publication.

When Wyatt Earp died in 1929 with his wife of 47 years, Josephine, by his side, newspapers across the country carried reports of his passing. The Breakenridge and Burns books would serve as models for innumerable books and articles that would be published after Wyatt's death, some glorifying him as an invincible defender of justice, others vilifying him as a contemptible killer. The following books represent only a fraction of those published over the last 75 years, but they serve as examples of the polarity still engendered by Wyatt Earp.

John Clum's account entitled "It All Happened in Tombstone" was published in *The Arizona Historical Review* nine months after Wyatt's death and has the benefit of the well-respected journalist's direct knowledge of the controversial events. Stuart Lake's biography, *Wyatt Earp, Frontier Marshal* (Houghton Mifflin; 1931), established Wyatt's

Bat Masterson and Wyatt Earp

reputation as the embodiment of a Wild West lawman. Based in small part upon interviews with Wyatt, Lake's book would serve as the basis of the image of Wyatt that survived for at least three decades. Unfortunately, Lake's tendency to insert first-person quotations which he attributed to Wyatt is often used to discredit his subject. While there is little doubt that Lake exaggerated and invented some facts, current research has proven that the book still contains far more truth than the books of the debunkers.

It is ironic that later researchers, who disregard the Lake book because of its positive bias, readily accept as truth the negative bias of the anti-Earp books. Breakenridge's self-promoting *Helldorado* is often used as a legitimate source to prove various charges against Wyatt despite the author's exaggeration of his own importance as well as his friendliness with the outlaws. In contrast, debunkers with an agenda will quickly dismiss the Lake book and the works of Clum and Burns simply because their view of Wyatt is favorable. Such debunkers adapt a Catch-22 attitude in which they assume that if something good is written about Wyatt it cannot be true but anything negative simply has to be true.

Some film historians are guilty of the same error and, though knowledgeable about movies, display incredible ignorance of historical facts. In *The Western* (A.S. Barnes; 1975) Allen Eyles writes that Wyatt was an "exhibitionist and card cheat." In *The Filming of the West* (Doubleday; 1976), Jon Tusca writes that Wyatt "managed to pursue his marshalling with a minimum of personal involvement, surrounding himself with deputies who were invariably deadly shots." In Brian Garfield's *Western Films: A Compete Guide* (Rawson Associates; 1982), the author writes that Wyatt only wore a badge once as a tax collector and allegedly resorted to murder while getting rich. He further writes that "as many as 600 shots seem to have been fired" at the O.K. Corral gunfight. In *John Ford: The Man and His Films* (University of California Press; 1986), Tag Gallagher writes that "Earp, Holliday and the Clantons were leagued in a holdup racket," that the O.K. Corral fight was a "massacre" and that the "Clantons' bodies were left hanging in a butcher's shop." Such statements, for which there are absolutely no foundations of truth, seem to get more fantastic with the passing of time. It is a wonder that Wyatt hasn't been accused of killing Abraham Lincoln.

Wyatt Earp was not a saint and is not above criticism, but that criticism should be honest. Unfortunately, Wyatt was the kind of man who during his lifetime inspired extreme emotions. People either loved or hated him; there was no middle ground with Wyatt. Debunkers have carried on the tradition of hating him and this damages their credibility. Their intent is not to discover the truth but to destroy his reputation and this seems to stem from a pathological loathing for the man and what he symbolizes. In 1907, Bat Masterson possibly explained such vicious attacks when he wrote the following: "Much has been written about Wyatt Earp that is the veriest rot." He adds that, "Wyatt, by his display of great courage, has excited the envy and hatred of those small-minded creatures whose sole delight in life seems to be fly-specking the reputations of real men."

In the early 1960s, when revisionism was fashionable, the anti-Wyatt movement gained considerable ground with the publication of Frank Waters' *The Earp Brothers of Tombstone* (Clarkson N. Potter; 1960.) This book is based upon interviews with people who didn't like Wyatt, including Virgil's widow, Allie, and recounts and disseminates every false story, misstatement, innuendo, rumor and lie ever told about Wyatt. The book is a biased and warped version of the facts and, from a historical perspective, has no value. Interestingly, Allie later withdrew her support of Waters after realizing how her words were being distorted. However, despite its fraudulence, the book was very influential and was subsequently referenced and quoted by debunkers ceaselessly.

Ed Bartholomew's *Wyatt Earp: the Untold Story* (Frontier Books; 1963) and *Wyatt Earp: the Man and the Myth* (Frontier Books; 1964) are filled with such blatant untruths and vitriol toward Wyatt that the books are worthless. It is difficult to account for such bias masquerading as history. Perhaps one of Bartholomew's ancestors was buffaloed by Wyatt.

Ramon F. Adams' *Burs Under the Saddle* (University of Oklahoma Press; 1964) is a critique of books of the West. In his introduction, the author criticizes careless writers who "seem to delight in repeating frequently untrue stories" without investigation. In then critiquing the Lake book, Adams spends 22 pages attacking Wyatt and Lake by repeating numerous frequently untrue stories without investigation, relying on Frank Waters and other anti-Earp writers as evidence for his charges. His account of the O.K. Corral fight as "wholesale murder" alone disqualifies him as a reliable historian. Throughout the book, so many false accusations appear that have since been proven untrue by objective researchers that the entire book loses its value as an authoritative reference work while the author's reputation is forever tarnished.

Fred Dodge was a Wells Fargo detective who posed as a gambler while working undercover in Tombstone. No one knew of Dodge's secret identity and it is revealing that this lawman praised Wyatt and his brothers to his superiors and, indeed, often rode with Wyatt on various posses. In 1969, his papers were edited by Carolyn Lake and published by Houghton Mifflin as *Undercover for Wells Fargo*, which provides invaluable first-hand accounts of the Tombstone troubles. In view of Dodge's identity, there is simply no way that he would have supported the Earps if they had been responsible for any criminal activity, as later implied by debunkers. The fact that he remained a lifelong friend to Wyatt is extremely helpful in uncovering the truth.

I Married Wyatt Earp (University of Arizona; 1976) was edited by Glenn Boyer and based upon the memoirs of Josephine Marcus Earp. Though the text is naturally favorable toward Wyatt, it often reads like a romance novel. It is difficult to take seriously text in which she searches for words to explain her feelings as a teenage girl who is shocked to discover that her town is a "haven of thieves and murderers." From all accounts of Josie, this wide-eyed innocent doesn't seem accurate. Her account of the O.K. Corral gunfight is equally suspect. While she places the blame for the gunfight on Johnny Behan as well as on Billy Clanton and Frank McLaury, she also claims that Doc and Morgan fired first and that Virgil's warning that he didn't want a gunfight was addressed to them and not the Cowboys. In reality, Morgan's history suggests he was never the hothead she claims and, prior to the gunfight, had never shot anyone. The account doesn't ring true and Josie probably would have made a good novelist. The book, however, is still an invaluable source of historical data due primarily to the editor's exhaustive research and comprehensive annotations which follow every chapter.

More recent books have added to the debate. *And Die in the West* (William Morrow; 1989) by Paula Mitchell Marks purports to be a detailed examination of the O.K. Corral fight, but her reliance on debunkers exposes an anti-Wyatt bias. This is obvious, for instance, when she labels George Parsons "an Earp partisan," thus dismissing his diary, and defines Wells Spicer as being "friendly to the Earp faction," thus impugning his objectivity as a judge. She writes that Fred Dodge was "a gambler who later claimed to have been a Wells Fargo detective," thus discrediting his memoirs. She also belittles respected journalist John Clum as "he of the amateur theatricals and purple pen." Some of the author's conclusions are absurd. For instance, her explanation of Doc's maneuvers with a rifle and pistol during the gunfight are nonsensical. She also seems to depend heavily upon Josie's memoirs, since she claims that Doc and Morgan were chiefly responsible for starting the battle. Further, her socioeconomic conclusion that the Cowboys were symbols of downtrodden agrarian innocents who were victimized by industrialist and capitalist interests as symbolized by the Earps is simply ludicrous.

However, such a theory shows how Wyatt can be perceived as a symbol of evil by the far left. Ironically, the far right also views Wyatt as a symbol of evil in view of his rules on gun control and his status as a federal officer. The fact that both extremes view Wyatt as villainous should alone be evidence of his integrity.

Marks' book was published by a mainstream publisher which, combined with her status as a university professor, gives it a perceived legitimacy denied to authors and publishers specializing in the Old West. Such books are rarely reviewed in conventional newspapers or magazines. Nevertheless, the authors have in many cases spent years and even decades researching the subject and have uncovered invaluable data which is often utilized by more mainstream authors. But despite the legitimacy of their research, such authors are routinely dismissed because of their favorable conclusions regarding Wyatt, though they can be critical of Wyatt if evidence warrants it.

In contrast, when some university professors research Wyatt, they approach the subject with condescension. They feel compelled to display independence from traditional beliefs by demolishing popular images embraced by the masses, whether accurate or not. They must condemn Wyatt to prove that they would never share perceptions associated with the popular media. This attitude is typical of revisionists who selectively interpret data to prove their agenda while ignoring other facts. Such academics, perhaps unconsciously, proceed with an agenda that predetermines their opinions and conclusions. It also makes their books historically inaccurate.

Far more worthwhile and objective than the Marks book is Michael Hickey's *Streetfight Trilogy*, three large-size paperback books published between 1992 and 1994 by Talei Press. The first book, *Streetfight in Tombstone, Near the O.K. Corral* is a second-by-second, shot-by-shot account of the gunfight and includes some conclusions with which both pro-Wyatt and anti-Wyatt forces may disagree. But the author has no agenda and is merely seeking the truth.

The most authoritative account of the post-gunfight legal action can be found in *The O.K. Corral Inquest*, edited by Alford E. Turner (Creative Publishing; 1981) which contains not only the text of the inquest and hearing, including the statements of eyewitnesses and participants, but thoroughly researched historical notes and editorial comments. On the same subject and of far less value is *Murder in Tombstone: The Forgotten Trial of Wyatt Earp* by Steven Lubet (Yale University Press; 2004). The author blames an inept prosecution for the acquittal of the Earps and Doc, thus implying that if he were prosecuting the case, Wyatt would have been convicted. His speculations seem to indicate so much partiality against Wyatt that the book emerges as another example of Bat Masterson's "fly-specking."

The Illustrated Life and Times of Wyatt Earp (Tri-Star-Boze; 1995) by Bob Boze Bell, who is not half as witty as he thinks he is, has interesting illustrations and photographs, but the text is often ridiculous, such as when he praises Johnny Behan and Billy Breakenridge. This is the same Behan who lied to the Earps when he said that he had disarmed the Cowboys and, if he had done his job, could have prevented the gunfight. This is the same Behan who deputized Johnny Ringo and Ike Clanton to kill Wyatt. This is the same Behan who turned a blind eye to the repeated violations of the law by the Cowboys and thereby allowed organized crime to flourish. This is the same Breakenridge who invented the story of Wyatt wearing a steel vest, which is so absurd that it makes his entire book suspicious. And this is the same Breakenridge, primarily a tax collector and jailer, who hired Curly Bill Brocius to collect taxes.

The Truth About Wyatt Earp (O.K. Press; 1994) by Richard Erwin is excellent reading because it utilizes virtually everything written about Wyatt in contemporaneous newspapers, court documents and public records and then objectively analyzes many of the subsequent books on Wyatt to try to unearth the true facts. The author's neutrality is commendable, neither bashing nor idolizing his subject, though he perhaps makes the mistake of assuming that if something wasn't printed it didn't happen. It is also regrettable that he apparently didn't have access to Clara Brown's articles.

More flyspecking was apparent in Steve Gatto's *Wyatt Earp: A Biography of the Western Lawman* (San Simon; 1997), a one-sided attempt to deflate Wyatt that is more of a diatribe than a biography as he carefully selects incidents to support his agenda. It was followed by *The Real Wyatt Earp: A Documentary Biography* (High Lonesome; 2000), which is equally sketchy and partial. The author seems to have contempt for Wyatt, and the transparency of this emotion makes both books worthless.

In the late 1990s, mainstream publishers published two major biographies of Wyatt Earp. *Wyatt Earp: The Life Behind the Legend* by Casey Tefertiller (John Wiley & Sons; 1997) is a diligently researched book that dispassionately analyzes its subject's life without any preconceived agenda. The book is admirably impartial in its approach and is based in part upon many newly discovered documents. Significantly, the author illustrates the extent of the organized criminality that infected Tombstone and in fact created a national security issue that almost instigated war with Mexico. The account of the O.K. Corral gunfight, along with the factors that preceded it and the events that followed, is riveting. He also convincingly demolishes the fiction that Doc fired the first shot at the gunfight. The resulting portrait of Wyatt Earp as an outstanding man with natural human flaws is supported by documentation and facts, which are undeniable.

Inventing Wyatt Earp by Allen Barra (Carroll & Graf; 1998) is as much an examination of the development of Wyatt's legendary status as a biography. The author's intent is simply to uncover the truth about his subject and, as a result, he has produced an extremely well-researched and balanced book. Once again, the O.K. Corral gunfight is presented with a fresh and authoritative approach that is supported by factual documentation. Most significantly, the author's analyses of the significant events of Wyatt's life and their impact upon American culture are perceptive and fascinating. His exposition of the reasons for anti-Earp criticism is also illuminating. Much to the dismay of debunkers of the Earp legend, the man who emerges from these pages was a remarkable and admirable person who is deserving of his legendary status.

Wyatt Earp: A Biography of the Legend — Volume 1: the Cowtown Years by Lee A. Silva (2002; Graphic Publishers) is a monumental book based upon meticulous research and is the first of four volumes on the complete life of its subject. Silva evaluates every incident in Wyatt's life and provides in-depth, detailed information on not only the events but on the social and environmental factors that influenced them. Scrupulously objective, the author provides all versions of disputed incidents and draws his own conclusions based upon the evidence while allowing the reader to do the same. Based on the first volume, Wyatt Earp indeed was an admirable man who served as a lawman with distinction and courage in Wichita and Dodge City from 1874 to 1879.

Adding further luster to Wyatt's legend was the publication of *Wyatt Earp: The Biography* by Timothy W. Fattig (Talei Publishers; 2003), which boasts top-quality research, and analysis of the various suppositions and theories of Wyatt's life. This massive book provides new and detailed documentation in support of Wyatt's legendary status.

In view of the Barra and Tefertiller books combined with the Fattig and Silva encyclopedic works, debunkers might as well give up the fight. These four books qualify as definitive biographies and certify the legitimacy of Wyatt's deserved reputation. Nevertheless, it wouldn't be surprising in the future if a book was published alleging that Wyatt went to London at the end of the century and became Jack the Ripper.

Wyatt Earp lived long enough to see the birth of motion pictures. While living in the Los Angeles area, he visited many Hollywood sets and formed close friendships with such Western stars as Tom Mix and William S. Hart, for whose films he often served as technical advisor. In fact, Hart paid tribute to Wyatt by having an actor identified by Lee Silva as Bert Lindley portray him in the 1923 film, *Wild Bill Hickock*, though apparently his character was not central to the plot. Charles Brinkley as

Doc Holliday also does not seem to have figured prominently in the story, though Jack Gardner as Bat Masterson has a fairly large role. It is more than likely that Wyatt was on the set to view the filming and, while his thoughts on seeing himself portrayed on film are unknown, a letter from Josephine to Hart indicates her approval of the film.

As a result of the Hart film, Wyatt must have realized that events of his life would eventually be brought to the screen. However, even in his wildest imagination, he could probably never have envisioned just how many versions, variations, revisions and interpretations of his life would be depicted on film and how many times the infamous gunfight at the O.K. Corral would be recreated.

In 1932, less than three years after the death of Wyatt Earp, his first screen incarnation as the central character appeared in the Universal production of *Law and Order*, which was based on the novel *Saint Johnson* by W.R. Burnett (Dial Press; 1930). The realism of the characters and the explanation of the environmental causes of violence that would be evident in Burnett's more famous gangster novels (*High Sierra, The Asphalt Jungle, Little Caesar*) are prominent in this nontraditional Western novel, which is obviously a fictionalization of Wyatt Earp's exploits as the author explains in a forward to the novel.

Although the names of the characters and the town are changed, the novel reveals the author's knowledge of the historical facts of the saga of Tombstone. Wayt Johnson is a former lawman of Dodge City who wants to be sheriff of the booming silver mining town of Alkali, Arizona. Opposing him is a corrupt Sheriff Wingett, who is aligned with the criminal gang led by the Northrup family and their allies, the Todd brothers. Wayt is a rigid man who wears black and has few vices, earning him the epithet of *Saint* Johnson from his enemies, who resent his attempts to enforce the law. Wayt is aided by his close friend, gambler Ed Brandt, and his two brothers, Luther and Jimmy. A series of increasingly violent incidents, combined with the apathy of the townsfolk, push the normally peaceful and controlled Wayt into a dangerous frame of mind. The Northrups' continued violation of the law and threats against Wayt lead to a bloody gunfight at the North End Corral, the subsequent murder of Jimmy and Wayt's vengeance.

The film version changes the storyline to some degree but retains the general theme of the novel. The protagonist of *Law and Order*, renamed Frame Johnson, is the famous ex-marshal of Wichita and Dodge City who is tired of the violence that comes with being a lawman. With his close friend, gambler and gunfighter Ed Brandt, younger brother Luther and another friend, Deadwood, Frame travels to Tombstone and finds the town under the domination of an outlaw family, the Northrups, who control the local sheriff. Frame doesn't want to become involved in the town's problems, but when the local citizens beg him for help, he reluctantly becomes marshal. However, the citizens express their resentment of Frame's harsh methods by

accusing him of trying to take over the town. When the Northrups murder Ed, Frame angrily lashes out at the hypocritical citizens and promises them that they can have their lawless town back but only after he gets revenge. The following morning, Frame, Luther and Deadwood meet the Northrups at the O.K. Barn in a brutally realistic gunfight which leaves him the only survivor. Tormented by his grief and the violence he tried to avoid, Frame berates the citizens for their cowardice and dejectedly rides away.

Law and Order is a starkly graphic and austere Western that is totally bereft of any romanticism of the Old West or its people. It is deliberately bleak and primitive to emphasize the lawlessness that permeates Tombstone when Frame arrives and will probably return after he leaves. It is a very unremitting view of the price society has to pay for justice if it allows, either through indifference or acquiescence, savagery to rule.

The performances are excellent, particularly Walter Huston as Frame. Huston powerfully conveys the weariness, the sadness and the inherent goodness of Frame as well as the violence that is forced from him. The rage in his face and the fury in his voice after Ed is killed is spellbinding in its impact. And the grief and disgust he conveys at the end as he rides away, victorious but broken-hearted and alone, is haunting. Harry Carey is equally forceful as Brandt, whose weary tone and expression seem to express the despair inherent within the town as well as his life.

John Huston, Walter's son, and Tom Reed co-wrote the solid screenplay which brings the authentic names of Tombstone and the O.K. Corral back to the story, though for some inexplicable reason, Wayt's name is changed to Frame which, in the novel, is the name of one of the outlaw brothers. The movie is the first directorial effort for Edward Cahn, who does such a superb job that it is surprising that he never did anything of distinction after this. *Law and Order* is the first and one of the best Wyatt Earp movies. It received good reviews (*The New York Times* said that it was "a superior specimen of Western heroics") and, though Westerns were not especially popular at the time, struck a chord with audiences in part because lawlessness was as rampant in the early 1930s as it was in 1880s Tombstone.

In a different class is Fox's 1934 production of *Frontier Marshal*, based upon Stuart Lake's biography. In this loose adaptation of the book, George O'Brien portrays Michael Wyatt, who rides into a lawless town and becomes involved in an artificial romantic triangle while defeating an outlaw gang led by the corrupt mayor. He also has a friend named Doc Warren who is played by Alan Edwards. Filled with cardboard heroes and villains, the movie is ineffective and sags, despite its short running time of just over an hour. It is an undistinguished oater and a typical example of the kind of B Western that defined the genre throughout the 1930s.

In 1937, Universal used Burnett's *Saint Johnson* as the basis of a serial starring Johnny Mack Brown entitled *Wild West Days*. Brown portrays Kentucky Wade, who travels to the town of Brimstone with two friends to save a mine-owning couple from an outlaw leader who wants their ore. The thin plot is hardly noticeable amidst the numerous gunfights, chases, Indian raids and cliffhanger endings, all of which delighted juvenile audiences. Only fleeting connections exist to the 1931 adult film or its source novel, but since it is officially based upon a Wyatt Earp novel, it must be included.

In 1935, RKO produced a film entitled *The Arizonian*. This movie falls into the gray area of not being officially or unofficially a Wyatt Earp movie and is a good example of many others that would follow. Such films, though changing the names of characters and places, take incidents from Wyatt's life plus incidents from other movies and mix them in with various Western clichés. If the film has enough clearly identifiable elements pertaining to Wyatt, then it could be included in his filmography. The hero of *The Arizonian* is Clay Tallant, who rides into Silver City, saves a woman from outlaws, is hired as marshal and defeats the outlaws in a gunfight. These are clichés but he is also a famous lawman, is aided by a former outlaw named Tex Randolph, has a brother named Orin and is involved in a romantic triangle with the crooked sheriff. Such plot elements in the original script by Dudley Nichols suggest that he may have read the various books on Wyatt thus far published. Richard Dix is Tallant and Preston Foster is Randolph in this fast-moving action film, which just barely qualifies as a Wyatt Earp movie.

Series star Buck Jones starred in and co-directed *Law for Tombstone* in 1937, one of his series of programmers he made for Universal. He stars as Alamo Bowie, a stagecoach agent hired to stop gold shipment robberies. This is not really a Wyatt Earp movie and is another example of how series Westerns often borrowed themes and characters from major Westerns. It is only mentioned because Wyatt worked for Wells Fargo on occasion and Doc Holliday, as played by Harvey Clark, is a character in the movie. Also, one of the villains is named Bull Clanton. The movie is less than an hour long and played second-tier theaters.

In 1938, Columbia pictures released *In Early Arizona,* which features Wild Bill Elliot as Whit Gordon, a former Dodge City lawman who wants to hang up his guns but puts on a badge once again in Tombstone to do battle with an outlaw gang. Obviously inspired by Wyatt's exploits, the movie is the first of the studio's Elliot series and would be routine if not for the presence of the star who looked like he belonged in the saddle and was one of the more believable heroes of low-budget films. The movie is only 53 minutes long and played on the B circuit.

In 1939, 20th Century Fox filmed Stuart Lake's book a second time, again titled *Frontier Marshal,* but with the names of the two main characters and others true to the source. Randolph Scott plays a hero named Wyatt Earp for the first time on screen, introducing audiences unfamiliar with the books to the legendary lawman. The movie begins with Wyatt's arrival in Tombstone and, after subduing a drunken Indian, being persuaded by helpless citizens of the lawless town to become marshal. Doc Holliday, as portrayed by Cesar Romero, is a disgraced medical doctor from Boston with a bad heart whose life Wyatt saves when a coughing spasm gives an opponent in a gunfight the edge, thus beginning their friendship. Romantic escapades, including friendly rivalry between Wyatt and Doc for the same woman, are only brief intrusions between several confrontations with Curly Bill and his outlaw gang that lead to an inaccurate though exciting showdown at the O.K. Corral.

Randolph Scott as Wyatt Earp in the 1939 *Frontier Marshal*

Scott's natural acting style makes his Wyatt Earp a very likeable character, the soft-spoken and polite yet sturdy hero that would become Scott's trademark. It is a very effective performance and is integral to the film's success. Cesar Romero is convincing as Doc Holliday, though his character as conceived is not historically accurate. In this version, he is killed before the O.K. Corral shootout. Directed by Alan Dwan from a screenplay by Sam Hellman, the movie is filled with action and excitement and is a big improvement over the first version. *Frontier Marshal* is a solid and unpretentious Western with rousing action scenes. It proved to be a popular movie and was one of the year's several films (*Stagecoach, Jesse James, Destry Rides Again,* etc.) that heralded the return of the Western as adult entertainment.

Also in 1939, *The Arizonian* was remade by RKO as *Marshal of Mesa City,* an entry in the George O'Brien series of programmers. O'Brien is Mason, a former marshal who cleans out a group of outlaws who have taken control of a town's political offices. Henry Brandon plays his outlaw friend, named Allison, who becomes one of the good guys to help the marshal. It is barely over an hour long and played neighborhood theaters. It departs further from the facts than the first version since the script changes plot elements from the original Dudley Nichols script. It is even further removed from being a Wyatt movie than the original.

Warner Bros. released *Dodge City* in 1939, but though some film historians claim that the main character is based upon Wyatt, there are no resemblances other than the fact that he cleans up the lawless cowtown. Errol Flynn plays a reluctant lawman who could just as easily have been based upon Bat Masterson, Bill Tillgham or any other lawman if he wasn't totally fictional, as is the entire movie. This is not a Wyatt Earp movie.

Universal got more mileage out of the Burnett novel in 1940 with yet another adaptation entitled *Law and Order* but, as in the second version, the adult storyline of the 1932 film is converted into a juvenile programmer. The story was sufficiently different from the serial to enable Johnny Mack Brown to again play the lead, this time as Bill Ralston, an ex-lawman who finds that the town he has chosen for a life of peace is in dire need of his marshalling skills. With the help of an ex-gambler played by James Craig, Ralston soon cleans up the town. The movie is poorly conceived and little opportunity exists within the 57-minute running time for anything other than the usual ingredients of a formula Western, including romance and a comedy sidekick. Any relation to the source novel is purely coincidental.

In 1942, Paramount released its own version of the story, this one based upon the Walter Noble Burns book, *Tombstone: An Iliad of the Southwest*. Entitled *Tombstone, The Town Too Tough to Die*, ex-lawman Wyatt Earp must once again accept the job of marshal after finding the toughest town in Arizona under the control of the Clanton gang, which has the local sheriff under its control. Romance alternates with action as Wyatt, with the help of his brothers and Doc Holliday,  gradually asserts his authority on the town. The finale once again is the battle at the O.K. Corral, which is fairly exciting.

Tombstone is filled with good action scenes but has its share of clichés. The direction by William McGann makes little use of the more interesting elements of the script by Edward Paramore and Albert LeVino, which adds Virgil and Morgan Earp and a Johnny Ringo character called Johnny Duane as well as the Clantons and McLaurys (here called the McLowerys) to differentiate itself from *Frontier Marshal* of three years earlier. Richard Dix is convincing as "the Lion of Tombstone" and is more sincere as an authentic Wyatt than he was as an imitation in *The Arizonian* seven years earlier. Kent Taylor accurately plays Doc as a dentist turned gunfighter and gives a good performance. Victory Jory as Ike Clanton and Edgar Buchanan as Curly Bill Brocius provide colorful portrayals while Rex Bell and Harvey Stephens are stalwart as Virgil and Morgan. This was a big-budget film from producer Harry Sherman, known for his Hopalong Cassidy series, and the film was sufficiently popular to increase the name-recognition factor of Wyatt Earp as one of the West's most fearless lawman, an image accepted by the public.

The following year, Harry Sherman produced a movie for United Artists called *The Kansan*, also with Richard Dix. The film's setting of a cattle town in Kansas has led to it being often incorrectly labeled a Wyatt Earp movie. Dix is John Bonniwell, a wandering cowboy, who is on his way to Oregon when he foils a robbery by the James Gang in the town of Broken Lance. He is then made town marshal and is pitted against a local politician who wants control of the town. It is based upon a novel by Frank Gruber entitled *Peace Marshal* and neither the film nor the book has any relation to Wyatt (except that, in the novel, Wyatt is mentioned as a young buffalo hunter and possible candidate for position of marshal until the hero, Bonniwell, takes the job).

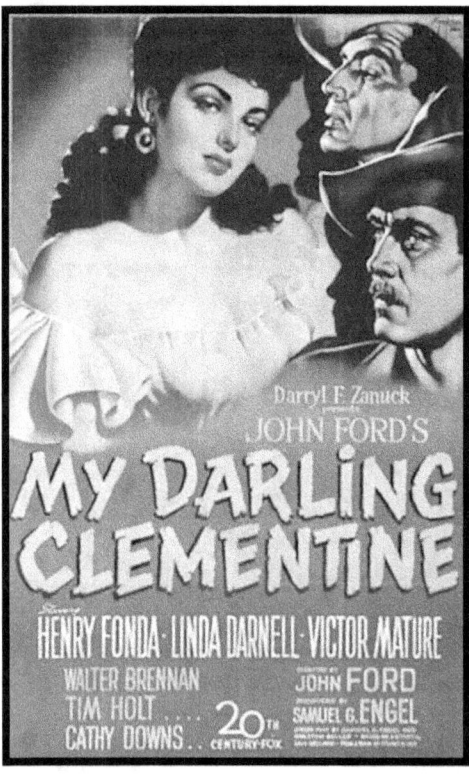

In 1946, Stuart Lake's book was filmed a third time when John Ford directed *My Darling Clementine* for 20th Century Fox. Although using the 1939 Sam Hellman screenplay as a basis, Ford's film is totally different in style and execution. On the surface, the screenplay by Samuel G. Engel and Winston Miller is familiar. Wyatt Earp, after having tamed Dodge City, wants only to settle down with his brothers and live a life of peace as a rancher. In Tombstone, he once again disarms an intoxicated Indian (played by the same actor from the 1939 version, Charles Stevens) but refuses the badge that the town elders implore him to take. When Old Man Clanton and his murderous sons kill Wyatt's younger brother James, Wyatt once again becomes a lawman. He meets and befriends Doc Holliday and becomes romantically involved with Clementine, the teacher from the East who has come west in search of Doc. Following the murder of Virgil, Wyatt defeats the Clantons at the O.K. Corral and then rides away from Tombstone.

Historically, this film also departs from accuracy and uses only the general facts as basis for the story. Though the director claimed that his reconstruction of the O.K. Corral fight was based on the recollections of Wyatt, whom he knew from his early filmmaking days, it is inaccurate due perhaps to Wyatt's reluctance to relive the battle or to reveal secrets. Newton Clanton, known as Old Man Clanton, was killed a few months prior to the gunfight and his death is believed by some to have been another factor that led to the bloody showdown. James Earp was actually the oldest of the five brothers and had been seriously wounded in the Civil War. However, Ford was intent on telling a story of more significance than a feud, a gunfight or even a legend. He expands the familiar story to depict not only the taming of Tombstone but the bringing of civilization to the American frontier.

Ford's Wyatt Earp is more than a single man or even a folk hero. He is a symbol of the idealism and the sacrifice that tamed the savage land as well as the savagery of man. Wyatt is a genuine hero who is chosen by fate and circumstance to be Tombstone's savior and accepts the responsibility as though it is his destiny. Due to his influence and actions, Tombstone is gradually transformed from a lawless outpost to a place where children can grow and people can worship. Yet Earp also has his personal needs and enjoys being a part of the new society, embracing all of its values. However, his

Doc Holiday (Victor Mature) and Wyatt Earp (Henry Fonda) in *My Darling Clementine*

Fonda's casting as Earp furthered the image of Earp as the archetypal Western lawman.

duty to his family takes precedence over his duty to society and, in destroying the evil of the Clantons, he is avenging his family honor. But he cannot enjoy the fruits of his labors and, grieving for his brothers, he must ride away from Tombstone.

Doc Holliday is again an ex-surgeon and killer from Boston who is slowly dying of consumption and is intent on hastening his death through liquor. He seems to have loathing for himself and everyone else until he meets Wyatt and this friendship becomes his redemption. However, his past life of violence necessitates his death, though in dying while helping his only friend, he cleanses himself and washes the blood from his soul.

The performances are uniformly fine, including Henry Fonda's quiet and commanding presence as Wyatt. Fonda already had an image that was the essence of American and his casting as Wyatt furthered the image of Wyatt as the archetypal Western lawman. He is honest and proud in a straightforward manner but can be grim and determined

when pushed too far. Victor Mature provides an unappreciated tour de force as the haunted and self-destructive Doc. He fully captures the moody, withdrawn and dangerous aspects of his character but still projects his suppressed intelligence and cultured background. He puts just the right amount of emotion into the barroom scene in which he completes the Shakespearean soliloquy. It is obvious from his tone and expression that the "undiscovered country" is his desired destination.

In support, Walter Brennan (who had a small role in the 1932 *Law and Order*) is an exquisite representation of evil as Old Man Clanton and John Ireland is notable as Billy Clanton. Ward Bond (who was in both previous versions of Lake's book) is Morgan, with Tim Holt as Virgil and Don Garner as James. As two opposite types of women, Linda Darnell as the sensuous Chihuahua and Cathy Down as the innocent Clementine of the title both contribute fine characterizations.

My Darling Clementine is a rich and beautiful movie. Ford's cinematic artistry is evident throughout the entire film, from the restrained yet emotional visual style and the subtle character detail to the honest sentiment of the Earp brothers and the genuine tenderness of the romantic scenes. In the filmography of Wyatt Earp, however, *My Darling Clementine* is significant on another level. It is with this film that Wyatt Earp is certified in the public consciousness as the essence of frontier heroism and law enforcement. However, he transcends that image and becomes more than a legend, more even than a folk hero. He assumes the stature of a classical hero, chosen and cursed by the gods to reap the rewards of his status but to suffer the pains as well.

Critics also praised *My Darling Clementine*. Bosley Crowther in *The New York Times* called it "a dynamic composition of Western legend." It was also a commercial success with post-war audiences, who embraced the image of Wyatt as a frontier savior.

This image of Wyatt was embraced by a public who now viewed their country as divinely protected and as the salvation of the entire world. It earned $2.75 million in North American theatrical rentals, which was notable for 1946.

Howard Hughes' controversial *The Outlaw* was released in 1947, though it was filmed years earlier. This is not a Wyatt Earp movie but it is only mentioned because Walter Huston, who played a character modeled on Wyatt in 1932's *Law and Order*, plays Doc Holliday in this totally fictional movie, making him the first actor to play both Wyatt and Doc.

Three years later, Wyatt had a brief appearance in Anthony Mann's 1950 film, *Winchester '73*, released by Universal-International. In a brief scene, Will Geer plays Wyatt as the Dodge City Marshal whose presence at the July 4th rifle competition ensures that there will be no trouble. By this time, the name was so familiar to moviegoers that audiences fully understand why James Stewart's character and other competitors

respond with caution and respect when Wyatt introduces himself. The film, incidentally, is based upon a story by Stuart Lake.

In 1953, two more disguised interpretations of Wyatt, both based upon previously filmed books and both departing radically from their sources, were released. 20th Century Fox's *Powder River* is yet another variation of Stuart Lake's *Frontier Marshal* and, to a larger degree, the 1939 Sam Helllman screenplay. In this version, Rory Calhoun plays Chino Bullock, a mine owner who becomes sheriff to find the killer of his friend and partner. Cameron Mitchell is Mitch Hardin, an ex-doctor who is no longer able to practice because of a brain tumor. The two men become friends until Chino learns that Hardin is the killer he is seeking, and in the climactic duel Hardin is faster on the draw but collapses from the tumor before firing. The movie has a fair amount of character development and tension as the two men edge toward the inevitable showdown. *Powder River* is a modest but pleasing minor effort.

That same year, *Law and Order* was remade once again by Universal-International, this time with Ronald Reagan as Frame Johnson. In this version, after taming Tombstone, the famous marshal retires to ranching with his fiancée and brothers only to find his new community in the grip of an old outlaw enemy and his sons. When the citizens ask him to be marshal, he politely declines, but his brother takes the badge and is killed by one of the outlaw brothers. Frame then pins on the badge and quickly cleans up the town. Once again, it is difficult to connect the original Burnett novel or the first film version to this tedious feature.

Also in 1953, Wyatt was a supporting character in the George Montgomery movie, *Gun Belt*, released by United Artists. James Millican is Wyatt in this low-budget feature about a reformed outlaw trying to go straight. Montgomery gives a sincere performance as the outlaw but the film is thoroughly routine. The following year, Wyatt also supported Montgomery, who had the title role in Columbia's *Masterson of Kansas*. Bruce Cowling, who was Virgil Earp in *Gun Belt*, is Wyatt and James Griffith is Doc Holliday in this juvenile movie about how Bat cleaned up Dodge City with some help from his friends. This was one of the many inept Westerns directed quickly by William Castle and released as bottom-of-the-bill programmers.

DeForest Kelley as Ike Clanton in *You Are There*.

Television was taking audiences away from theaters in the early 1950s and it was inevitable that Wyatt would appear on the small screen. *You Are There* was a weekly program that recreated historical events in a documentary manner. In 1953, the O.K. Corral gunfight was dramatized with Robert Bray as Wyatt and Barry Atwater as Doc, with DeForest Kelley as Ike Clanton. Walter Cronkite narrated the episode.

The saga was obviously the inspiration for *Dawn at Socorro*, released by Universal-International in 1954, with Rory Calhoun playing a Doc Holliday variation. This supporting feature begins with "The Shooting at Keene's Stockyards," in which Marshal Harry McNair, his brother and their friend, gambler and gunfighter Brett Wade, defeat the notorious Old Man Ferris and his three sons. Wade, who coughs incessantly due to an old wound, then travels to Colorado for his health and becomes involved in a romantic triangle and one last fight. Calhoun plays Wade and the Wyatt character (Marshal McNair) is played once again by James Millican. The movie is interesting and well-acted. Technically, Calhoun cannot be listed as having played both Wyatt and Doc, as Walter Huston did, but he did play a character that was modeled on Wyatt in *Powder River* the year before and a character modeled on Doc in this movie.

Thus far, Wyatt's earlier days as a lawman had been neglected, with most films concentrating on his more renowned Dodge City and Tombstone adventures. But *Wichita*, released by Allied Artists in 1955, rectified that oversight. In this movie, Joel McCrae as Wyatt is hired by the town elders to put an end to the lawlessness of the wide-open cattle town in which even a child is gunned down. He meets some initial resistance, particularly when he insists on banning all guns from the city limits, but the accidental killing of a woman justifies his methods. Gradually, the townspeople, including a romantic interest, accept his ways and the outlaws are eventually rousted. Wyatt's brothers, Morgan and James, as well as a young Bat Masterson, are also on hand to assist Wyatt. Stuart Lake served as technical advisor on this movie.

Jacques Tourneur's stylish direction keeps *Wichita* moving at a fast pace. The many well-staged action scenes are exciting and the romantic subplot is believable. Daniel Ullman's script is efficient and well-constructed. Though mostly fictional, particularly regarding the romance, the story does contain a basis of truth. Wyatt did serve with distinction as a lawman in Wichita, and he earned a reputation as an honest and fearless officer who was repeatedly successful in preventing violence in the wild cattle town and who helped to keep peace while never having to take a life. But he was only a deputy, whose tenure on the force ended when the town council reluctantly fired him after an altercation with a politician. Despite this, a few years later, many of the town's leading citizens would praise Wyatt's integrity in the legal affidavit that was used in his defense following the O.K. Corral gunfight.

Joel McCrae is excellent in the main role, bringing his usual sincerity and quiet strength to the character. Though the actor was, at 50 years old, almost twice as old as Wyatt, who was in his mid-20ss during his Wichita days, McCrae still projects the innate integrity and courage attributed to Wyatt. He is aided by a fine supporting cast, including Keith Larsen as a young Bat Masterson, Edgar Buchanan (who was Curly Bill Brocius in *Tombstone*) in another villainous role and Lloyd Bridges as a trigger-happy gunman. Peter Graves and John Smith as brothers Morgan and James also contribute to the film's appeal. (In reality, James was never involved in law enforcement.) *Wichita* is highly enjoyable. It was a commercial success for Allied Artists, earning $2.4 million in domestic theatrical rentals, and was the minor studio's biggest hit of the year.

If the public learned from *Wichita* that there was more to Wyatt's life than Dodge City and Tombstone, they were about to learn still more, and in their own living rooms. In September 1955 *The Life and Legend of Wyatt Earp* premiered on the ABC television network. Based on Stuart Lake's book, the series didn't pretend to be totally factual, as evident from its full title, but it did present a fair amount of authentic material in addition to fictional embellishments. Indeed, the half-hour series was quite remarkable since it was not only based upon the life of an actual historical person but followed him along the various stages of his life as they occurred.

Thus, the first season depicts his beginnings in Ellsworth and Wichita, while later seasons take him to Dodge City and Tombstone. In each setting, the pertinent historical characters are featured as regulars. For instance, the Thompson brothers and Dr. Fabrique are regulars during the first season but disappear after Wyatt moves to Dodge City and are replaced by such persons as Jim "Dog" Kelley, Bat and Jim Masterson and eventually Doc Holliday, who would remain until the end of the series. And when Wyatt sets up residence in Tombstone, among those who became regulars are John Clum, Johnny

Behan, the Clantons and McLaurys as well as the Earp brothers.

While each episode of the series was a story in itself, it was also part of a continuing saga. Characterizations and relationships develop over a period of weeks, even months. Of particular interest is the relationship of Wyatt and Doc Holliday which gradually evolves from initial distrust to devoted friendship. Wyatt's romantic relationships are for the most part not included, though some episodes feature a romantic rivalry between Wyatt and Johnny Behan for a showgirl. The relationship with the Clantons and McLaurys also gradually and realistically develops from minor skirmishes to increasingly bad blood and eventual gunplay. The O.K. Corral gunfight is depicted over a period of five weeks as Wyatt testifies in court. The series ended with the acquittal of Wyatt, his brothers and Doc.

The Life and Legend of Wyatt Earp was televised for six years and was very popular, being in the Top 20 highest-rated shows for four seasons and in the Top 10 for two years. Part of the credit for the success of the series has to be given to Hugh O'Brian, whose portrayal of Wyatt convincingly depicted the gradual growth of the character from an initially unassuming and reluctant lawman to a living legend. Moreover, it was a different kind of Western hero that he skillfully portrayed. Dressed in a black suit and wearing a tie, he projected a different image than the one associated with virtually every other Western hero. Instead of firing his gun, he would prevent trouble by buffaloing his opponent with the barrel of his gun, as the real Wyatt did. O'Brian successfully brought this legendary character to life and helped to make Wyatt Earp the most renowned frontier lawman to emerge from the Old West. Along with considerable talent, O'Brian projected a likeable screen presence and became a genuine star of the small screen.

In support, Douglas Fowley colorfully portrayed a cranky and quick-tempered Doc Holliday, except for a brief period when the role was assumed by Myron Healey. Unlike the usual sidekick of the hero of television Westerns, Doc was not a humorous character and indeed was quite often unlikeable, though his recklessness often made him admirable. John Anderson and Dirk London played Virgil and Morgan Earp while Alan Dinehart was Bat Masterson.

The series remains unique due to the determination of the producers to remain true to Wyatt's life by changing settings and characters in the midst of the series' popularity. Despite such changes, the series maintained continuity as it depicted the development of the principal character and his evolving relationship within the different settings and the people within them. Consistency was maintained for the entire 226 episodes and recognition for this difficult achievement must be given to the chief writer Frederick Hazlitt Brennan, noted novelist and playwright. It is unfortunate that the series didn't continue to depict the events after the O.K. Corral hearing. However, it is unlikely that the most violent part of Wyatt's life would have made palatable viewing.

Also deserving of mention is the show's theme song entitled "The Legend of Wyatt Earp," which was recorded in several versions and included lyrics and a refrain which became familiar and identifiable in households throughout the nation. The real Wyatt, who was always unassuming and taciturn, would probably have been embarrassed to hear youngsters singing how brave, courageous and bold he was.

"The Legend of Wyatt Earp" can be found on various TV Western song collections.

Incidentally, four days after the premiere of the Wyatt Earp series, *Gunsmoke* premiered on CBS-TV and would remain on the air for 20 years. What is interesting about this program is that the character of Marshal Matt Dillon was reportedly a composite of Wyatt Earp, Bat Masterson and Bill Tillgham.

As the Wyatt Earp series began its third year, *Bat Masterson* premiered on NBC-TV. Since Bat had been a semi-regular on Wyatt's series, usually depicted as an inexperienced apprentice to Wyatt, it was only natural that Wyatt would make an occasional appearance on Bat's series. Ron Hayes played Wyatt in four episodes during the third and fourth seasons. In one episode, obviously a swipe at the rival network's series, Wyatt is portrayed as a likeable grandstander who takes credit for one of Bat's heroic feats, much to Bat's amusement. The series ran for four years.

Wyatt's next appearance on the big screen was in 1957 when Paramount released its big-budget production of *Gunfight at the O.K. Corral*. Directed by John Sturges from a screenplay by Leon Uris, the movie is an exciting and dramatic rendition of the story which focuses as much on the relationship of Wyatt Earp and Doc Holliday as on the infamous battle with the Clantons. Burt Lancaster portrays a puritanical and rigid lawman whose dedication to the law and to his brothers costs him the woman he loves. Kirk Douglas is the tubercular ex-dentist and killer who tries to escape the shame he brought upon his aristocratic family with liquor. The development of the relationship between the two men from mutual enmity to respect and friendship is portrayed believably.

Although the film contains a liberal amount of fiction, some historical basis lies behind many of the events depicted. Wyatt and Doc did meet in Fort Griffin, Texas, though Wyatt was on the trail of outlaws other than the Clantons. Doc's escape from detention with the help of Kate Fisher is based upon fact, though the specific details are not clear and Wyatt was not a participant. Doc's explosive relationship with Kate is

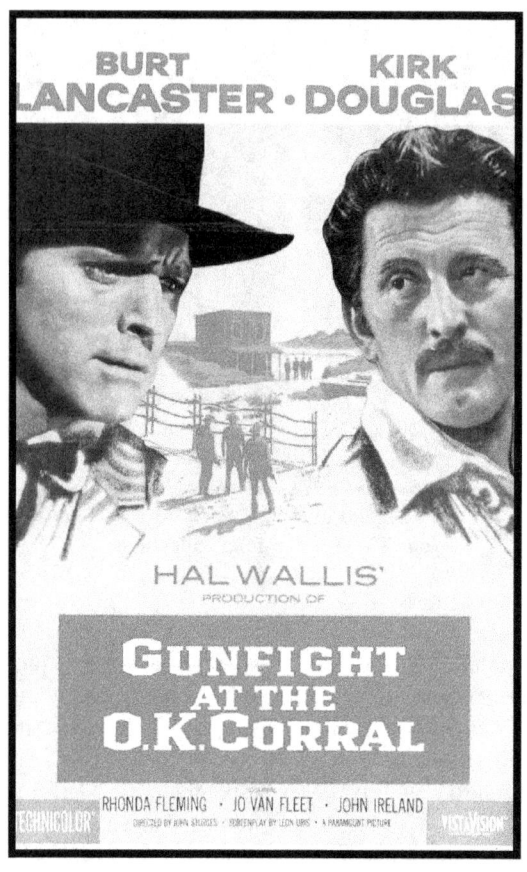

by most accounts not exaggerated. Besides the Clantons and McLaurys, other historical characters in the movie are Johnny Ringo, Jim Kelley, John Clum, Bat Masterson, Charlie Bassett and Shanghai Pierce as well as Virgil, Morgan and James Earp. While the romantic relationship between Wyatt and Laura Denbow is fictional, the character of the woman gambler is based on an actual person, Lottie Deno.

Most of the film's first half takes place in Dodge City, with the concluding half in Tombstone. After taming Dodge, Wyatt is ready to give up his badge and settle down with Laura until he is summoned to Tombstone by his brother, Virgil. Once again, family duty is more important to Wyatt than personal happiness and he is forced to leave Laura. Doc accompanies Wyatt westward, which causes concern among brothers Virgil, Morgan and James, who again is depicted as the youngest brother. However, by this time the friendship is close and Wyatt makes it clear that Doc deserves his trust. In this version, Billy Clanton is a troubled youngster whom Wyatt befriends and tries to dissuade from following his outlaw brothers. It is a futile attempt, for the Clantons and McLaurys are determined to maintain their control of the territory. When the outlaws ambush James, the stage is set for the climactic battle. As the factions meet at the O.K. Corral, it is as much a personal battle as a legal showdown. Wyatt, Virgil and Morgan must avenge their brother's murder while Doc's loyalty to Wyatt is his only reason for living.

The gunfight itself is largely inaccurate, occurring over several minutes and extending from the corral to a storeroom in town where Doc kills Billy Clanton to save a hesitating Wyatt. Because the film is somewhat episodic, the Clantons don't appear until relatively late and as a result the gunfight lacks the dramatic impact it should have. The screenplay attempts to provide cohesion by establishing friction between Wyatt and the Clantons in the Fort Griffin prelude, as well as between Doc and Ringo in Dodge; it also has Ringo taking part in the shoot-out. It only partially works.

Nevertheless, *Gunfight at the O.K. Corral* is very entertaining, due in no small part to the splendid performances of Lancaster and Douglas. As Wyatt, Lancaster convincingly projects the pride and solidity of a rigid lawman whose lack of tolerance for anyone who doesn't met his idealistic standards is shaken first by Doc and then by a

woman. Douglas is excellent at projecting self-contempt and bitterness. Since Doc has a wider range of emotions to display, from an explosion of ferocious of anger toward Kate to sudden helplessness in the depth of a coughing spasm, Douglas perhaps is more memorable, but both actors shine in their roles. The gradual manner in which these two distinctly different types of men come to develop respect and affection for one another is depicted very believably by the two actors.

Excellent support is provided by Jo Van Fleet as Kate, Dennis Hopper as Billy and John Ireland (who was Billy Clanton in *My Darling Clementine*) as Johnny Ringo. DeForest Kelley, John Hudson and Martin Milner capably portray the Earp brothers. Don Castle (who was Johnny Duane in *Tombstone*) has a small role as a drunken cowboy in this movie, and Kenneth Tobey makes an appearance as Bat Masterson.

Direction by John Sturges is effectively paced, initially concentrating on the relationship between Wyatt and Doc and then building to the action-filled climax. Another asset is a rich and thunderous score by Dimitri Tiomkin, which includes a title song by Frankie Laine that is sung throughout the film and becomes part of the narrative.

In the mid-1950s, the public wanted to believe in heroes and the image of Wyatt Earp presented in this movie fit that mold. The movie was a tremendous commercial success, earning almost $5 million in domestic theatrical rentals. Since the television series was achieving high ratings during the same period, it appeared that the public could not get enough of Wyatt Earp.

Also in 1957, another variation of the story was released, this one with a sex-change for the outlaw chief, entitled *Forty Guns*. Jessica Drummond is the leader of an outlaw gang that runs Cochise County in 1880s Arizona with an iron fist. The 40 guns of the title refer to her band of lawless cowboys, which includes her trigger-happy younger

brother Brock. Since the country sheriff is under Jessica's control, U.S. Marshal Griff Bonnell and his brothers Wes and Chico are assigned to bring an end to the outlaw band. Because of remorse for his past as a gunfighter, Griff hopes to complete his mission without gunplay. The issue becomes complicated when Griff and Jessica fall in love. However, when Wes is killed by Brock, Griff discards his principles as well as his feelings for Jessica and seeks vengeance. In the climactic gunfight, Brock holds Jessica in front of him as a shield but Griff without hesitating shoots Jessica and then kills Brock.

Forty Guns is written and directed by Samuel Fuller and has been praised in Europe as a masterpiece and condemned by some critics in the United States as dehumanizing trash. It is neither but it is fascinating in spots, though annoying in others. While the narrative is straightforward on the surface, it is marred by the director's overuse of huge close-ups, bizarre angle shots and rapid cutting, which tend to distract from the sound characterizations and engrossing plot. The performances are very effective. Barbara Stanwyck brings authority as well as femininity to the role of Jessica while Barry Sullivan is suitably grim and determined as Griff. They are given fine support by Gene Barry (television's Bat Masterson) as Wes and John Erickson as Brock. The film is more than worthwhile, if only for Sullivan's classic line at the finale as he walks by the wounded Jessica. The film should have ended then and eliminated the scene that follows, which implies a happy ending for the lovers.

A television series called *Tombstone Territory* premiered on ABC-TV in 1957. The main character is Sheriff Clay Hollister, played by Pat Conway, and his close ally is the editor of the *Tombstone Epitaph*. But it still doesn't qualify as even a disguised Wyatt Earp series, although Doc Holliday, as played by Gerald Mohr, made an appearance in one episode, as did Billy Clanton. The series lasted one season on the network and then became a syndicated series for another year.

In 1958, George Montgomery once again received assistance from Wyatt in *Badman's Country*, released by Warner Bros. This is another low-budget B movie destined to play the bottom of a double feature. Montgomery plays Pat Garrett, who is aided by Buster Crabbe as Wyatt in tracking down Butch Cassidy and the Sundance Kid. Buffalo Bill Cody and Bat Masterson also make appearances in this historically erroneous programmer, which is also boring.

Also in 1958, Montgomery starred in *The Toughest Gun in Tombstone*, released by United Artists. He plays Matt Sloane, a U.S. Marshal who is sent to Tombstone to clean up the town that is ruled by a gang of rustlers who previously killed his wife and may be trying to kill his son. It is not a Wyatt Earp movie but is only mentioned because it includes Ike Clanton and Johnny Ringo as outlaws. Obviously the names were added to give the story an appearance of authenticity, but it is another forgettable B movie.

Wyatt made a humorous appearance in the Bob Hope comedy, *Alias Jesse James*, released by United Artists in 1959. Hope plays an insurance salesman who sells a life insurance policy to the notorious outlaw. The climax has Hope aided by several television heroes, including Hugh O'Brian as Wyatt (as well as James Arness as Matt Dillon).

Joel McCrae starred in a television series entitled *Wichita Town* that premiered in 1959. Once again the connection to Wyatt is somewhat questionable. Though the show was inspired by McCrae's Wyatt Earp movie of four years earlier and in fact shares the same producer, he plays Marshal Mike Dunbar while his son, Jody, plays his deputy. Since Wyatt is the best-known lawman from Wichita's days as a wild cattle town, his spirit probably influenced the creation of Dunbar. But the individual episodes of the series, which only lasted one season, could pertain to any lawman of the Old West.

The year 1959 witnessed the release of a film that, at the time of its release, was not considered a Wyatt Earp movie, officially or unofficially. But it is one and it is one of the finest Westerns ever made. It is based upon a novel by Oakley Hall called *Warlock*, which had been published the previous year by Viking Press. The novel received almost universal acclaim and is a literary achievement of rare distinction.

Warlock is a mining town in the Southwest in 1880 that is being terrorized by a gang of lawless cowboys from the McQuown ranch just off the nearby San Pablo River. The cowboys had originally been hired by mine owners to quash labor problems, but they extended their power to forcefully rule the town while pursuing their illegal activities. Frustrated by the incompetence of official law, the town citizens hire legendary gunfighter Clay Blaisedell to bring law and order to their community. Blaisedell and his close friend, gambler and killer Tom Morgan, arrive and set in motion a series of confrontations that explore the foundations of the legends and myths of the Old West. It is a powerful narrative with compelling and realistic characters and events, one of which is the hotly disputed "Gunfight at the Acme Corral."

If readers of the novel found the story familiar, it was definitely by design. In his preface to the novel, author Hall states that while the town of War-

Richard Widmark, as Johnny Gannon, gives an excellent performance in *Warlock*.

lock is a fabrication, many of the characters "are composites of figures who still live on the frontier between history and legend" and that "by combining what did happen with what might have happened, I have tried to show what should have happened." And Hall's version of what should have happened emerges as a major novel of the American West.

The novel was bought by 20th Century Fox and the film version was released in 1959. Directed by Edward Dmytryk from a screenplay by Robert Alan Aurthur, *Warlock* stars Henry Fonda as Clay Blaisedell and Anthony Quinn as Tom Morgan. Richard Widmark also stars as Johnny Gannon, a member of the McQuown gang who quits the outlaw life to become deputy sheriff and Blaisedell's antagonist. Though some of the characters and subplots of the long novel, such as the military martinet and the labor problems, had to be eliminated, the film is a faithful adaptation and captures the complex characterizations and relationships that made the original work so enthralling.

Warlock begins with the humiliation of the town sheriff by the McQuown gang, who celebrate their victory over law and order with a night of hellraising which ends with the senseless killing of a barber. The stage is set for the arrival of a savior as the desperate and frightened citizens realize that they need someone to do their killing for them. But Clay Blaisedell is not a professional killer; he is a man with his own code of honor who will try to avoid killing as he enforces his brand of law upon the town. He is also a practical man who knows that the money he is being paid to endanger his life will hardly pay for his ammunition. Since his objective is not only to bring law to the town but to make money, Clay and Tom bring not only their guns but a deed to the local gambling palace. They see Warlock as just another town to tame while increasing their bankrolls. They have no premonition that Warlock will be the last town they will tame together, that their relationship will be torn apart and that one will have to kill the other.

A sense of inevitable tragedy surrounds Clay Blaisedell. He knows that civilization is gradually encroaching upon the frontier and that a professional gunfighter will soon no longer be needed. But he accepts his fate with grace, figuring that there will be enough towns in need of his services to last his lifetime. Cultured and sophisticated, he is gratefully welcomed by the citizens who place all their hope in him, though he correctly predicts that they will eventually turn against him. Like the criminals he is hired to destroy, he is also outside the official law. But though he has no legal status, he is righteous and takes pride in his professional ethics not as a hired gunfighter but as a hired marshal. He has no organization and no person to rely upon for help, except for Tom Morgan, and soon even he will be gone.

Clay is extremely loyal to Tom, whose physical disability doesn't prevent him from being fast on the draw whenever Clay needs him. Crude, unmannered and crippled by a clubfoot, Tom is reluctantly accepted by the townspeople as part of the arrangement. Embittered and shunned, Tom cares about nothing except his devotion to Clay. Tom will do anything to keep Clay's friendship, partially because Clay is the only person who ever looked at him and didn't see a cripple.

But in Warlock that friendship is about to be threatened by the arrival of Lilly Dollar, Tom's former mistress, as well as by the presence of town resident Jessie Marlow, who though initially disapproving of Clay finds herself gradually attracted to him. Meanwhile, Gannon's guilt over past crimes propels him to seek repentance by challenging Clay as well as McQuown, a challenge that will also affect the longstanding friendship.

The intricate relationships are never confusing and the reasons for each character's actions become gradually understandable. Despite the unexpected twists and changing loyalties, the simultaneous plots are interwoven seamlessly. And at the center of it all is the friendship of two legendary figures whose trust of one another is the basis of their close relationship. Thus, it is a shattering moment when Clay learns of Tom's duplicity and the pain in each man's face is highly distressing. Tom's shame as he pleads understanding for what he knows is unforgivable becomes one example of the film's ability to reveal the very soul of its characters.

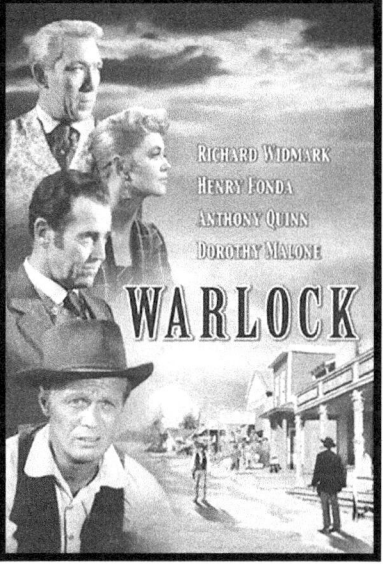

In Clay's case, such exposure is startling simply because he is the living legend whose exploits have already made him seemingly infallible. One of the many virtues of *Warlock* is its ability to mythologize Clay Blaisedell while at the same time display his humanity. A profound sadness exists about Clay, who is content to be a legend until he falls in love with Jessie. But like a mythological hero of Greek tragedy, he is forced to realize that a man can become a legend but a legend cannot return to being a man.

An abundance of memorable scenes occur in *Warlock*: the initial confrontation between Clay and McQuown when it becomes immediately clear that the two will not be able to co-exist; the gunfight (which in the movie takes place in the center of town and not at the Acme Corral) in which Clay and Tom face McQuown's cowboys when Clay almost pleads with young Billy Gannon not to draw before having to kill him; McQuown's infuriated reaction to Gannon's challenge. Certainly one of the most dramatic highlights of the film is the duel between Clay and Tom. Very rarely has a gunfight been filled with as many conflicting emotions as this one. Clay, angry and hurt, feels betrayed by Tom and yet responsible for him. Tom, grief-stricken at the loss of his only friend, wants to strike out at everyone but mostly at himself. Neither man wants to kill the other, but they both have to fire.

The scene that follows the duel is one of the most poignant in the history of the Western film. As Clay, tears streaming down his face, carries Tom's body into the saloon and forces the citizens to sing a hymn in homage, his inner torment is painfully visible. When he kicks the crutch out from under the hypocritical Judge Holloway and then forces him to crawl for it, his suffering seems unbearable. And when he smashes the lantern against the curtain, burning the building down around Tom's body, he sets the stage for the final confrontation, between the past and the future, between his humanity and his legendary status, between the civilization he brought about and the violence he now represents.

At the end of the film, when Clay appears with his celebrated gold-handled guns, walking down the street to meet Gannon, he knows that he is totally alone. The people who begged for his help are now totally against him. The town he has tamed has no room for him. His only friend is dead. And the woman he loves cannot travel with him from town to town just as he cannot stay with her. When he throws away the symbols of his legendary fame, smiles sadly at Gannon and then rides away, it is one of the most memorable evocations of a fallen hero that has ever been captured on film.

Warlock is a superb film with top-notch performances. Henry Fonda is one of the few actors who can so believably convey all of the facets of Clay Blaisedell. Throughout the entire film, Fonda displays his extraordinary ability to realistically bring to life such a complex character. Self-assured and proud, melancholy and laconic, calm and deadly, Fonda perfectly captures all sides of Blaisedell. It is an unforgettable portrayal that deserves as much praise as his more celebrated roles.

Anthony Quinn as Tom Morgan and Richard Widmark as Johnny Gannon are also excellent. Quinn provides a blistering portrait of a man who desperately tries to return to a past that is gone forever due in part to his own actions, while Widmark perfectly conveys the anguish of a decent man whose conscience forces him to finally take a stand.

Dorothy Malone and Dolores Michaels are equally fine as, respectively, Lilly and Jessie. Of the many standout supporting performances, Tom Drake as McQuown, Wallace Ford as Judge Holloway, Walter Coy as Sheriff Canning and Deforest Kelly as Curly all register strongly. Each actor in the movie, no matter how small the role, creates a believable three-dimensional character.

The direction of Edward Dymtryk, who also produced, is one of the highlights of his long and distinguished career. He derives as much tension from the emotional conflicts as from the physical ones. His confident treatment of the complex material and character exploration combined with the surprising density implicit in even the action sequences is nothing short of magisterial. A good deal of the effectiveness of the film is also due to Robert Alan Aurthur's literate and poetic screenplay with its perceptive dialogue that captures both the strengths and weaknesses of the main characters.

Some reviewers foolishly tried to inject a homosexual theme into the film. For the record, such a theme is dismissed by the film's director in his autobiography, *It's a Hell of a Life But Not a Bad Living*, published in 1978 by Times Books. Dmytryk, who was also the film's producer, worked on the script with Aurthur throughout its development, so his opinion should be the definitive one. And, of course, no such theme appears in the novel. But some critics bring their own agendas to their reviews and are simply incapable of understanding the concept of a deep friendship.

Another definite asset is the fine score by Leigh Harline. Accompanying the main titles is a thunderous and darkly dramatic theme that suggests menace and a potential for violence within a group of men riding across the landscape. This theme will reoccur at appropriate scenes of suspense and tension. But the score's main theme is the beautiful one for Clay Blaisedell that underscores the dignity and heroism of the character. When it initially appears during Clay's introduction, it suggests hope, but at the end of the film it will convey the essential tragedy and loneliness of the character as it builds in poignancy to the resolution.

It is interesting to compare Henry Fonda's portrayal of Wyatt Earp in *My Darling Clementine* with his portrayal of the fictional composite, Clay Blaisedell, in *Warlock*, particularly since both films are totally different interpretations of the same historical events with the same actor playing variations of the same real-life person. In *My Darling Clementine*, Wyatt Earp is the famous marshal without any taint of corruption. Sincere, idealistic and forceful, he is a noble figure. He brings civilization to Tombstone and fits in perfectly with the pioneers who endure hardships to build a future out of the wilderness. When he dances with Clementine on the foundation of the church, his place in that future is assured. He is a model and an inspiration for everyone else. Yet after he has rid the community of evil, he cannot stay in Tombstone even though the people want him. He has fulfilled his destiny and no longer has a purpose to stay. He must ride away and never appear again, except in legend.

In *Warlock*, Clay Blaisedell is already a legend, but one that is tainted by his reputation as a professional gunfighter. He becomes the town's savior not because of destiny or idealism but because he is being paid for his professional skills. During the course of his stay in Warlock, the decay at the core of his profession is exposed. Jesse can fill the emptiness within him, but he is forced to realize that it is too late for him to enjoy the happiness she can give him. Clay cannot fit into Warlock the way Wyatt fits into Tombstone. The people of Warlock are not grateful to him the way the citizens of Tombstone are to Wyatt. And as Clay rides away, there is no Clementine smiling and waving to him; there is only Jessie, crying bitter tears of sorrow and loss.

Unfortunately, *Warlock* was a commercial failure, earning only $1.3 million at the box office. It was 55th on *Variety*'s annual list of top-grossing films, beneath such movies as *Gidget* and *House on Haunted Hill*. It received many good reviews, including that of Bosley Crowther in *The New York Times*, who called it "good, solid, gripping Western fare (and) pretty exciting." The reviewer for *Newsweek* wrote that, "If Henry James had ever written a Western, he probably would have produced something like *Warlock*." But audiences stayed away, primarily because the timing was wrong.

In 1959, *Warlock* had to compete with numerous other adult Westerns released that year, along with an even larger number of Western series on television that ruled the prime-time hours. The most successful Westerns at the box office in 1959 were two John Wayne movies, *Rio Bravo* and *The Horse Soldiers*, with over $5 million and $4 million respectively. Other Westerns ranking higher on the list were *The Hanging Tree* and *Last Train from Gun Hill*. It got lost in the large surplus of Westerns available on both large and small screens. If *Warlock* had been released a few years earlier, prior to the explosions of Westerns on television, or a decade later when fewer Westerns were being made, it would perhaps have had a better opportunity to receive acclaim and attract audiences. If it had been released in 1969, along with such films as *The Wild Bunch* and *True Grit*, it would certainly have stood out. Unfortunately, it was released before its time. Nevertheless, *Warlock* is a classic Western and deserves to be called, as Phil Hardy labels it in his 1983 book, *The Western*, "Dmytryk's masterpiece."

Wyatt made an appearance on the television series *Maverick* in 1962. In an episode entitled "Marshal Maverick," a timid bartender steals Wyatt's gun, pretends to be the famous lawman and is hired by Bart Maverick as deputy. The real Wyatt, as played by Med Florey, shows up in town to retrieve his weapon. Peter Breck played Doc Holliday, and repeated the role four times during the series' last two seasons.

John Ford provided a different interpretation of Wyatt Earp in his *Cheyenne Autumn*, released by Warner Bros. in 1964. The somber story about mistreatment of Indians is interrupted by a brief comic interlude in which James Stewart as Wyatt and Arthur Kennedy as Doc Holliday try to conduct a poker game in Dodge City despite interruptions from unwelcome cowboys and hysterical citizens. Unlike the idealist in *My Darling Clementine*, this Wyatt appears to be a self-centered cynic, which suggests that Ford may have been influenced by the anti-Wyatt books published in the early 1960s. Ford's last Western is not one of his classics.

Also in 1964, a movie entitled *Gunmen of the Rio Grande* was released with ads proclaiming Guy Madison as Wyatt Earp. This was actually an Italian-Spanish-French co-production originally titled *Jennie Lees Ha Una Nuova Pistola* and also known as *El Sheriff del O.K. Corral*. At the beginning of the movie, Madison states in dubbed English that he is the famed lawman traveling incognito in response to a plea from a woman whose mine is being threatened by a crooked land baron. The standard plot suggests that the producers may have used Wyatt's name to hopefully attract audiences who would normally avoid European Westerns. The movie is indistinguishable from the dozens of other foreign Westerns that were flooding the market during this period.

Death Valley Days was a Western anthology series that was syndicated for several years on television. In 1964, Jim Davis and Dan Stafford played Wyatt and Doc in a half-hour episode entitled "After the O.K. Corral," which depicts the attacks upon the Earp brothers following the gunfight.

The Three Stooges went west in 1965 when Columbia released *The Outlaws Is Coming*, a typical slapstick juvenile farce. Being protectors of animals, the Stooges attempt to stop the slaughter of buffalo and meet several famous and infamous legends of the Old West, including Wyatt Earp, played by Bill Camfield.

In 1967, 10 years after *Gunfight at the O.K. Corral*, director John Sturges returned to the saga with *Hour of the Gun*, released by United Artists. Sturges, who functioned just as director on the 1957 film, is also the producer of this one, making it more of a personal work. In terms of storyline, this film is a sequel to the earlier one since it begins with another version of the gunfight that ended the earlier film. But otherwise, the films are completely different, this one being more of a character study of Wyatt than an adventure movie. Edward Anhalt's screenplay concentrates on the bloody aftermath

of the shoot-out and the effect it had on Wyatt, as well as the effect the shootout had on his friendship with Doc Holliday. The staging of the gunfight is the most accurate to date, taking as much time as the actual fight with the participants as well as the outcome based upon historical accounts. The inquest that follows, which includes some actual court testimony, establishes Wyatt as being on the side of justice, though perhaps not the paragon previously depicted. The political aspects of the feud are presented for the first time and Wyatt is shown to be basically honest but pragmatic as well. The acquittal of Wyatt and Doc is followed by the attempted murder of Virgil and the murder of Morgan, which precedes Wyatt's sustained vengeance against the Clanton gang.

The action scenes are secondary to the internal conflicts that motivate the characters. Wyatt Earp is a tragic character whose grief for his brothers causes his moral decline. Seemingly rigid and unfeeling, he does not publicly display his emotions to anyone, even his closest friend. Violence becomes the only outlet for his anguish and the pain thrust upon his family. In contrast, though filled with self-contempt, Doc Holliday functions as Wyatt's conscience, regretfully watching as Wyatt lies to himself and to his friends while pursuing his quest for vengeance. Doc's futile attempts to save his only friend slowly give way to the painful acceptance that the man he admires has become a mirror-image of himself.

There are some departures from historical accuracy. The role of Curly Bill Brocius is minimized and his killing by Wyatt, in reality one of the most dramatic and heroic acts of Wyatt's life, is inaccurately depicted. The movie also invents a final confrontation between Wyatt and Ike Clanton, who in real life was eventually killed while rustling cattle as shown but not by Wyatt. Otherwise, the movie provides a fairly accurate depiction of events that followed the gunfight. The Johnny Behan character, called Jimmy Bryan

in this film, is correctly shown to be an ally of the Clanton gang. Bryan and Clanton cleverly manipulate the law to make Wyatt a fugitive, which by all objective accounts is what Behan actually did. The public display of the bodies of Billy Clanton and the McLaurys actually occurred as Clanton drummed up public support against the Earps and Holliday. The funeral parade down the main street of Tombstone is another example of the film's historical accuracy.

Wyatt's three controversial killings are each suspensefully staged. The killing of Frank Stillwell at the Tucson train station is particularly memorable as the close-up of Wyatt's face signals the ferocity of an avenging angel. Equally impressive is the scene in which Wyatt challenges Andy Warshaw (a stand-in for Florentino Cruz, also known as Indian Charlie) to a duel after slowly seething while hearing of the details of his brother's murder. Only the expression on his face and the tone of his voice give any indication as to whether he is defending himself or executing the men. It is after the third killing that Doc finally confronts Wyatt and angrily forces him to admit the truth, though not until after Wyatt violently strikes him. It is a powerful scene, not only because of the legendary aspects of the friendship but also because of the realization that a folk hero's fallibility is being mercilessly exposed.

The movie ends with Wyatt realizing that he has violated his own principles and giving up the law as well as the political future that his friends were helping him to achieve. As Doc sits on the porch of the Colorado sanitarium and takes a swig of liquor that he knows will hasten his death, he glances sadly at Wyatt riding away for the last time. And Wyatt, his face emotionless and drained, rides away from his friends and his past, a barren future ahead of him. It is a bitter, downbeat ending that almost suggests an elegy for the ignoble end of a once heroic figure.

Perhaps because of the bleakness of the film, *Hour of the Gun* was a failure at the box office. It didn't even earn the minimum amount of one million dollars to qualify for inclusion on *Variety*'s annual list of top-grossing films. The biggest Western hits of the year were, once again, two John Wayne movies, *El Dorado* and *The War Wagon*, with domestic earnings of approximately $6 million each. Another factor, once again, was the period of the film's release. *Hour of the Gun* is another film released before its time.

During the mid-1960s, Italian Westerns with graphic violence that glorified killing and bloodshed were the rage. The anti-heroes of these movies lived outside the law and killed either for money or for the fun of it. In direct contrast, a character study of a lawman who suffers internally because of his bloodlust was not what audiences wanted during this period. Critics also didn't like it. A typical review was Bosley Crowther's in *The New York Times*, in which he called it "a totally conventional Western drama." He concluded the review by writing that, "The wonder is that John Sturges has made such an obvious, slow film and that James Garner is a nobody as the legendary Mr. Earp."

However, *Hour of the Gun* is a very underrated movie, directed solidly and efficiently by John Sturges without any of the romanticism of the earlier film, which may also have been a factor affecting its commercial performance. Balancing known facts with speculation, Edward Anhalt's taut script creates a very believable Wyatt Earp who is neither heroic nor villainous but simply human. Sturges and Anhalt masterfully balance scenes of brutal violence with scenes of introspective tension, all the while gradually delineating the character of Wyatt Earp. A sense of the real American West permeates the entire film, from the grittiness of the outdoor scenes to the raw realism of the streets, courtrooms and pool halls of Tombstone. Each of the supporting characters, major and minor, is carefully etched and throwaway touches add authenticity, such as

the offended bartender who doesn't recognize Doc or the pained expression on Sherm McMasters' face when Wyatt unintentionally insults him.

James Garner gives one of his finest performances as Wyatt Earp. Because Wyatt's motivations are obscure for much of the film, Garner has to project his inner torment in subtle ways, through his eyes and voice and conveying just a hint of the suppressed anger that lies beneath the calm exterior. He does this so expertly that only repeated viewings, with the knowledge of what is actually occurring within the character, can reveal the depth of the actor's portrayal. Jason Robards is also exceptional as Doc Holliday. His coughing spasms, so familiar to moviegoers by this time, could easily have become a cliché but instead seem to tear his body apart from the inside, particularly the one that occurs during his violent confrontation with Wyatt. As with Garner's Wyatt, Robards must convey Doc's feelings in an understated manner, particularly his reluctant but gradual disillusionment with his only friend, and he does this superbly. Unlike the Wyatt and Doc of Sturges' earlier film, no warmth or humor occurs between the two men in this movie, but the friendship still is equally genuine because of the credible and relaxed manner in which the two men relate to one another.

Robert Ryan gives his usual dependable performance as Ike Clanton, providing just the right amount of menace but tempered by an innate stateliness that the real Ike never had. Fine support is provided by Larry Gates as John Clum, Karl Svenson as Dr. Goodfellow and Monte Markham as Sherm McMasters, with Frank Converse and Sam Melville both effective as Virgil and Morgan Earp. Steve Ihnat as Andy Warshaw, and Michael Tolan as Pete Spence also register strongly as Clanton gang members

Also adding to the overall excellence of the film is an exceptionally fine score by Jerry Goldsmith. The score not only captures perfectly the tone and flavor of the drama, but it actually expands the range of the film and its characterizations. The main title theme is particularly memorable and, from the very beginning, projects a sense of ominous danger as the Earps and Doc join together and then start their fateful walk toward the O.K. Corral. As the four men approach their destiny, the theme gradually increases in volume and density and finally punctuates with a vivid concluding note that leaves no doubt of the violence that will erupt. Throughout the film, the score projects a sense of tragedy that precisely complements the sense of foreboding that surrounds Wyatt and eventually engulfs him.

The one fault of the movie is due to the cutting of integral explanatory scenes by the production company prior to release. The elimination of scenes of Wyatt's soul-searching and introspection damages the essence of the film that Sturges and Anhalt so carefully developed. Nevertheless, *Hour of the Gun* still emerges as a superior Western and is a credit to all of the creative personnel involved.

On the surface, incidentally, this movie presents a less laudable image of Wyatt than the one usually presented on screen. But the debunkers didn't like it because, instead of depicting a truly nasty villain, it depicts an honorable man pushed by forces of evil to the breaking point. The creators of this movie, unlike the debunkers, did not set out to destroy the memory of the man but to try to explain him. The fact that he emerges as flawed but still heroic to some degree was not enough for the debunkers. The fact that his culpable behavior was shown as being understandable was not acceptable. They wanted a despicable scoundrel and nothing less would satisfy them. They would have to wait four years for their version to reach the screen, though they probably derived some pleasure from Wyatt's appearance on the small screen the following year.

One of Wyatt Earp's strangest appearances on film was on television in 1968 when he met the crew of the Starship Enterprise in an episode of *Star Trek* entitled "Spectre of the Gun." An alien intelligence entraps the crew within the bodies of the Clantons

Kirk and co. are trapped in the bodies of the Clanton Gang before the shootout at the O.K. Corral in the *Star Trek* episode "Spectre of the Gun."

just before the O.K. Corral gunfight and creates phantom images of the Earps and Doc Holliday from Captain Kirk's subconscious. Apparently Kirk has a low opinion of the Earps and Doc because they are presented as reprehensible, mean-tempered killers. Ron Soble and Sam Gilman play Wyatt and Doc in this rather insipid teleplay from the series' third and worst season. The episode is trashy and presumptuous because it has no foundation in fact and because it assumes a superior attitude by having its characters, through simpleminded dialogue, lecture those members of the audience who are lacking their allegedly superior knowledge on the subject. The episode's writer, Lee Cronin, may have read one of the anti-Wyatt books or perhaps he was trying to appeal to equally uninformed fans of the series who considered themselves too sophisticated to believe in Western heroes. Incidentally, this would be series regular DeForest Kelley's fourth and last encounter with the saga.

Will Henry's novel *Who Rides with Wyatt* was published in 1955 and was another fictional account of the Tombstone saga based upon the actual events. On his way to Tombstone to be marshal, Wyatt saves the life of a young Johnny Ringo and tries to save the young man from a life of crime by offering him a deputy's badge. But as Wyatt becomes involved in the business of cleaning up the lawless town, he soon realizes that Ringo has a killer instinct within him, particularly after the young gunman aligns himself with crooked sheriff Johnny Behan and the outlaw element led by Curly Bill Brocius. Wyatt also becomes involved with two women in the town, showgirl Lilly Belloit, who is involved with Behan, and Evvie Cushman, who has personal problems of her own. Events escalate in violence until the showdown at the O.K. Corral and the bloody aftermath, including the mysterious death of Ringo.

Henry's novel served as the basis of *Young Billy Young*, released by United Artists in 1969. It is possible that the name of Wyatt Earp was so familiar to moviegoers by

this time that the film's producers considered it lacking in commercial value. Whatever the reason, the name of the main character is changed from Wyatt to Ben Kane and Ringo becomes the Billy Young of the title. Robert Mitchum plays Kane, who saves Billy's life on his way to the town of Lordsburg where he will be the new marshal. Kane is hunting his son's killer, Frank Boone, who is aligned with the town's corrupt boss, John Behan. Hoping to keep Billy from a life of crime, Kane offers him the job of deputy, which Billy refuses but later accepts. Kane receives help from dance hall girl Lilly Belloit while Billy romances Evie Cushman, daughter of the town doctor. Kane's arrest of Boone's son leads to a gunfight in which both Behan and Boone are killed, leaving Kane with Lilly and Billy as the new marshal. It is difficult to determine any connection between novel and film, except for the familiar plot of a new marshal cleaning up a lawless town as well as the names of Behan, who is converted into a standard villain, and the two women, who are converted into standard romantic interests. Basically a readable and interesting novel is turned into a tedious and uninteresting film. If not for the novel basis, this film would not be recognizable as even an unofficial Wyatt Earp movie.

In 1971, the anti-Wyatt faction had reason to rejoice. Debunking popular heroes was fashionable by this time and Wyatt Earp was a natural target for those who were intent on defaming legendary idols, either for personal or political reasons. *Doc*, directed by Frank Perry from a screenplay by Pete Hamill, presents its Wyatt Earp as a sadistic murderer while Doc Holliday wallows in self-pity. As evident from the title, Doc Holliday is the main character of this movie and therefore is less despicable than Wyatt, who has no redeeming qualities. Filmed in Spain, *Doc* clumsily tries to draw an allegory between the O.K. Corral gunfight and the My Lai massacre in Viet Nam in which U.S. troops slaughtered innocent civilians. Thus, the Clantons and McLaurys become innocent victims of Wyatt's political opportunism and repressed homosexuality.

Doc features a couple of good actors, Stacy Keach and Harris Yulin, in the main roles of Doc and Wyatt, but no amount of acting talent can save this mess. The movie is terrible, not because it features a Wyatt who is the epitome of evil and not because the screenplay is so pretentious and not even because the direction is amateurish and unimaginative. It is terrible primarily because it possesses an abundance of ignorance of the American West and its people. The inane dialogue, graphic violence, hypocritical piousness and one-dimensional characters seem to exist not in any believable semblance of Tombstone of the 1880s but in a patently phony setting which serves only to provide a forum for the personal and political beliefs of the screenwriter and director.

Doc tried to appeal to fans of revisionist Westerns through its debunking image of Wyatt and to fans of Italian Westerns through its graphic violence, but the movie appealed to no one. It is a rancid mess and played to empty theaters.

As Westerns gradually lost their popularity with audiences throughout the 1970s, Wyatt would remain absent from theater screens until the late 1980s, though he would make occasional appearances on the small screen.

In 1972, the television series titled *Appointment with Destiny* featured a segment called "Showdown at the O.K. Corral." This was a pseudo-documentary series in which various historical events were reenacted while voice-over narration provided alleged facts as they may have been reported at the time of the event. David Vowell played a less than heroic Wyatt and Tim James was Doc, while Lorne Greene narrated.

Cameron Mitchell as Wyatt Earp in *Alias Smith and Jones'* "Which Way to the O.K. Corral?"

Also in 1972, Cameron Mitchell played Wyatt in an episode of the television series, *Alias Smith and Jones*, entitled "Which Way to the O.K. Corral?" The plot revolves around the two heroes trying to avoid Wyatt while passing through Tombstone. Mitchell, incidentally, is another actor who though he didn't technically play both Wyatt and Doc, did play a variation of Doc in 1954's *Powder River*. In view of this, he is a member of the exclusive club occupied by Walter Huston and Rory Calhoun.

Wyatt's next appearance was also on the small screen in 1983 in a television movie called *I Married Wyatt Earp*, based on the book edited by Glenn Boyer. The movie presents Wyatt as a dedicated lawman who admits his love for Josephine only after his alcoholic wife dies. In this slightly feminist version of the O.K. Corral fight, Josephine saves Wyatt's life by getting the drop on two Clanton gang members who were hiding in a shack adjacent to the corral. This, of course, did not happen, either in reality or in the book. Though reports of shots possibly being fired from an adjacent alley surfaced, Josie was nowhere near the fight. The television movie ends with Wyatt and Josephine leaving after

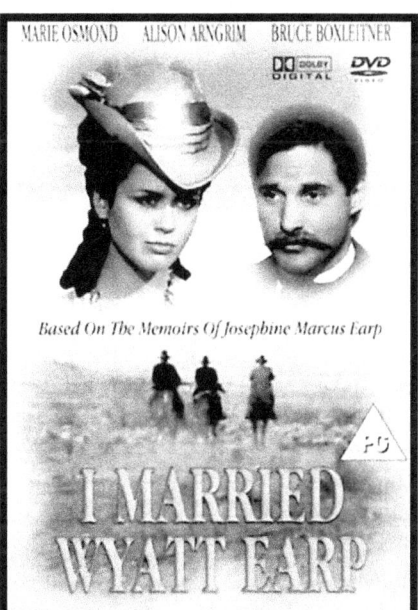

Good Movies; Bad Timing

the gunfight for a life of wedded bliss. The film is dull and undistinguished, though it does present the familiar story from a different perspective and it was the first version to depict the significance of the romantic rivalry between Wyatt and Johnny Behan. Bruce Boxlietner played Wyatt in this movie with Marie Osmond as Josie and Jeffrey DeMunn as Doc.

In 1988, James Garner played Wyatt Earp for the second time on movie screens in *Sunset*. Written and directed by Blake Edwards from a story by Rod Amateau, *Sunset* is a fictional story about how an elderly Wyatt and movie star Tom Mix, played by Bruce Willis, solve a notorious murder in Hollywood in 1928. Garner adds more humor to his characterization than he did 21 years earlier. In the sunset of his years, Wyatt is able to look back upon his life with some amusement as the movie industry transforms his life into myth. Yet while watching a filming of the O.K. Corral gunfight, in which Mix plays Wyatt, a close-up of his solemn expression followed by a brief flashback to the actual gunfight reveals an indication of his true feelings. This Wyatt accepts his status as a living legend not out of conceit but out of resignation. He knows that his past is concealed by "a lie or two" but any doubts by cynical studio executives about his courage are banished by confrontations which establish his physical as well as moral superiority. However, only the Western movie within the film has a happy ending, for while Wyatt with the help of Mix succeeds in bringing the killers to justice, he is unable to save the life of the woman who loves him. After bidding farewell to Mix, Earp, the most famous lawman of the Old West, rides away on a train, the symbol of progress, while the most popular Western movie star of his era and his horse salute him. It is a poignant end not only to a bittersweet movie but to an era.

Incidentally, while the mystery plot of *Sunset* is fictional, the basis of the relationship is factual. Wyatt's friendship with Tom Mix is a matter of historical record. In fact, Mix and the equally popular early Western movie star, William S. Hart, along with John Clum and George Parsons, served as pallbearers at Wyatt's funeral in 1929.

Interestingly, Casey Tefertiller reports that John Wayne told Hugh O'Brian that he met Wyatt on a Hollywood set in the late 1920s and used the lawman as a model for some of his characters. So Wyatt's influence and spirit that began in the silent era continued in one form or another in Westerns that have no direct connection with him.

Another aged Wyatt appeared on television in 1989, essayed once again by Hugh O'Brian in a two-part episode of the CBS-TV series *Paradise*. In this fictional story, Wyatt comes out of retirement to aid the hero of the series, who has been falsely imprisoned. After this plot is resolved (with the aid of Bat Masterson, who is again played by Gene Barry), Wyatt is then challenged by a surviving Clanton brother who seems determined to avenge the O.K. Corral killings. The chief interest of the teleplay was in seeing O'Brian and Barry return to the roles they had made famous three decades earlier.

Two years later, O'Brian and Barry, along with several other television heroes from the past, returned as Wyatt and Bat in the television movie, *The Gambler Returns: The Luck of the Draw*. In this third telefilm about the gambler of the title, Wyatt makes a brief appearance to help the hero who is on his way to a big poker game.

Wyatt made another appearance on the small screen in a television movie entitled *Four Eyes and Six Guns*, which was presented on the TNT cable network in 1992. This alleged comedy concerns an optometrist who journeys to Tombstone to open an eyeglass store and helps Wyatt Earp restore justice and his reputation. Fred Ward broadly plays Wyatt in this forgettable telefilm that plods along without a single laugh. But this depiction of Wyatt on the small screen was only a prelude to two major but rival Wyatt movies which would soon burst upon theater screens.

Westerns had fallen out of favor in the 1980s but the success of *Dances with Wolves* in 1990 was responsible for rekindling interest in the genre. In 1993, announcements were made by two studios that major motion pictures about Wyatt Earp were in simultaneous development. Warner Bros. was preparing a biography to star Kevin Costner, while Universal was planning a film entitled *Tombstone* which would focus on the lawman's exploits in that town. Universal eventually passed on their project, which was then taken over by Hollywood Pictures, a subsidiary of Buena Vista.

Tombstone appeared in theaters first and was released in 1993. Outlaws known as the Cowboys, led by Curly Bill Brocius and Johnny Ringo, are in control of the territory when former lawman Wyatt Earp arrives in town with his brothers and wives to make their fortune in the prosperous boom town. Wyatt also reunites with his close friend, Doc Holliday, the tubercular gambler who values Wyatt's friendship above everything else. Though the extent of criminality in the town quickly becomes obvious to the Earps, Wyatt seems interested only in getting rich. He is also frustrated by his wife Mattie's dependence upon laudanum and consequently becomes attracted to actress Josephine Marcus, who is also involved with corrupt Sheriff Johnny Behan. But Virgil and Morgan follow their consciences and again become lawmen. Friction between the two camps steadily escalates and eventually erupts at the O.K. Corral, which leads to the deadly revenge by the Cowboys and Wyatt's Vendetta Ride. The film ends with Wyatt's farewell to Doc on his deathbed and his subsequent joyous reunion with Josie.

In *Tombstone*, action predominates from the beginning massacre of a peaceful Mexican village by the Cowboys to the annihilation of the outlaw gang by Wyatt's posse. Director George Cosmatos brings exceptional verve to these action scenes and injects the film's highpoint, the O.K. Corral gunfight, with tremendous excitement. The build-up to the gunfight is filled with tension as well as historical accuracy. Ike Clanton's clashes with Virgil and Doc at the Oriental saloon the night before, along with Wyatt's buffaloing of Tom McLaury the next morning, all happened as depicted. As the Cowboys gather near the corral and the Earps and Doc meet on Hafford's Corner, it is obvious that the time for talking is over. Wyatt's reluctance to force a showdown adds a new twist to the story, but when he finally accedes and returns to his room for his gold-handled gun, he knows that bloodshed is inevitable.

The gunfight, besides being historically accurate, is depicted with extraordinary power. When the four men start marching down Fourth Street, a burning building appears behind them, suggesting that the fires of hell are accompanying them. As they approach the vacant lot next to the corral, the Cowboys stare at them with defiance and hatred. Several suspenseful moments occur during which the men face one another and the tension builds rapidly until the cowboys reach for their guns. The gunfight lasts

slightly longer than the actual battle but is authentic concerning who shot whom and in what order. Some speculation is also present regarding the mysterious shots that were reportedly fired from the adjacent building and, in this film, are attributed to Ike, who fled after the shooting started.

Numerous other scenes are equally exciting. Interestingly, the ambush of Virgil is not shown, though the aftermath, where Virgil staggers into the saloon to tell Wyatt, actually happened. The murder of Morgan is also depicted accurately and is particularly poignant. Other memorable scenes include Wyatt's confrontation with Curly Bill and Doc's duel with Ringo. In reality, no one knows who actually killed Ringo, whose body was found as depicted, though Doc and Wyatt are both good candidates for the honor.

The Wyatt Earp of *Tombstone* is a sensitive and emotional man who hopes that family togetherness will bring him peace. He is an honorable man who tries to resist his attraction to Josie out of consideration for Mattie. He has feelings of guilt over the killing of one man in Dodge City and is determined to avoid having to kill again. When he starts the fateful march toward the O.K. Corral, it is more out of loyalty to his brothers than duty. He will not realize until later, after personal tragedy has struck, that it is his destiny to become the avenging rider on a pale horse who will cleanse the territory of evil.

In this film, Doc Holliday has a sense of humor and seems to regard his life and the lives of others with irony. He can be likeable and charming but he is ready to kill at the slightest instigation. Except for Wyatt, he has affection for no one, including his companion, Kate Fisher. He has only contempt for himself, whom he sees as a mirror-

image of the murderous Johnny Ringo. At the film's end, lying on the sanitarium bed, Doc recalls the love of his life and his loss of her, thus explaining the reason for his despair. But his last salvation is a book that Wyatt has written in his honor. In reality, Wyatt never wrote such a book, but it is a highly poignant touch.

Kurt Russell brings remarkable authority to the role of a hardened lawman and yet is still able to project warmth and tenderness in his personal relationships. He is especially heartrending when Morgan is murdered and particularly frightening after the Stillwell killing, when he visibly becomes the prophesied angel of death. It is an exceptionally fine and persuasive performance that is perfectly complemented by Val Kilmer's portrayal of Doc. Kilmer is quite extraordinary, superbly conveying both danger and frailty. From the sweat on his face to his dazed expression, he projects perfectly the image of a dying man, yet the coldness in his eyes still suggests the deadliness inside. Even in those moments when he appears relatively healthy, a sense of sadness and regret exists in his tone and expression. Doc's death scene alone is evidence of the actor's singular skill and brings the film to an emotional climax, aided immeasurably by the poignancy conveyed by Russell's Wyatt. Together, the performances of Russell and Kilmer definitively convey the genuine affection that confirms the legendary friendship of Wyatt and Doc.

In support, Sam Elliot and Bill Paxton make strong impressions as Virgil and Morgan. Dana Delaney is effective as Josie, though her characterization at times seems too modern. Joanna Pacula makes her presence felt as Kate and Dana Wheeler Nicholson makes Mattie believably shrewish. On the opposite side of the law, Stephen Lang nicely plays Ike Clanton, who is reduced to secondary status in the gang and is

believably portrayed as a cowardly agitator. Joe Tenney also registers as Johnny Behan, who is correctly shown to be a corrupt political hack. However, it is Powers Boothe and Michael Biehn who stand out as Curly Bill Brocius and Johnny Ringo, and it is the conviction they bring to the roles that makes them worthy adversaries to Wyatt and Doc.

Also deserving of praise is Bruce Broughton's beautiful score that includes a powerful main theme that is not heard in its full glory until the end credits. The romance of Wyatt and Josie is accompanied by a lovely melody which is reminiscent of a theme Broughton wrote for an episode of *Gunsmoke* in 1974 called "In the Performance of Duty."

Kevin Jarre, who wrote the screenplay, started the film as director but was replaced shortly after filming began, with his script subsequently revised and shortened. His original unfilmed script for *Tombstone* is highly praised by both Allen Barra and Casey Tefertiller. In the completed film, the dialogue is sprinkled with factual references, such as the Town Site Company, which suggests that the original script might have expounded upon this major symbol of the town's political corruption and Behan's participation in it. Other references mentioned in passing indicate that the original script, if filmed, could have been the definitive movie on the Tombstone saga and Wyatt's participation in it, encompassing all of the political and social factors as well as the numerous events that led to the O.K. Corral.

As an indication of what also may been cut, it was announced prior to production that Robert Mitchum had been signed to play Old Man Clanton. In the finished movie, the Clanton patriarch is nowhere to be seen and neither is Mitchum, whose narration

is heard at the beginning and the end. Also missing from the film is a cameo scene with Hugh O'Brian that was filmed before Jarre was replaced as director. One cut scene that appears on the home video expanded edition is particularly welcome. As Doc leaves Kate to join Wyatt on his Vendetta Ride, he asks her if she has any kind words to say before he rides away. As any fan of Western film themes knows, these lines are taken from the ballad sung by Frankie Laine in the 1957 movie, *Gunfight at the O.K. Corral*.

However, the revised script for the completed film still indicates extensive research by Jarre and includes many characters from Wyatt's life that are usually excluded from the films, including Fred White, Billy Breakenridge, Cawley Dake and Henry Hooker. The major characters and their relationships are finely detailed, particularly for Wyatt and Doc but also for Wyatt and his brothers and the two women in his life. The interaction between Johnny Ringo and Doc is also quite absorbing. The dialogue has an authentic ring to it throughout the entire film. *Tombstone* succeeds as both a glorious Western adventure and an emotionally moving human drama.

Special mention should be given to the film's last scene, which is a particularly fitting tribute to Wyatt as well as to his brothers and Doc. As the end credits appear, Wyatt, Virgil, Morgan and Doc once again take their fateful walk toward the O.K. Corral but this time they are framed not by the fires of hell but by a clear blue sky. And they are looking straight ahead, toward the screen, toward the audience. It is almost like, as Wyatt has just told Josie, the camera is looking into heaven where the four men are together once again, ready to bring justice to one and all. It is a beautiful accolade to Wyatt Earp.

Tombstone was very popular with audiences and was a huge hit at the box office, thus making the names of Wyatt Earp and Doc Holliday familiar to another generation. The movie's popularity surprised many in the industry, who believed that the name of Wyatt Earp belonged to previous generations. But the image of Wyatt presented here resonated with the public, who had become desirous of an old-fashioned hero who, when pushed too far, will bring a deserved justice to evildoers.

In 1994, six months after the release of *Tombstone*, the Warner Bros. production of *Wyatt Earp* was released. This is the first full-scale biography of Wyatt and depicts his life from adolescence to late middle-age. It encompasses within its time span all of the familiar incidents that have been previously told but from the perspective of his personal development. By depicting the people and events that shaped his maturity, the film delves deeply into Wyatt's personality to explain in detail why and how he became the famed lawman of legend.

After a brief Tombstone prologue, *Wyatt Earp* begins in 1863 with a teenage Wyatt yearning to join his two older brothers in the Civil War. For the first time, Wyatt's complete family is presented and includes his parents, sister and brothers James, Virgil, Morgan and Warren. As the family treks westward, Wyatt becomes afflicted with wanderlust, though he is nauseated by the brutality he witnesses. At age 21, he marries his hometown sweetheart, Urilla Sutherland, and happily settles down with no desire to wander. However, the deaths of his wife and unborn child precipitate his descent into despair and wrongdoing. He eventually rejoins the human race to be close to his brothers and becomes a lawman in part because it suits his hardened personality.

This Wyatt Earp will not allow any emotional contact. He has no sense of humor and he exudes no warmth. Even his brothers' wives think that he is cold and heartless and despise him because of his influence over their husbands. Former prostitute Mattie Blaylock, who lives with him as his wife, cannot break through his shell and is kept at a distance. Only one man, Doc Holliday, detects the loneliness within Wyatt and senses a kinship with him, thus sealing their friendship. His harsh methods are proven to be the only ones that can tame Wichita and Dodge City and his fame spreads. When Wyatt decides to move on once again, his brothers and Doc follow him further west to a boom town rich with opportunity for business success. The town is called Tombstone.

However, Wyatt's dreams of attaining financial success are not realized and the brothers once again become lawmen. At this stage in his life, Wyatt has no tolerance for lawbreakers, particularly the Clantons and McLaurys, whose gang of Cowboys is more organized and powerful than any of his previous adversaries, due in part to their alliance with County Sheriff Johnny Behan. Also, for the first time since Urilla's death, he is emotionally attracted to a woman, Josephine Marcus, who happens to be Behan's fiancée. Mattie, sensing that she is losing Wyatt, becomes increasingly suicidal through her use of laudanum. Continued criminality by the Cowboys heightens the tension between the two factions and leads to the O.K. Corral.

This Wyatt Earp who meets his brothers and Doc on the fateful day of the gunfight is an emotionally scarred man who has hardened himself to survive and who has filled

the emptiness of his life with a devotion to the cold concept of the law. The Cowboys represent all of the outlaws he has encountered his entire life. Not only are they violating the law but they are also threatening his life and the lives of his brothers. He has never forgotten the words of his father, who instilled in him the importance of family unity, and he will not allow his family to be destroyed by outlaws.

The gunfight at the O.K. Corral is naturally a highlight of the film. As the Earps and Doc start their famous walk into history, the excitement once again builds with each step until the two parties face one another. Included during the walk is Morgan's dubious "let 'em have it" remark to Doc, which was reported by a woman in a butcher's shop, followed by Doc's assent. Many researchers believe that, if the words were actually said, they could have been the end of a sentence that was preceded by something like, "If they go for their guns...." Also included is Morgan's challenge to the Cowboys, which was reported by Ike Clanton and Billy Clairborne, not exactly impartial witnesses.

Nevertheless, the staging of the gunfight is historically accurate and is a terrific action sequence. After several tense moments in which the parties stare at one another, the battle begins with precipitate ferocity. And when the violence explodes, it is as chaotic and bloody as the actual gunfight. Within half a minute, almost 30 shots are fired and then it is over. In this film, because of the changes in Wyatt's life and in his personality, the bloody event takes on a new significance.

The wounding of Virgil and the murder of Morgan are again depicted accurately (though the attacks didn't occur on the same evening) but also with new impact. As Wyatt holds Morgan's body in his arms and then helplessly tries to comfort a wounded Virgil, the devastation that he experienced upon Urilla's death revisits him and again tears him apart. Increasing his agony is the fact that he blames himself for bringing the family to Tombstone. The loss of Urilla hardened him, but the loss of Morgan will turn him into an implacable killing machine. As he vows revenge, the innocent boy that he once was no longer exists. The lawman that respected the law and avoided killing will now make his own law and enforce it his own way.

Thus, the infamous Vendetta Ride begins. The horror on Warren's face as Wyatt empties a shotgun and pistol into Frank Stillwell's body is a forceful indication of Wyatt's deterioration, for Warren is the boy that Wyatt used to be. Only Josie's promise never to leave him keeps him from descending into complete savagery. One by one, his brother's killers are cut down by Wyatt and his posse. At Mescal Springs, as an enraged Curly Bill marches toward Wyatt and fires repeatedly at him, Wyatt stands fearlessly and cuts the outlaw in half with his shotgun. Wyatt can then only look blankly ahead, lost in his memories, wondering why everything turned out so wrong.

In the film's epilogue, a young admirer asks an elderly Wyatt about a fabled incident that contributed to Wyatt's fame. Did it happen the way the boy had been told or was it part of the myth surrounding the legendary figure? Wyatt can remember holding off a lynch mob by himself even though people are denying that it happened. But the heroic act is meaningless to him. He smiles faintly as he holds Josie. They are looking toward the Alaskan shore. He is still wandering.

Wyatt Earp is both an intimate character study and an epic adventure. It is a story of heroism and courage and it is a story of love, both family and romantic. Since the script covers so many events over an extended period of time, the film appears episodic. However, it retains continuity if we look within the personality of Wyatt. Gradually, the boy who is inspired by the warmth of a close-knit family gives way to a lonely wanderer's endless quest for something he has lost. Outwardly, Wyatt emerges from all of his travails triumphant but inwardly his soul has been tarnished. He is a hero to his country but not to himself, for he has paid too high a price for his fame.

Ironically, the screenplay for *Wyatt Earp* suffered the same fate as the one for *Tombstone*. Originally, the original script by Dan Gordon was envisioned as a six-hour event for pay television, but when the decision was made to produce it as a theatrical feature, director Lawrence Kasdan rewrote and shortened the script.

A comparison of the final screenplay with the Gordon novel gives an indication of the changes. In the film, more emphasis is given to Wyatt's early years and less time is spent in Tombstone. Missing from the film are many historical persons who figure prominently in the novel, including Old Man Clanton as well as the politicians who were an integral part of the corruption of the boom town along with the fraudulence attached to the Town Site Company. However, the novel and film share the theme of Wyatt's devotion to his family, the destruction of which causes his moral deterioration.

Once again, as in *Tombstone*, historical references in the film are mentioned and not elaborated upon, giving an indication of the larger scope of the original script. For instance, a significant event leading to the bloodshed was the Benson stage hold-up by the Cowboys, who tried to implicate Doc. The subsequent arrest by Wyatt's posse of one of the robbers and his escape from Behan's custody is mentioned briefly by Wyatt to Behan, but the reference is puzzling to the moviegoer unaware of its significance.

An unfortunate consequence of the abridgement is that some significant characters in Wyatt's life, particularly in Tombstone, are given too little screen time. Among the Cowboys, Curly Bill Brocius and Ike Clanton become recognizable but others like Frank and Tom McLaury, Frank Stillwell, Pete Spence and Indian Charlie make only a minimal impression. Johnny Ringo is practically nonexistent except to get shot by Doc at Mescal Springs, which is historically inaccurate. The one-dimensional aspect of the Cowboys lessens the dramatic impact of their confrontations with Wyatt.

However, the revised script still presents an abundance of factual new data. The importance of Urilla to Wyatt is presented on screen for the first time. Marshals Mike Meagher and Larry Deger, whom Wyatt served under in Wichita and Dodge, are given overdue recognition. Minor characters such as Rowdy Dubbs, Mannen Clements and John Shanssey existed in the real Wyatt's world. Many familiar names from other films also make appearances, including John Clum, Wells Spicer and Kate Fisher. Wyatt's only killing prior to Tombstone is shown to have been unavoidable, though it is perhaps glossed over too quickly. The events following the gunfight include details not usually presented, such as the siege of the Earp party in the Cosmopolitan Hotel.

In the title role, Kevin Costner gives a multi-layered performance that captures the stages of Wyatt's growth as well as his psychological complexities. As a young

man, his open sincerity invites affection, but as he becomes increasingly unfeeling, he deliberately discourages sympathy and invites resentment. His Wyatt does not care if he is liked and will not compromise for anyone. Costner's performance covers a range of emotions from unbridled love to deranged fury. And beneath the implacability is a suggestion of sadness, initially for what he has experienced but eventually for what he has become. Costner's performance is an introspective one and it is excellent.

As Doc Holliday, a gaunt and emaciated Dennis Quaid projects pathos as well as menace. Encumbered with a deathly voice and rasping cough, this Doc has no sense of humor and no warmth. He projects irascibility overshadowed by self-pity and a suggestion of loneliness that is difficult to discern because, like Wyatt, he has erected a shell around himself. When he meets Wyatt, his guarded tone suggests that he discerns the same loneliness in Wyatt and this makes his offer of friendship quite moving. Since Wyatt is the film's focus, Doc's screen time is more limited than usual, but Quaid still invests total commitment into his scenes. It is an impeccable performance.

There are over a hundred speaking parts in the movie but creating distinct characterizations are Michael Madsen, Linden Ashby, David Andrews, James Caviezel as the Earp brothers and Catherine O'Hara, JoBeth Williams and Alison Elliot as the Earp wives. Mark Harmon makes a slimy Behan while Joanna Going is an appealing Josie and Mare Winningham makes Mattie both pathetic and demanding. Also making notable impressions are Ian Bohen as young Wyatt, Annabeth Gish as Urilla, and Isabella Rossellini as Kate.

Director Lawrence Kasdan keeps the sprawling story interesting and cohesive, despite the numerous characters and settings, by maintaining the focus at all times on the character of Wyatt Earp. The movie makes it clear that Wyatt's life offered much more than violence alone. Many scenes of lyrical quality stand out, including Wyatt and Urilla tilling in their garden or a young Wyatt sharing a happy meal with his family, his future full of hope and promise. And the film has an atypical ending, in which a flashback scene is used after the main story is completed to illustrate the truth behind the legend.

The score by James Newton Howard begins with a striking main title theme, an almost heraldic statement which encompasses the grandeur of the adventurous and tragic life that about to follow. Throughout the film, the music ideally complements the action scenes as well as the romantic ones while bridging the various stages of Wyatt's development. It is a stunning score which adds immeasurably to the film's splendor.

Regarding the unofficial contest between *Tombstone* and *Wyatt Earp*, the two films perhaps should not be judged against one another for, despite sharing the same main character and many of the same events, they are different kinds of movies. They also feature different interpretations of Wyatt as well as Doc, both of whom are brought to life in both films by flawless performances. And they are both very good movies.

Wyatt Earp failed at the box office, in part because it was released so soon after *Tombstone* and because its second half told the same story as the earlier film. In the 1990s, a Western had to be perceived as having something unique to offer audiences, who believed incorrectly that they had seen it all in *Tombstone*. The movie had additional competition from the small screen.

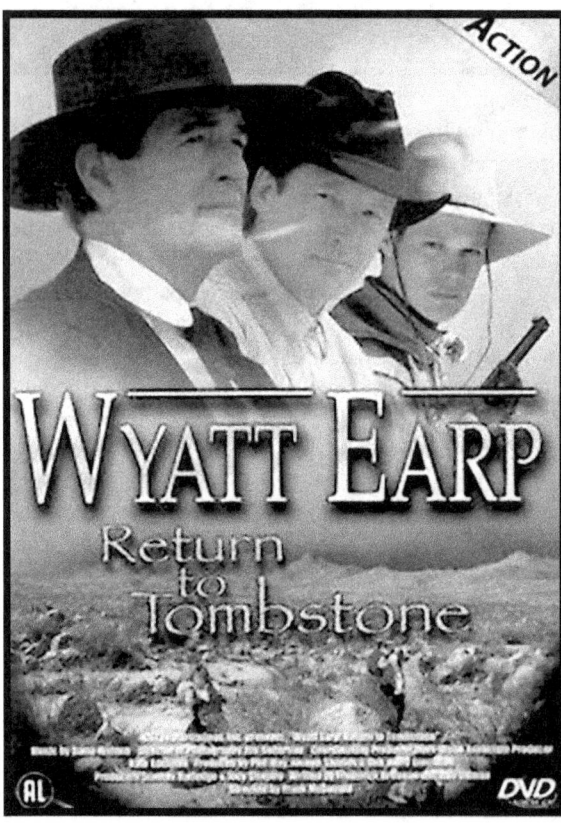

Also in 1994, Hugh O'Brian again reprised the role that made him famous in *Wyatt Earp: Return to Tombstone*, which was televised on CBS-TV. This is a fictional story of how the retired lawman returns to the scene of the infamous battle to help a young man who is revealed to be Virgil's son. (In reality, Virgil discovered late in his life that he had a daughter from his first marriage.) Footage from the series occupies a good portion of the telefilm as Wyatt recalls some of his more turbulent adventures. O'Brian's performance and the flashbacks are pleasantly nostalgic, though the film was obviously made to take advantage of the publicity given to the theatrical movies.

In fact, the movie was televised the same week that *Wyatt Earp* opened in theaters and *Tombstone* was released on home video. The television movie achieved high ratings while *Tombstone* became a top seller in video stores. Thus, it is not surprising that *Wyatt Earp* didn't attract audiences. Warner Bros. should have delayed the release of the movie until a more opportune time, when it didn't have to compete with rival depictions of Wyatt. In the three-way race, it came in third. It was a film released at the wrong time.

Incidentally, the debunkers had been dismayed by both *Tombstone*, which presented a valiant Wyatt, and *Wyatt Earp*, which presented a darker but still courageous Wyatt. Since the scripts of both films were based on objective and extensive research, they could only fume and look for other flies to speck.

Wyatt made another appearance on the small screen in 1994, though a brief one, in a television movie entitled *Young Indiana Jones and the Hollywood Follies*. While working for director John Ford, the young hero of this teenage series meets several of the director's friends, including an aged Wyatt Earp, played by Leo Gordon.

That same year, the cable network Arts & Entertainment presented a pseudo-documentary entitled "Justice at the O.K. Corral." This was an episode of a series entitled *The Real West* which pompously claimed to expose the truth about celebrated events in the Old West. It was another attempt to defame Wyatt but the attempt was futile. By this time, the laudable image of Wyatt Earp was supported by unassailable factual data.

The real Wyatt Earp never wanted to become the most enduring legend of the American West. After Tombstone, he tried to avoid the publicity that his reputation decreed would follow him everywhere. Nevertheless, he would not exploit his name. While visiting Hollywood studios, he was often asked to appear in front of the cameras but declined.

Wyatt probably knew that lies would continue to be told about him and his brothers. But he also probably realized that truth would eventually win out, as it usually does. He would be gratified to know that in 1991, the Southern California Paraders Association would dedicate a memorial and headstone in honor of Morgan Earp at his gravesite in a ceremony attended by a delegation from the U.S. Marshal's posse and an Honor Guard from the 7th U.S. Cavalry. He would be equally delighted to know that, in 1994, Virgil Earp would be the subject of a laudatory biography. Even Warren Earp's life and murder would be thoroughly explored in a book published in 2000.

However, Wyatt Earp will always be the most famous of the Earp brothers. His name is one of the most recognizable ones in the history of the country. It is a name that is known throughout the United States and in many parts of the world. The name

Wyatt Earp Birthplace Historic House Museum

is referenced in movies, on television shows, on news programs and by politicians. He remains the most renowned symbol of the fearless lawmen of the Old West. Tombstone today is a popular tourist attraction because of the name of Wyatt Earp as much as the O.K. Corral gunfight. In today's Dodge City, one of the main thoroughfares is Wyatt Earp Boulevard.

In 1986, the house in which Wyatt was born in Monmouth, Illinois was restored and established as the Wyatt Earp Birthplace Historic House Museum, which has since been visited by tourists from 49 states and 30 foreign countries. The house has been placed on the National Register of Historic Places and, in 2005, was recognized by the state of Illinois as the recipient of the Governor's Home Town Award.

In Los Angeles, a plaque in tribute to Wyatt stands in front of his former residence and a similar plaque stands in front of the San Francisco cottage in which he lived. At the Hills of Eternity Cemetery in Colma, California, his gravesite is visited so frequently that directions to the tombstone are on the door of the cemetery office. And 65 years after his death, Wyatt Earp was awarded the distinction of a U.S. Postage Stamp in his honor.

Wyatt would have preferred anonymity but this was denied him. That is the price one must pay for becoming a legend. And he achieved that status for one very good reason. He deserves it.

Wyatt Earp is an American hero. He may not have been the noble hero of *My Darling Clementine* or the tragic hero of *Warlock*. Perhaps the dejected and weary hero of *Law and Order* is an accurate portrayal of how he really felt after Tombstone. Or possibly the embittered and empty Wyatt at the end of *Hour of the Gun* is closer to the truth. It would be nice to think that the joyful, dancing Wyatt at the end of *Tombstone* is factual. Or perhaps the prosperous Wyatt whose expression at the end of *Wyatt Earp* suggests that he has found inner peace is more accurate. Quite probably, some degree of truth exists in all of these films.

Most likely the complete truth will never be known, though Hollywood will probably continue to provide its versions.

Mortals die, but legends live on.

Law and Order [Universal/1932]
CREDITS: Director: Edward Cahn; Screenplay: John Huston, Tom Reed based on the novel *Saint Johnson* by W.R. Burnett; Cinematographer: Jackson Rose; Editor: Phil Cahn
CAST: Walter Huston (Frame Johnson); Harry Carey (Ed Brandt); Russell Hopton (Luther Johnson); Raymond Hatton (Deadwood); Ralph Ince (Poe Northrup); Russell Simpson (Judge Williams); Harry Woods (Walt Northrup); Richard Alexander (Kurt Northrup; Andy Devine (Johnny Kinsman); Walter Brennan (Lanky Smith)

My Darling Clementine [20th Century Fox/1946]
CREDITS: Producer: Samuel G. Engel; Director: John Ford; Screenplay: Samuel G. Engel and Winston Miller, from a story by Sam Hellman, based on the book *Wyatt Earp, Frontier Marshal* by Stuart Lake; Cinematographer: Joseph P. MacDonald; Editor: Dorothy Spencer; Music: Cyril Mockridge
CAST: Henry Fonda (Wyatt Earp); Victor Mature (Doc Holliday); Linda Darnell (Chihuahua); Walter Brennan (Old Man Clanton); Tim Holt (Virgil Earp); Ward Bond (Morgan Earp); Cathy Downs (Clementine Carter); John Ireland (Billy Clanton); Grant Withers (Ike Clanton); Don Garner (James Earp); Russell Simpson (John Simpson); Alan Mowbray (Granville Thorndyke)

Gunfight at the O.K. Corral [Paramount/1957]
CREDITS: Producer: Hal Wallis; Director: John Sturgis; Screenplay: Leon Uris, based on the article *The Killer* by George Scullin; Cinematographer: Charles Lang, Jr.; Editor: Warren Low; Music: Dimitri Tiomkin
CAST: Burt Lancaster (Wyatt Earp); Kirk Douglas (Doc Holliday); Rhonda Fleming (Laura Denbow); Jo Van Fleet (Kate Fisher); John Ireland (Johnny Ringo); Lyle Bettger (Ike Clanton): Dennis Hopper (Billy Clanton); John Hudson (Virgil Earp); DeForest Kelley (Morgan Earp); Martin Milner (James Earp); Frank Faylen (Cotton Wilson); Kenneth Tobey (Bat Masterson); Earl Holliman (Charlie Bassett)

Warlock [20th Century Fox/1959]
CREDITS: Producer-Director: Edward Dmytryk; Screenplay: Robert Alan Aurthur, based upon the novel *Warlock* by Oakley Hall; Cinematographer: Joe MacDonald; Editor: Jack W. Holmes; Music: Leigh Harline
CAST: Henry Fonda (Clay Blaisedell); Anthony Quinn (Tom Morgan); Richard Widmark (Johnny Gannon); Dorothy Malone (Lilly Dollar); Dolores Michaels (Jessie Marlowe); Wallace Ford (Judge Holloway); Tom Drake (Abe McQuown); DeForest Kelley (Curly Burne); Frank Gorshin (Billy Gannon); Richard Arlen (Bacon); Regis Toomey (Skinner); Whit Bissell (Petrix); Walter Coy (Sheriff Thompson); Vaughn Taylor (Richardson); Donald Barry (Calhoun); Don Beddoe (Dr. Wagner)

Hour of the Gun [United Artists/1967]
CREDITS: Producer-Director: John Sturges; Screenplay: Edward Anhalt; Cinematographer: Lucien Ballard; Editor: Ferris Webster; Music: Jerry Goldsmith
CAST: James Garner (Wyatt Earp); Jason Robards (Doc Holliday); Robert Ryan (Ike Clanton); Steve Ihnat (Andy Warshaw); Michael Tolan (Pete Spence); Frank Converse (Virgil Earp); Sam Melville (Morgan Earp); Larry Gates (John Clum); Karl Svenson

(Dr. Charles Goodfellow); Bill Fletcher (Jimmy Bryan); Monte Markham (Sherm McMasters); Charles Aidman (Horace Sullivan); William Windom (Texas Jack Vermillion); Lonny Chapman (Turkey Creek Jack Johnson); William Schallert (Judge Spicer); Robert Phillips (Frank Stillwell); Jon Voight (Curly Bill Brocius)

Tombstone [Hollywood Pictures/1993]
CREDITS: Producers: James Jacks, Sean Daniel, Bob Misiorowski; Director: George P. Cosmatos; Screenplay: Kevin Jarre; Cinematographer: William A. Fraker; Editors: Frank Urioste, Roberto Silvi, Harvey Rosenstock; Music: Bruce Broughton
CAST: Kurt Russell (Wyatt Earp); Val Kilmer (Doc Holliday); Sam Elliot (Virgil Earp); Bill Paxton (Morgan Earp); Powers Boothe (Curly Bill Brocius); Michael Biehn (Johnny Ringo); Dana Delaney (Josie); Joanna Pacula (Kate); Stephen Lang (Ike Clanton); Jon Tenney (Johnny Behan); Dana Wheeler-Nicholson (Mattie); Jason Priestley (Billy Breakenridge); Michael Rooker (Sherm McMasters); Billy Zane (Mr. Fabian); Thomas Haden Church (Billy Clanton); Thomas Arana (Frank Stillwell); Buck Taylor (Turkey Creek Jack Johnson)

Wyatt Earp [Warner Bros./1994]
Producers: Jim Wilson, Kevin Costner, Lawrence Kasdan; Director: Lawrence Kasdan; Screenplay: Dan Gordon, Lawrence Kasdan; Cinematographer: Owen Roizman; Editor: Carol Littleton; Music: James Newton Howard
CAST: Kevin Costner (Wyatt Earp); Dennis Quaid (Doc Holliday); Gene Hackman (Nicholas Earp); Michael Masden (Virgil Earp); Linden Ashby (Morgan Earp); David Andrews (James Earp); James Caviezel (Warren Earp); Annabeth Gish (Urilla); Joanna Going (Josie); Mare Winningham (Mattie); Tom Sizemore (Bat Masterson); Bill Pullman (Ed Masterson); Ian Bohen (Wyatt, age 15); Mark Harmon (Johnny Behan); Jeff Fahey (Ike Clanton); Isabella Rossellini (Kate); Betty Buckley (Virginia Earp); JoBeth Williams (Bessie Earp); Catherine O'Hara (Allie Earp); Louis Smith (Curly Bill Brocius); Kirk Fox (Pete Spence); J.D. Johnson (Frank Stillwell); Randall Mell (John Clum)

Wyatt Earp on Film

Theatrical Movies
1) *Wild Bill Hickock* (1923) Bert Lindley
2) *Law and Order* (1932) Walter Huston
3) *Frontier Marshal* (1934) George O'Brien
4) *The Arizonian* (1935) Richard Dix
5) *Wild West Days* (1937) Johnny Mack Brown
6) *In Early Arizona* (1938) Bill Elliot
7) *Frontier Marshal* (1939) Randolph Scott
8) *Law and Order* (1940) Johnny Mack Brown
9) *Tombstone, the Town Too Tough to Die* (1942) Richard Dix
10) *My Darling Clementine* (1946) Henry Fonda
11) *Winchester '73* (1950) Will Geer
12) *Powder River* (1953) Rory Calhoun
13) *Law and Order* (1953) Ronald Reagan

14) *Gun Belt* (1953) James Millican
15) *Masterson of Kansas* (1954) Bruce Cowling
16) *Dawn at Socorro* (1954) James Millican
17) *Wichita* (1955) Joel McCrae
18) *Gunfight at the O.K. Corral* (1957) Burt Lancaster
19) *Forty Guns* (1957) Barry Sullivan
20) *Badman's Country* (1958) Buster Crabbe
21) *Alias Jesse James* (1959) Hugh O'Brian
22) *Warlock* (1959) Henry Fonda
23) *Cheyenne Autumn* (1964) James Stewart
24) *Gunmen of the Rio Grande* (1964) Guy Madison
25) *The Outlaws Is Coming* (1965) Bill Camfield
26) *Hour of the Gun* (1967) James Garner
27) *Young Billy Young* (1969) Robert Mitchum
28) *Doc* (1971) Harris Yulin
29) *Sunset* (1988) James Garner
30) *Tombstone* (1993) Kurt Russell
31) *Wyatt Earp* (1994) Kevin Costner

Television Series
The Life and Legend of Wyatt Earp (1955-1961) Hugh O'Brian

Television Episodes
1) *Bat Masterson* (1960-1961) Ron Hayes; four episodes
2) *Maverick* (1962) Med Florey; one episode
3) *Death Valley Days* (1964) Jim Davis; one episode
4) *Star Trek* (1967) Ron Soble; one episode
5) *Alias Smith and Jones* (1972) Cameron Mitchell; one episode
6) *Paradise* (1989) Hugh O'Brian; two episodes

Television Documentaries
1) *You Are There* (1953) Robert Bray; one episode
2) *Appointment with Destiny* (1972) David Vowell; one episode
3) *The Real West* (1994); one episode

Television Movies
1) *I Married Wyatt Earp* (1989) Bruce Boxleitner
2) *The Gambler Returns: The Luck of the Draw* (1991) Hugh O'Brian
3) *Four Eyes and Six Guns* (1992) Fred Ward
4) *Wyatt Earp: Return to Tombstone* (1994) Hugh O'Brian
5) *Young Indiana Jones and the Hollywood Follies* (1994) Leo Gordon

Twelve "A" Westerns of the 1950s

The 1950s could justifiably be called the Decade of the Western. From 1950 to 1959, Westerns reached the zenith of their popularity with the public and with the critics. Never before and never since have so many A Westerns been produced and released by the major studios.

Westerns had been a part of the film industry since its inception, with the degree of popularity fluctuating due to public tastes. During the silent era, the genre was popular due to stars like William S. Hart and Tom Mix, but by the late 1920s Westerns were losing their appeal to adults. In the 1930s, though occasional major Westerns were produced, the genre was dominated by series Westerns stars oriented toward a younger audience. At the end of the 1930s, Westerns made a comeback due to the popularity of films like John Ford's *Stagecoach* with John Wayne and Henry King's *Jesse James* with Tyrone Power. Their commercial success led to more stars and directors riding west.

In the early 1940s, films such as William Wyler's *The Westerner* with Gary Cooper and William Wellman's *The Ox-Bow Incident* with Henry Fonda added further prestige to the genre. As a result, the number of Westerns gradually increased during the 1940s, especially after World War II. In mid-decade, Ford's *My Darling Clementine* and Raoul Walsh's *Pursued* were representative of the new adult Westerns being produced. By the end of the decade, the popularity of Ford's *Fort Apache, 3 Godfathers* and *She Wore a Yellow Ribbon* along with Howard Hawks' *Red River* was a significant factor in the genre's explosion the following decade; the fact that John Wayne starred in all four films was undoubtedly a factor in his ascendancy to all-time leading star of the genre.

By the early 1950s, series Westerns that had remained popular with youngsters during the 1940s were losing their appeal due in part to the rise of science fiction movies. More significantly, Gene Autry, Roy Rogers and William Boyd, the reigning kings of series Westerns, successfully entered the world of television. Since youngsters could now watch their favorite stars on the small screen, Hollywood targeted its Westerns at an older audience who desired movies with more substance.

Another factor was the steadily decreasing numbers of audiences in theaters, due to the impact of television. As a result, Hollywood began to emphasize films with adult themes not permitted on the small screen, a trend which extended to Westerns. Accompanying these mature themes were heroes whose psychological complexities reflected their perilous environments. By the middle of the decade, the success of such Westerns convinced the television industry of the public's desire for similarly adult fare on the small screen. The public's appetite for Westerns seemed to be insatiable.

An A Western of the 1950s can be defined as a big-budget movie from a major studio produced with prominent talent on both sides of the camera. Virtually every major star and director ventured into the genre in the 1950s due to the commercial success and critical esteem of many of these movies.

From 1950 to 1959, over 125 A Westerns were released, averaging 12 major Westerns every year. With so many releases, the quality naturally varied and included the two greatest Westerns of all time, *Shane* and *The Searchers*. Many others received justified acclaim. But still many others were neglected due to the surplus of Westerns in the marketplace. Such films deserved a better fate and probably would have received more praise and bigger profits if not for the period in which they were released.

Thus, these unheralded Westerns could be called timeless. Many of these movies may have played just one week in theaters before disappearing. The following 12 Westerns, though they may not be the best Westerns of the era, are examples of such movies generally ignored and deserving of more critical notice.

Each year of the decade had its share of great Westerns as well as many good ones. In 1950, among the most significant Westerns were Henry King's *The Gunfighter* with Gregory Peck, Delmer Daves' *Broken Arrow* with James Stewart and Anthony Mann's *Winchester '73* with Stewart. John Ford completed his cavalry trilogy with *Rio Grande* starring John Wayne and also made *Wagonmaster*. And there were many others that were notable but not as renowned.

The year 1950 was an important one for director Anthony Mann. Previously, he had distinguished himself with modest B movies which were fine examples of film noir. In 1950, Mann graduated to A movies and made three Westerns: *Winchester '73*, *The Furies* with Barbara Stanwyck and *Devil's Doorway* with Robert Taylor. *Devil's Doorway* was the first Western he directed but was released after the other two due to the studio's concern over the profitability of the film's pro-Indian message. The successful release of 20th Century Fox's *Broken Arrow* prompted MGM to finally release the movie. It is an uncompromising study of injustice and prejudice.

Anthony Mann

Robert Taylor had been a star since the mid-1930s but, prior to 1950, he had only made one Western, playing the title role in *Billy the Kid* in 1941. *Ambush,* his second Western, immediately preceded this film. In *Devil's Doorway*, he stars as Shoshone Indian Lance Poole, who was awarded the Medal of Honor while fighting for the Union during the Civil War. He returns home to encounter prejudice and legalized discrimination that confiscates the land of his people. Having no other recourse, he leads a rebellion against the cavalry that he served so honorably and which he and his followers have virtually no chance to defeat. This leads to a disastrous ending for Lance and his people.

Devil's Doorway features a sensitive and intelligent performance from Taylor. The feeling he imparts to his portrayal of Lance creates a tragic character, particularly as he appears lost between two worlds. The last scene, in which he appears in his Army uniform, is heartrending as his expression reveals both love and shame for his country as well as pride and anguish. In support, Louis Calhern is very good as an Indian-hating lawyer and Edgar Buchanan provides his usual dependable performance as the sheriff. Mann's direction is reminiscent of his noir films, such as when he frames Poole against a cloud of black smoke, and is perfectly suited to Guy Trosper's eloquent original script. The intimate scenes of Poole with his people are handled with warmth while the climactic battle sequence is harshly realistic.

Though *Broken Arrow* had been a box office success, its unhappy ending was accompanied by optimism. The ending of Mann's film is hopeless, which is probably the reason for its commercial failure. *Devil's Doorway* did not earn the minimum of $1 million to qualify for inclusion on *Variety*'s annual list of top-grossing movies. *Samson and Delilah* topped the list with $11 million in domestic theatrical rentals followed by *Battleground* and *King Solomon's Mines* with $4.5 million each. *Broken Arrow* was Number 9 with $3.5 million while *Winchester '73* earned $2.2 million.

Throughout the 1950s, Mann directed 10 Westerns that comprise a unique and distinctive body of work. Taylor made nine Westerns in the 1950s, including films for John Sturges, William Wellman, Richard Brooks and Michael Curtiz. Taylor and Mann never worked together again.

The year 1951 witnessed two Westerns that are good but might have been great if they hadn't been butchered by the studio, which in both cases was MGM: John Huston's *The Red Badge of Courage* with Audie Murphy and William Wellman's *Across the Wide Missouri* with Clark Gable. Raoul Walsh's *Distant Drums* with Gary Cooper and Gordon Douglas' *Only the Valiant* with Gregory Peck are good movies that were released and forgotten. They are not the only ones.

Tyrone Power, like Robert Taylor, had been a very popular star since the mid-1930s but, excluding the biographical *Brigham Young* in 1940, he had only starred in one Western, ironically as another famous outlaw, *Jesse James*, in 1939. Henry Hathaway started his directorial career in the early 1930s and made several B Westerns prior to *Brigham Young*. Eleven years later, Hathaway and Power reunited for *Rawhide*, a suspenseful Western about a man, a woman and a child being held hostage at the Rawhide relay depot by a gang of outlaws who plan to rob the gold shipment due to arrive. During the course of the ordeal, the couple unites to survive, but no contrived romance intervenes due to the menacing threat posed by the outlaws, who have already killed one person.

Hathaway's direction is brisk and creates increasing tension within the claustrophobic atmosphere of the station in which most of the movie takes place. Power brings conviction to the role of Tom, a different kind of Western hero. He is an Easterner who has traveled west to learn the business of managing a stage line. He has no intention of staying in the West and aspires only to a desk job back where he came from. Playing the role with humility and without false heroics, Power provides a powerful portrayal of an average man forced into a desperate fight for his life. Susan Hayward is also believable as Vinnie, a former riverboat entertainer who knows how to take care of herself, but is also learning how to take care of her sister's baby. Edgar Buchanan is again on hand to make Sam, the manager, a likeable character before he is gunned down. Standout support is provided by Hugh Marlowe as Zimmerman, the cultured outlaw leader, and Jack Elam as Tevis, a deranged killer whose bizarre facial expressions hint at the ferocity that can erupt at any moment.

Deliberately small in scope with little use of the landscape, the movie concentrates on the concisely developed characterizations. *Rawhide* is a good example of how the Western genre can be utilized to provide the suspense of a crime thriller. According to some sources, Dudley Nichols' script was loosely based upon a 1935 crime drama *Show Them No Mercy,* which was about a group of kidnappers holding a couple and their baby hostage in an abandoned home. Though some similarities exist, Nichols' script for *Rawhide* is essentially an original one and the Western is more effective than the modest thriller.

Audiences did not respond overwhelmingly to this suspenseful Western. On *Variety*'s annual list, *Rawhide* ranked 46th with theatrical rentals of $1.9 million, below such movies as *Ma and Pa Kettle* and *Francis Goes to the Races*, both of which earned $2.3 million. The top movie of the year was *David and Bathsheba* with $7 million while the top Western was *Across the Wide Missouri* with $2.9 million. Other Westerns scoring higher were *Branded* with Alan Ladd and *Tomahawk*, a B Western with Van Heflin.

After *Rawhide*, Power only made one more Western, *Pony Soldier*, in 1952, which is routine. Hathaway made two more Westerns in the 1950s, one of which co-starred Susan Hayward, but he and Power did not work together again.

In 1952, *The Greatest Show On Earth* and *Quo Vadis* were the top-grossing films of the year with, respectively, $12 million and $10 million in North American theatrical rentals. Fred Zinneman's *High Noon* with Gary Cooper ranked 8th and was the top-grossing Western of the year with $3.4 million. Anthony Mann's second Western with James Stewart, *Bend of the River,* is another exceptional film which earned $3 million to rank 13th on the list. Other Westerns of the year included Howard Hawks' *The Big Sky* and Fritz Lang's *Rancho Notorious*, which are both flawed but still interesting. Elia Kazan's *Viva Zapata* with Marlon Brando and William Wellman's *Westward the Women* with Robert Taylor both expanded the horizons of the genre in different directions.

The year 1953 was a banner year for Westerns due to the release of George Stevens' magnificent *Shane,* with Alan Ladd giving the performance of his career. Also noteworthy are John Farrow's *Hondo* with John Wayne, John Sturges' *Escape from Fort Bravo* with William Holden, and Anthony Mann's *The Naked Spur*, considered by some to be the pinnacle of his collaborations with James Stewart.

Sympathetic portrayals of Indians did not start with *Broken Arrow* and can be found in Westerns from the 1930s and 1940s. However, Daves' movie can be credited with starting a trend that became popular in the 1950s. In view of this, it was surprising to see the characterization of Toriano, who is depicted as a bloodthirsty Apache leader whose only desire is to kill white men. Played by Jack Palance, he is the leader of an Apache uprising in Charles Marquis Warren's *Arrowhead* starring Charlton Heston as U.S. Army scout Ed Bannon. The story begins at an Army post where preparations are being made to transport the defeated Apaches to Florida. Although the Army believes that Toriano, who has just returned from an Eastern school, intends to honor the peace treaty, Bannon distrusts him. His suspicions prove correct when Toriano leads his men on a rampage against the whites, which eventually leads to a fight to the death between the two men.

On the surface, the story sounds fairly simple, a battle between good and evil. However, as the film progresses, it becomes clear that the characterizations of Bannon and Toriano are not so clear-cut. Bannon's loathing of all Apaches borders on the pathological and Toriano's reprehensible actions are to some degree understandable when his people are herded like cattle prior to their forced relocation to a reservation thousands of miles away. Little difference can be found between the scout's callous reaction to the suicide of Anita, his Indian lover, and the Apache's killing of his white friend. Hatred is the emotion that drives the two men, who do not seem capable of any other feeling.

Arrowhead is based upon a novel by W.R. Burnett entitled *Adobe Walls*. The hero of the novel is Walter Grein, Chief of Scouts for the U.S. Cavalry who, as the author explains, is based in part upon legendary scout Al Sieber. Grein is an independent, self-confident man who rarely shows emotion. He is disliked by soldiers because of his expertise at killing Apaches and is distrusted by politicians, who feel that he is an obstacle to peace. He has no friends except for fellow scout Reb MacKinnon, who is a skillful tracker. When two bands of Apaches escape from the reservation, Grein is summoned to the Army post by Colonel Wainwright and assigned the mission of tracking them down. Grein's life is complicated by Wainright's young wife, Amelia, who dislikes him. An incident involving Amelia's Indian maid, Alice, leads to a change in their relationship and, for the first time in his life, Grein has feelings he cannot control.

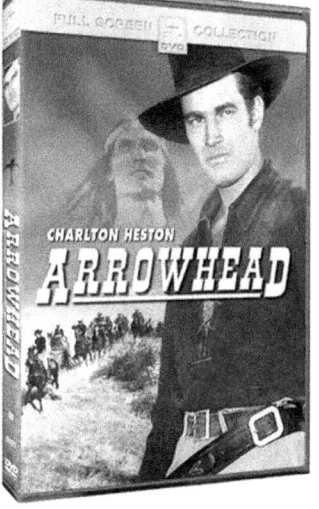

The novel is concerned with Grein's attempts to catch Toriano but the mission is complicated by political pressures, traitorous scouts and inefficient army officers. After his first mission fails through no fault of his own, Grein is dismissed due to pressure from the Bureau of Indian Affairs representative. Colonel Wainwright's career is in jeopardy because of the Apache uprising and Grein's respect for the commanding officer influences his decision to resume command, though on his terms, when the politicians realize he is the only man for the job. The final pursuit of Toriano is fraught with peril as Grein leads his men over very hazardous terrain. By the novel's end, Grein emerges as a tragic figure, a hero to the people but in reality a lonely man who has lost his only friend and the only woman he could ever love.

Since *Adobe Walls* is an exciting novel with intriguing characterizations, it is not surprising that Paramount bought the film rights. However, it is surprising that Warren's screenplay uses the novel as merely an inspiration for a different story. The movie changes the title and the name of the main character, although it is stated in the opening credits that Ed Bannon is also based upon Al Sieber. (Incidentally, according to Burnett, Toriano is based in part upon the Apache leader, Vittorio, who is depicted far more admirably in *Hondo*, which was released two months after *Arrowhead*.) The movie eliminates every other major character, substitutes new ones and enlarges the role of Toriano, who only appears at the end of the novel. Since the movie was released the same year as the publication of the novel, it is probable that film rights were purchased prior to publication, but this doesn't explain the new storyline.

Judged independently, *Arrowhead* is a very good Western that still packs a punch, thanks in part to the hard-hitting script as well as the performances of Heston and Palance. There is also good support from Brian Keith as a cavalry officer and Katy Jurado as Anita, whose role at times parallels that of Alice in the novel. Warren's direction moves the story along at a nice pace and nary a dull moment occurs in the film. Nevertheless, a faithful adaptation of Burnett's novel would have been more gratifying.

Arrowhead barely made *Variety*'s annual list with domestic theatrical rentals of $1.2 million to rank 107th. By comparison, *Shane* ranked Number 3 with $8 million and *Hondo* earned $4 million. The top films on the list were *The Robe* with $17 million and *From Here to Eternity* with $12 million.

Prior to *Arrowhead*, Heston had appeared in two Westerns in the 1950s and, afterward, would star in three more during the decade. Warren, originally a novelist, followed this movie with several B Westerns but made his mark in television as producer and writer of *Gunsmoke* during its first year.

The year 1954 saw the release of several acclaimed Westerns, including Edward Dmytryk's *Broken Lance* with Spencer Tracy, Nicholas Ray's *Johnny Guitar* with Joan Crawford, Henry Hathaway's *Garden of Evil* with Gary Cooper and William Wellman's *Track of the Cat* with Robert Mitchum. Robert Aldrich directed two fine Westerns, *Apache* with Burt Lancaster and *Vera Cruz* with Cooper and Lancaster. And Delmer Daves made another Indian Western, one that is not as well-known as *Broken Arrow*.

Delmer Daves directed nine Westerns in the 1950s. His second was a contemporary Western, *The Return of the Texan* in 1952, and his third was *Drum Beat*, which he also wrote. Like *Broken Arrow*, this movie is based on fact and deals with attempts to negotiate a peace treaty with the Modoc Indian tribe. Alan Ladd plays Johnny McKay, a former Indian fighter who is assigned to capture a renegade known as Captain Jack. Unlike the peaceful Modocs who are represented by Chief Manok and his sister Toby, Captain Jack wants only to make war and kill the whites who have invaded his homeland.

Daves brings an unusual degree of realism to the story, which is aided by well-developed characterizations. The film has many compelling scenes, including the

treacherous attack upon the peace committee, in which suspense and tension gradually escalate as the hostile Modocs slowly surround the committee. His screenplay is devoid of the romanticism of his earlier Western and has an air of authenticity that is evident from the lack of clichés and the unpredictable storyline. The final scene between McKay and Jack in his prison cell is unexpectedly poignant because both characters are believable. It is to the credit of the actors and director that Captain Jack emerges as a sympathetic figure despite his murderous actions. Daves brings forth an appealing performance from Ladd, who is solidly heroic when he needs to be yet can be deferential and shy in the romantic scenes. Charles Bronson stands out in a showier role of Captain Jack and took his first tentative steps toward stardom.

White Christmas was the top film of the year with $12 million in theatrical rentals followed by *The Caine Mutiny* with $8 million. The highest grossing Western of the year was *Vera Cruz* with $4 million while other Western hits were *Bend of the River* and *Broken Lance*, both at $3.8 million. *Drum Beat* scored a hit with $3 million. Nevertheless, it was soon forgotten and, for inexplicable reasons, is not as well regarded as Daves' other Westerns of the decade.

Daves and Ladd reunited in 1958 for *The Badlanders*, a Westernized remake of W.R. Burnett's *The Asphalt Jungle*, which is competent but disappointing for fans of both Daves and Ladd. Prior to the 1950s, Ladd had only starred in one Western. However, in the 1950s, he made nine Westerns. Besides *Shane*, which stands alone, some are good and some are routine. *Drum Beat* is one of the good ones.

In 1955, Anthony Mann's *The Man from Laramie* with James Stewart and John Sturges' contemporary Western *Bad Day at Black Rock* starring Spencer Tracy were standout films, but the year also saw the release of Raoul Walsh's *The Tall Men* with Clark Gable and Mann's *The Far Country*, also with Stewart, among many other noteworthy oaters, including one from veteran director King Vidor.

King Vidor started directing in the silent era and made infrequent forays into the Western genre. During the 1930s and 1940s, he directed four Westerns, including *Northwest Passage* in 1940 and *Duel in the Sun* for David O. Selznick in 1946. It would be nine years before he directed another Western, one smaller in scale than the Selznick film but more rewarding. Kirk Douglas made three Westerns prior to 1955. His first had been Raoul Walsh's *Along the Great Divide* in 1951, in which he looked like a greenhorn pretending to be a cowboy. Four years later, he inhabits the old West like an old glove.

Man Without a Star is the story of Dempsey Rae, a drifter who keeps wandering further west to escape the advancing tide of civilization. After saving the life of naïve farm boy Jeff Jimson, who yearns to be a cowboy, Dempsey proceeds to teach him the art of Western survival. Dempsey and Jeff are hired by ranch foreman Strap Davis, whose employer, cattle baroness Reed Bowman, soon arrives from the East to

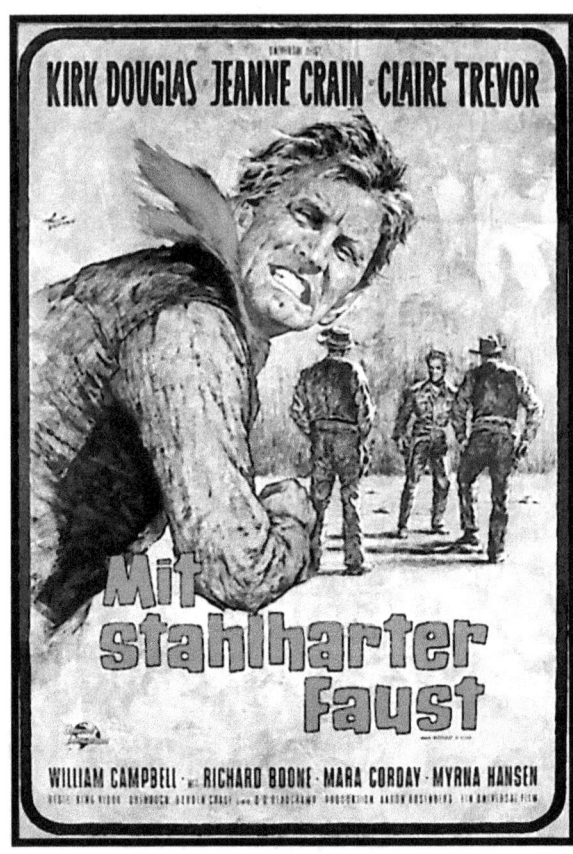

make as much money as she can out of the ranch, regardless of the effect her plans have upon smaller ranchers. Dempsey romances Reed but quickly becomes repelled by her ambitions, which involve hiring gunfighter Steve Miles to get rid of her neighbors. Reluctant to get involved in a range war, he quits his job but cannot convince Jeff, who is infatuated with Reed, to leave with him. He drifts into town and renews an acquaintance with saloon hostess Idonee but circumstances, including a savage beating from Miles and his men, force him to join the smaller ranchers, despite his hatred of their barbed wire.

Vidor's muscular direction brings a special intensity to the action scenes but he also generates eroticism with Dempsey and Reed, whose relationship seems to hover between mutual attraction and mutual contempt. A genuine feeling of the West occurs throughout the film and this is undoubtedly due to the incisive screenplay co-written by Borden Chase, whose previous credits included *Red River, Winchester '73* and *Bend of the River*. Credited as co-writer is D.D. Beauchamp, but since he is mostly associated with undistinguished B Westerns (*Jesse James' Women, Son of Belle Starr*, etc.), it can probably be assumed that Chase is responsible for the most of the screenplay, particularly since the themes presented here are themes associated with Chase's other scripts (an individual's self-worth and his place in society).

Man Without a Star is based upon a novel of the same name by Dee Linford, which was published in 1952. Once again, the script is only loosely based upon the novel and is a totally different story. The novel's hero is Jeff Jimson, while Dempsey Rae is a secondary character. Jeff starts out as an innocent 17-years old runaway who meets Abby Garrett, daughter of one of Wyoming's biggest ranchers, and he is instantly enamored of her. He also meets Dempsey Rae, who saves his life and teaches him the ropes about being a cowhand. Dempsey and Jeff are hired by Garrett, but Dempsey's dishonesty causes Garrett to fire them. After Dempsey stakes his claim on a small homestead, he is killed by one of Garrett's gunmen, Strap Bowman. The novel then covers several years of Jeff's life as he matures from an ambitious cowhand into a defender of the dispossessed ranchers, including Dempsey's brother, who have been victimized by Garrett's attempts to take over the territory. The novel is moderately entertaining but Jeff's journey toward maturity is full of plot twists, which weigh down the story.

The film version relegates Jeff to a supporting character, condenses the story and elevates Dempsey Rae into one of the most memorable characters in the genre of Western film. Dempsey, like so many of Chase's other Western heroes, is a complex man with psychological conflicts that need to be resolved. Despite the amiable face he presents to everyone, Dempsey is haunted by events from his past. His scars are physical as well as emotional and the scene in which he rips off his shirt to show the effects of barbed wire is chilling. More poignant is the gentle scene in which he explains to Jeff how a man must have a star to guide him throughout his life or he will end up an aimless wanderer who will never belong anywhere.

Kirk Douglas is charismatic as Dempsey and perfectly brings to life the character created by Chase. He conveys his affability and even strums a banjo while singing a cheerful ditty. But he is also very persuasive as a tortured man who is slow to anger but becomes ferocious when he is pushed too far. And he convincingly projects Dempsey's loneliness, which is evident in the last scene in which he has to ride away from the fences and the wire which are gradually destroying the open range he loves. Jeanne Crain and Claire Trevor provide good support as, respectively, Reed and Idonee, while Richard Boone, always a great villain, stands out as Steve Miles. Only William Campbell seems miscast as Jeff, failing to convey his character's innocence, but his performance doesn't impair the film.

The movie also features a rousing title song sung by Frankie Laine that was not available as a recording at the time of the film's release, probably due to the fact that Laine recorded for Columbia Records while Decca Records owned a controlling interest in Universal-International, the studio that released the movie. A version of the song by Martin Newman was released by Decca and this was the only recording available for years. Decca also released a recording by Kirk Douglas of the tune he sang in the movie, "And the Moon Grew Brighter and Brighter." When Laine recorded his album "Gunfighter Ballads and Trail Songs" in 1957, which included many Western film songs, "Man Without a Star" was not one of them. It would not be until the year 2000 that Laine's version became available on a Bear Family CD entitled "Rio Bravo and Other Movie and TV Themes," one of four CDs devoted to Western themes released by the German label.

In 1963, Universal remade the story as an episode of the television series *The Virginian* entitled "Duel at Shiloh." In this lackluster version, which credits the Chase-Beauchamp screenplay, series regular Steve Hill, played by Gary Clarke, visits the grave of Johnny Wade, the Dempsey Rae character, and then remembers how he met Wade. The story's beginning is similar to that of the movie and then takes a different direction. After Wade, played by Brian Keith, saves Steve's life, they are hired by a greedy

woman rancher who is feuding with neighbors. In this version, Steve leaves the ranch in disgust but Wade stays and this eventually leads to a showdown between the two men. The episode lacks credibility and debases the original film.

In 1969, Universal again filmed the story, this time for a theatrical remake titled *A Man Called Gannon*. Anthony Franciosa plays the title character and Michael Sarrazin is the naïve youth called Jess Washburn. The screenplay of the original film is utilized again, this time practically scene-for-scene. However, this version lacks the vitality and realism of Vidor's film and looks like it was filmed quickly on sound stages. Franciosa is a good actor, but he is miscast as a Westerner and lacks the authority that Kirk Douglas brings to the role. The supporting actors are undistinguished, except for John Anderson, whose performance equals that of Richard Boone. The movie is substandard and forgettable.

When *The Lusty Men* was released in 1952, it set a standard for rodeo movies. This contemporary Western was directed by Nicholas Ray and starred Robert Mitchum and Susan Hayward. Two years later, Ray directed *Johnny Guitar*, a unique Western that has become a cult favorite. The following year, Ray directed James Cagney and John Derek in *Run for Cover*, probably the least known of his four Westerns and, on the surface, his most conventional. But few of Ray's films are conventional and this one, from a screenplay by Winston Miller which is based upon a story by Irving Ravetch and Harriet Frank, is no exception.

Cagney is former gunfighter and wrongly imprisoned ex-convict Matt Dow, who is hoping to start a new life. On the trail, after he befriends Davey Bishop. A trigger-happy posse ambushes the two men and leaves the younger man wounded. To atone for their mistake, the townspeople elect Matt sheriff and Davey his deputy. But Davey, who has been permanently disabled, retains a bitterness that will lead to betrayal, a manhunt and a climactic shootout that leaves several men dead. A synopsis of the story doesn't convey the complex relationships that form the core of the film. Matt yearns for a paternal relationship with Davey, who resents the older man's feelings, which he mistakes for pity. Simultaneously, Matt's romance with Helga Svenson reflects Matt's need for a genuine family, with Helga a mother figure for Davey. However, Matt's personal desires and his refusal to see Davey's weaknesses set the stage for his treachery. Davey is also tortured by inner conflicts. He covers his true feelings, showing only hostility and resentment to those who care for him. It is only at the end of the movie, with one man dying in the arms of the other, that their emotions rise to the surface.

The feeling of sadness runs throughout *Run for Cover*. Davey is doomed from the beginning because of a miscarriage of justice. It is the actions of the self-righteous townspeople that lead to his despair and wrongdoing. Matt's guilt is more palpable than the posse's because he made Davey ride ahead of him. Davey's redemption comes with a terrible price for Matt because, despite the uplifting ending, he will most likely blame himself for finishing what the townspeople started with his own miscarriage of justice because he misinterpreted Davey's last action. And with this deed, Davey expressed the feelings toward Matt that he could never admit to Matt or to himself. These repressed emotions and human frailties make this underrated movie linger in the memory.

Cagney made his first Western in 1939, *The Oklahoma Kid*, and his discomfort was apparent, which is probably why it would be 16 years before he made another oater. By this time, he looked authentic in a Western setting and contributes an energetic and intense portrayal. Cagney would make his last Western, *Tribute to a Bad Man*, the following year. John Derek appeared in five Westerns in the 1950s, usually as the hero. As Davey, he projects persuasively the moral weakness that drives his character. Viveca Lindfors, as Helga, also creates a believable characterization, particularly as it relates to her relationship with her father, played by veteran actor Jean Hersholt. All of the actors shine under Ray's direction, which accentuates the violence beneath the surface of the relationship between Matt and Davey while capturing the gentility of the romance.

In 1955, in addition to *The Man from Laramie* and *The Far Country*, a third Anthony Mann Western was released. *The Last Frontier* is different due to its setting and its main character. Unlike most of Mann's Westerns, which feature traditional Western heroes, this one deals with mountain men on the fringe of civilization during the period of the Civil War. And, unlike his other Westerns, this one ultimately disappoints due to a script that deviates from the source novel.

The Last Frontier is based upon the novel, *The Gilded Rooster*, by Richard Roberts, which was published in 1947. The novel's setting is an Army post on the Western frontier that is in danger of being exterminated by the Sioux. The main character is Jed Cooper, a primitive man who has been raised in the wilderness. He is an Indian fighter but has even less fondness for the white men, whom he views with disgust. His only friend is Rideout, another mountain man who found him as a boy after his family had been killed and raised him as his son. Rideout is worried about Jed and, hoping that close contact with other whites will tame his savagery, persuades him to be a scout for the Army. But Jed has no desire to live like a white man and constantly fights with the soldiers who despise him. Because he trounces all of them, he is known as the Gilded Rooster, a title of which he is very proud.

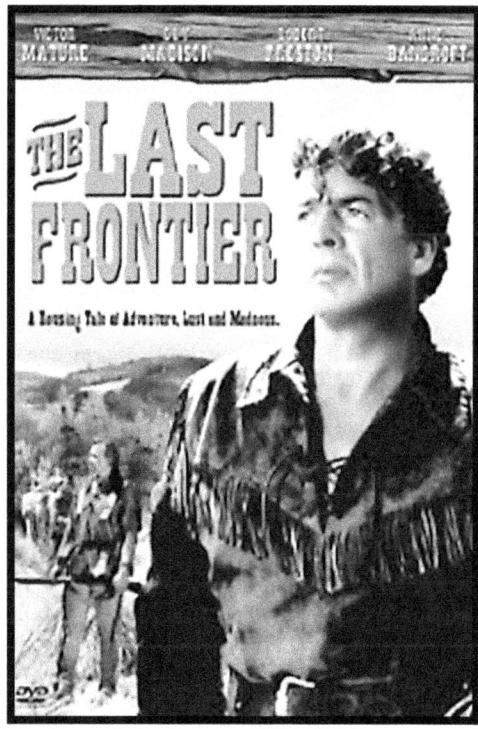

Because Jed is constantly the source of trouble, the post commander Major

Bonwitt dismisses him, but the wounding of Rideout forces the major to ask Jed to stay. Jed is about to leave when Captain Charles Gunne and his wife, Corrine, arrive at the fort. Gunne is a brutal man who has been sent out West because of his drunken behavior in the war, but Corrinne's delicacy attracts Jed, who decides to stay at the fort. Jed becomes obsessed with Corrine and will do anything to possess her, including killing her abusive husband. Corrinne also attracts the attention of Major Bonwitt, an educated man who translates foreign works of literature and recognizes in Corrinne a similar patron of the arts. But Corrinne, who is becoming increasingly despondent due to her husband's humiliation of her as well as his beatings, begins to see Jed as her only salvation, while also sensing a kinship with Bonwitt. She knows that Jed will kill Gunne if she asks him to, but she also knows that she will have to pay the price of such an act.

Jed is a tragic figure, a man who cannot adjust to any kind of human society. He is accustomed to surviving on his own and has never needed anyone. His feelings for Corrinne are the first indication of the humanity that is buried within him. But he knows that he would be unable to live in her society and that she would be unable to live with him in the wilderness. His inability to adapt to civilization combined with his desire for Corinne causes him to make a strategic mistake that results in the loss of troops under his guidance. More harmful to his self-esteem, his mistake also leads to loss of the title he cherishes, the Gilded Rooster. Broken and dejected, and knowing that he can never have Corrinne, Jed embarks on a mission which saves the fort but completes his destruction.

The Gilded Rooster, if filmed faithfully, could have been a great movie. Unfortunately, the screenplay written by Philip Yordan and Russell Hughes uses the main character and the plot of the novel as the basis for a different story. The characterizations and storyline are altered to such a degree that it seems likely that the studio, in this case Columbia, bought an idea and not a novel. Since Yordan's credits include *Johnny Guitar* and *The Man from Laramie*, it is puzzling that he misses the mark here, which leads to the suspicion that the studio executives dictated a standard story with a happy ending.

The Last Frontier begins with Jed Cooper and fellow mountain men, Gus and Mungo, being warned by the Indians to stay off their land. However, the army is building a post nearby and the uneasy truce between the trappers and the Indians is quickly broken. At the fort, they meet Captain Riordan, who offers them jobs as scouts to make up for their losses. Jed, who likes the blue uniform of the soldiers, convinces the others to stay at the fort. Jed meets Corrinna Marsten, and becomes immediately attracted to her, but her husband, Colonel Frank Marsten, soon arrives and assumes command of the fort from Captain Riordan. Marsten, desperate to atone for a disaster he caused in the Civil War, believes that he can defeat the Sioux by attacking them. The movie culminates with a fierce battle between the soldiers and the Sioux that solves everybody's problems.

The changes in the screenplay are almost all detrimental to the story. Jed's desire to be a soldier makes his character the antithesis of the novel's Jed. Except for Marsten and one sergeant, Jed seems to be liked by all of the soldiers, quite unlike the novel's Jed. The Jed of the movie wants to be civilized but the Jed of the novel would rather be dead, a fate he achieves. The drunken and brutal Gunne is more despicable and complex than his counterpart, Marsten, a standard by-the-book military officer. Gunne despises his wife but Marsten wants his wife's respect and pride. The novel's Corrinne is more sympathetic than the film's Corrinna, whose characterization is inconsistent. She initially cares for her husband and is repelled by Jed but then is disgusted with her husband and attracted to Jed, with no explanation other than the contrived revelation of the Civil War blunder.

Mann's Westerns tend to contain a fatalistic sensibility. The inherent good within his heroes seems to be waging a battle against not only the evil of others but also against their own sinful tendencies. Despite the pessimism, the films end on an uplifting tone with the heroes triumphing, though at a cost. The endings are satisfying because, after enduring suffering and pain, the heroes deserve peace and happiness. The ending of *The Last Frontier*, with Jed wearing a sergeant's uniform while Corrinna smiles at him, is nonsensical and atypical for Mann. Though Jed has learned to adapt to military life, he simply doesn't belong there, just as the fort doesn't belong in the wilderness. This tends to confirm the suspicion that Mann, like Yordan, worked under a studio decree.

Nevertheless, the movie has its virtues. Mann's direction beautifully captures the grandeur of the environment and contrasts the ramshackle look of the fort with the beauty of the natural surroundings, which may have been a subversive message on his part. His camera moves continually in some scenes, many of which are at night, recalling his noirs. He also obtains capable performances from his cast, including Robert Preston as Marsten, Guy Madison as Riordan and Anne Bancroft as Corrinna. In a class by himself, James Whitmore looks like he actually lived in the mountains to prepare for his role as Gus.

However, it is the performance of Victor Mature as Jed that that indicates just how great the movie could have been. Unjustly disparaged as an actor, Mature has provided some excellent performances throughout his career. He was equally credible in a film noir, a biblical spectacle, an adventure film or in any of the five Westerns he made. When presented with challenging material and a good director, he was more than competent. In John Ford's *My Darling Clementine,* he was a brooding and introspective Doc Holliday, his expression and tone flawlessly suggesting a desire to die. In a totally different characterization, not many actors could convincingly play a Sioux chief, but Mature did when he played the title role in *Chief Crazy Horse*, also released in 1955.

As Jed Cooper, Mature is fascinating, conveying his character's innocence as well as his savagery. He approaches the perfect embodiment of the novel's Jed, despite the changes in characterization. When Corrinna calls him an animal, his expression of pain immediately elicits sympathy. When Mungo leaves him, he is unable to understand why, and when Gus tries to explain how Corrinna will destroy him, he is unwilling to understand how. All of these confused and troubling emotions are evident in his insightful performance. He brings a depth to the character that the tone of the movie doesn't sustain and that deserved an equally complex script which adhered to the novel. If he could have played the Jed Cooper of the novel, it is evident from his portrayal that Mature could have fully realized the character's tragic persona and would have surpassed all expectations as an actor. His performance alone makes the movie worthy.

Another asset of the movie is the stirring title song which, in the film, is sung by Rusty Draper but also was recorded by Tex Ritter and Rex Allen. The lyrics don't really apply to the content of the movie, being more appropriate for a frontier settlement than an Army post, but when a movie misses its potential, anything of merit is appreciated.

Cinerama Holiday topped *Variety*'s annual list with $10 million in theatrical rentals followed by *Guys and Dolls* with $9 million and *Mister Roberts* with $8.5 million. There are 12 Westerns on the list, the highest grossing one being *The Tall Men* at Number 21 with $4.5 million followed by *The Man from Laramie* at Number 29 with $3.3 million. *Man Without a Star* is 49th on the list with $2.2 million and *Run for Cover* is 85th with $1.5 million. *The Last Frontier* did not earn the minimum amount to be included.

The year 1956 saw the release of John Ford's masterpiece, *The Searchers,* which features John Wayne's most towering performance as Ethan Edwards. But other notable Westerns appeared, including Richard Brooks' *The Last Hunt,* with Robert Taylor excelling in a rare villainous role. Delmer Daves directed two fine films, *Jubal* with Glenn Ford and *The Last Wagon* with Richard Widmark. And among the many others were two modest Westerns that disappeared quickly but deserved a better fate.

John Sturges directed five traditional Westerns and one contemporary Western in the 1950s, as well as a Revolutionary War drama. In many of his films, including Westerns, he places a group of characters in a closely knit situation and concentrates on their interactions, the development of their relationships and the impact of the environment upon them. *Backlash* would be the only movie he directed from a Borden Chase script and it proved to be a fruitful collaboration.

Richard Widmark is Jim Slater, a tormented man searching for knowledge of his father, who was reportedly killed along with five other men by Apaches. Jim believes that if he finds the lone survivor of the massacre he will learn the truth about the father he never knew. Since the survivor escaped with a supply of gold, other relatives of the murdered men are also looking for him. Among them is Karyl Orton, a bitter widow who seems more interested in the money than in her late husband. The journey is hampered by Indian attacks and a range war which is related to the mystery. Jim's quest is as much an internal as external one as he struggles to learn the truth about himself.

Backlash is a fine example of how the Western genre can be used for still another kind of story, a psychological drama. Sturges directs in the style of a thriller and builds

tension gradually as the emotional make-up of his characters is revealed. While the human conflicts dominate the story, the action sequences are exciting and serve to further illuminate the course of the relationships. Widmark contributes a plausible portrayal and is especially effective when he meets the object of his search. Donna Reed capably complements him as the enigmatic Karyl, though John McIntire gives perhaps the film's most memorable performance as Jim Bonniwell, in part due to his character's degeneracy but also due to the authority he brings to all of his roles. Also giving a colorful portrayal is William Campbell who, in this film, is not miscast as flashy gunman Johnny Cool.

Incidentally, the credits for *Backlash* state that Chase's screenplay is based upon a novel of the same title by Frank Gruber, and this is repeated in contemporaneous reviews as well as current reference books. However, the novel doesn't seem to have ever existed, at least in book form. The April 1956 issue of *Library Journal* features a section entitled "Books into Film" which includes a brief review of the movie and a notation by the reviewer that the credited source novel could not be found anywhere. Currently, no library in the entire country has or has ever had such a novel.

In 1967, Gruber published his autobiography entitled *The Pulp Jungle*. The book features a list of his published novels, which includes 19 Westerns, with a special notation for those that were filmed under the same or a different title. No mention is made of *Backlash*. Interestingly, Gruber writes about his friendship with Borden Chase. It seems unusual that, in discussing Chase's work at Universal in the 1950s, Gruber does not mention the 1956 Universal movie which is the only one in which the two writers share credits. Gruber also wrote many stories for Western pulp magazines and it is

possible that the movie originated in one of these pulps. Nevertheless, in discussing his fondness for Chase, it seems that Gruber would have mentioned their only collaboration. It is a mystery that perhaps only Simon Lash, Gruber's detective hero, can solve.

Regardless of the origin of the movie, the screenplay of *Backlash* features such familiar Chase subjects as family conflicts and the hero's struggle to find his personal identity. These themes are not present in Gruber's mostly pulp novels. Most of the Western movies based upon Gruber's works are the cinematic equivalent of pulp stories. These include *Dakota Lil* in 1950, adapted from a Gruber story, *Denver and the Rio Grande* in 1952, for which Gruber wrote the screenplay, and *Rage at Dawn* in 1955, based on a story by Gruber. Chase's Westerns are far more adult and complex and *Backlash* has all the earmarks of a Chase Western.

This was the third of six Westerns Widmark made in the 1950s. Sturges made five Westerns in the decade, including another with Widmark. The following year, Chase wrote the screenplay for *Night Passage,* which Anthony Mann was supposed to direct, but Mann withdrew just prior to filming.

The practice of a Hollywood studio buying the film rights to a Western novel and then changing its story was a familiar one in the 1950s, with varying results. *The Proud Ones* by Verne Athanas was published in 1952 and became a motion picture four years later. The novel is the story of two men, Cass Silver and Thad Ogilvie. Cass is the town marshal of a Kansas town and Thad is a young drover whose impulsive act saves the marshal's life. But Thad is wounded in the leg and, since he is unable to resume life as a cowhand, Cass makes him a deputy. Meanwhile, Cass is facing a challenge to his authority by a prosperous saloon owner, Martin Dupre, whose ambitions to take over the town are thwarted by Silver's authoritarian rule. Thad gradually learns how to be a lawman from the marshal, who will have to fight Dupre's hired gunfighters as well as political corruption to keep the town safe. When Dupre sets a trap that kills Cass, Thad enforces justice for the murdered lawman.

Cass Silver is a proud man who states that he has never needed anyone and cares for no one, including his mistress, Nancy, owner of a local brothel, as well as Thad. He is a cold, hard man who reads Shakespeare and other works of literature but will not admit to any emotion. Thad Ogilvie is also proud, despite his disability, and admires the independent Cass. When he meets Dorothy Markham at a dance and begins to court her, he will not admit to any feeling for her, wanting to be as independent as Cass. But by the end of the novel, Thad will discover that love is worth more than pride and a letter that Cass left with Nancy will reveal the truth about the marshal's feelings. It is a good novel with distinctive characters, though the ending is almost too downbeat with Thad's near-suicidal act occurring after Cass' murder.

In the film version, Cass Silver is a grim and determined lawman who is too proud to admit that his eyesight is failing. Thad Anderson is a cowboy who becomes a deputy because he wants vengeance for his father, whom he believes was unjustly killed by Cass. Honest John Barrett is the saloon owner who wants to open up the town and resents Silver's strict enforcement of the law. When his political influence fails to get rid of Cass, Barrett is willing to hire gunfighters to do the job. Sally is the owner of the local hotel who loves Cass and wants him to give up the law and settle down. These parallel plot lines converge in a gun battle that teaches Thad the truth about his father's death.

Edmund North's adaptation of the Athanas novel, co-written with Joseph Petracca, uses the plot and characters as a basis for a story that has some similarities to the novel but more differences. The film's Cass is more emotional than his counterpart in the novel. He appears to have genuine feelings for Sally, who has a more respectable occupation than Nancy. The relationship between Cass and Thad remains the focus of the movie. However, by giving Cass a disability instead of Thad, the nature of the relationship is changed. The film's Cass is forced to realize that he needs someone in both his personal and professional life. He is willing to accept his failing powers and give up his badge for Sally while, in the novel, only death can release him from his duties. The film's Thad assumes Cass' position after Cass rides away with Sally, thus affirming the lawman's principles, while the novel's Thad ultimately realizes that Cass was wrong in his rigidity and in his priorities. The addition of a revenge motive for Thad was probably intended to increase the tension but it emerges as a cliché. Basically, the movie would have been more original with a faithful adaptation, but it is still pleasant entertainment with an emotionally satisfying ending.

The performances are all compelling. Robert Ryan is an extremely fine actor who comfortably inhabited the world of film noir with his haggard looks and penetrating eyes. His skill allowed him to be equally believable in Westerns and he was great as the sniggering, manipulative killer in *The Naked Spur* and as the more deliberate but equally deadly racist in *Bad Day at Black Rock*. Yet, with his ability to elicit sympathy, he could also project a weary kind of heroism. As Cass, Ryan's subtle yet powerful portrayal is the center of the movie. If allowed to play the novel's Cass, who is in some ways a Westernized version of his film noir protagonists, Ryan could have believably conveyed his intellectualism and emotional rigidity. Playing North's softer version of the character, he brings

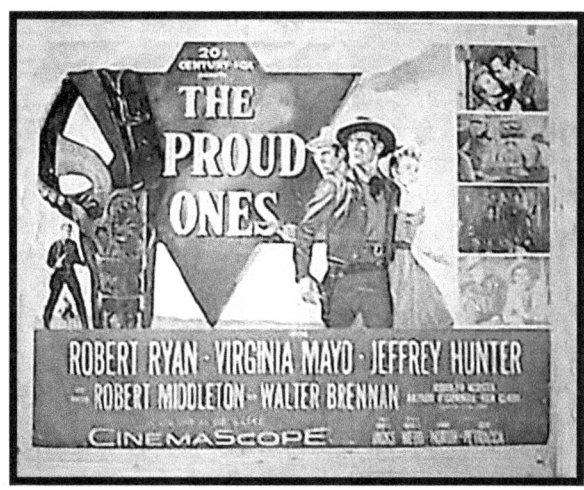

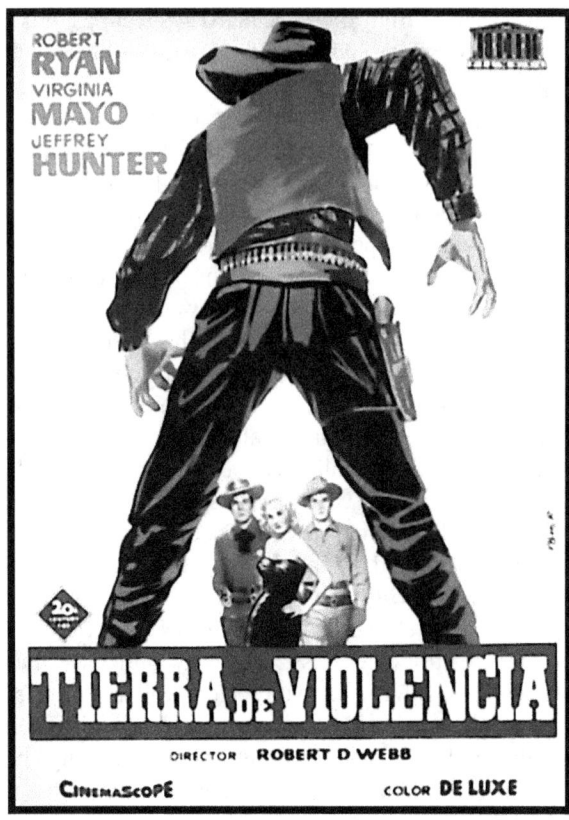

warmth to his portrayal, conveying fatigue and sadness beneath the harsh exterior. Jeffrey Hunter is effectively sincere as Thad, who begrudgingly develops admiration for the man he formerly despised. Providing competent support are Virginia Mayo as Sally, Robert Middleton as Honest John, and as deputies, Arthur O'Connell and Walter Brennan, whose presence in a Western never failed to enliven it.

Robert D. Webb, who was a house director at 20th Century Fox, helmed *The Proud Ones*. He was given his assignments and brought a level of competence to them but little else. The quality of his films usually depended upon the script and the actors. In 1955 and 1956, he directed four Westerns, three of which featured Jeffrey Hunter. Ryan starred in six Westerns in the 1950s, his presence elevating all of them. Hunter appeared in eight Westerns in the 1950s, the highpoint being *The Searchers*.

Adding to the film's pleasure is the score by Lionel Newman, which features a beautiful main title theme accompanied by the whistling of Muzzy Marcellino. It was recorded on Columbia records, which pleased fans of Western film themes.

On *Variety*'s annual list, the spectacles *The Ten Commandments* and *Around the World in 80 Days* topped the list with $33 million and $23 million in North American theatrical rentals. To provide a more reasonable comparison, the top Western of the year was *The Searchers* at Number 10 with $4.8 million. *Love Me Tender* (which is technically a Western but is actually in a class by itself since it is Elvis Presley's first movie) made $4.2 million. *The Indian Fighter* with Kirk Douglas earned $2.4 million. *The Proud Ones* ranked 76th with $1.4 million while *Backlash* did not earn the minimum amount of $1 million to make the list.

In 1957, adult Westerns continued to appear steadily in theaters. Some of the more notable releases included Delmer Daves' *3:10 to Yuma* with Glenn Ford and Van Heflin, John Sturges' *Gunfight at the O.K. Corral* with Burt Lancaster and Kirk Douglas, Anthony Mann's *The Tin Star* with Henry Fonda and Anthony Perkins, and Nicholas Ray's *The True Story of Jesse James* with Robert Wagner and Jeffrey Hunter. Simultaneously, adult television programs dominated prime-time programming. For the 1957-1958 season, the highest-rated program on television was *Gunsmoke*, starring James Arness as Marshal Matt Dillon. This was the third year of its record-breaking 20-year run. Prior to its appearance on the small screen, *Gunsmoke* had been a successful radio program and was still being heard weekly in 1957. During its nine-year run from 1952 to 1961, William Conrad played Matt Dillon. Conrad often appeared as a villain in movies and was occasionally a producer.

During its first season in 1952, the 10th episode of the *Gunsmoke* radio program was entitled "The Ride Back." It was a two-character story about Marshal Dillon escorting a prisoner back to Dodge City. During the long and grueling trek, Matt tries to keep the upper hand but is not always successful, and the two men learn to respect one another. The episode was written by Anthony Ellis and, although many of the radio episodes were later adapted for television, this one was not. However, five years later it was adapted into a motion picture produced by and co-starring William Conrad.

The Ride Back stars Anthony Quinn as Bob Kallen, a suspected murderer, and Conrad as Sheriff Chris Hamish, whose job it is to capture Kallen in Mexico and bring him back across the border for trial. During the four-day journey through Apache territory, Kallen constantly challenges the anxious lawman's authority and courage. Complicating the journey is the threat of an Apache attack and a little girl, the lone survivor of a massacre, they find along the way. The two men gradually develop mutual respect that will be tested when Apaches wound one of them and the other has a momentous decision to make.

Antony Ellis adapted his radio episode into a screenplay, expanding the story, adding characters and changing the personality of the lawman. The overweight Sheriff Hamish is about as far from Matt Dillon as possible. He is an insecure, frightened man who considers himself a failure. He is not respected by either the people of the town he serves or his wife. He has to complete this mission to prove to himself that his life is not a total waste. Kallen, in contrast, is self-confident and unafraid, even when he is in chains. He is liked by everyone and has a woman who is willing to die for him. Though he is the captive, he appears more in control than the lawman and he seems to have no doubt that he will eventually best his captor, a feeling that Hamish inevitably shares.

The Ride Back is a suspenseful movie and, although it has its share of action scenes, it is the interaction of the two men that propels the story. Quinn is appropriately jovial and brash as Kallen while Conrad's tone and expression perfectly suggest that his grim determination is slowly crumbling. The movie is directed frugally by Allen H. Miner, who directed only one other movie, a B Western called *Black Patch*, and who spent most of his career in television. Miner was a protégé of director Robert Aldrich, whose company produced the movie with Conrad. The movie also has a good title theme sung by Eddie Albert, who often acted in Aldrich's movies.

The Ride Back disappeared quickly and didn't earn enough at the box office to qualify for inclusion on *Variety*'s annual list. The top Western on the list was *Gunfight at the O.K. Corral* at Number 12 with $4.7 million. *The Bridge On the River Kwai* topped the list with $18 million, followed by *Peyton Place* with $12 million.

Major Westerns of 1958 included Anthony Mann's *Man of the West* with Gary Cooper, John Sturges' *The Law and Jake Wade* with Robert Taylor and Richard Widmark, Delmer Daves' *Cowboy* with Glenn Ford, Henry Hathaway's *From Hell to Texas* with Don Murray, and William Wyler's *The Big Country* with Gregory Peck and Charlton Heston. Three months before the release of Wyler's large-scale movie, Peck starred in another Western, one that was more modest and far grimmer.

Excluding silent films and the Indian love story *Ramona* in 1936, veteran director Henry King made only three Westerns in his lengthy career, His first was *Jesse James* in 1939, followed by *The Gunfighter* in 1950. Prior to *The Gunfighter*, Peck starred in two Westerns, King Vidor's *Duel in the Sun* and William Wellman's *Yellow Sky*. In 1951, he made *Only the Valiant* for Gordon Douglas and didn't venture out west again until he reunited with Henry King for *The Bravados*.

Jim Douglas is an embittered man who has been hunting four men for the rape and murder of his wife. When he hears that they have been jailed for another murder, he rides to the town in which they are held to watch them hang. However, the four men escape and kidnap Emma Steinmetz, the daughter of a local storekeeper. Thus begins the manhunt with Jim leading the posse to recapture the outlaws and rescue Emma. But it is hatred, not justice, that drives Jim, and as he catches up with three of the men, one by one, he executes them. After being captured by the fourth man, Jim is forced to face the truth about his wife's death and about himself, which leads to his moral collapse.

The Bravados is based upon a novel of the same name by Frank O'Rourke published in 1957. Once again, though the book and the film share the names of some characters as well as the plot of a manhunt for escaped killers, they are different stories. The novel begins in a New Mexican border town where two killers, Zachary and Taylor, and four other men are being held in the local jail by Sheriff Sanchez. Among the prisoners is Jim Douglas, who has been falsely accused of nonpayment of debts by local businessman Gus Steinmetz, who resents the fact that Jim outbid him on a mining contract and is also courting his daughter Emma. When the prisoners kill a jailer and escape, they also kidnap Emma and steal valuable horses from a wealthy rancher, Josefa Valarde. Jim remained in jail to establish his innocence and, since he is an excellent tracker, Gus pleads with him to rescue his daughter. Jim also wants Emma back and coordinates a plan with Sanchez to track down the killers. He also reluctantly accepts the help of Josefa, who wants her horses back.

During the course of the manhunt, the novel alternates between the hunters and the hunted. Zachary and Taylor are willing to kill anyone to elude the posse and Emma is becoming increasingly hysterical over the threat posed by the killers, especially Zachary. Meanwhile, Josefa cannot conceal her attraction to Jim and earns his respect when she sacrifices her most valuable mare to secure Emma's safe return. The posse gradually closes in on the fugitives, who separate in an attempt to stay free. Individually, the fugitives are tracked down, resulting in bloody confrontations and Emma's rescue. But Emma's response to her experience betrays her true character to Jim, who realizes that his destiny is with Josefa.

The novel was adapted into a screenplay by Philip Yordan, who has more successful results than he did with *The Last Frontier*. Most significantly, he transforms a standard hero into an angry executioner who will not let anything prevent him from satisfying his need for vengeance. In the novel, Jim's courtship of Emma seems contrived, particularly in view of her later kidnapping, while in the film he seems to have no feeling for her other than as a means to find the killers. The addition of a religious subtheme to the movie adds emotional resonance and contributes to the impact of Jim's distressed plea for help at the film's end. The character of Josefa is also changed, with only the name remaining the same. Gus and Emma Steinmetz lose their unsavory characteristics on screen while killers Zachary and Taylor retain their unrepentant villainy. Generally, the novel is average while the movie is haunting and intriguing.

King's direction expertly balances scenes of tension and suspense with scenes of action, all the while focusing on the internal torment of Jim Douglas. Peck projects the customary authority associated with his screen persona which, in this instance, crumbles into despair and self-loathing. He plays his character with the level of intensity and suppressed passion of a coiled rattlesnake. It is a severe and uncharacteristic performance from an actor accustomed to projecting moral truth. Stephen Boyd, Lee Van Cleef, Henry Silva and Albert Salmi all create distinctly individual portraits of the fugitives, while Andrew Duggan is persuasive as the town priest. Only Joan Collins seems to belong somewhere else since she seems so uncomfortable on horseback.

Once again, music adds tremendously to the film's impact due to an exciting score that captures the action of the story and also reflects its spirituality and moral uncertainty. Though credited to Lionel Newman, the score was composed by Hugo Friedhofer and Alfred Newman, whose main title theme perfectly conveys the protagonist's obsession with revenge. The score would not be available as a recording until four decades later when FSM (Film Score Monthly) released a CD of the soundtrack and provided information on who actually composed the music.

The Big Country was the top grossing Western of the year with $5 million to rank 11th on *Variety*'s list. *The Bravados* earned $2.2 million to rank a disappointing Number 39. *South Pacific* was a big favorite of the year with $15 million in theatrical rentals.

During the year 1959, Howard Hawks' *Rio Bravo* with John Wayne and Dean Martin and Edward Dmytryk's *Warlock* with Henry Fonda and Richard Widmark were both dismissed by critics upon release, but the former is now justly recognized as a classic while the latter is on its way to such deserved status. Delmer Daves directed his last Western, *The Hanging Tree*, with Gary Cooper. John Ford's *The Horse Soldiers* with John Wayne and William Holden and John Sturges' *Last Train from Gun Hill* with Kirk Douglas and Anthony Quinn were also released, along with an unusual Western that was neither a critical nor financial success, but it deserves to be rescued from oblivion.

In pre-Civil War Kansas, Luke Darcy has a grandiose dream to build an empire that he intends to rule as a peaceful despot. To establish his kingdom, he has organized a group of men known as the Jayhawkers who have been terrorizing the region. Cam Beeker breaks out of prison as part of a plan to infiltrate Darcy's gang and bring his reign of terror to an end. Cam also has a personal reason for hating Darcy since he blames him for the death of his wife. The first part of Cam's plan is successful, and Luke not only makes him a Jayhawker but a friend. The second part of the plan is more difficult as Cam is faced with difficult moral decisions. This is the plot of *The Jayhawkers*, a distinctive Western about friendship and loyalty.

The film stars Jeff Chandler as Darcy and Fess Parker as Beeker. After his breakthrough role as Cochise in *Broken Arrow*, Chandler starred in numerous movies at Universal, most of them conventional programmers. In the 1950s, he starred in 10 Westerns, most of which played the top half of double bills and rarely allowed him to stretch himself as an actor since his roles were those of standard heroes. After he left Universal, he began to get more challenging roles, such as the title character in *Drango* (1957), which he also produced.

However, the role of Luke Darcy in *The Jayhawkers* is his finest and gave him the opportunity to excel as an actor. Darcy could have been portrayed as a demented and callous dictator with a lust for power who raids and kills for his own ambitions, which is partially suggested by the script. But Darcy is a more complex character than a killer with a Napoleon complex. He also has an altruistic desire for peace and a sincere belief that his ambitions will benefit the people. A sense of loneliness surrounds Darcy, a feeling that he has finally found a kindred spirit in Beeker. He appears to be an emotionally cold man, yet can be capable of warmth with someone he likes and trusts. Chandler contributes a restrained yet perceptive performance that brings out all of these qualities and manages to make Luke likeable and even sympathetic, particularly at the

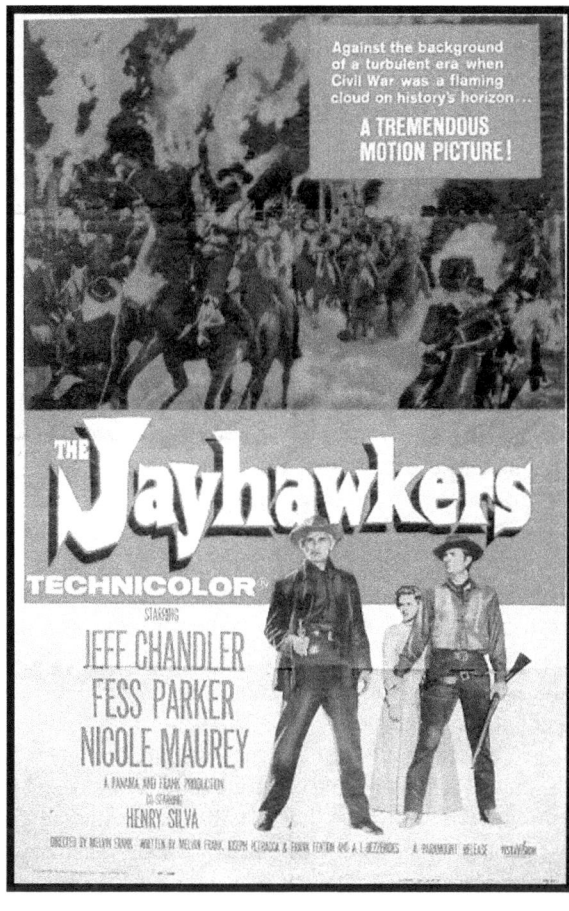

finale. It is understandable why Beeker develops a fondness and respect for Darcy and why his conflicting loyalties create such a personal dilemma for him.

Fess Parker plays Beeker in a low-key manner, which contrasts with Chandler's more colorful role. Nicole Maurey plays a woman who is living at Beeker's former ranch, but the role is unnecessary and distracts from the main plot. Henry Silva and Leo Gordon both stand out as Jayhawkers, managing as they always did to make their villains distinct. Direction is by Melvin Frank, who spent most of his career in comedies. This was his only Western, excluding a modern comedy *Callaway Went Thataway* in 1951, and his unfamiliarity with the genre is occasionally apparent since some of the action scenes don't seem to reach their potential. However, the thunderous rides of the rampaging Jayhawkers are sumptuously and excitingly staged. Frank also co-wrote the script with Joseph Petracca, Frank Fenton and A.I. Bezzerides and the intriguing story could probably have been more completely realized by a director experienced with Westerns. But it is still a good Western with an inspired performance by Jeff Chandler.

The top-grossing Westerns of the year were *Rio Bravo* with $5.2 million and *The Horse Soldiers* with $4 million. *The Jayhawkers* was at the bottom of *Variety*'s annual list with estimated theatrical rentals of $1 million. The blockbuster *Ben-Hur* was the year's top hit with $36 million. It was followed by the comedies, *Some Like It Hot*, *Pillow Talk* and *The Shaggy Dog* with about $8 million each.

Westerns ruled the film industry in the 1950s. Never again would there be a decade filled with an abundance of such treasures for Western fans. Westerns continued to be made in the 1960s but their number started to decline from the peak in the 1950s. Approximately 80 major Westerns were released by the Hollywood studios from 1960 to 1969. Not coincidentally, many of these were comedy Westerns, a trend which perhaps was one symptom of the public's gradual disinterest in traditional Westerns.

The decade started off excitingly with John Sturges' influential *The Magnificent Seven* with Yul Brynner. In 1962, two classics were released: John Ford's *The Man Who Shot Liberty Valance* with John Wayne and James Stewart and Sam Peckinpah's *Ride the High Country* with Randolph Scott and Joel McCrae. Also released in 1962 was David Miller's memorable contemporary Western, *Lonely Are the Brave* with Kirk Douglas. Mid-decade saw the release of Howard Hawks' majestic *El Dorado* with Wayne and Robert Mitchum and Richard Brooks' *The Professionals* with Burt Lancaster and Lee Marvin. Henry Hathaway's *True Grit* with Wayne and Peckinpah's *The Wild Bunch* with William Holden and Robert Ryan graced the end of the decade. The fact that these films lamented the vanishing West or dealt with the deteriorating capabilities of their aging heroes was perhaps another sign that the end of the traditional Western was near. It was as though great artists like Ford and Hawks were aware of their own mortalities and were creating nostalgic finales to the genre to which they had given so much respect and glory.

While these films and others indicate that great Westerns were still being made, the factors that would eventually kill the genre began in the 1960s. One factor was the saturation of the market in the 1950s. Such a high degree of popularity was impossible to maintain in the following decade. Another factor was the popularity of James Bond and his numerous imitators, who began to edge Westerns out of the market. Heroes of espionage in super-charged cars with high-tech weapons gradually became more fashionable than cowboys on horseback with six-guns.

However, the most regrettable factor was the introduction into the American market of the Italian Westerns, which had an extremely detrimental impact upon the genre due to their emphasis upon amoral anti-heroes and gratuitous violence. These movies were supposedly made for adult audiences but in fact were made for adults with primitive needs and expectations. Dozens of Italian Westerns were released in the U.S. and their effect was to considerably lower the artistic as well as moral standards of the Western. The two movies that established the formula serve as perfect examples.

Sergio Leone's *A Fistful of Dollars* with Clint Eastwood was filmed in 1964 and released in the U.S. in 1967, followed a few months later by the 1965 sequel, *For a Few Dollars More*. These movies are hopelessly amateurish but they were influential in the manner in which they inspired laughter and cynicism about the values of traditional Westerns. The protagonist of these movies is a combination of a cowboy, a gangster and a sadist. Scenes depicting Eastwood gunning down multiple opponents while chewing on a cigar are constructed to provoke pleasure and endorse killing. When audiences watched these movies or the innumerable imitations, they didn't have to think. They could just see how good it was to solve problems with violence and how enjoyable it was to kill people.

This was a radical change from the morality of earlier Westerns in which, for instance, Shane would regrettably strap on his guns and then tell Joey that there was no living with a killing. Shane would not be able to live in the valley after using his guns, just as Ethan Edwards would be unable to enter the cabin at the end of *The Searchers* because of his violent past.

Totally aside from the depravity, however, is the lack of originality in all of the Italian Westerns. The extreme close-ups of characters with expressions suggestive of silent films are overly melodramatic. The choreographed compositions of gunfights are comparable to the choreographed musical numbers of the singing cowboy Westerns of the 1940s, only wailing trumpets and screeching flutes accompa-

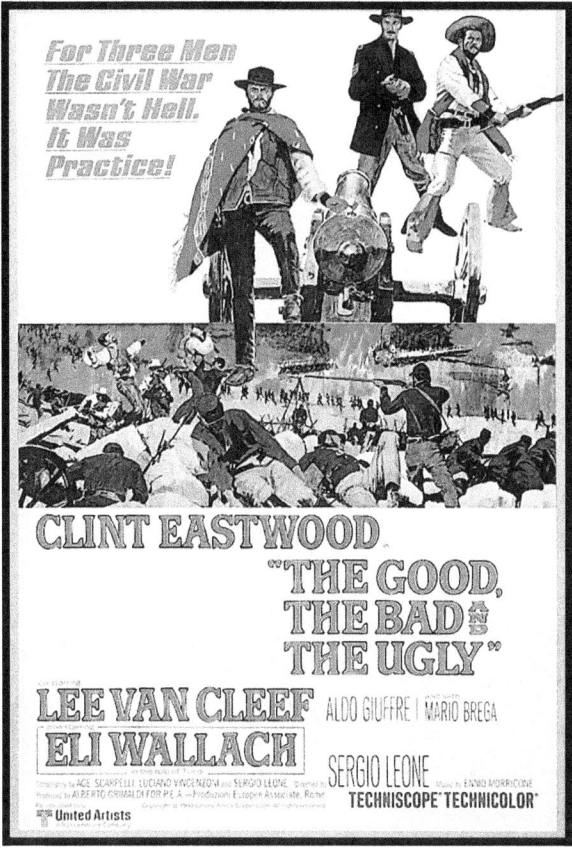

nied them instead of songs. The films contain virtually every cliché familiar to juvenile series Westerns of the same era. When Eastwood rips off his poncho after being shot and reveals a metal plate, it is reminiscent of the old serials in which the hero, shot at the end of one chapter, would survive at the beginning of the next chapter by revealing armor under his shirt. The only allegedly modern element is the anti-hero's cynicism and even this is fraudulent, since it is not based upon a characterization or a thematic reason but on a calculated attempt by the filmmakers to appeal to a mocking audience.

Leone's *Once Upon a Time in the West* is the most absurd of all the imports. If a 1950s Western featured a hero who confronted his opponent and then started playing a harmonica, it would have been laughed off the screen. Filled with interminable scenes and redundant dialogue that would have made Sturges or Daves physically ill, this elephantine would-be-epic makes every point bluntly and hammers in each cliché, indicating that Leone was incapable of comprehending the artistry with which Ford and Mann conveyed messages and themes. Nor was he capable of approaching the skill with which Peckinpah used violence to deplore the death of honor and morality in *The Wild Bunch,* which was released within a month of his fiasco.

The 1970s witnessed a continuation of the decline with fewer than 50 major Westerns released, many of these anti-Westerns that emulated Italian Westerns and ridiculed traditional virtues but with a total lack of creativity. Arthur Penn's *Little Big Man*, Frank Perry's *Doc*, Ralph Nelson's *Soldier Blue* and Penn's *The Missouri Breaks* are dreadful

movies, not necessarily because they are untraditional, but because they replaced artistry, creativity, realistic characters and involving plots with caricatures, self-importance, condescension toward the genre and messages that were designed to appeal to whatever was culturally fashionable and politically correct.

There were laudable exceptions, including Mark Rydell's *The Cowboys* in 1971, but it is not insignificant that John Wayne's character, who symbolizes traditional morality, is a victim of brutal violence in that movie. And when Wayne dies at the end of Don Siegel's *The Shootist* in 1976, it signaled the end of a Western icon, and in some ways, the end of the American Western.

By the 1980s, Westerns were simply no longer relevant, with few being produced and none worth mentioning, except for director Clint Eastwood's embarrassingly inept *Pale Rider*, which is a contemptible offense to the memory of *Shane*. In the 1990s, Kevin Costner's *Dances with Wolves* and Eastwood's *Unforgiven* both won Academy Awards, but they are anti-Westerns, which made them appealing to Academy members who chose to ignore the two-dimensional simplicity of the former and the hypocritical pretentiousness of the latter. However, the ability to make good Westerns still existed. George Cosmatos' *Tombstone* and Lawrence Kasdan's *Wyatt Earp* are notable and the only commendable Westerns of the entire decade. In the 21st century, Westerns are a rare event, with only Kevin Costner's *Open Range* in 2003 capturing the splendid flavor of the great Westerns of the past.

The 1950s are a distant memory now, but fortunately the Westerns of that decade survive on cable television, on videocassettes and on DVD. And they survive in our memories. One indication of the impact these movies had is the fact that so many of their heroes achieved a degree of reality off the screen, as though they actually existed. They are so real that we not only remember them with fondness but we wonder what happened to them after they left us. It is not difficult to imagine their fates. A few fortunate ones found happiness. John T. Chance, after making the town of Rio Bravo safe, settled down with Feathers. Will Kane no longer has to look anxiously at the clock as it approaches high noon.

But most of them can never belong anywhere. Ethan Edwards will forever wander between the winds with no home to call his own, cherishing the memory of holding little Debbie in his arms. Shane will always be riding over a hill in the distance, remembering the warmth he shared for a brief time with little Joey and with Marian and Joe. And Clay Blaisedell, alone and despised by even the people he serves, will never forget the town of Warlock, where he lost his only chance for happiness. They are all permanently ingrained within the cultural heritage of the American Western. They exist forever somewhere in a world within our collective consciousness.

It is heartbreaking that so many of them are alone. But that's the way it has to be. That's the way they are. That's why we miss them. But it is not all sadness. If you listen closely, you can hear Dempsey Rae singing a tune as he strums on his banjo. He is still searching for a star to call his own, somehow knowing that he will never find it.

Devil's Doorway [MGM/1950]
CREDITS: Producer: Nicholas Nayfack; Director: Anthony Mann; Screenplay: Guy Trosper; Cinematographer: John Alton; Editor: Conrad A. Nervig; Music: Daniele Amfitheatrof
CAST: Robert Taylor (Lance Poole); Louis Calhern (Verne Coolan); Paula Raymond (Orrie Masters); Marshall Thompson (Rod MacDougall); James Mitchell (Red Rock); Edgar Buchanan (Zeke Carmody); Rhys Williams (Scotty MacDougall); Spring Byington (Mrs. Masters); James Milllican (Ike Stapleton); Bruce Cowling (Lieut. Grimes)

Rawhide [20th Century Fox/1951]
CREDITS: Producer: Samuel G. Engel; Director: Henry Hathaway; Screenplay: Dudley Nichols; Cinematographer: Milton Krasner; Editor: Robert Simpson; Music: Sol Kaplan; Song: "A Rolling Stone" by Lionel Newman
CAST: Tyrone Power (Tom Owens); Susan Hayward (Vinnie Holt); Hugh Marlowe (Zimmerman); Dean Jagger (Yancy); Edgar Buchanan (Sam Todd); Jack Elam (Tevis); George Tobias (Gratz); Jeff Corey (Luke); James Millican (Tex); William Haade (Gil); Ken Tobey (Lieut. Wingate); Louis Jean Heydt (Fickert); Dan White (Gilchrist)

Arrowhead [Paramount/1953]
CREDITS: Producer: Nat Holt; Director: Charles Marquis Warren; Screenplay: Charles Marquis Warren, based on a novel by W.R. Burnett; Cinematographer: Ray Rennahan; Editor: Frank Bracht; Music: Paul Sawtell
CAST: Charlton Heston (Ed Bannon); Jack Palance (Toriano); Katy Jurado (Nita); Brian Keith (Capt. Bill North); Mary Sinclair (Lee); Milburn Stone (Sandy MacKinnon); Richard Shannon (Lieut. Kirk); Lewis Martin (Col. Weybright); Frank DeKova (Chief Chattez); Robert Wilke (Sgt. Snow); Peter Coe (Spanish)

Drum Beat [Warner Bros./1954]
CREDITS: Producer: Delmer Daves; director: Delmer Daves; Screenplay Delmer Daves; Cinematographer: J. Peverell Marley; Editor: Clarence Kolster; Music: Victor Young
CAST: Alan Ladd (Johnny McKay); Audrey Dalton (Nancy Meek); Marisa Pavan (Toby); Robert Keith (Bill Satterwhite); Rudolfo Acosta (Scarface Charlie); Charles Bronson (Captain Jack); Warner Anderson (Gen. Canby); Elisha Cook, Jr. (Crackel); Anthony Caruso (Manek); Frank DeKova (Modoc Jim); Richard Gaines (Dr. Thomas)

Man Without a Star [Universal-International/1955]
CREDITS: Producer: Aaron Rosenberg; Director: King Vidor; Screenplay: Borden Chase, D.D. Beauchamp, based on a novel by Dee Linford; Cinematographer: Russell Metty; Editor: Virgil Vogel; Music: Joseph Gershenson; Songs: "Man Without a Star" by Arnold Hughes and Frederick Herbert, "And the Moon Grew Brighter and Brighter" by Jimmy Kennedy and Lou Singer

CAST: Kirk Douglas (Dempsey Rae); Jeanne Crain (Reed Bowman); Claire Trevor (Idonee); William Campbell (Jeff Jimson); Richard Boone (Steve Miles); Jay C. Flippen (Strap Davis); Myrna Hansen (Tess Cassidy); Mara Corday (Moccasin Mary); Eddy Walker (Tom Cassidy); Sheb Wooley (Latigo)

Run for Cover [Paramount/1955]
CREDITS: Producer: William H. Pine, William C. Thomas; Director: Nicholas Ray; Screenplay: Winston Miller, based on a story by Harriet Frank, Jr., Irving Ravetch; Cinematographer: Danile Fapp; Editor: Howard Smith; Music: Howard Jackson; Song: "Run for Cover" by Jack Brooks and Howard Jackson
CAST: James Cagney (Matt Dow); Viveca Lindfors (Helga Swenson); John Derek (Davey Bishop); Jean Hersholt (Mr. Swenson); Grant Withers (Gentry); Jack Lambert (Larsen); Ernest Borgnine (Morgan); Ray Teal (Sheriff); Irving Bacon (Scotty); Trevor Bardette (Paulsen)

The Last Frontier [Columbia/1955]
CREDITS: Producer: William Fadiman; Director: Anthony Mann; Screenplay: Philip Yordan, Russell Hughes, based on a novel by Richard Emery Roberts; Cinematographer: William Mellor; Editor: Al Clark; Music: Leigh Harline; Song: "The Last Frontier" by Lester Lee and Ned Washington
CAST: Victor Mature (Jed Cooper); Guy Madison (Capt. Glenn Riordan); Robert Preston (Col. Frank Marsten); James Whitmore (Gus); Anne Bancroft (Corrinna Marsten); Russell Collins (Capt. Bill Clarke); Peter Whitney (Sgt. Major Decker); Pat Hogan (Mungo); Guy Williams (Lieut. Benton)

The Proud Ones [20th Century Fox/1956]
CREDITS: Producer: Robert L. Jacks; Director: Robert D. Webb; Screenplay: Edmund North, Joseph Petracca, based on a novel by Verne Athanas; Cinematographer: Lucien Ballard; Editor: Hugh S. Fowler; Music: Lionel Newman
CAST: Robert Ryan (Cass Silver); Jeffrey Hunter (Thad Anderson); Virginia Mayo (Sally); Robert Middleton (John Barrett); Walter Brennan (Jake); Arthur O'Connell (Jim Dexter); Ken Clark (Pike); Rudolfo Acosta (Chico); Whit Bissell (Sam Bolton); Edward Platt (Dr. Barlow); George Mathews (Dillon)

Backlash [Universal-nternational/1956]
CREDITS: Producer: Aaron Rosenberg; Director: John Sturges; Screenplay: Borden Chase, based on a novel by Frank Gruber; Cinematographer: Irving Glassberg; Editor: Sherman Todd; Music: Herman Stein
CAST: Richard Widmark (Jim Slater); Donna Reed (Karyl Orton); William Campbell (Johnny Cool); John McIntire (Jim Bonniwell); Barton Maclane (Sgt. Lake); Edward Platt (Sheriff Marson); Harry Morgan (Tony Welker); Robert Wilke (Jeff Welker); Regis Parton (Tom Welker); Robert Foulk (Sheriff Olsen); Roy Roberts (Maj. Carson)

The Ride Back [United Artists/1957]
CREDITS: Producer: William Conrad; Director: Allen H. Miner; Screenplay: Anthony Ellis; Cinematographer: Joseph Biroc; Editor: Michael Luciano; Music: Frank DeVol; Song: "The Ride Back" by Frank DeVol
CAST: Anthony Quinn (Bob Kallen); William Conrad (Sheriff Chris Hamish); Lita Milan (Elena); Victor Millan (Fr. Ignatius); George Trevino (Border Guard); Ellen Hope Monroe (Little Girl); Joe Domingues (Luis); Louis Torres (Boy)

The Bravados [20th Century Fox/1958]
CREDITS: Producer: Herbert B. Swope, Jr.; Director: Henry King; Screenplay: Philip Yordan, based on a novel by Frank O'Rourke; Cinematographer: Leon Shamroy; Editor: William Mace; Music: Bill Henry
CAST: Gregory Peck (Jim Douglass); Joan Collins (Josepfa Velarde); Stephen Boyd (Bill Zachary); Albert Salmi (Ed Taylor); Kathleen Gallant (Emma Steinmetz); George Voscovec (Gus Steinmentz); Barry Coe (Tom); Henry Silva (Lujan); Lee Van Cleef (Parral); Herbert Rudley (Sheriff Sanchez): Andrew Duggan (Padre); Gene Evans (John Butler); Ken Scott (Primo)

The Jayhawkers [Paramount/1959]
CREDITS: Producers: Melvin Frank, Norman Panama; Director: Melvin Frank; Screenplay: A.I. Bezzerides, Frank Fenton, Melvin Frank, Joseph Petracca; Cinematographer: Loyal Griggs; Editor: Everett Douglas; Music: Jerome Moross
CAST: Jeff Chandler (Luke Darcy); Fess Parker (Cam Beeker); Nicole Maurey (Jeanne Dubois); Henry Silva (Lordan); Leo Gordon (Jake); Herbert Rudley (Gov. Clayton); Frank DeKova (Evans); Jimmy Carter (Paul); Don Megowan (China)

Twelve "B" Westerns of the 1950s

In the 1930s, during the Depression, studios and theaters began to offer audiences two movies for one price in an effort to entice patrons back into theaters. The double-feature consisted of a main attraction, which was usually a major studio's A movie, and a supporting feature, referred to as a B movie. The B movies could be low-budget independent programmers made by and with second-string personnel and which lacked the production qualities of an A movie. The B movies could also be the products of so-called Poverty Row studios, such as PRC or Monogram, which lacked the finances, status and quality personnel of the major studios. Quite often, the B movies were produced by subsidiaries of the major studios for the express purpose of supporting A movies in studio-owned theaters.

In many cases, B movie personnel spent their entire careers in this second-class area of filmmaking, particularly if they were associated with the minor studios. The class system in Hollywood was extremely rigid and, once such personnel became identified with low-grade product, they were permanently associated with that kind of film. However, the B movies, especially those produced by the subsidiaries of major studios, could also be training and testing grounds for personnel on both sides of the camera who were hoping to display the kind of talent that would elevate them to A movies. Some fortunate artists, through fate or talent, realized this dream while different fates could account for some others being demoted to B movies.

Regardless of their origin or the talents involved, B movies were second-class product. Their plots were often formulaic or imitative of A movies and their running times were relatively brief. In many cases, the absence of talent was obvious even to the average moviegoer, but expectations for such movies were not very high. B movies usually served their purpose of supporting more prestigious features and were expected only to provide minor entertainment for audiences waiting for the main feature. Since most B movies were genre films, they might also serve the purpose of attracting less discriminating patrons who were immune to the appeal of the main feature. For instance, a Western or a mystery might bring into the theater patrons who had no interest in the drama or romance that topped the bill.

During the 1950s, however, a new development occurred within the field of the B Western. Of course, trends do not necessarily follow calendar years and the factors that impacted upon the genre really began in the late 1940s. It was during that period that Westerns with more complex themes began to capture the attention of a public that had just finished fighting a world war. Additionally, two other major factors led to the explosion of such films during the following decade.

By the 1950s, the advent of television combined with the divestiture of theaters by studios signaled the beginning of the end of B movies. Since studios could no longer own theaters, a major reason for the existence of B movies ceased to exist. Also, television was providing the kind of genre entertainment in which B movies specialized. Many series and juvenile Western heroes who had formerly attracted youngsters to theaters had moved to the small screen and now kept their young fans glued to their television sets. With television cornering the juvenile market, major studios began producing an increasing number of A Westerns aimed toward adult audiences.

An increasing number of Westerns of the 1950s treated subjects such as racism, sexuality and psychologically complex characters in a flexible manner that expanded the genre's perimeters. Ambivalence appeared about the Old West that was reflected in many of the A Westerns of the 1950s, which questioned some of the more traditional foundations of Westerns of previous decades. Following the trend set by these A Westerns, producers of B Westerns were inspired to feature equally mature subjects and themes. As a result, B Westerns of the 1950s became more intricate and sophisticated and attempted to be equally stimulating and thought provoking.

Another new development in the B Western field was the presence of actors who had formerly starred in A movies and who brought class to their less prestigious films. Whether due to their status as leading men having passed its peak or due to their replacement by newer stars, the presence of such actors gave their B movies an appearance of respectability denied some of the other films in the genre.

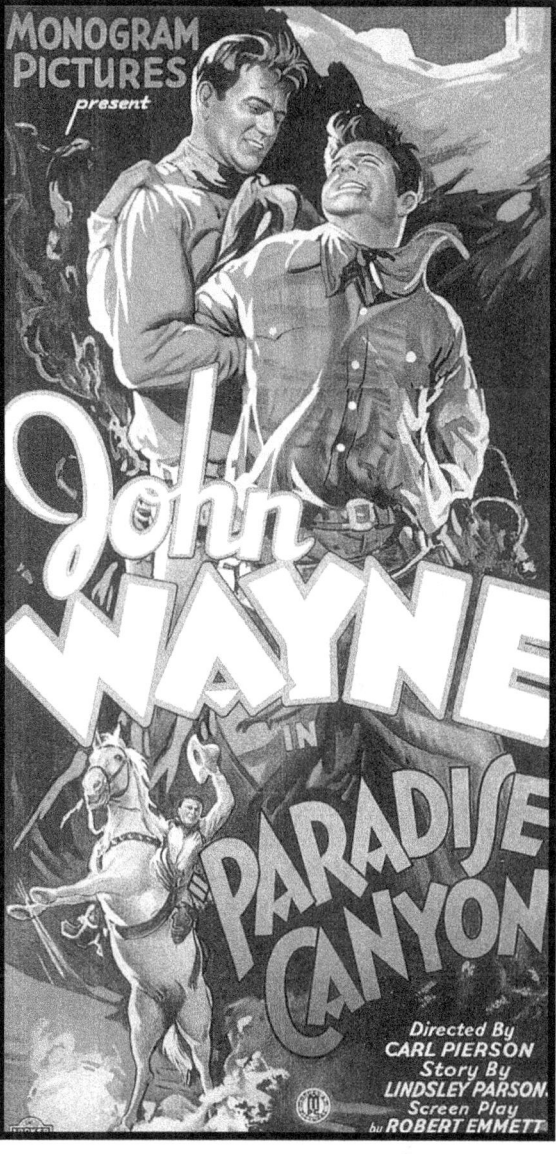

John Wayne began his career in B programmers

However, in spite of the tendency to imitate A Westerns and despite the restrictions imposed by limited budgets and brief production schedules, some creative personnel within the framework of the B Western strove for quality, rose above expectations and realized personal ambitions to create a commendable motion picture. The fact that these movies were not recognized for their qualities is due to the period in which they were released. In the 1950s, B Westerns were simply not considered worthy of consideration. Unfortunately, the factors that stimulated the higher quality of some B Westerns had no effect upon their status as second-class movies.

In another period, when they could perhaps have rated more than a line or two in advertisements below the main feature, they might have received some acclaim, or at least, some notice. In the 1940s, possibly their adult elements could have merited some top-of-the-bill engagements since they were so clearly different than the typical B movie of that decade. And in the late 1960s, with the number of B movies rapidly decreasing, such fare might have had more of an opportunity to stand out. But, in the 1950s, there was a surplus of B Westerns emulating A Westerns, with most of them failing in their objectives. However, many succeeded. The following is a list of 12 noteworthy B Westerns of the 1950s.

The Showdown, released by Republic Pictures and starring Bill Elliott, is typical of the nuanced B production that stands apart from the typical B fare. Shadrack Jones and his brother had been planning to start their own ranch, but his brother is murdered and his money stolen. Shadrack's quest for vengeance leads him to the saloon where his brother spent his last evening. He meets the owner of the saloon, Adelaide, who sells her business for part of a cattle herd owned by Cap Mackellar. Suspecting that one of Mackellar's crew is the killer, Shad signs on as the new trail boss. He is determined to exact vengeance and drives all of the men cruelly, ignoring the words of Mackellar, who preaches to him to leave vengeance to the Lord. Hatred consumes Shad, who has no compassion for anyone, Determined to make the killer expose himself, he sadistically

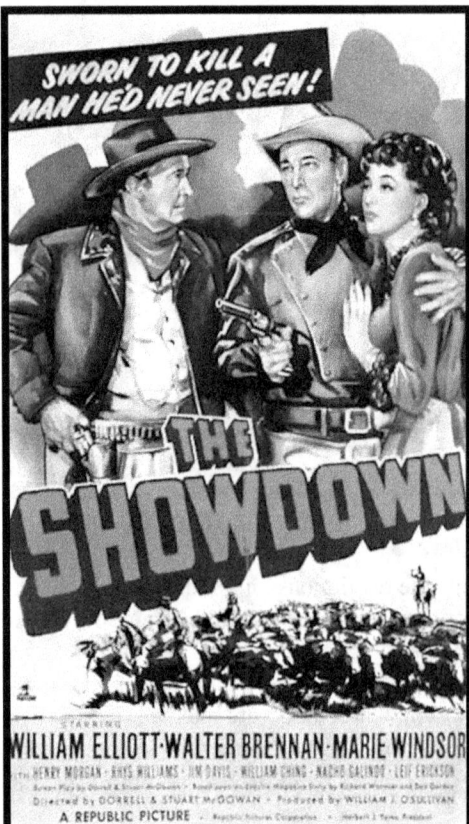

humiliates everyone, even a crippled cowhand who had tried to keep his disability hidden from his friends. Eventually, Cap is revealed to be the killer and his fate is indeed one of divine retribution that cleanses Shad of his hatred.

Herbert J. Yates created Republic Pictures during the mid-1930s when three Poverty Row studios merged into one film company. The studio became known for producing quality B movies and serials including the lucrative series of Westerns starring Gene Autry, Roy Rogers and other juvenile heroes, including a young John Wayne. When Wayne became a major star, his association with Republic allowed the studio to produce some notable A movies. The success of the Wayne films combined with a diminishing market for series Westerns in the late 1940s was the impetus for Republic to inject more adult elements into their B Westerns.

Prior to becoming a Western star, Bill Elliott had appeared in numerous minor roles, usually billed as Gordon Elliott. In 1938, he starred in the serial *The Great Adventures of Wild Bill Hickock* and, as a result of its popularity, was thereafter billed as Wild Bill Elliott. Over the next several years, he starred in several B series, playing Hickock, then Red Ryder and eventually using his own name in *Calling Wild Bill Elliott*, the first of his Republic Westerns in 1943. Unlike other Republic series stars, Elliott possessed a tougher screen image, which made him a good choice to star in programmers that included more adult elements than the usual second feature.

The plot of *The Showdown* may seem somewhat familiar, particularly since it seems to combine a traditional Western theme of a cattle drive with the plot of a mystery thriller. Indeed, some of the scenes are obviously filmed on a sound stage instead of on location, which adds to the artificiality of the film. However, the movie still emerges as a terrific little Western for several reasons, not the least of which is its star.

The Showdown was his last Republic movie and is arguably his best. Children who were fans of his juvenile movies must have been surprised and even a bit alarmed at the brutal persona he displays in this movie. He is so obsessed with vengeance and blinded by hatred that he doesn't seem to care how many innocent men he tramples on. It is perhaps deliberately ironic that his hero is far less likeable than the killer.

The movie is directed and written by Dorrell McGowan and Stuart McGowan, brothers who had collaborated on numerous B Westerns at Republic since the 1930s. They became producers in the late 1940s and this was the first film they directed. Their script is sparse yet contains deep undertones that were naturally not present in the many Westerns they wrote for Gene Autry and Roy Rogers. Direction is equally expressive and, as befitting the dark tone of the film, many key scenes take place at night. In fact, the predominance of night scenes combined with the moral ambivalence of the hero clearly places the movie into the category of a Western film noir. And while there are some obligatory action scenes, tension and suspense more clearly define the tone of this film.

German program for *The Showdown*

The cast is quite good. Walter Brennan is pleasant and sympathetic, which makes the revelation that he is the killer almost regrettable. He doesn't make Mackellar evil and despicable as, for instance, his Ike Clanton was in Ford's *My Darling Clementine* four years earlier. His Cap Mackellar projects genuine sincerity as he cautions Shad against personal vengeance, and this appears to be due to affection for Shad as well as regret for his own actions. As Adelaide, Marie Windsor gives another dependable performance as she did in innumerable B movies. Jim Davis and Harry Morgan provide good support as drovers and the rest of the cast is equally convincing. However, the movie belongs to Elliott, whose stoic tone and grim visage create a memorable character whose transformation at the film's end doesn't erase the memory of his ruthless anti-hero.

At the Stadium Theater in Woonsocket, Rhode Island, *The Showdown* was the supporting feature for a Warner Bros. movie called *Breakthrough*. The Republic Western received little notice, with only the title and star being listed in small letters beneath a large advertisement for the main feature. Today, no doubts exist that the B Western is a far more satisfactory movie than the routine war movie.

Lippert Pictures was an independent company that was formed by Robert Lippert in the mid-1940s to produce and distribute inexpensive programmers. During its 10-year existence, Lippert released over a 100 movies, some of which are pleasant time-fillers but most of which are forgettable. Occasionally, Lippert produced a movie that could take its place alongside any major studio product. One example was *Rocketship X-M*, a memorable science-fiction movie released in 1950. The following year, an equally memorable Western was released and, though it disappeared rather quickly, it deserves to be better known than it is.

Little Big Horn is the story of a small group of cavalry troopers who attempt to reach General Custer and warn him that he is leading his command into an ambush. The leader of the patrol is Captain Philip Donlin, who is torn between his duty to try to warn Custer and his responsibility to his men, whom he believes may well die during the course of their dangerous trek. Also complicating his mission is the fact that he believes his subordinate, Lieutenant John Haywood, has been having an affair with his wife. As he leads the patrol through hostile Indian territory, his men are killed one by one by an invisible enemy. Finally, only Donlin and Haywood are left and it is quite possible that they will kill one another before the Indians can kill them.

The movie is directed and written by former Western novelist Charles Marquis Warren. This was the first film Warren directed and he fully realizes his script's ambitions by focusing on the characterizations, forcing each of the troopers to confront his previously unexplored feelings about duty and honor. Even though it is known by audiences that the patrol will never reach Custer in time, the movie still maintains suspense because the men have no such knowledge and this increases sympathy for them, regardless of their human failings. The action is often quite brutal, which increases the tension as the hopelessness of the mission becomes increasingly obvious. Warren also effectively uses the black and white photography to reflect the starkness of the surroundings. It is an impressive directorial debut (that would lead to his first A Western, *Arrowhead*, two years later).

Lloyd Bridges and John Ireland bring total commitment to their roles of, respectively, Donlin and Haywood. It is easy to believe that these two men have little use for one another and would probably not care if the other is the next victim of an arrow appearing out of nowhere. Bridges convincingly plays an ordinary soldier who is almost forced against his will to perform a heroic act while conveying his own personal misgivings and doubts. Quite underrated as an actor, Bridges had only the year before played with equal conviction a despicable kidnapper and murderer in *The Sound of Fury*. In that film, he invited contempt and anger from audiences, but in this film he invites admiration and sympathy. Ireland is equally good, using his somewhat sinister countenance to make audiences believe that he might be guilty of adultery but yet simultaneously rising to gallantry that perhaps he never thought he possessed.

Marie Windsor is once again on hand as Celie Donlin, though her role is limited, and Jim Davis also brings his usual dependability to his role as one of the troopers. As other troopers, Reed Hadley is an authoritarian sergeant major while Hugh O'Brian, Wally Cassell, King Donovan and Richard Emory bring believability to their characters. While the individual troopers may seem to some degree stereotypical, including the frightened kid, the veteran grumbler and even an obligatory though brief comic relief, they achieve some degree of freshness because of the assurance each actor brings to his role as well as the eventual fates of their characters.

The Laurier was a second-run theater in Woonsocket that played major films after they finished their first-run engagements. But the theater was the first to show *Little Big Horn* and used it as a supporting feature to the second run of *That's My Boy*, a Dean Martin and Jerry Lewis hit comedy. In New York City, it suffered perhaps a more lamentable fate. It played at the RKO Palace, where it received second billing to a live stage show publicized as "10 Swell Vaudeville Acts." It is doubtful that any person in the audience bought a ticket to see the movie, which received little notice in newspaper ads. But it remains a stark, memorable Western that lingered in the mind long after it disappeared into the vaults of the forgotten Lippert Pictures.

The exciting *War Paint* begins with a pre-credits sequence in which two Indians, Taslik and Wanima, entrap and kill a soldier and Commissioner Kirby, who has brought a treaty for peace to be delivered to Chief Grey Eagle. As it will later become clear, the two Indians are brother and sister and are children of Grey Eagle. It is also clear that they have no desire for peace with the white men, who have subjected their people to abuse and humiliation.

Nevertheless, the film's protagonist, Lieutenant Billings, remains unwavering against increasingly difficult obstacles to deliver the treaty to the chief before the deadline elapses. Unaware of Taslik's true feelings, Billings asks him to lead his troops to the Commissioner. With Wanima trailing behind, Taslik sabotages the mission at every opportunity and is eventually killed by one of the men when his treachery is exposed. Without water or horses, the men become increasingly desperate and begin to turn against Billings. When Wanima leads them to an abandoned gold mine, greed pushes three of the troopers to mutiny and murder. By the end of the journey, Billings is virtually alone except for an unlikely ally, Wanima, who has been persuaded to help him by his sincerity and his willingness to die for peace.

The United Artists release is directed by Lesley Selander, prolific veteran of dozens of B Westerns beginning in the 1930s. Many of his Westerns are juvenile programmers, including several with Buck Jones in the 1930s, even more with Tim Holt in the 1940s, and over two dozen Hopalong Cassidy movies. Generally, his direction was energetic if uninspired and his skills seemed suitable to series Westerns. However, when presented with a script of substance, he displayed the appropriate talent required for the project. *War Paint* is his best Western and stands out in a career devoted largely to the genre. Following the gripping opening, the movie builds a terrific tension and never lets up until the conclusion. The action scenes are ruggedly realistic, but tension arises from the interaction of the characters and this propels the story. Selander also uses location photography in Death Valley quite effectively, as the harsh landscape (photographed in AnscoColor) impacts the actions of the characters.

The screenplay by Richard Alan Simmons and Martin Berkeley is distinguished by a stark realism in its depictions of the various characters, all of whose fates are contrary to the usual requirements of the B Western. The soldier whose wife just had a baby and is promised by Billings that he will see his child is not expected to die from drinking poisoned water. The jovial, good-natured trooper is not expected to turn into a cold-blooded murderer. The heroic trooper who volunteers to save the patrol is not supposed to be killed by the female warrior. Yet all of this happens in scenes that are quite shocking and unpredictable. And the script is also free of romantic complications that would have been unrealistic and intrusive within the context of the story.

War Paint contains very strong performances from the entire cast. Third-billed Charles McGraw, who had starred the previous year in what would eventually become his most renowned movie, *The Narrow Margin*, brings his customary power to the role of the loyal Sergeant Clarke. With his grizzled features and rasping voice, McGraw believably conveys the type of authority that is necessary to keep the troops in line and that his lieutenant, it is implied, may lack.

Joan Taylor brings restrained emotion to her role of Wanima and it is to her credit that her character achieves some degree of sympathy despite having killed one of the more likeable troopers. The manner in which she describes the reasons for her hatred and distrust of the soldiers, whose weaknesses are gradually exposed, clearly indicates that neither side is completely right or wrong.

As Taslik, Keith Larsen is also quite effective, his words dripping barely concealed venom as he leads the soldiers into a death trap. The individual troopers are given distinct personalities by the supporting actors. Notable are Robert Wilke and Peter Graves, but John Doucette, Paul Richards, Douglas Kennedy and Walter Reed all have individual scenes that add to the film's raw impact.

However, Robert Stack's performance as Lieutenant Billings is the focal point of the movie. Prior to this film, Stack had been known primarily for giving Deanna Durbin her first screen kiss in 1939. Subsequently, he starred in two minor Westerns but was soon reduced to playing supporting roles in comedies and romances. By 1950, his career was at a low point with a role in a B Western dud called *My Outlaw Brother*. However, in 1951, he gave a very good performance in *The Bullfighter and the Lady* and, the following year, brought some credibility to *Bwana Devil*, which began the 3-D craze of the 1950s. *War Paint* proved that he was a far more capable actor than had been presumed. His increasingly haggard appearance fully conveys the urgency of the mission and the desperation of his character. He makes Billings not only admirable but sympathetic, particularly when he is discussing his estranged wife. This effective performance from Stack would lead to more demanding roles.

Perhaps one false note sounds in the movie. During a campfire sequence early in the movie, the soldiers sing a pleasant melody entitled "Elaine." The scene doesn't quite fit in with the grim tone of the rest of the movie or with the subsequent characterizations of the troopers. Little demand existed for the song, which was not recorded. The score by Emil Newman and Arthur Lange is an original one, somewhat atypical for a B Western, and is quite efficient.

At the Park Theater in Woonsocket, *War Paint* played the bottom-of-the-bill to a United Artists A movie, *Act of Love*, with Kirk Douglas. In newspaper advertisements, the main feature occupied most of the allotted space with the supporting feature receiving just enough space to list the title in small letters.

Hannah Lee is an interesting movie based upon the novel *Wicked Water* by MacKinlay Kantor, which was published by Random House in 1949. Among Kantor's previous works was the novel in verse, *Glory for Me*, which was the basis of the classic 1946 film *The Best Years of Our Lives*, and he would later win the Pulitzer Prize for his novel *Andersonville* in 1955.

Hannah Lee was released by Realart Pictures.

Wicked Water is subtitled *An American Primitive,* which refers to the main character, Bus Crow, an obvious fictionalization of the legendary Tom Horn, a genuine hero who turned evil and was eventually hung for murder. Former Army scout and lawman Crow is primarily a killer and is hired by wealthy cattlemen to dispose of settlers. Crow quickly murders several homesteaders, thus spreading fear throughout the territory. While he has always resisted emotional attachments, he is attracted to former saloon singer and teacher, Mattie McCloud, who reluctantly falls in love with him. Meanwhile, U.S. Marshal Steve Rochelle suspects Crow of the murders but can find no evidence due to Crow's cleverly established alibis. As the killings mount, Mattie also becomes suspicious of Crow but is torn between her love for him and her conscience. After Crow unintentionally kills a settler's young son, Rochelle is able to trick him into confessing to the murders by getting him drunk and using his fear of dripping water to admit his guilt. And it is dripping water that plunges Crow to his death on the gallows, though not until he has expressed his hatred of Mattie for disclosing his secret fear to Rochelle.

In adapting his novel to the screen as *Hannah Lee*, Kantor and co-writer Alford Von Ronkle retain the plot but simplify characterizations and change the ending. In the novel, the author's portrait of a merciless killer is fleshed out by details of his abusive childhood. The background events as well as the complexities of the relationship between Bus and Mattie are eliminated from the completed film, though enough remains to indicate that Kantor attempted to infuse the low-budget production with some degree of sophistication. It is also possible that Kantor's original script was too literary for the filmmakers' intentions. In Macdonald Carey's autobiography, *The Days of My Life*, published by St. Martins Press in 1991, the film's star relates how he and co-star John Ireland rewrote many scenes during filming. Though this may have had a detrimental effect upon the integrity of the script, the completed film remains intriguing.

In *Hannah Lee*, which in the credits is also subtitled *An American Primitive*, Bus Crow is hired by ranchers to kill homesteaders and earns a hefty payment for each man he murders. He displays his brutality to everyone, including saloon hostess Hallie, who falls in love with him. Marshal Sam Rochelle suspects Crow of the murders but is unable to prove his suspicions. Hallie is aware of Crow's guilt but is reluctant to help Rochelle because her testimony once helped Rochelle to send her own brother to the gallows. After Crow shoots a boy, Rochelle tracks him through the countryside and discovers the hiding place in which Crow keeps his special rifle. But Crow gets the drop on the lawman and is about to shoot him when Hallie, who has followed them, kills the man she loves.

Hannah Lee was released by Realart Pictures, an independent company that was chiefly known for theatrically rereleasing old Universal films, particularly horror movies. After having success with the reissues, Realart president Jack Broder formed his own production company to make B movies and quickly turned out numerous supporting features, mostly genre movies. Since a large market existed for Westerns and since three-dimensional movies were popular in 1953, Realart financed the production of *Hannah Lee*, which would be filmed in Pathecolor and 3-D.

Hannah Lee is co-directed and co-produced by John Ireland and Lee Garmes. Ireland, who had received an Academy Award nomination for his supporting performance in *All The King's Men* in 1949, had been equally impressive in supporting roles in two classic Westerns, John Ford's *My Darling Clementine* (1946) and Howard Hawks' *Red River* (1948). Subsequently, he starred in many B movies, such as *Little Big Horn*, while also continuing to play second leads and villains in A movies. This was his first effort at directing. Lee Garmes had directed previously but was primarily known for his innovative cinematography, which over the previous two decades had earned him an Academy Award for *Shanghai Express* in 1932 and widespread acclaim for numerous other films, including Alexander Korda's magnificent production of *Jungle Book* in 1942.

The decision to film the movie in 3-D was certainly a commercial one. When *Bwana Devil* was released in late 1952, its success took Hollywood by surprise. Advertisements showing a lion jumping out of the screen attracted huge audiences, who didn't object to wearing special glasses to get the full effect of the three-dimensional images.

All of the major studios and many independent production companies jumped on the bandwagon and announced plans to make 3-D movies. During 1953, 28 movies were released in 3-D, 10 of which were Westerns. They included such movies as *The Moonlighter* with Fred MacMurray, *Gun Fury* with Rock Hudson, and *The Stranger Wore a Gun* with Randolph Scott. Short subjects, including a couple with The Three Stooges and numerous cartoons, were also filmed in 3-D. Lippert Pictures even filmed the heavyweight championship fight between Rocky Marciano and Joe Walcott in 3-D.

Several 3-D films were A movies with major directors and stars that utilized the process to its best effect, such as John Farrow's *Hondo* starring John Wayne. However,

Hannah Lee was retitled *Outlaw Territory* and released without 3-D a year after its debut.

the majority of 3-D productions were B movies which attained top-of-the-bill status because of the process. The quality of these movies was generally dependent upon the quality of other production values combined with effective use of the process. Unfortunately, too many 3-D movies used the process simply as a gimmick which was added onto cheap, hackneyed productions which would alienate audiences and hasten the end of the process.

Ireland and Garmes had a good script by a prestigious author, good actors (including Ireland, Carey and Joanne Dru) and a good cinematographer (Garmes). Their intent obviously was to make a good movie in three-dimension, not a quickie exploitation film. However, they apparently had difficulty with the StereoCine 3-D process. In his autobiography, Macdonald Carey writes about the movie's premiere in Philadelphia, during which patrons left the theater after complaining about headaches, due perhaps to poor projection or possibly improper aligning of the dual 35mm cameras during filming. Since a major studio was not involved, the movie subsequently received poor distribution and only had sporadic playdates in 3-D.

This is unfortunate because Ireland and Garmes efficiently direct *Hannah Lee*, and it is obvious, even when seen in standard flat version, that the directors attempted to use the three-dimensional process to enhance the mood of the story and not simply as a gimmick. The directors keep the focus of the film on Crow and Hallie while Rochelle doesn't appear until more than a half hour into the movie. The action scenes, particularly the murders, are handled quite effectively. The scene in which Hallie assumes the upper hand and seduces Crow in the darkened saloon is charged with erotic tension. The story is absorbing and the characters are not the typical stereotypes found in programmers. While Rochelle may be a standard lawman, Crow and Hallie are not as familiar and their relationship does not follow the usual format. The ranchers project realistic self-righteousness while at least one homesteader is not free of guilt. And the climax, though not as historically authentic as that of the novel, is still poignant.

The movie also has the added advantage of good performances from the three leads. Macdonald Carey is cast against type as the cold-blooded killer and is very good. In his first scene, his character is established when he slaps a small boy who doesn't do his bidding. He forcefully projects a man who seems to have nothing but ice in his veins. The only emotion he displays, even in his love scenes, is anger. Even the trace of regret he shows after shooting the boy is more infected with anger than sorrow. It is a very chilling performance. Joanne Dru, who was married to Ireland at the time, is appealing as Hallie and projects convincing emotional torment in her key scenes, particularly when she discovers that the man she loves is a vicious killer. Ireland, though usually more effective as a shady or villainous character, makes a fine hero.

Hannah Lee may be flawed due to the apparent script revisions during filming as well as an obvious low budget, but it remains entertaining and memorable for more than its ambitions. It is certainly superior to some other 3-D Westerns released during the same period. Movies such as *Fort Ti*, *The Nebraskan* and *Jesse James Vs. the Daltons* are terrible even with arrows and knives popping out of the screen, but they had the benefit of major studio distribution. Realart Pictures had no distribution clout and the movie quickly disappeared, at least in its original format.

Over one year after its original release *Hannah Lee* finally arrived in Providence, Rhode Island, at the RKO Albee Theater as a supporting feature to 20th Century Fox's *Carmen Jones*. Retitled *Outlaw Territory* and shown in black and white and two dimensions, the movie still proved to be more interesting than Otto Preminger's musical drama, though it is unlikely that any prospective patrons were aware of its existence. In advertisements for the movies, the title of the Western was printed in very small letters beneath a large ad for the musical.

And not to be forgotten is an infectious title ballad sung under the credits by Ken Curtis and the Pioneers and throughout the film by Stan Jones, William Lue and Richard Cherney. "Hannah Lee" was recorded by Guy Mitchell and was not a hit, though at least one die-hard collector still has his copy of the 45 rpm record about "the pretty devil," who shot her cruel husband and almost sent her lover to the gallows for her crime. The lyrics were irrelevant to the storyline but still, with its tale of love and death, fit the mood of the film. Thanks to Bear Family Records of Germany, the song has had renewed life. In 1989, they released a version by Johnny Western on a CD of Western themes entitled *Gunfight at O.K. Corral* and, in 1999, Guy Mitchell's original version was included on the CD entitled *Wanderin' Star and Other Movie and TV Songs*.

In *Three Hours to Kill*, Jim Guthrie returns to his hometown where the townspeople greet him with fear and anger. Three years before, Guthrie had almost been lynched for the murder of his fiancée's brother but managed to escape, though he was left with a permanent scar around his neck. Determined to clear his name, he has now returned to find the actual killer who ruined his life and to reclaim his fiancée, Laurie Hendricks. His anger and bitterness increase when he learns that Laurie has given birth to his son and has married another man.

Jim receives no sympathy from Laurie or anyone else. His former neighbors still think he is guilty and his only friend, the

deputy sheriff, gives him only three hours of freedom before he is arrested. Eventually, Jim is able to expose the murderer, who is revealed to be the only man he trusted. After being forced to kill his friend, he is almost lynched again but this time is vindicated by the testimony of witnesses. However, his victory is a bitter one. Though he has found justice, he knows that he has lost the woman he loves and can never be a father to his son. Realizing that neither he nor the townspeople can ever forget what they did to him, he leaves his hometown with some satisfaction but little happiness.

Three Hours to Kill is a Columbia Pictures release in Technicolor and is directed by Alfred Werker, a reliable craftsman who began his directing career with silents in the mid-1920s. Over the next three decades, with a few medium-budget exceptions, he helmed mostly B movies with only a couple of Westerns under his belt early in his career. Of his last seven movies, six are B Westerns. His direction is more than competent, particularly with the action scenes. The lynching, shown in flashback, is depicted with excruciating detail as Guthrie escapes on a runaway wagon with the noose still around his neck and the dangling rope trailing behind, catching and pulling him backward at various points.

A solid screenplay by Richard Alan Simmons and Roy Huggins that is well constructed, with atypical characterizations, aids Werker. Jim Guthrie is not a standard hero. Prior to the murder, he appears to have been irresponsible, quick-tempered and a heavy drinker. Nevertheless, the eagerness with which his former friends hasten to judge and hang him is effectively disturbing. A bitter tone permeates the story, which is only partially alleviated by the vindication of Jim at the end. Only the last scene seems artificial. As Jim rides out of town, the saloon girl who has always loved him rides after him. Her character seems to have been included only for this purpose and the implication of eventual happiness for Jim does not fit in with the downbeat tone of the story.

However, the movie remains engrossing entertainment and its success is due in large part to the presence of Dana Andrews. One of Hollywood's most underrated actors, Andrews starred in many A movies of the 1940s and gave fine performances in films by Elia Kazan, Lewis Milestone, Jean Renoir and Otto Preminger, who directed him in four movies throughout the decade as well as a fifth in the 1960s. He gave a memorable portrayal in Preminger's *Laura* (1944) but surpassed it as a brutal cop in the director's *Where the Sidewalk Ends* (1950). His superb performance in William Wyler's *The Best Years of Our Lives* in 1946 deserved an Academy Award, or at the very least a nomination, but the performance was unjustly ignored.

Prior to the 1950s, Andrews appeared in only a few Westerns. He played supporting roles in his debut film *Kit Carson* and in William Wyler's *The Westerner*, both in 1940. He gave a poignant performance in his breakthrough role as the doomed victim in William Wellman's *The Ox-Bow Incident* (1943) and he proved to be a sturdy hero in Jacques Tourneur's flawless *Canyon Passage* (1946). In the early 1950s, his career began to slide and *Three Hours to Kill* is perhaps his first B movie, but he brings his customary authority to the role of Jim Guthrie. His is particularly convincing in projecting the grim-faced, smoldering anger combined with moral ambivalence embodied by his character, which is reminiscent of many of his film noir portrayals.

Andrews receives fine support from Donna Reed. Reed just won an Academy Award for her supporting role in *From Here to Eternity*. After that acclaim, Reed reportedly was not too happy about being assigned by studio boss Harry Cohn to a B Western, but she still gives a professional performance, believably conveying the resentment and sorrow of her character.

At the Park Theater, *Three Hours to Kill* played the top half of a double bill over another Columbia B Western, *The Black Dakotas*, a typical below-average programmer that gave B Westerns a bad name.

Joel McCrae's screen presence conveyed dignity and integrity. In a film career which spanned over three decades, he provided dependable performances in A movies for Alfred Hitchcock, William Wyler, George Stevens, William Wellman and was one of Preston Sturges' favorite actors. He was equally adept at serious drama and light comedy. In the 1930s and early 1940s, he starred in a few Westerns, the most prominent being Wellman's *Buffalo Bill* in 1944. In the late 1940s, he began to work almost exclusively in the genre, starring in such notable A Westerns as *Ramrod* (1947), *Colorado Territory* (1949), and *Four Faces West* (1948). In the 1950s, except for one movie, he starred only in Westerns and the majority of them are B movies, all of which are enjoyable due to his presence.

In 1950 McCrae starred in *Stars in My Crown*, a gentle and delicate story of a year in the life of a preacher and his family in a Southern town. McCrae gave a very genial and unpretentious performance as a man of faith who was not above using his fists and even his gun to rid the town of evil and prejudice. This was his first of three movies with Jacques Tourneur, a director with an unassuming style and who was noted for making films that are visually innovative through his use of light and movement. Among his films are *Canyon Passage* and the classic film noir *Out of the Past* in 1947, as well as the horror films he directed for producer Val Lewton.

McCrae enjoyed working with Tourneur and chose him to direct *Stranger On Horseback*, filmed in AnscoColor and released by United Artists. It is a modest and

narratively simple film about Rick Thorne, a circuit judge who finds the town of Bannerman controlled by land baron Josiah Bannerman. After investigating a mysterious death, Thorne arrests Bannerman's son Tom, who had been romancing the dead man's wife. The townspeople, including the sheriff, are too frightened of Bannerman to tell the truth about the killing. The conflict between Thorne and Bannerman is actually between archaic law and official law. Though he is subjected to pressure and threats, Judge Thorne with the help of Bannerman's daughter secretly takes Tom out of town to another jurisdiction where he will get a fair trial. The plan almost succeeds until Bannerman and his gunmen force a showdown, but Thorne's determination, after he seems to back down in the face of overwhelming power, even wins the respect of his enemy.

The script by Herb Meadow and Don Martin is fairly straightforward. Any journeyman director would have found ways to pad out the story with unnecessary exposition, but Tourneur keeps the focus on the plot and characterization. He uses lighting and camerawork, particularly during the numerous night scenes, to increase atmosphere. The manner in which he frames scenes tends to emphasize the psychological passions below the story's surface that are only implied by the dialogue. The relationships between Bannerman and his adult children, in particular, are given a resonance that increases involvement in the story. As a result, the film has an emotional intensity that builds steadily until the satisfying conclusion.

McCrae projects strength and decency in the role of Judge Thorne, which makes the gradual willingness of the sheriff and others to put their trust in him believable. Though his acting appears effortless, McCrae's understated portrayal masks a definite skill at bringing total sincerity to his role. He can have water thrown in his face and still suggest through his eyes that he doesn't have to fight to prove how tough he is. And at the climax when he appears to be intimidated by Bannerman's show of force and starts to ride away, his bearing and expression suggest an inner strength that will asset itself in some way. It is a typically fine performance.

Kevin McCarthy consistently gave good performances which added to any movie in which he appeared, whether it was the film version of *Death of a Salesman* in 1952 or a minor Western. He is as convincing as the morally weak Tom as he would be the following year as the morally resolute hero of Don Siegel's *Invasion of the Body Snatchers*. John McIntire brings some degree of sympathy to the role of his father, a man who is not necessarily evil as much as accustomed to having everyone do his bidding. McIntire is one of those character actors who could always be depended upon to add clout to any role he portrayed. His deep and raspy voice could be used to project decency as in that same year's *The Phenix City Story* or outright villainy, as in Anthony Mann's *The Far Country* the year before.

At the Loew's State Theater in Providence, *Stranger On Horseback* was on the bottom of the bill for MGM's *Kismet* and, once again, advertising for the co-feature was practically nonexistent. Beneath a large ad for the musical, the title of the Western was listed in small letters followed by the tag line: "He tamed the West with a .45." Not only is the line an inaccurate description of the film but also it makes the film appear to be a formulaic juvenile Western. Ironically, the main feature turned out to be one of director Vincente Minnelli's less inspired musicals while the co-feature was worth the price of admission.

In 1953, a story entitled "My Brother Down There" by Steve Frazee appeared in *Ellery Queen's Mystery Magazine* and was subsequently anthologized in *Best American Short Stories: 1953*, published by Houghton-Mifflin. It is a contemporary Western about a manhunt in the Northwestern wilderness for three escaped convicts. The story's protagonist is Deputy Sheriff Ben Melvin, whose feelings toward the convicts gradually change during the course of the hunt. The posse also includes Syd James, who has an inclination for killing, especially if his prey is a running target. But it is the humanity of one of the convicts, Myles Kaygo, and not the savagery of Jaynes that forces Melvin to realize that all men, even ruthless killers, are his brothers.

Three years later, the film version of Frazee's story was released and quickly disappeared, which was an undeserved fate for an engrossing modern Western. Entitled *Running Target*, the movie adds a woman, Smitty, as a member of the posse, but is generally a faithful adaptation of the story. The deputy sheriff, here called Scott, remains the center of the story and it is his perception of events which serve as the movie's focus. Refreshingly, Smitty is not added to the film as a romantic interest for the hero. She is not a traditional female character and seems to avoid any trace of femininity while having little use for men. Initially, it appears that she has joined the posse to avenge her suspected humiliation by the convicts who robbed her store, a crime only alluded to in the story. Thus, it is puzzling when it is discovered that

she has a bright red dress hidden among her belongings. As the hunt progresses, two of the convicts are captured and the true motivations of Jaynes and Smitty are revealed to Scott. The final confrontation, involving the killing of Kaygo, achieves an added dimension in the film because of the revelation of Smitty's romantic attachment to him. As in the story, Scott becomes aware of his shared humanity because of the events that have unfolded.

Running Target is filmed in Deluxe Color and was released by United Artists. Marvin Weinstein directed and co-wrote the screenplay with producer Jack Couffer and Conrad Hall, who would have an illustrious future career as a cinematographer. Weinstein's direction is quite sophisticated for a first film. Tense and taut, with a gloomy mood of desolation, the movie is very effective in conveying a sense of pessimism that is gradually supplanted by a feeling of hope, despite the ambivalent outcome. And all the while, the magnificent surroundings of the wilderness are used to project a counterpoint to the human mayhem taking place against them. Many fine sequences occur throughout the film, from the first killing by Jaynes at the beginning to the poignant one in which Scott views Smitty's rendezvous with Kaygo from afar. Despite this impressive directorial debut, Weinstein never again directed or wrote a film and his only other credit is as cinematographer on a 1958 film called *Edge of Fury*.

The perceptive screenplay is equally successful. During the course of the movie, the personalities of the posse members are carefully delineated and even Kaygo, an apparently callous killer, is allowed some degree of sympathy. The story moves purposely toward the inevitable conclusion as the characters gradually expose their inner feelings. Interestingly, Jaynes emerges as the real villain because he obviously enjoys killing, and the climactic scene in which Scott destroys the symbol of Jaynes' manhood is particularly satisfying. It is perhaps a testament to the script's quality that author Frazee subsequently expanded his original story into a novel, basing it on the script and using its title.

The actors, mostly B veterans, all provide sharply etched performances. Arthur Franz spent most of his film career starring in B movies while playing supporting roles in A movies. He is probably best remembered for his lead role in William Cameron Menzies' science fiction gem *Invaders from Mars* in 1953. However, he gave a terrific performance in *The Sniper*, directed in 1952 by Edward Dmytryk, and the director must have been pleased with Franz since he gave him roles in eight more of his movies over the next 25 years. More of an urban type than a Westerner, Franz appeared in only one conventional oater and one other contemporary Western. As Scott, he lends quiet authority to the pivotal role and underplays to allow the other characters more of an emotional range, though his angry outburst at the end of the film is very effectual.

Doris Dowling, who never quite made her mark in A movies, credibly conveys Smitty's complexities. Richard Reeves sharply projects the uncertain masculinity of Jaynes while familiar heavy Myron Healey has enough of a screen presence to make his role as Kaygo stand out, despite his limited screen time. But this is one of those low-budgeted movies in which all of the actors seem to sense that the material and filmmakers deserve more than simply walking through their roles and, as a result, add to the film's force by going that extra yard.

At the Stadium Theater in Woonsocket, *Running Target* was the supporting feature to MGM's service comedy, *Don't Go Near the Water*, but a magnifying glass was necessary to see in newspaper advertisements that a second feature was on the bill. It was obviously felt that the comedy was enough of a draw for audiences, who probably weren't even aware of the name of the second feature until it appeared on screen. In fact, many of them may not have even seen it, planning their schedule to arrive in time for the main feature. Perhaps this may help to explain why Weinstein never directed again.

In 1956, John Wayne was responsible for launching the film careers of director Andrew McLaglen and writer Burt Kennedy. Three movies produced by Wayne's Batjac Productions were released during the year. McLaglen co-produced *Seven Men from Now* and directed the other two Batjac films, *Man in the Vault* and *Gun the Man Down*, both B movies. Kennedy, who had previously written for radio and television, received his first theatrical screen credits for the three movies.

John Wayne was also responsible for bringing James Arness to stardom. In the early 1950s, Arness had played small roles in many B movies but had not attracted attention. His most prominent roles were as a villain in John Ford's *Wagonmaster* (1950) and as the title role in Howard Hawks' *The Thing* (1951). His presence in the Ford movie first brought him to the attention of the Duke, who later saw him in a community theater production and, not intimidated by his height as other actors may have been, signed him to a personal contract. Wayne subsequently provided Arness with supporting roles in several of his movies. This exposure led directly to his co-starring role in the terrific giant ant movie *Them*, released in 1954.

The story of how Arness became famous is reported in the book, *Gunsmoke: A Complete History* by Suzanne Barabas and Gabor Barabas (McFarland; 1990). When the Duke heard that CBS-TV was looking for an actor to star in a television series called *Gunsmoke*, based upon the popular radio show, he contacted a network executive and recommended Arness for the starring role. The producer of the show was Charles Marquis Warren, who had gotten the assignment because of his experiences with writing and directing Westerns, including *Little Big Horn* and the equally fine *A Western Arrowhead* in 1953. Warren was familiar with Arness, having previously directed him in *Hellgate* in 1952. But Arness preferred acting in movies and had to be persuaded by the Duke to do a screen test. Meanwhile, Denver Pyle was virtually set to play Dillon until Arness tested and was immediately offered the role. Even then, he wanted to back out of the deal and it was only after Wayne had several drinks with him and convinced him to sign the contract that he became Marshal Matt Dillon.

Thus, in September 1955, John Wayne made a rare television appearance to introduce the first episode of *Gunsmoke* and introduce his friend, Jim Arness, whom he predicted would be a big star. Over one year later, after Arness had become a household name, United Artists released *Gun the Man Down*, starring television's heroic marshal as an ex-convict out for revenge.

Rem Anderson has sworn vengeance against his two ex-partners, Ranking and Farley, who deserted him after he was wounded during a bank robbery. Freed after serving his sentence, Anderson finds the two men with his former mistress, Janice, in a town on the border, but instead of killing them he taunts them with his presence. Janice is tormented by guilt for betraying Rem and tries to make amends, but Rem is unforgiving. Their nerves shattered, Ranking and Farley hire a gunman to kill Rem but their plan backfires. In the action-filled climax, Rem achieves his revenge, but it is a hollow victory, for Janice is killed saving his life.

Gun the Man Down is an exciting, action-packed Western that is also strong on character and atmosphere. Filmed in black and white, the movie has the gritty, stark look of a low-budget film but uses the lack of frills to complement the bleakness of the story as well as the ultimate futility of the main character's quest for vengeance. Andrew McLaglen directs assuredly and creates a genuine sense of increasing tension that is punctuated by a thrilling climax. Burt Kennedy's script avoids clichés as well as a happy ending and contains dialogue that is crisp and direct.

James Arness delivers a compelling performance as Rem Anderson, quite unlike the stalwart Matt Dillon who was then appearing in living rooms every Saturday night. Angie Dickinson is introduced in this film and makes an impression as Janice. Familiar villains, Robert Wilke and Don Megowan, register strongly as Ranking and Farley, while Emile Meyer and Harry Carey, Jr. add support as the town's lawmen. All of the actors add to the effectiveness of this crisply made Western that fully achieves its intended purpose of providing unpretentious entertainment.

Gun the Man Down debuted at the Metropolitan Theater in New York City as a co-feature to, ironically, a second-run of the John Wayne-John Ford MGM movie, *The Wings of Eagles*, which had just finished an exclusive engagement at the Radio City Music Hall. As usual, the supporting feature was allotted little space with only the title and star listed along with the words, "First New York showing." Well, maybe the Duke and Jim toasted a few more drinks to celebrate sharing a double bill.

Joseph Cotten is another major actor whose career began to slide in the 1950s and subsequently starred in many B movies. He began his film career auspiciously with Orson Welles in *Citizen Kane* (1941) and *The Magnificent Ambersons* (1942). Though he proved to be a popular romantic lead in such movies as *Since You Went Away* (1944) and *Portrait of Jennie* (1948), he was perhaps more inspired when playing unconventional characters and excelled in such classics as Alfred Hitchcock's *Shadow of a Doubt* (1943) and Carol Reed's *The Third Man* (1949). He also managed to distinguish himself in David O. Selznick's bloated production of *Duel in the Sun* (1946), his only Western prior to the 1950s.

In contrast, Ward Bond was never a leading man. In the 1930s, he appeared in small roles in dozens of movies, including many minor Westerns, and by the 1940s had achieved a reputation as a versatile character actor. Over the course of his career, he was directed 22 times by John Ford, in whose Westerns he gave his most memorable performances, and he was in 19 movies with John Wayne. In the Ford movies, Bond usually projected genial authority and traditional values. Yet, like Cotton, he displayed additional capabilities when challenged by more complex Western roles, such as the weak-willed leader of a lynch mob in Nicholas Ray's *Johnny Guitar* (1954) or the crooked sheriff in Ray Milland's *A Man Alone* (1955).

Since both Cotton and Bond had worked with acknowledged masters of A movies, it was perhaps appropriate that they would co-star in a B Western directed by Joseph H. Lewis, who has been called a master of the B movie. Lewis is primarily known for his B noirs, including *Gun Crazy* (1949), which had a superb screenplay co-written by MacKinlay Kantor based upon his own story. Though he had directed juvenile Westerns in the early 1940s, Lewis stayed away from the genre until the end of his theatrical career. His last four movies are B Westerns and *The Halliday Brand* is the best of the quartet. It is a brutal yet poignant drama about a family torn apart by prejudice and hatred.

The Halliday family is ruled by Big Dan Halliday, who has unrelentingly carved an empire out of the wilderness and treats his three adult children with the same severity. Since he has also appointed himself the county sheriff, he has total authority throughout the territory and abuses his power to enforce his will. When he discovers that his daughter Martha is romantically involved with one of his cowhands, Jivaro, who is half-Indian, he furiously manipulates subsequent events to sanction the lynching of the man. His dictatorial policies gradually alienate his eldest son Daniel, who eventually leaves the family home. Daniel also falls in love with Jivaro's sister Aleta, but his hatred for his father is stronger than his love for Aleta. Determined to destroy the Halliday brand and all it stands for, Daniel engages in equally vicious acts which place him outside the law. When Daniel returns to his home to reconcile with his father, whom he believes is repentant, he is greeted only with lies and a gun.

Since *The Halliday Brand* is told in flashback, a pervading sense of bitterness bathes the movie. The original script by George W. George and George Slavin is perceptive in its depiction of the complex family relationships. The austere black and white photography also helps to create a feeling of despair. The opening scenes establish the enmity between father and son which contrast with the flashback, in which Big Dan and Daniel appear initially to have a warm and close relationship. The drama inherent in the story is enhanced by the director's striking visual style, particularly notable in the scenes of

A sense of bitterness bathes *The Halliday Brand*.

friction between family members during which the intensity increases due to the absence of cutting. Some outdoor scenes, particularly the one in which Daniel and Aleta edge toward closeness, are obviously filmed on a sound stage, but the director's stylistic approach creates an almost poetic feeling. At the other extreme, the fight between father and son is exceptionally brutal.

In an earlier and unremarkable B Western, *Untamed Frontier* (1952), Joseph Cotton merely walked through his part and gave the impression that he knew the material was beneath his talents. As Daniel Halliday, however, he perfectly conveys the anguish of the moral quandaries that drive his character to the violence he supposedly detests. As a further indication of the complexities of his motivation, it is left unclear whether he engages in his acts of violence for justice or because of his own feelings for Aleta. Knowing that his father has destroyed his sister's chance for happiness, his motivations may not be as pure as he pretends. Cotton's expressions suggest that he is aware that he is more like his father than he may want to admit.

Ward Bond gives one of his finest performances as Big Dan, projecting a viciousness bordering on sadism. Many scenes forcefully indicate the conflicting emotions that exist within his character. When he leaves the jail to the mercy of the mob that is crying for Jivaro's blood, his insincere explanations to Dan clearly suggest that he knows his daughter's lover will be lynched, though he will not admit this to his sons. The scene in which the friction with Daniel begins is evident of his understanding of his character. Warmth coats his voice when he tells Daniel that he has given him his own name, but immediately afterward suppressed violence surfaces in his lowered tone when he tells his son not to threaten him. In the climactic scene, the hatred in his eyes as he tries to summon the strength to kill his eldest son is frightening in its intensity.

Viveca Lindfors as Aleta and Betsy Blair as Martha provide sensitive portrayals to balance the savagery practiced by father and son. Bill Williams is also very good as Clay, who cannot summon the courage to go against his father until he is able to see through his lies. The performances make the family relationships believable and enhance the feeling of sadness throughout this somber movie.

In Providence, *The Halliday Brand* was the supporting feature at Loew's State Theater to the United Artists A movie, *The Strange One,* with Ben Gazzara. The military school drama received all of the publicity and it was difficult to discern in newspaper advertisements that a co-feature existed.

Once again, Western icon John Wayne deserves to be given credit, in this case for generating the notable series of Randolph Scott-Budd Boetticher B Westerns of the late 1950s. In 1956, the Duke's Batjac company produced *Seven Men from Now* at Warner Bros. Wayne had intended to star in the movie, and he had signed Boetticher to direct and Burt Kennedy to write the screenplay.

Boetticher had previously directed *The Bullfighter and the Lady* (1951) with Robert Stack for producer Wayne. He had subsequently directed some routine action movies. His most recent film had been a suspenseful B noir *The Killer Is Loose*, with Joseph Cotton. Wayne had liked Boetticher's work on his earlier production and entrusted him to direct him in *Seven Men from Now*. However, when other commitments prevented the Duke from starring in the film, he asked his former co-star Randolph Scott to take his place. Scott accepted and worked for the first time with Boetticher. The result was an excellent movie that is superior to Scott's other Westerns of the period, including *Tall Man Riding* (1955), directed by Lesley Selander, as well as *A Lawless Street* (1955) and *Seventh Cavalry* (1956), both directed by Joseph H. Lewis.

Since 1948, Scott and Harry Joe Brown had been co-producing low-budget Westerns at Columbia. These movies were, for the most part, average programmers that benefited from Scott's imposing presence. (Brown also produced other Westerns, including *Three Hours to Kill*.) Pleased with his initial collaboration with Boetticher, Scott asked both Boetticher and Kennedy to work on his next production with Brown. Over the next five years, Boetticher would make five Westerns at Columbia with Scott and Brown, three of which were written by Kennedy and two by Charles Lang, Jr., who had scripted *The Magnificent Matador* for Boetticher in 1955. Though the films have common themes and characterizations, only two are original screenplays, both by Kennedy. Of the other three, two are based on novels and one is based upon a short story.

The films can be viewed as morality tales in which good and evil exist in shades of gray while the hero and villain share many traits. Usually, the hero is a lonely man who, because of something that has occurred in his past, has imposed upon himself a rigid code of honor and behavior that may place him at the mercy of events beyond his control. The villain is, at least on the surface, more extroverted but has his own code of morality and is often equally powerless to change his behavior. Scott's characterization is one that obviously appealed to both actor and director and would be explored to the limits in their films together.

The Tall T was their first Columbia production and it is a marvelous little film in which Scott and Richard Boone play two sides of the same coin. Scott is the hero and Boone is the villain, but they both have dreams, they both live by codes of honor and they both do what they have to do to survive. Scott plays Pat Brennan, who hitches a ride on a stage occupied by a wealthy bride and her husband, who has married her for her money. Believing the stage is carrying a payroll, Frank Usher and his gang kill the driver and, with the help of the cowardly groom, decide to hold the bride for ransom. As the captives try to stay alive, the excitement escalates steadily. By the time they face one another at the end of the film, Brennan and Usher have developed a begrudging respect for one another. Neither really wants to kill the other but they have to live by their code or die.

Italian poster for *The Tall T*

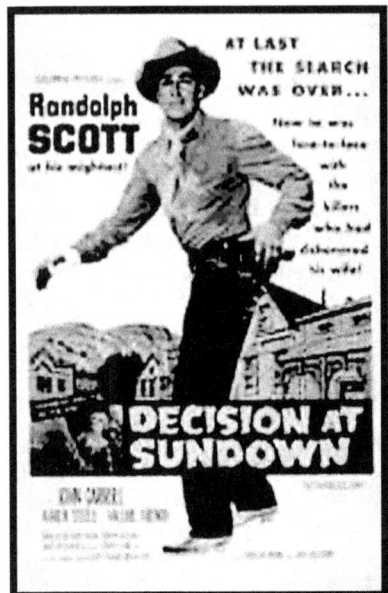

The Tall T was followed by *Decision at Sundown* (1957), *Buchanan Rides Alone* (1958), *Ride Lonesome* (1959), and *Comanche Station* (1960). The movies are all filmed in Technicolor, which the director uses cleverly to contrast the pessimism of most of the films. They are very well crafted and compact with tight editing and small casts which emphasize the interaction of the characters. Interestingly, in 1959 Scott and Boetticher also made *Westbound* at Warner Bros., but it is mediocre and lacks the passion of their other collaborations.

It is unfortunate that Boetticher chose to leave Hollywood after his last Scott film and spend the next several years directing a documentary about Mexican bullfighter Carlos Arruza. This decision virtually ended his Hollywood career. His body of work, best represented by the Scott films, indicates a unique talent. It is difficult to choose one of the series above the others, but *Decision at Sundown* is a personal choice as the finest.

At the beginning of *Decision at Sundown*, Bart Allison arrives in the town of Sundown with his friend Sam Ridgely to kill Tate Kimbrough, whom Allison blames for seducing and causing the suicide of his wife Mary. Ironically, Bart and Sam arrive on the day that Tate is going to marry Lucy Summerton, the daughter of the town's most respected citizen. Bart promptly interrupts the ceremony and informs Kimbrough and the wedding guests of his intentions and the reasons for them. This naturally inflames Tate and his corrupt sheriff Swede Hanson, whose gunmen force Bart and Sam to take refuge in a stable. It is during the course of this siege that personalities and failings of the principal individuals are pitilessly exposed.

While besieged, Bart resists attempts by the townspeople, including Lucy and her father, to leave town peacefully. Bart and Sam are also visited by the town physician, Doc Storrow, who seems almost sympathetic to Bart and Sam as he informs them of the means by which Kimbrough corrupted his once-decent town. Meanwhile, Tate gets some comfort from his mistress Ruby despite the fact that he is leaving her for Lucy. He then attempts to assure Lucy and her father that Bart's charges are untrue and it is soon revealed that he may be correct. This is suggested initially by Sam who, aware now of the reasons for Bart's hatred of Kimbrough, tries to tell his friend of Mary's infidelities. Bart refuses to listen and strikes Sam, who then angrily leaves the stable after being assured by Swede that he won't be harmed. But Swede has lied and Sam is killed, which increases Bart's fury to an almost frenzied level.

Due to the savagery of Sam's murder, Bart receives help from Kimbrough's enemies, who disarm Swede's gunmen and allow Bart to leave the stable. Bart promptly outdraws Swede and kills him, though he injures his gun hand. Tate now no longer has anyone to protect him and is forced to face Bart in a fair gunfight. But Ruby shoots her lover to wound him and save him from Bart's vengeance. Bart is unable to kill the wounded man and is forced to listen as Doc Storrow tells him of Sam's last words, which condemn Mary. Finally forced to realize the worthlessness of his quest and perhaps his entire life, Bart retreats to the local saloon where he drowns his anger in liquor. He berates the townspeople for allowing Sam's murder and then leaves town, more alone and embittered than when he arrived.

While Lang's insightful script for *Decision at Sundown* contains variations of themes featured within the other Scott-Boetticher films, it is also based to a large degree upon the source novel of the same title by Charles Carder, published by Macrae Smith in 1955. The novel contains the main plot and some of the characterizations of the movie, but the novel has a different resolution and different fates for the main characters. Basically, the screenplay eliminates some of the novel's clichés, particularly the romantic ending as well as the subplots involving Tate's blackmailing of Lucy's father and Lucy's true parentage, while it expands upon the familiar Scott-Boetticher themes. Lang would later adapt another novel, Jonas Ward's *The Name's Buchanan,* in the same manner for the film *Buchanan Rides Alone,* just as Burt Kennedy had previously adapted Elmore Leonard's story "The Captives" into *The Tall T.*

A summary of the novel by Carder, a pseudonym for Vernon L. Fluharty, illustrates the basic differences between novel and film version. The first part of the novel is adapted fairly faithfully to the screen, though the reader learns more of Bart's background. He is a Texan who, upon his release from a Union prison camp, returned home to learn of his wife Belle's suicide after Tate Kimbrough supposedly lied to her of Bart's death and then seduced and deserted her. Bart has since been searching for Kimbrough and, after three years, has found him in Sundown. The confrontation at the wedding is the same as in the film, as is the fight between Bart and Sam in the stable. In the novel, Sam is Belle's brother but he still had hoped never to have to tell Bart of her infidelities. His death occurs under slightly different circumstances but is still the result of Bart's refusal to believe that his image of his wife may be erroneous.

Decision at Sundown **features a small cast, led by Randolph Scott, which emphasizes the interaction of the characters.**

After this incident, the novel takes a different course than the film as the author converts an intriguing plot into a standard Western romance. (Actually, the novel originally appeared in *Ranch Romances Magazine*.) Lucy Summerhill, now that she is free of her obligation to marry Tate, is attracted to Bart, but Bart clings to the image of his dead wife. Doc Storrow, unlike his counterpart in the movie, is elderly and a drunkard, partly because he lost Lucy's mother to Charles Summerton. Tate Kimbrough is clearly a coward, first hiring two men to kill Bart and then trying to sneak out of town. When Tate is forcibly returned, Bart challenges him to a gunfight and kills him. His mission completed, Bart starts to leave town but Tate's mistress shoots him, though he survives to start a new life with Lucy. Thus, in the novel, Tate is subjected to a villain's death, neither deserving nor receiving redemption as in the movie, and Bart can look forward to love and happiness, a fate denied his counterpart in the movie.

The film version of *Decision at Sundown* is the most harsh and uncompromising of the Scott-Boetticher films. Like most of the other protagonists Scott played in the series, Bart Allison is living in the past but in this case the past is a fantasy. He has deceived himself into believing that Tate Kimbrough destroyed his marriage and wife when in fact the marriage was a fraud and his wife a cheat. Believing himself to be on a quest for justice to avenge a wrong, he is actually determined to murder a man who is innocent of this particular charge. Indeed, as the film progresses, the roles of hero and villain are increasingly blurred as each man takes on the characteristics of the other.

At the beginning of the film, Tate rules Sundown with an iron fist and callously discards his mistress to marry into an influential family. By the end of the day, he develops courage and integrity as he walks out to face Bart and certain death. And it is Tate, not Bart, who is allowed a happy ending as he rides away with the woman who loves him. No such happiness exists for Bart Allison. He is not even allowed a trace of nobility since it is suggested that it was his crippled hand and not a moral awakening that prevented him from killing a wounded man. And afterward, he has to get drunk to block out the truth that he has been forced to hear. As he bitterly leaves town, it is doubtful that he will ever find peace and his future is very bleak.

Decision at Sundown is directed simply yet masterfully by Budd Boetticher, who economically uses his camera to tell the story while allowing the pathos of Bart Allison and the pointlessness of his quest to gradually unfold. The director's stark approach emphasizes the emotional pain of the two main characters, who initially seem to be in control of their destinies but in fact are revealed to be helpless pawns at the mercy of a cruel fate. Considerable action erupts in the movie but it is subordinate to the inner torment of both Bart and Tate, who have been deceiving themselves and who lose what they cherish most dearly. But only Tate is given something of value to replace what he has lost, while Bart is left desolate. Boetticher would create variations of this theme with his star and writers in other films in the series, but never with such little sympathy for the hero. Not a false note sounds in this minor masterpiece.

The film contains fine performances from its entire cast, but most notably its star. As Bart Allison, Randolph Scott is outstanding. Initially, Scott projects the grim-faced, heroic qualities associated with his screen persona. But it is gradually becomes clear that the cold smile on his face, as he announces his hatred of Kimbrough, masks a sadistic eagerness to inflict pain upon his prey before killing him. This eagerness is quickly replaced by a blind obstinacy that develops into a homicidal fury. After Sam is killed, he appears deranged with hatred and grief, his eyes filled with tears while his voice quivers with rage. In the closing scenes, his total despair is fully conveyed by his expression and manner, both of which suggest that he has lost the will to live. Scott's performance is truly exceptional.

Providing fine support is John Carroll at Tate Kimbrough. In the 1940s, Carroll had played the lead in many programmers and supporting roles in more important films, but his career as a leading man seemed to be over in the 1950s. Considered a lightweight actor, he gives a distinctive performance as Tate, persuasively displaying a viciousness that is a cover for marked insecurities. Noah Beery is also good as Sam, his subtle expressions when discussing Mary clearly indicating that he is hiding a secret. Andrew Duggan makes a smooth villain as Swede while Karen Steele and Valerie French as, respectively, Lucy and Ruby, effectively etch two different types of femininity.

At Woonsocket's Park Theater, *Decision at Sundown* was the supporting feature to Columbia's *The Long Haul*, a tired British programmer with Victor Mature, another good actor whose talents in numerous A movies had been denigrated. Earlier in the year, *The Tall T* suffered a more disgraceful fate at the same theater by playing the bottom of the bill to Columbia's *Hellcats of the Navy* with Ronald Reagan and Nancy Davis, who had no talents to denigrate.

Fred MacMurray, another major star of the 1940s as well as the 1930s, was a versatile leading man who starred in comedies, romances and dramas. Early in his career, he starred in two A Westerns, *Trail of the Lonesome Pine* (1936) and *The Texas Rangers* (1936), as well as *Rangers of Fortune* (1940), which has the trappings of an expensive B movie. In these Westerns, he displayed an affable charm, not unlike his other roles. However, he gave his best performances where he displayed a brittle masculinity beneath a rough exterior and was superb in Billy Wilder's classic *Double Indemnity* (1944). After two decades in films, MacMurray's leading man status had faded somewhat and, beginning in the mid-1950s, he made several B Westerns, including the interesting *At Gunpoint* (1955), directed by Alfred Werker. The Universal-International release, *Gun for a Coward*, is worthy of his talents.

Will Keough is the eldest of three brothers who has had to assume responsibility for his family and their ranch upon the death of his father. This is not an easy task since the ranch has not been profitable. His two younger brothers are the sensitive Bless, who abhors violence, and the rebellious Hade, who has a penchant for gunplay. Bless has not

Gun for a Coward explores the complicated lives of the Keough brothers (Jeffrey Hunter and Fred MacMurray).

only to contend with his undeserved reputation as a coward but also must endure his domineering mother, who has made him feel guilty for his father's death. Bless's guilt is increased when another death occurs during the cattle drive. Will's responsibilities, which include dealing with rustlers and Indians, force him to postpone his marriage to Audra Niven. The postponement displeases Audra, who alone seems to understand Bless. Will's determination saves the ranch but costs him the woman he loves.

Fred MacMurray brings the same conviction to the role of Will Keough that he brought to so many major roles in A movies. Will could have been an unpleasant character because of his insensitivity to Bless's dilemma but, due to the actor's understated performance, he emerges as ultimately sympathetic. MacMurray's expertise is more than evident throughout the movie but particularly in the scenes in which he becomes aware that he has lost Aud and his inner pain is unmistakably conveyed. MacMurray is another one of those great actors who made acting look easy and brought a high degree of professionalism to every performance.

As Bless Keough, Jeffrey Hunter projects both sensitivity and inner strength in a difficult role. Hunter was an earnest actor who seemed to radiate honesty, and this trait made him popular in such Westerns as John Ford's classic *The Searchers* (1956) and Nicholas Ray's *The True Story of Jesse James* (1957), a 20th Century Fox A Western that was released in Providence on the same day as the Universal B Western. Janice Rule makes Aud's change of heart understandable through her growing displeasure with Will's harsh actions, and Josephine Hutchinson turns in a nice portrayal as the well-meaning but embittered mother. Only the overly intense acting style of Dean Stockwell as Hade doesn't quite blend in with the naturalism of the other actors.

Gun for a Coward is directed efficiently in Eastmancolor and CinemaScope by Abner Biberman and features a literate screenplay by R. Wright Campbell. Biberman was a character actor (and acting coach) who played many villains and exotic roles from the 1930s to the 1950s, when he started directing, doing most of his work in television. Campbell was also an occasional actor whose screenplays are

mostly for B movies. The dialogue has an authentic ring to it and the characterizations are nicely developed. A good amount of action occurs in the movie, some of it perfunctory, but it is secondary to the relationships between the family members and the effect of their feelings upon their behavior. The difficulty of running a ranch is depicted realistically, which makes Will's giving priority to business over personal happiness understandable, though regrettable. The movie should have ended on a downbeat note with Will's realization of the cost of his sacrifice instead of the happier ending in which Will rides away to seek some fun. It doesn't ring true, but the movie remains a solid piece of Western entertainment.

At the Park Theater, *Gun for a Coward* was the supporting feature to Universal-International's *Mister Cory*, an early Blake Edwards-directed vehicle with Tony Curtis, one of the studio's most popular stars of the 1950s. MacMurray's movie was advertised with the tag line, "The saga of the Keough brothers who fought together, faced death together, till a red-haired woman drove them apart!" Such a line, complete with exclamation point, is a totally erroneous description of the movie, indicating that studio executives probably didn't even bother to see it.

War hero Audie Murphy's film career lasted for over two decades, during which he appeared in several A films, including his most successful movie, *To Hell and Back* (1955), based upon his autobiography. In the 1950s, he also branched out in his career, starring in a boxing film *The World in My Corner* (1956), a service comedy *Joe Butterfly* (1957), and the political drama *The Quiet American* (1958). However, the majority of his 44 movies are B Westerns, some of which are good examples of the genre and others which are forgettable. In 1959, he starred in the two best B movies of his career.

The Wild and the Innocent is a different kind of Western in which Murphy plays a trapper, Yancy Hawks, who travels from the wilderness to a frontier town to sell his furs. Along the way, he is persuaded by an irresponsible father to take his teenage daughter Rosalie into town with him. Once in town, Sheriff Bartel befriends them but Bartel is also the town boss who disguises his own reasons for giving Rosalie a job with his mistress Marcy. Yancey doesn't understand the kind of establishment Rosalie will be working in or what kind of woman Marcy is, particularly since he is attracted to her. When Yancy finds out the truth, he has to pay a painful price to rescue Rosalie.

This is an appealing and bittersweet movie that concentrates on character development while providing a portrait of people on the brink of civilization that is both mellow and cynical. Jack Sher directs *The Wild and the Innocent* from an original screenplay he wrote with Sy Gomberg. Murphy perfectly conveys just the right amount of naiveté combined with innate wisdom to make Yancy both likeable and believable. As his character matures and learns the ways of civilization, he deftly displays a variety of emotions. In the climactic scenes, his expressions, his speech and even his manner of walking after he has been humiliated by Bartel are indicative of a first-rate actor.

Gilbert Roland gives a fine portrayal of an aging lothario whose dream for his youth masks his tendency to use and discard women. His smooth, seemingly sincere Bartel suggests the dark-shadowed side of roles he played so often since his silent film star days. Joanne Dru gives a poignant performance as a woman who would also like to recapture her innocence but knows it is too late, while Sandra Dee is engaging as Rosalie. The movie is an underrated Western that deserves reevaluation.

Released in the same year, *No Name on the Bullet* stars Murphy in a totally different role but one in which he also excels, thus displaying in these two films the wide range of talent that was generally undeveloped and unappreciated in most of his movies. Audie plays John Gant, a hired killer whose arrival in town causes fear and panic among the residents. Everyone knows by his reputation that Gant kills only for money, and several townspeople appear to have a dark secret in their past that makes them likely candidates to be Gant's next victim.

Gant is not the usual type of killer. He articulately justifies his occupation and he is intelligent enough to avoid arrest for his killings by psychologically pressuring his victims to draw first. As he plays a waiting game and is seemingly amused by the terror he is causing, the townspeople become edgy and paranoid. Alone and aloof from most people, Gant forms an unusual but not unfriendly relationship with Dr. Luke Canfield, with whom he engages in a series of philosophical conversations on the nature of good and evil as well as the right to kill. No clear-cut answers to these questions exist and, as the story progresses, Gant appears more reasonable and honest than most of the townspeople. As the weaknesses and guilt of the citizens are gradually exposed, it becomes clear that they are responsible for their fates. One man commits suicide, two others try to kill one another and several other supposedly law-abiding citizens form a lynch mob that collectively fails to match Gant's courage. All appear to be guilty of something and Gant's presence

appears to be increasingly justified, almost as if he were an avenging angel.

At the film's climax, Gant's intended target is revealed to be the town judge, a model of respectability with a dark past. However, Gant doesn't kill the judge directly. Aware of his victim's failing health, Gant pretends to assault the judge's daughter, which provokes the elderly man into a fatal collapse. Ironically, the self-righteous doctor assumes that Gant has killed the judge and throws a hammer at him, crippling his gun arm. In effect, Gant becomes the sacrificial victim of the sins committed by the townspeople. However, he accepts his fate with his usual cynicism. Indeed, he emerges as morally superior to even Luke as he absolves the repentant doctor of any guilt and rides away to face probable death.

No Name on the Bullet features Audie Murphy in an atypical anti-hero role.

Director and co-producer Jack Arnold is best known for his memorable science fiction films, including two 3-D movies, *It Came from Outer Space* (1953) and *Creature from the Black Lagoon* (1954), as well as *The Incredible Shrinking Man*. Arnold didn't restrict himself to the science fiction genre and, as a studio contract director, helmed virtually all other kinds of movies, including comedies, romances, mysteries and three Westerns. He contributed a natural skill to all of his movies, but he needed a good script and a cast of equal quality to illustrate his expertise.

Filmed in Cinemascope and Eastmancolor, *No Name on the Bullet* has these elements and Arnold's direction allows the drama to unfold smoothly while suspense builds to the harrowing climax. He develops tension, not with action but with the conflict of character between Gant and Luke, as well as between the various possible victims as they interact with one another. The movie has a drive and an impact that is due in part to the sense of fatalism that becomes increasingly predominant as the story progresses. Especially effective is the scene in which Gant visits the judge, who has been awaiting this fateful day for years due to his guilt and shame.

A great deal of the success of the movie comes from the discerning script by Gene Coon. The characterizations are insightful, particularly in presenting the weaknesses of the townspeople as contrasted with Gant's psychological strengths. The dialogue is quite intelligent and thought provoking, yet it never lessens the pace of the story. Virtually every line has a purpose within the context of the story and even scenes without dialogue speak volumes, including the one at the beginning when the elderly frontier couple stares after Gant, who has asked directions. The fear and suspicion in their expressions says all that has to be said and establishes the sense of doom that pervades the film.

The movie is another example of how even studio contract players seem to sense that they are in something other than an average assignment and deliver fine performances. Charles Drake registers moral strength as Dr. Canfield while Warren Stevens and Whit Bissell have excellent individual scenes as possible victims. Joan Evans also makes the judge's daughter a truly sympathetic character as she slowly discovers her father's secret past. And Edgar Stehli is memorable as Judge Benson, projecting self-disgust and shame as his public façade slowly disintegrates.

However, it is Audie Murphy who achieves genuine stature as John Gant in this superior Western. It isn't just the penetrating stare and the sadistic smile that sends chills throughout the townspeople. It is also the deliberately calm manner in which he speaks his lines and the condescension with which he addresses everyone. He projects an arrogant air of self-confidence that contrasts with the quivering voices and shivering figures who come before him, whether singly or in groups. It is an incisive performance from an immensely underrated actor.

At the Park Theater, *No Name on the Bullet* supported Universal-International's A movie *This Earth Is Mine* with Rock Hudson, who was the studio's biggest star, which explains why the overblown soaper got all of the attention. Although only the title and star of the B Western were listed in small letters beneath a large advertisement for the dull main feature, Murphy's movie proved to be far more rewarding. *The Wild and the Innocent* didn't even get to play first-run in Woonsocket and eventually played the bottom of the bill to various features in drive-in theaters in surrounding areas.

As the 1950s passed into history, the end of the B movie was in sight. B Westerns continued to be made in the 1960s but in diminishing numbers. Theaters gradually returned to showing single features as studio executives realized that more showings per day of major features increased their profits. The need for supporting features no longer existed, particularly since television now seemed to provide that kind of less demanding entertainment formerly provided by B movies. In fact, many of the personnel associated with the best B Westerns would eventually venture into television.

However, during the 1960s, the disappearance of the B movie was gradual. In 1962, Randolph Scott and Joel McCrae starred in Sam Peckinpah's classic *Ride the High Country,* which in San Diego played the bottom of the bill to *The Tartars*, an Italian pseudo-spectacle. Scott retired after this movie and McCrae semi-retired, making only a guest appearance in a 1970 movie and starring in his last film in 1976. In 1960, Audie Murphy played a supporting role in an A Western, *The Unforgiven,* and stole the film with a searing performance. He continued to make B Westerns, including a series of above-average movies for Universal, but he also made several trivial movies for other studios. In 1969, Murphy produced and co-starred in a Western for Budd Boetticher entitled *A Time for Dying* after the director's return to Hollywood, but it received only limited distribution. It was the last movie for Murphy, who died soon afterward, and for Boetticher who couldn't rebuild his career.

The 1960s also witnessed the arrival of dozens of Italian, German and Spanish Westerns, which were the equivalent of substandard American B Westerns, only more violent. For marquee value, they often starred American actors, among them Joseph Cotton, John Ireland, Jeffrey Hunter and Audie Murphy, whose Spanish Western was directed at least nominally by Lesley Selander. By the end of the decade, B Westerns were extinct.

With the success of adult television Western series in the mid-1950s, many stars of adult B Western movies made the same journey to home screens that juvenile Western heroes had made earlier in the decade. None of them could dethrone James Arness, who reigned as television's most popular Western star in *Gunsmoke*, which became a television phenomenon during its record-breaking 20-year run. Andrew McLaglen, who had directed Arness in *Gun the Man Down*, subsequently directed over 90 episodes of *Gunsmoke*. Also, Jospeh H. Lewis of *The Halliday Brand* directed two episodes of the series and Abner Biberman of *Gun for a Coward* directed a single episode.

Charles Marquis Warren became producer of *Gunsmoke* for its first year and also produced *Rawhide* and *The Virginian* for limited periods. During the 1960s, Jacques Tourneur concluded his career directing in television, except for a couple of competent but undistinguished programmers.

Jack Arnold worked extensively in television as a producer as well as director throughout the 1960s and 1970s. He also continued to make occasional theatrical films, none of which approached the quality of his work in the 1950s. Andrew McLaglen and writer Burt Kennedy, both of whom graduated to directing A movies in the 1960s and 1970s, eventually returned to television when theatrical Westerns entered a modernist phase.

Surprisingly, Joel McCrae and Audie Murphy failed in their Western series attempts, respectively *Wichita Town* and *Whispering Smith*, due in part to poor scheduling by the networks. Ironically, Ward Bond, who was never the major Western star that McCrae and Murphy were, achieved television fame as the star of the highly successful series, *Wagon Train*. Two episodes featured his former co-star Joseph Cotton. After his death, Bond would be replaced by John McIntire, McCrae's co-star from *Stranger on Horseback*. William Elliott, after retiring from movies in the late 1950s, hosted a weekly television show in Las Vegas in which he presented old movies and interviewed guests. His co-star from *The Showdown*, Walter Brennan, starred in his own successful non-Western series, *The Real McCoys*.

Fred MacMurray, after returning to A movies thanks to Walt Disney and Billy Wilder, had a huge success with *My Three Sons*. Robert Stack was equally successful with *The Untouchables*. His co-star from *War Paint*, Charles McGraw, appeared often on the small screen and was the star of an unsuccessful series based on the movie,

Casablanca. Dana Andrews made numerous guest appearances on dramatic series and starred in a soap opera entitled *Bright Promise* for three years. Joseph Cotton hosted a pair of anthology series and also made frequent guest appearances on dramatic series. John Ireland appeared in over 150 episodes of various series and also became a regular on the Western series *Rawhide* for a couple of years. Ireland's co-star from *Little Big Horn*, Lloyd Bridges, starred in a syndicated series *Sea Hunt*, for several years. His co-star from *Hannah Lee*, Macdonald Carey, also became a star of the soap opera *Days of Our Lives*, remaining with the show for an incredible 30 years. And Arthur Franz made over 200 appearances on various shows over three decades.

The double feature is now a distant memory. Huge movie palaces like the Park Theater in Woonsocket with balconies and giant screens with curtains have been replaced by multiplexes that show single features as many times as possible each day. However, for over three decades, the double feature and the B movie were an enjoyable part of moviegoing. And literally dozens of B Westerns were made every year. The juvenile B Westerns predominated in the 1930s and 1940s, but the adult B Western reached its zenith in the 1950s. Many of these B Westerns are at best average movies that provide minor entertainment. And many are the products of hacks and have no value.

However, some are very fine films that deserve recognition for achieving against all odds an admirable degree of quality and even artistry.

The Showdown [Republic/1950]
CREDITS: Producer: William J. O'Sullivan; Directors: Dorrell McGowan, Stuart McGowan; Screenplay: Dorrell McGowan, Stuart McGowan, based on a story by Dan Gordon and Richard Wormser; Cinematographer: Reggie Lanning; Editor: Harry Keller; Music: Stanley Wilson
CAST: William Elliott (Shadrach Jones); Walter Brennan (Cap Mackellar); Marie Windsor (Adelaide); Henry Morgan (Rod Main); Rhys Williams (Chokecherry); Jim Davis (Cochran); Leif Erickson (Big Mart); William Ching (Mike Shattoy)

Little Big Horn [Lippert/1951]
CREDITS: Producer: Carl K. Hittleman; Director: Charles Marquis Warren; Screenplay: Charles Marquis Warren, based on a story by Harold Schumate; Cinematographer: Ernest W. Miller; Editor: Carl Pierson; Music: Paul Dunlap; Song: "On the Little Big Horn" by Maurice Sigler and Larry Stock
CAST: Lloyd Bridges (Capt. Philip Donlin); John Ireland (Lt. John Haywood); Marie Windsor (Celie Donlin); Reed Hadley (Sgt. Major Grierson); Jim Davis (Cpl. Moylan); Wally Cassell (Pvt. Zecca); Hugh O'Brian (Pvt. DeWalt); King Donovan (Pvt. Corbo); Richard Emory (Pvt. Shovels); John Pickard (Sgt. McCloud)

War Paint [United Artists/1953]
CREDITS: Producer Howard W. Koch; Director: Lesley Selander; Screenplay: Richard Alan Simmons, Martin Berkeley, based on a story by Fred Freiberger and William Tunberg; Cinematographer: Gordon Avil; Editor: John F. Shreyer; Music: Emil Newman, Arthur Lange; Song: "Elaine" by Johnny Lehmann and Emil Newman
CAST: Robert Stack (Lt. Billings); Joan Evans (Wanima); Charles McGraw (Sgt. Clarke); Keith Larsen (Taslik); Peter Graves (Trooper Tolson); Robert Wilke (Trooper Grady); Walter Reed (Trooper Allison); John Doucette (Trooper Charnofsky); Douglas Kennedy (Trooper Clancy); Paul Richards (Trooper Perkins)

Hannah Lee (aka *Outlaw Territory*) [Realart/1953]
CREDITS: Producer: Jack Broder; Directors: Lee Garmes, John Ireland; Screenplay: MacKinlay Kantor, Alford Von Ronkel, based upon a novel by MacKinlay Kantor; Cinematographer: Lee Garmes; Editor: Chester W. Shaeffer; Music: Paul Dunlap; Song: "Hannah Lee" by Stan Jones
CAST: Macdonald Carey (Bus Crow); Joanne Dru (Hallie Mclaird); John Ireland (Sam Rochelle); Harold J. Kennedy (Bainbridge); Stuart Randall (Montgomery); Frank Ferguson (Britton); Ralph Dumke (Alesworth); Peter Ireland (Willie Stiver); Don Haggerty (Crashaw); Tristram Coffin (Paulson); Tom Powers (Sheriff)

Three Hours to Kill [Columbia/1954]
CREDITS: Producer: Harry Joe Brown; Director: Alfred Werker; Screenplay: Richard Alan Simmons, Roy Huggins, with additional dialogue by Maxwell Shane, based on a story by Alex Gottlieb; Cinematographer: Charles Lawton, Jr.; Editor: Gene Havlick; Music: Paul Sawtell
CAST: Dana Andrews (Jim Guthrie); Donna Reed (Laurie Hendricks); Diane Foster (Chris Palmer); Stephen Elliot (Ben East); Richard Coogan (Niles Hendricks); James Westerfield (Sam Minor); Richard Webb (Carter Mastin); Carolyn Jones (Polly); Whit Bissell (Deke)

Stranger on a Horseback [United Artists/1955]
CREDITS: Producer: Robert Goldstein; Director: Jacques Tourneur; Screenplay: Don Martin, Herb Meadow, based on a story by Louis L'Amour; Cinematographer: Ray Rennahan; Editor: William B. Murphy; Music: Paul Dunlap
CAST: Joel McCrae (Judge Rick Thorne); Miroslava (Amy Lee Bannerman); Kevin McCarthy (Tom Bannerman); John McIntire (Josiah Bannerman); Nancy Gates (Caroline); John Carradine (Colonel Streeter); Emile Meyer (Sheriff Bell); Robert Cornthwaite (Arnold Hammer)

Running Target [United Artists/1956]
CREDITS: Producer: Jack Couffer; Director: Marvin R. Weinstein; Screenplay: Marvin R. Weinstein, Jack Couffer, Conrad Hall, based on a story by Steve Frazee; Cinematographer: Lester Schorr; Editor: Carl Lodato; Music: Ernest Gold
CAST: Arthur Franz (Scott); Doris Dowling (Smitty); Richard Reeves (Jaynes); Myron Healey (Kaygo); James Parnell (Pryor); Charles Delaney (Barker); James Anderson (Strothers); Gene Roth (Holeworth); Frank Richards (Castagna)

Gun the Man Down (aka *Arizona Mission*) [United Artists/1957]
CREDITS: Producer: Robert E. Morrison; Director: Andrew V. McLaglen; Screenplay: Burt Kennedy, based on a story by Sam Freedle; Cinematographer: William H. Clothier; Editor: A. Edward Sutherland; Music: Henry Vars
CAST: James Arness (Rem Anderson); Angie Dickinson (Janice); Robert Wilke (Rankin); Don Megowan (Farley); Emile Meyer (Sheriff Morton); Michael Emmett (Billy Deal); Harry Carey, Jr. (Deputy Lee)

The Halliday Brand [United Artists/1957]
CREDITS: Producer: Collier Young; Director: Joseph H. Lewis; Screenplay: George W. George, George F. Slavin; Cinematographer: Ray Rennahan; Editor: Michael Luciano; Music: Stanley Wilson
CAST: Joseph Cotton (Daniel Halliday); Ward Bond (Big Dan Halliday);Viveca Lindfors (Aleta Burris); Betsy Blair (Martha Halliday); Bill Williams (Clay Halliday); Jay C. Flippen (Chad Burris); Christopher Dark (Jivaro Burris); Jeanette Nolan (Nante); Peter Ortiz (Manuel)

Decision at Sundown [Columbia/1957]
CREDITS; Producer: Harry Joe Brown; Director: Budd Boetticher; Screenplay: Charles Lang Jr., based upon a novel by Vernon L. Fluharty; Cinematographer: Burnett Guffey; Editor: Al Clark; Music: Heinz Roemheld
CAST: Randolph Scott (Bart Allison); John Carroll (Tate Kimbrough); Karen Steele (Lucy Summerton); Valerie French (Ruby); Noah Beery (Sam Ridgely); John Archer (Dr. John Storrow); Andrew Duggan (Sheriff Swede Hanson); James Westerfield (Otis); John Litel (Charles Summerton); Ray Teal (Morley Chase); Vaughn Taylor (Baldwin)

Gun for a Coward [Universal-Internatiional/1957]
CREDITS: Producer: William Alland; Director: Abner Biberman; Screenplay: R. Wright Campbell; Cinematographer: George Robinson; Editor: Edward Curtis
CAST: Fred MacMurray (Will Keough); Jeffrey Hunter (Bless Keough); Janice Rule (Aud Niven); Dean Stockwell (Hade Keough); Josephine Huchinson (Hannah Keough); Chill Wills (Loving); Betty Lynn (Claire); Iron Eyes Cody (Chief); Robert Hoy (Danny); Jane Howard (Marie); Marjorie Stapp (Rose); John Larch (Stringer)

No Name on the Bullet [Universal-International/1959]
CREDITS: Producers: Howard Christie, Jack Arnold; Director: Jack Arnold; Screenplay: Gene L. Coon, from a story by Howard Amacker; Cinematographer: Harold Lipstein; Editor: Frank Gross; Music: Herman Stein
CAST: Audie Murphy (John Gant); Charles Drake (Luke Canfield); Joan Evans (Anne Benson); Edgar Stehli (Judge Benson); Warren Stevens (Lou Fraden);Virginia Grey (Roseanne Fraden); R.G. Armstrong (Asa Canfield); Willis Bouchey (Sheriff Hastings); Simon Scott (Henry Reeger); Karl Svenson (Earl Stricker); Whit Bissell (Thad Pierce)

Two Hammer Horror Classics: Dracula Meets the Werewolf

In the middle of the 20th century, two of the best horror movies ever made were produced by Britain's Hammer Film Productions and featured, respectively, Count Dracula and a werewolf. *Dracula*, called *Horror of Dracula* in the United States, was released in 1958 and *The Curse of the Werewolf* was released in 1961. Universal-International, which released the films in the North American market, used lurid advertisements to attract teenage audiences, but the films were totally adult in their approach. *Horror of Dracula* (the U.S. title will be used to differentiate it from other films also titled *Dracula*) was a commercial success, but only by the standards of exploitation films and because it was a relatively inexpensive film to produce. *The Curse of the Werewolf* was a commercial disappointment. Both films are superior to the big-budget horror films of later decades but did not approach the high earnings of those more expensive films because they were produced during a period in which horror movies were not considered worthy of critical discussion or artistic merit. However, these two movies are not only horror classics but classics of filmmaking.

In the history of world cinema, horror movies have enjoyed varying degrees of popularity and critical acceptance. During the silent era of the 1920s, horror movies were lightweight fare in the United States, except for Lon Chaney's films and a few other exceptions, while European cinema produced darker and more imaginative product. In the 1930s, while European films declined in quality, Hollywood product achieved prominence and acclaim with such films as *Dracula*, *Frankenstein* and *The Mummy*, all produced by Universal, the studio that became noted for its horror films. Also during the 1930s Enrique Carreras and William Hinds, who acted under the name of Will Hammer, founded a small British company that came to be known as Hammer Films. The small company produced minor crime thrillers that attracted little attention and most were not exported to the United States.

By the 1940s, the horror genre had lost some of its adult attraction and Hollywood fright films generally declined in quality. A few exceptions appeared, including Universal's *The Wolf Man* in 1941 and the series of films produced by Val Lewton for RKO. But Universal eventually cheapened its classic monsters by putting them all together in monster rallies. In Europe, few horror films were made. In England, World War II interrupted Hammer's production schedule that resumed in the

late 1940s with inexpensive programmers, many based upon successful British radio programs.

By the early 1950s, the horror genre was perhaps at a nadir throughout the world. Universal, the studio that had been the premier producer of horror films, had completed its destruction of its monsters by using them as comedic characters. The European film industry produced some serious films but none that received international distribution. Even younger audiences seemed bored with horror movies and were more interested in science fiction movies, which seemed more imaginative and were perhaps more suitable to the atomic age. By the middle of the decade, mainstream audiences and film critics considered horror movies to be cheap entertainment for undemanding audiences. Considering the quality of product released, this was perhaps an accurate description. And the major studios tended to agree, with the result that few if any serious horror films were released.

That was all about to change due primarily to Hammer Film Productions, which in the mid-1950s began the renaissance of horror films by embarking upon a policy of remaking the great horror classics of the 1930s. In the early 1950s, under the new management of Michael Carreras and Anthony Hinds, sons of the original founders, Hammer's future was uncertain. The film industry around the world was in trouble due to the emergence of television, and a small studio like Hammer was having difficulty making any kind of profit on their undistinguished fillers. However, continuing their policy of adapting successful radio programs to the screen, the company produced a film version of Nigel Kneale's television serial, *The Quatermass Experiment*, a decision which would shape the studio's future. Another significant factor that would influence the company's development was the fortuitous decision to hire director Terence Fisher, whose style would largely be responsible for Hammer's emergence as a premier producer of Gothic horror movies.

Fisher had started in the film industry as a clapper boy, worked his way up to editor and then directed his first film *Colonel Bogey* in 1947. Subsequent films included some A movies which he co-directed (*The Astonished Heart*, *So Long at the Fair*) and various B movies which were mostly thrillers. Though not especially noteworthy, these movies would display an increasing degree of skill as Fisher developed his talents. He joined Hammer in 1951 and continued to make programmers, including two efficient but bland science fiction movies, *Four Sided Triangle* and *Spaceways*. Neither film is notable but they introduced the company to the genre of science fiction, which led to *The Quatermass Experiment* (U.S. title: *The Creeping Unknown*), directed by Val Guest in 1955. This film and a sequel, both of which had horrific elements, were fairly successful, not only in Britain, but also in the lucrative American market. This success led to the decision of Hammer executives to cancel plans for other types of movies and produce their first horror film, a remake of Mary Shelley's novel *Frankenstein*.

Universal's 1932 version of *Frankenstein*, directed by James Whale with Boris Karloff, was and remains a classic horror movie and the idea of remaking it seemed foolhardy. But Hammer was prepared to give the tale a new twist and would add new ingredients of color and graphic detail. Hammer assigned Terence Fisher to direct the movie and it proved to be a perfect blending of subject and director. Fisher was assisted by gifted actors, cinematographers, production designers, film editors and other artisans who displayed talent as well as professionalism in their respective fields. With this film, Fisher helped to develop the style that would become known as "the Hammer look." This consisted of voluptuous use of color to create mood, a carefully calculated atmosphere related to each specific film's theme, authentic recreations of period settings, and precise compositional balance within each sequence.

The movie was titled *The Curse of Frankenstein*. Heading the cast was Peter Cushing, a highly respected actor who had achieved acclaim for television work in England but was not known elsewhere. Ironically, Cushing had made his film debut in the 1939 version of *The Man in the Iron Mask*, directed by James Whale. The man-made creature was played by an unknown actor, Christopher Lee.

When *The Curse of Frankenstein* arrived in 1957, it surprised the industry by becoming a worldwide commercial success, despite some critical condemnation for its relatively gruesome detail in glorious color. Though the film does not approach the classic status of the Whale-Karloff version, it is entertaining. However, it has more than its share of flaws, most prominent of which is the subplot involving Dr. Frankenstein and his maid, which is unnecessary and intrusive. But the adaptation is intelligent and brought new dignity to Mary Shelley's creature, who had been subjected to unjust humiliations in cheap, unimaginative movies. *The Curse of Frankenstein* breathed new life into a much-maligned genre. More significant, it set the stage for the best Dracula film of all time and the studio's first genuine classic.

Flushed with the success of their first horror movie, Hammer immediately started their next production, perhaps inevitably choosing a horror novel as famous as *Frankenstein* for its second film. Bram Stoker's *Dracula* had over the years become linked with Shelley's monster as an equally renowned character of horror. The two creatures were also linked together because they had been the subjects of Universal's two most famous horror films of the early 1930s. However, unlike Universal's Dracula film of 1931, which was based upon the play of the same name, Hammer's version would be based directly upon the novel.

Published in 1897, Stoker's novel chronicles the vampire king's attempt to extend his reign of terror from his home country of Transylvania to Victorian England. The novel begins with lawyer Jonathan Harker's visit to Dracula's castle to complete the Count's purchase of a home in England. The Count initially makes a somewhat normal impression, being described as "a tall, old man, clean-shaven save for a long white moustache, thin with a pallor except for full red lips."

Stoker, who was famous in his lifetime as the manager of the Lyceum Theater in London, wrote numerous works of nonfiction in addition to romances and children's stories. He also wrote two other horror novels, *The Jewel of the Seven Stars* in 1903, which has been filmed twice, once by Hammer, and *The Lair of the White Worm* in 1911, which has also been filmed. However, *Dracula* is his masterpiece and the work for which he will always be remembered. Although upon its publication many literary critics considered it second-rate literature due to its subject matter, it has since been recognized for its merits. This recognition was long overdue, for the novel is exceedingly well-written. Told through journals, recordings, diaries and newspaper clippings, the novel skillfully depicts events through several perspectives, all of which eventually converge.

Stoker expertly touches upon the universal fear that human beings have always had of vampires, who have been a part of folklore in virtually every part of the world since the dawn of civilization. The author cleverly establishes a realistic background for his story by providing detailed descriptions of each locale, actual geographic statistics and even accurate train schedules. His characters are also credible, except possibly for Quincey Morris, who is almost a caricature. Stoker's fondness for America probably caused the inclusion of the character, though his presence does not destroy the mood of the novel. However, it is the character of Dracula, one of the most evil creations in the history of literature, and his effect upon all of the other characters and upon society that is responsible for the novel's enduring popularity.

In view of later film adaptations of the novel, it should perhaps be noted that Stoker's Dracula is not supposed to be the historical Vlad Dracula of the 15th century. In the novel, Dracula does provide allusions to Vlad in his conversations with Harker, and Van Helsing states in one passage that "he must have been that Voivode, Prince Dracula, who won his name against the Turks." But Stoker only used these references to provide a background of brutality for his character. Vlad Tepes was notorious for his savagery, which included torturing and murdering over a hundred thousand men, women and children. He delighted in inflicting excruciating agony and was not capable of any kind of love or devotion that is depicted in some films. Indeed, he butchered one of his many mistresses when she told him she was pregnant. He was also known as The Impaler because that was his favorite form of torture, and he impaled innumerable people near his castle just so he could listen to their screams

In her definitive biography of the author entitled *Bram Stoker* (Knopf; 1996), Barbara Belford illustrates the genesis of the novel and the development of the character of Dracula. "Dracula is not Vlad Tepes," Belford writes, "only a novelist's interpretation of him." Belford relates the factors involved in the creation of Dracula, including Stoker's lifelong fears, fantasies and interests as well as his research into vampire mythology. Stoker was also influenced by previous vampire fiction such as John Polidori's *The Vampire*, Sheridan Lefanu's *Carmilla* and James Roymer's *Varney the Vampire*. Actually, Stoker originally set his novel in Styria, the setting of *Carmilla*, and only later placed Dracula's castle in Transylvania, a province in Romania that was adjacent to Vlad's

Wallachia. Most significantly, despite the name and the background of extreme cruelty, Stoker never intended for any details of Vlad's personal life to have an impact upon the course of his novel. Stoker used Vlad's barbarism but not his life as a background for his fictional creation, a distinction that later screenwriters would miss.

Since its publication, *Dracula* has never been out of print. This fame has naturally extended to the motion picture screen. Indeed, Dracula has appeared in more than two hundred films from around the world. However, less than a dozen of these movies have actually been directly based upon the novel, due possibly to its length and scope as well as its large number of major characters and its period setting.

The first film version of the novel was *Nosferatu*, a German production directed by F.W. Murnau in 1921 which is often considered a classic of silent cinema. Since it was an unauthorized version, the names and settings were changed for legal reasons, through this did not stop Stoker's widow from successfully suing the producers. In *Nosferatu*, a real estate clerk named Hutter leaves his home in Bremen to travel to the castle of Count Orlock to complete the Count's purchase of a home in Bremen. Hunter ignores the strange behavior of the Count, who is soon revealed to be a Nosferatu (Slavic for vampire). Hutter becomes a victim of Orlock but escapes after discovering the vampire sleeping in his coffin. Orlock travels by ship to Bremen and kills everyone aboard. Once he arrives at his new home, pestilence and death follow him. Orlock is attracted to Hutter's wife, Ellen, who sacrifices herself to his bloodlust and forces him to stay with her until after the sun has risen. Ellen dies but not until after Orlock is destroyed by the rays of the sun.

Nosferatu is held in high esteem by film historians, due primarily to Murnau's Expressionistic direction. The movie unfolds in a darkly poetic manner as the director and his cinematographer create nightmarish images through the fusion of shadows and light. The physical appearance of Orlock is loathsome and quite unlike Stoker's description of Dracula. With his bald head, pointed ears, serpentine teeth and cadaverous facial features, he looks more animalistic than human. As portrayed by Max Shreck (reportedly a pseudonym for German actor Alfred Abel; "shreck" means terror in German), Orlock exudes evil and his appearance is accompanied by a feeling of nausea. In general, the other characters, including Van Helsing (called Professor Bulwer), are relegated to secondary status by the director's striking visual style and the overt allegorical aspects of the story. Melodramatic in spots, *Nosferatu* is worth seeing for the director's sheer technical virtuosity. However, the film doesn't retain the ability to fully satisfy as true silent classics like Murnau's own *Sunrise* (1927) or Alfred Hitchcock's *The Lodger* (1926) still do. This film, incidentally, is the first version to feature the destruction of a vampire by sunlight, which in the novel only weakens Dracula. This would subsequently become a part of vampire folklore, at least in movies.

In 1927, three years after it premiered in Derby, Hamilton Deane's stage version of Stoker's novel opened in London and was an immediate success. The playwright necessarily modified and condensed the novel's numerous settings and characters to make it acceptable for the theater stage. The entire play is set in 19th-century London, mostly in Jonathan Harker's home, with an epilogue in Dracula's home in Carfax. In 1929, Deane collaborated with John Balderston on an American version which opened on Broadway with Hungarian actor Bela Lugosi in the title role. This version, set in modern London, takes place in Seward's asylum, Lucy's bedroom and Dracula's vault.

Once again, the play was enormously successful and led to a film version two years later, with Lugosi repeating his portrayal.

The film version of *Dracula*, directed by Tod Browning, was Universal's biggest commercial success of the year and inaugurated the horror explosion in the cinema. Unfortunately, the movie follows the play closely, with the result that the film is stagebound. The first sequence in which Renfield, who takes Harker's place in this version, visits Dracula's castle is taken from the novel and has a suitably eerie atmosphere that the rest of the film lacks. Dracula's introduction and Renfield's encounters with the three vampire women are handled effectively, thanks in part to Karl Freund's cinematography. The next sequence aboard the ship that takes Dracula and his coffins to England is also skillfully helmed and builds enormously to the final shot of Renfield, who has been driven insane after helping his master feed off the ship's crew.

Once the setting shifts to England, the film becomes overly verbose and the pace falters. Indeed, much of the action takes place off screen and is related by various characters. The scenes in which Dracula attacks Lucy, turning her into one of the undead, and then turns his attention to Mina are not as compelling as they would be if they had been more cinematic. This also applies to the final scenes in which Van Helsing tracks Dracula to his vault and destroys him with a stake, freeing Mina of her curse.

However, Lugosi's performance is memorable and he is quite convincing at projecting pure malevolence. He occasionally appears to overact, but this is probably because he was more accustomed to acting on a stage than in front of a camera. Edward Van Sloane as Van Helsing also recreated his role from Broadway and is properly professorial, though he also is a bit hammy at times. As Renfield, Dwight Frye chews the scenery as gleefully as he chews bugs. Because of its theatrical origins, *Dracula* has lost some of its power and seems somewhat dated today, quite unlike Universal's production of James Whale's *Frankenstein* later in the year, which remains a superlative example of cinematic horror. The Spanish-language version of *Dracula*, with George Metford directing and Carlos Villarias imitating Lugosi in the title role, was filmed simultaneously and, although some scenes are not as static and the sensuality is slightly more overt, it is basically a reproduction of Browning's version.

The success of *Dracula* guaranteed sequels and imitators. *Dracula's Daughter* (1935) and *Son of Dracula* (1942) are both interesting but, as profits dwindled, Universal would soon put all of its monsters together in films like *House of Frankenstein* and *House of Dracula*, which were aimed at a younger audience. Universal was never a studio known for loyalty to its film characters or their fans and, as a result, both Dracula and Frankenstein would soon be reduced to menacing Abbott and Costello. As a final insult, during the 1950s, the studio used the images of their most famous monsters, including Dracula, as the basis for an unfunny comedy series *The Munsters*. In addition to Universal's deplorable treatment of the vampire king, the over-familiarity of Dracula's name in cheap, exploitation movies also helped to significantly reduce the stature of his name as a serious horror character.

In 1956, one attempt to treat the novel seriously arrived, but this was on television as an episode of *Matinee Theater*, a daily one-hour anthology show that was telecast live on NBC-TV. John Carradine, who had played Dracula in the two Universal monster rally sequels and who approximated Stoker's description of the Count in his physical appearance, again played Dracula in this truncated telecast.

It was at this point in time that Hammer films made the momentous decision to resurrect Dracula from the ashes of ignominy and treat him with the dignity and respect befitting one of literature's most enduring creations. At this period, when it seemed like the name Dracula had lost its ability to frighten even children, the vampire king was about to reclaim his throne with a fury and a passion that would terrify audiences all over the world. Having no desire to break up a winning team, Hammer assembled the production personnel and major actors from *The Curse of Frankenstein* to work on their second major horror film. These craftsmen had served their apprenticeship on the first film and had sharpened their skills while exploring new territory and becoming skilled artisans.

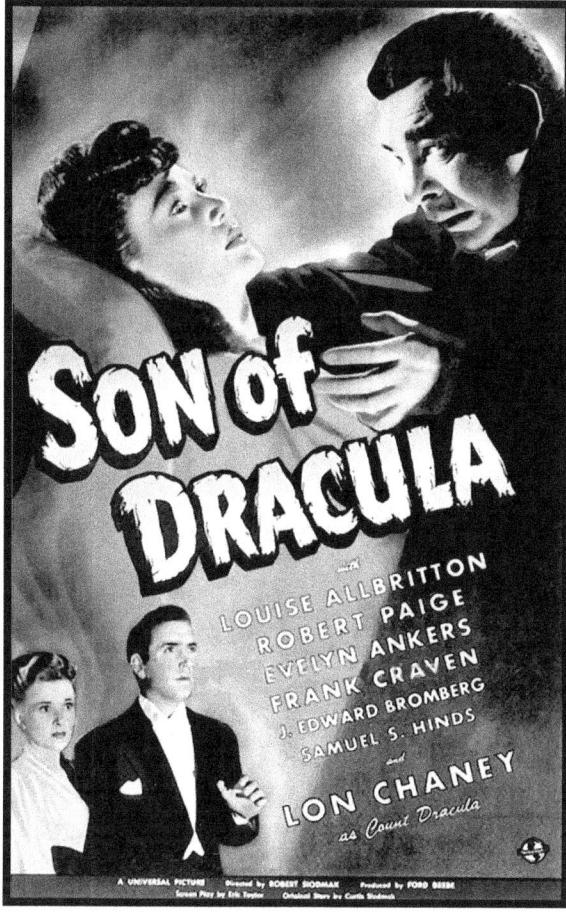

Hammer's production of *Horror of Dracula* was released in 1958 and it is this version by which all others pale in comparison. It is an excellent film by any standards and it was the inspiration for scores of other movies from around the globe that would follow. It certified Terence Fisher as a director of distinction and stars Peter Cushing and Christopher Lee as a horror team, as well as fine actors.

The expertise that permeates the movie begins with the superb screenplay by Jimmy Sangster, whose adaptation is a paradigm of efficiency. Many changes occur from the novel and the plot is considerably condensed. In this version, Lucy is Jonathan Harker's fiancée and Arthur Holmwood's sister while Mina is Arthur's wife. The motivations of major characters are altered significantly. Harker visits Dracula's castle to destroy him. Dracula attacks Lucy for revenge against Harker and then attacks Mina for revenge against Holmwood. The setting is also modified. Dracula's castle is near the village of Klausenburgh, as in the novel, but the other major characters live not in London but in Karlstadt, through their manners and appearance remain distinctly Victorian. They appear to be separated from Dracula's homeland by only a frontier border. No sea voyage is needed in this film, no Renfield and, thankfully, no Quincey Morris, while Dr. Seward is reduced to being a minor character. Nevertheless, such major changes do

not alter the basic substance of the novel. Sangster's script fully captures the essence of Stoker's work and remains true to the author's vision.

This also applies to the character of Dracula who, despite changes, remains Stoker's personification of evil. However, he is incapable of transformations, thus making his battle of wits and strength with his adversary more credible and exciting. It makes him more human as well and therefore more terrifying because of his thirst for blood. Van Helsing is also transformed from Stoker's elderly Dutch gentleman to a more vigorous opponent for the vampire king. The conflict between these two powerful and cunning antagonists, representatives of Christianity and evil, propels the film, as it does the novel.

The script also includes many subtexts that are present in the novel. For instance, the contrast between Dracula's initial appearance as a nobleman and his subsequent return from nocturnal bloodlust conveys the impression that he represents an aristocratic social order that preys upon the lower classes, feeding upon them to gratify his perverted desires. Stoker's implicit eroticism is more explicit and the attraction that evil offers for the virtuous is imparted quite distinctly. Also, the clear implication exists that, beneath the orderly and polite Victorian society that is proud of its scientific rationalism, demonic forces are constantly attempting to break through the fragile curtain that separates them. And the author's religious allegories are conveyed symbolically as well as overtly. It is interesting that the representatives of Christianity are depicted as being necessarily as equally brutal and destructive as the forces of darkness.

Horror of Dracula begins with Jonathan Harker's visit to Dracula's castle, ostensibly to catalog his library. Count Dracula initially appears to be a courteous host and is even solicitous about his guest's welfare. However, Dracula's true nature is quickly revealed to the unfortunate Harker, who pays the ultimate price for destroying the

Jonathan Harker (John Van Eyssen) meets a vampire (Valerie Gaunt) at Dracula's castle.

vampire's mate. Harker's colleague, Dr. Van Helsing, soon arrives and is able to release Harker from the fate of the undead, but he is unable to locate Dracula. The doctor brings the news of Harker's death to the Holmwoods and is suspicious upon learning that Lucy is suffering from an enigmatic illness. Van Helsing quickly realizes that she has become a victim of Dracula, who diabolically intends to replace the vampire bride that Harker destroyed with Lucy. Van Helsing is unable to convince a skeptical Holmwood of the vampire's existence and Lucy dies from Dracula's bloodlust. Soon afterward, the young child of a servant reports the presence of a strange woman near the graveyard who beckons to her. Under Van Helsing's guidance, Holmwood is shocked to learn that the woman is Lucy, and the two men free her from Dracula's curse by driving a stake through her heart. However, Dracula continues to outwit them and, despite their elaborate plan to protect Mina, Dracula is able to make Mina his next victim. But Van Helsing locates Dracula's resting place and sanctifies the coffin, forcing the vampire to race back to his castle with Mina as his captive. Van Helsing and Holmwood are only moments behind Dracula, who intends to conceal himself and Mina within the castle's many hidden dungeons. A vicious fight between Van Helsing and Dracula ensues in which the Count almost triumphs but is destroyed by sunlight and the symbol of the cross, thus freeing Mina's soul.

Terence Fisher's direction of *Horror of Dracula* is inspired. Though the movie was attacked upon its original release by critics for its allegedly graphic violence, which is mild by later standards, Fisher does not rely on such effects for horror. It is the film's haunting mood and uncanny atmosphere that creates a genuine sense of terror through-

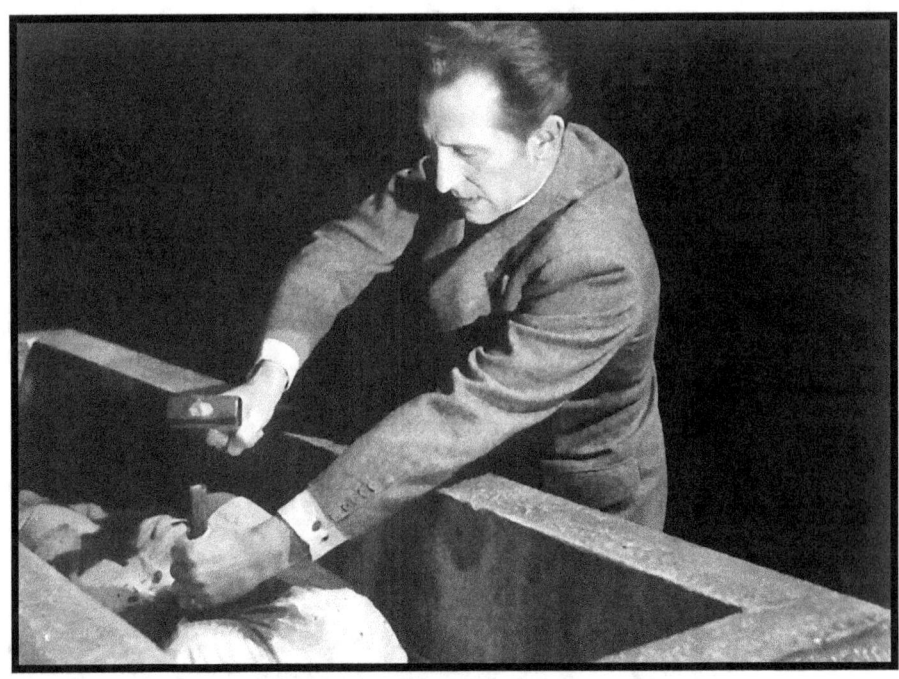

Peter Cushing is absolutely impeccable as Van Helsing.

out the story and affects the viewer on a visceral as well as external level. From the beginning, a sense of unease and discomfort accompanies Harker as he approaches and enters Dracula's castle, but it is not for the expected reasons. No cobwebs, no creaky stairs, no bats flying around. Indeed, the surroundings are quite elegant and the host appears rather cultured. Yet this feeling of unease never leaves and grows stronger during the course of the film, regardless of whether the setting is a dark vault or an orderly Victorian sitting room.

Far more horrifying than the explicit staking of Lucy, which caused much critical condemnation, is the sequence in Dracula's crypt in which Harker makes the fatal mistake of destroying the wrong vampire and then realizes that he is trapped by Dracula as he views his empty crypt. Equally memorable is the expression on Lucy's face as she awaits her dream lover, who is slowly killing her. And then Mina's suggestive smile appears as she greets her husband after becoming Dracula's latest victim. Such scenes illustrate that Fisher is equally adept at creating moments of emotional and psychological horror as well as physical horror. He also masterfully conveys subdued sensuality and imparts eroticism without gratuitous exploitation. Furthermore, each scene is imbued with an added dimension due to the director's unpredictable and occasional distracting sense of camera position. But this isn't just a horror film. It is a thriller and an adventure film in which the pace rarely stops. Exciting scenes alternate with scenes of unbearable tension. Conflicts and dangers gradually increase and the film accelerates to a climax that is positively cathartic.

Peter Cushing is absolutely impeccable as Van Helsing, despite the fact that he does not fit Stoker's description of the character. He brings sincerity and assuredness to the role and achieves stature equal to that of his adversary, a feat that is unique in a

Dracula movie in which the vampire usually dominates the proceedings. The integrity he conveys is essential in attaining audience believability. Cushing's Van Helsing is a determined man who is quite meticulous in his obsession to destroy the vampire king, and he will not allow anyone or anything to stand in his way. Impatient at times and arrogant at other times, he can also be gentle and compassionate. The performance not only inspires credibility but admiration. Audiences want him to win this battle, to succeed in his quest, even though the odds seem to be against him. Cushing's portrayal is so noteworthy that all other actors who would subsequently play the role, including such acclaimed luminaries as Laurence Olivier and Anthony Hopkins, have faded into the background with their inferior performances.

Complementing Cushing perfectly is Christopher Lee, whose interpretation of Dracula is mesmerizing. Though his appearance also does not fit Stoker's description, he completely projects the embodiment of evil which is the essence of the character. Lee's Dracula is demonic and bestial, yet he is also dignified and seductive. Initially appearing as a stately aristocrat whose only apparent interest is to enhance his aesthetics, he is later equally credible as a ferocious beast, hissing like a reptile and oozing blood from his mouth and eyes. Lee makes such a forcible impression in these opening scenes that, although he is subsequently on screen for a relatively brief period of time, his presence is powerfully felt throughout the entire film. This is remarkable since he does not have any dialogue after the opening scenes. (Dracula's appearances in this film are approximately the same in percentage as his appearance in print. In the original edition of the novel, he appears in 62 out of 390 pages.) And it is to Lee's credit that beneath the savagery is an occasional subtle implication of sadness. His vampire does not want sympathy or any kind of human emotion. He accepts his solitude just as he accepts his evil, but the connotation is part of his three-dimensional portrayal. Lee's Dracula is the definitive portrayal and has no peer.

Fisher, Cushing and Lee are surrounded by first-rate talent. Michael Gough as Holmwood, Melissa Stribling as Mina, Carol Marsh as Lucy and John Van Eyssen as Harker all bring commitment and depth to their roles. The superior production qualities of the film do not reflect its modest cost. The cinematography features liberal use of color that is often lush and sometimes muted, depending upon each scene's requirement. The production design contains irreproachable

Christopher Lee as Dracula complements Peter Cushing perfectly.

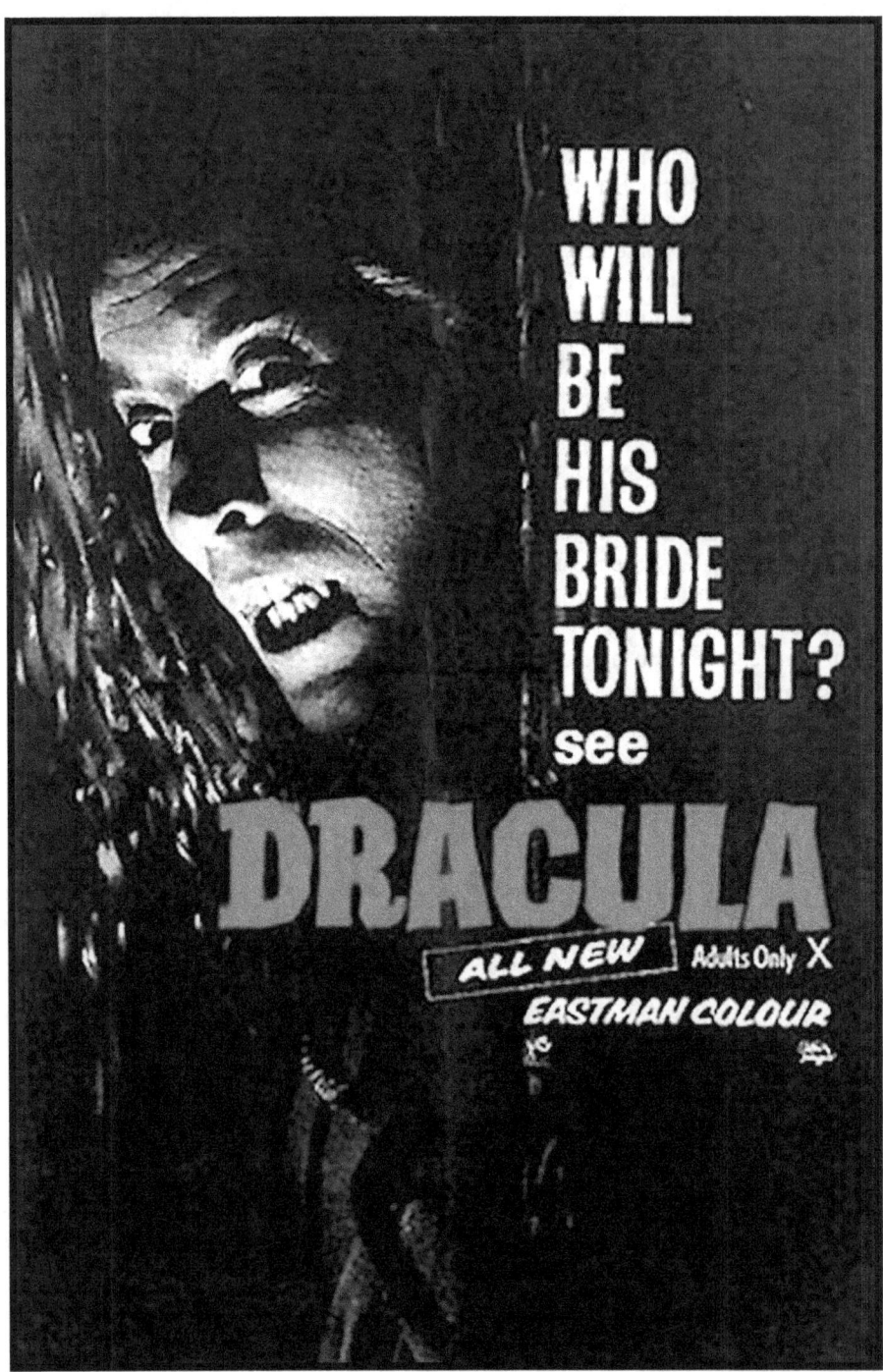

period detail; the domesticity of Victorian society exudes authenticity, while Dracula's castle conveys something sinister beneath the surface décor. The editing contributes immeasurably to the brisk pace of the film. James Bernard's richly textured score adroitly augments the macabre visuals, particularly with a resonant theme for Dracula. All of the members of the Hammer team merge their talents to create a superior piece of entertainment and a horror classic.

Horror of Dracula made a profit because of its relatively inexpensive cost. Its success in Great Britain was duplicated in the United States, but only compared to other horror films. Universal-International treated it as just another exploitation film, releasing it as the top feature of a double bill over *The Thing That Couldn't Die*, a cheap horror movie about a severed head. Most advertisements showed a menacing face with red dots for eyes staring down at a half-clad blonde woman who looks as though she is wearing a 1950s-type nightgown. The tag line asked the question: "Who will be his bride tonight?" Nothing in the ads indicated that the movie was an adaptation of Stoker's novel and there was nothing to distinguish it from *The Return of Dracula*, an inferior B movie released the same year, or even *Blood of Dracula*, a trashy teenage movie released the previous year.

In actuality, despite its merits, *Horror of Dracula* just barely made *Variety*'s Top Rental Films of the Year list at Number 72 with North American theatrical rentals of $1 million. While certainly good for a horror film in 1958, such earnings placed it at the bottom of the list, way beneath such movies as *The Geisha Boy* and *Rock-A-Bye Baby*, both with Jerry Lewis and which earned rentals of over $3.3 million. Other genre films of the year earned more money at the box office, including *The Fly* ($1.7 million) and *The Blob* ($1.1 million), while even such drivel as William Castle's *Macabre* ($1.2 million) was higher on the list. By comparison, the top movie of the year, *South Pacific*, earned $15 million. Sadly, in the year 1958, horror movies and the character of Dracula were considered juvenile fare and the movie was considered pure exploitation. *Horror of Dracula* was the right film at the wrong time.

Nevertheless, the success of *Horror of Dracula* led to several sequels. The first, *The Brides of Dracula* (1960), featured Cushing without Lee and the second, *Dracula—Prince of Darkness* (1965), featured Lee without Cushing. Both are directed by Terence Fisher and, though not up to the level of the first film, are distinctive horror movies well worth seeing. Subsequently, without Fisher and Cushing and with inferior scripts, the series steadily declined, though Lee repeatedly tried to invest his characterization with integrity. The two penultimate films in the series reunited Cushing and Lee but, with modern settings and youth-oriented plots, are terrible. The last film in the series takes Dracula to the Orient and, despite Cushing's presence, is a sad end to the series. (Hammer's Frankenstein series fared better, which is ironic since the first film in the series is not a classic. Fisher and Cushing kept the Frankenstein sequels refreshing and inventive. The two films in the series not directed by Fisher are notably inferior with Cushing's presence in one of them its only asset.)

Despite its premier position as the best Dracula film, *Horror of Dracula* did not pretend to be a completely faithful adaptation of the novel. In view of this, a Spanish-Italian-German-British co-production entitled *Count Dracula* was released in 1970 and was publicized as the first version to faithfully adapt the novel. Christopher Lee, who had been expressing dissatisfaction with the poor quality of his Hammer sequels as well as his desire to play the Count as envisioned by Stoker, once again portrayed the title role. However, with so many countries represented and with a low budget that was apparent, particularly in contrast to the Hammer productions that always looked more expensive than they were, the film turned out to be a muddle. The movie does attempt to adhere closely to the novel, through there are inevitable changes. Here again is Harker's visit to Dracula's castle, the three vampire women, and Dracula's journey to England. In this version, Van Helsing is the director of an asylum and Harker becomes a patient along with Renfield. No Arthur Holmwood, no Dr. Seward appears, though Quincey Morris is present. Dracula victimizes Lucy and attacks Mina before fleeing back to his castle with Van Helsing, Harker and Morris in pursuit. The heroes battle Dracula's Gypsy protectors and then destroy the vampire in his coffin with fire.

A summary of the plot sounds exciting but, on screen, it is dull and unconvincing, due in part to Jess Franco's dispiritingly routine direction which fails to convert Stoker's visions into cinematic terms. Despite some dialogue taken directly from the novel, the script is lackluster, while spurious sets and terrible music add to the film's negligible effect. Lee, sporting white hair and a long moustache before being gradually rejuvenated by the blood of his victims, fits Stoker's description and gives a good performance, but it is of no avail amidst the poor production qualities. Herbert Lom is only adequate as Van Helsing while the rest of the cast is dreary, except for Klaus Kinski, who seems to be enjoying himself as a maniacal Renfield. Actual horror is sparse and the turgid action scenes only serve to hamper the film's minimal momentum.

Also in 1970, the BBC in England presented a television adaptation of the novel as part of a mystery anthology series. Denholm Elliot was miscast in the title role and the production left little impression.

Jack Palance, an actor with a menacing presence, could have been quite imposing as Dracula in the right production. Regrettably, the 1974 television film based upon the novel is not that production. Telecast on CBS-TV and subsequently released theatrically in other countries, this is a disappointing version because the teleplay was written by Richard Matheson, one of the best writers of science fiction and fantasy. Matheson is the author of the 1954 novel, *I Am Legend*, an excellent story of modern vampirism which has been filmed twice as *The Last Man On Earth* (1964) and *The Omega Man* (1971), badly both times. He also wrote the memorable short story, "Blood Son," which is about a boy obsessed with Dracula.

In view of his credentials, Matheson should have had a firm understanding of the novel. Therefore, it is inexplicable that his Dracula is an evil but sympathetic figure who mourns for his lost love and who regrets

Jack Palance

his status as a vampire. This misconception is accompanied by absurd flashbacks of Dracula, incorrectly identified as Vlad Tepes, as a loving husband with the love of his life, Maria. Other scenes showing the Count's expression of self-disgust as he is about to sink his teeth into a victim's neck are equally absurd. Matheson's script also eliminates many of his supernatural abilities in a further attempt to make him more sympathetic.

Within this preposterous framework, the script follows the novel to some degree though it does not include Dr. Seward, Renfield or Quincey Morris. Harker visits Dracula in his castle, encounters the vampire women, and is turned into one of the undead. Dracula becomes obsessed with Lucy upon seeing her photograph and noting her resemblance to Maria. He then travels to England to recapture his lost love by turning Lucy into a vampire. After Lucy is destroyed by Van Helsing, Dracula is not pleased and wreaks vengeance upon everyone in his path, including Mina, who becomes his next victim. After Van Helsing sanctifies the Count's coffins, Dracula dashes back to his castle, where Van Helsing and Holmwood destroy him with sunlight and a stake.

It is not surprising that this film is directed by Dan Curtis, who had previously reduced vampire mythology to soap opera with his saccharine *Dark Shadows*, since so many soap operatic elements appear in this version. Palance tries hard and, though he is powerful in scenes in which he displays ferocity, he is not credible in other scenes in which Curtis requires him to be a warmer and fuzzier bloodsucker. Nigel Davenport is a sincere Van Helsing, but the other actors merely walk through their roles. Basically, the film fails because the routine material is bogged down even further by unimaginative direction. Soap opera and horror do not mix. Furthermore, Dracula is not supposed to be a reluctant vampire suffering from angst. More significantly, Vlad Tepes did not achieve infamy because of his benevolence or his romantic tendencies.

Incidentally, Dracula and Frankenstein always seem to follow one another. A few months earlier NBC-TV presented a television movie entitled *Frankenstein: The True Story*, which was also released theatrically in other countries. The movie contained little truth and less Shelley. It is regrettable that the estates of Bram Stoker and Mary Shelley cannot receive royalties from such bastardizations of the original works.

Ironically, Jack Palance with his distinctive features would fail as Dracula while the urbane Louis Jourdan would succeed, which validates the necessity of engaging first-rate production personnel and filmmakers who have an understanding of the novel. In 1978, the BBC presented a television adaptation of the novel with Jourdan in the title role. Entitled *Count Dracula*, the three-hour production was telecast on PBS in the United States and emerged as a terrifying experience. Director Philip Saville creates a disturbing atmosphere throughout the telefilm and, despite the limitations of the small screen, engenders some moments of pure horror. The teleplay followed the novel scrupulously and again depicted Harker's ill-fated journey to Transylvania and Dracula's subsequent attempt to populate England with vampires. All of the novel's major characters are here, including Quincey Morris, whose Texas accent seems more out of place than usual. The religious allegories of the novel receive emphasis and many lines of dialogue are taken directly from the novel. As Dracula, Jourdan conveys decadence and evil effectively while Frank Finlay makes a formidable Van Helsing. While restriction to studio sets and a slow pace hamper the overall effectiveness of the film, this production is the best television adaptation of the novel.

The year 1979 witnessed two cinematic versions of the novel. Two years earlier, the Deane-Balderston play had been successfully revived on Broadway with Frank Langella

Frank Langella provides a good performance as Dracula but is simply not Stoker's Dracula.

in the title role. (Strangely, a London revival with Terence Stamp, who should have been a great Dracula, failed dismally.) Langella recreated his role in Universal's new film version entitled *Dracula* with a portrayal that emphasizes his charm and seductive appeal at the expense of the character's evil side. The script by W.D. Richter, based on both the play and the novel, seems uncertain as to whether Dracula is a villain or a hero, leaving it up to Langella to emphasize his positive side. This conception might have provided an interesting variation of the theme if the film didn't also include an abundance of special effects illustrating Dracula's transformations into a bat and a wolf, making Lucy's romantic attraction to him somewhat absurd, if not kinky. The attractiveness of evil is one of Stoker's themes, but this film tries to make evil's appeal understandable by infusing it with love, which is not what Stoker intended. (Actually, the theme of a woman being attracted to Dracula is developed far more believably in Universal's 1943 movie, *The Son of Dracula*, which presents the heroine as always having been obsessed with perversion and the supernatural.)

Within the encumbrance of the script's many flaws, the movie presents the familiar plot developments, from Harker's ill-fated journey to Dracula's ocean voyage and to his encounters with Lucy, Mina, Dr. Seward and, of course, Dr. Van Helsing. In this version, Lucy is Van Helsing's daughter, who is supposed to make the conflict between the two adversaries more personal, but it doesn't work. The finale has Dracula being pursued by Van Helsing and company only to seemingly perish from the rays of the sun on the mast of a ship, with the hint of his survival delighting Lucy.

The unfocused script isn't aided by the conventional direction of John Badham, who seems incapable of creating the necessary atmosphere of terror. Since romance predominates, little suspense can be found and the thrills rely on special effects that are always a poor substitute for genuine horror. Transforming the female characters into liberated women may have been fashionable, but it negates the spirit of the novel in which the proper Victorian women were contrasted with the sensual vampire women. Also, in the novel, Mina disapproves of liberated women, whom she states "make a muddle out of things." Langella provides a good performance but it is simply not Stoker's Dracula. Laurence Olivier (who as a close friend of Peter Cushing gave him a role in *Hamlet* in 1948 and invited him to tour Australia with his Old Vic company) shamelessly overacts as Van Helsing. The rest of the cast is unremarkable and the film is unsatisfactory.

By this time, however, the major studios had embraced horror as a legitimate genre. The success of movies like *Rosemary's Baby* in 1968 and, especially, *The Exorcist* in 1973 had made horror not only acceptable but profitable. Horror was no longer restricted to inexpensive exploitation films and audiences were filling theaters showing horror movies. As a result, this *Dracula*, though not the blockbuster the studio had hoped for, was fairly successful and earned domestic theatrical rentals of $10 million with a gross of almost $25 million. The poor quality of the movie was irrelevant to its success, which was due to timing. If Hammer's superior version had been released during this period, it would have achieved the success and recognition it deserved.

Just a few months later, *Nosferatu the Vampire* was released. Directed by Werner Herzog, this German remake of the silent film is very funereal and somber. By this time, no legal obstacles remained to using Stoker's names, so the vampire is not Orlock but Dracula and, using virtually the same make-up as Max Shreck, again presents a subhuman appearance. This Dracula seems to be crying out for love and human contact that has been denied him due to his repugnant appearance. The plot is similar to the original and, indeed, many scenes seem to be painstaking replicates of those in the silent film. However, with the addition of color and sound, the sequences lack the dream-like quality of the original and some scenes, like the one in which Harker cuts his thumb, are unintentionally comical. As in the original, Dracula journeys to Bremen accompanied by disease and death until Harker's wife, Lucy, sacrifices herself to the vampire.

Klaus Kinski is effectively pathetic as Dracula, but it is Murnau's character, not Stoker's. Walter Ladengast is Van Helsing, but it is a supporting role since the character is ineffectual. Basically, this film seems more interested in paying reverent homage to its predecessor than in telling its own story. As a result, it is technically interesting but it fails as a horror movie. However, it attracted curious patrons on the art circuit.

In 1992, *Bram Stoker's Dracula* was released and proclaimed as the first totally faithful version of the novel. Actually, the film, directed by Francis Ford Coppola, is extraordinarily unfaithful to the novel and is probably the most ludicrous as well as the most expensive version. The film is scuttled by a gratingly modern and dishonest script, half-baked direction, rudimentary characterizations and wretched miscasting, particularly in the title role. As Dracula, Gary Oldman projects neither evil nor authority, only unintentional laughter when he overplays key scenes or when he is saddled with a bouffant hairdo that makes him look both matronly and loony. It is a ridiculous portrayal, certainly not Stoker's tall, clean-shaven old man with a long moustache. The supporting cast is equally unconvincing, with a particularly irritating Winona Ryder looking like a reject from *Gidget Meets Dracula* and having nothing at all in common with Stoker's Mina. Keanu Reeves as Harker gives the impression that he is looking for a surfboard. Only Anthony Hopkins tries to project some credibility to his role of Van Helsing, though he joins Olivier in Peter Cushing's shadow.

While all of the film versions of the novel have altered the source material to some extent, only this one vociferously pretended to be the definitive version. After an invented prologue involving Vlad Tepes which displays an ignorance of Stoker's intentions and establishes a fraudulent tone for the entire film, the script by James V. Hart follows the basic outline of the novel, but is filled with inaccuracies and infidelities which misinterpret the novel while mutating its themes and characters. Stoker's novel is about good versus evil, light versus darkness, Christianity versus Satanism. Dracula represents pure evil and bloodlust, not love and sentiment. Converting the vampire king into a bereaved husband who pines for the reincarnation of his lost wife totally miscalculates the author's intentions.

Coppola and his screenwriter classically misunderstood the novel and betrayed an appalling ignorance of Stoker as well as of history. Serious historians are probably still laughing over the film's invented motivation for Vlad's savagery. In this botch, Vlad tortures and murders thousands of innocents to defend his Catholic faith. Poor misunderstood Vlad never really enjoyed skinning or roasting people alive but was just being a good altar boy. Furthermore, Catholicism is responsible for Vlad's fate, since the Church's denial of salvation for his suicidal bride forces the grief-stricken bridegroom to forsake religion and become a vampire. In the novel, Dracula mocks Christian sacraments, not because his bride was denied salvation, but because he knows that Christianity is his enemy and can destroy him.

Direction is as misguided as the script. Coppola includes graphic sex scenes and nudity to patronize audiences who crave such elements, though such scenes are in opposition to the sexual symbolism of the novel. Another indication of the audience for which this film is aimed is the emphasis on odious special effects which nauseate rather than frighten and place the film into the category of an expensive macabre gore movie. Realistic monsters created by computers are designed for increasingly jaded audiences who demand sensationalism instead of imaginative horror. This movie is so absurd that it could perhaps be viewed as a comedy if it wasn't so inept and repellent. At least it has more laughs, though unintentional, than the unfunny 1995 parody by Mel Brooks.

Stoker's novel is effectively frightening because he cleverly cultivated human fears symbolized by the myths of vampires. Coppola's movie imbues these monsters with beneficial motives instead of harmful ones. Such a conception is not what Stoker intended for his creation and totally misunderstands the reasons for the superstitions that have exerted such an enduring impression upon humanity. This movie is an insult to Stoker's name and his novel.

Incidentally, as a horror film, *Bram Stoker's Dracula* is perhaps equaled only by Coppola's subsequent abysmal production of the equally misleadingly titled *Mary Shelley's Frankenstein*, which was released in 1996. As dreadful as these two movies are, they are eclipsed by *Van Helsing* (2004), an unbelievably atrocious film that includes Dracula, Frankenstein's monster and a werewolf battled by the hero of the title who has been transformed into a young, dashing adventurer. The makers of these expensive movies simply do not know how to make a genuine horror movie. They only know how to make movies designed to appeal to teenagers and make huge profits. *Bram Stoker's Dracula*, which cost more than every Hammer movie combined, ended up with a domestic gross of about $80 million. Despite its lack of quality, it had the advantage

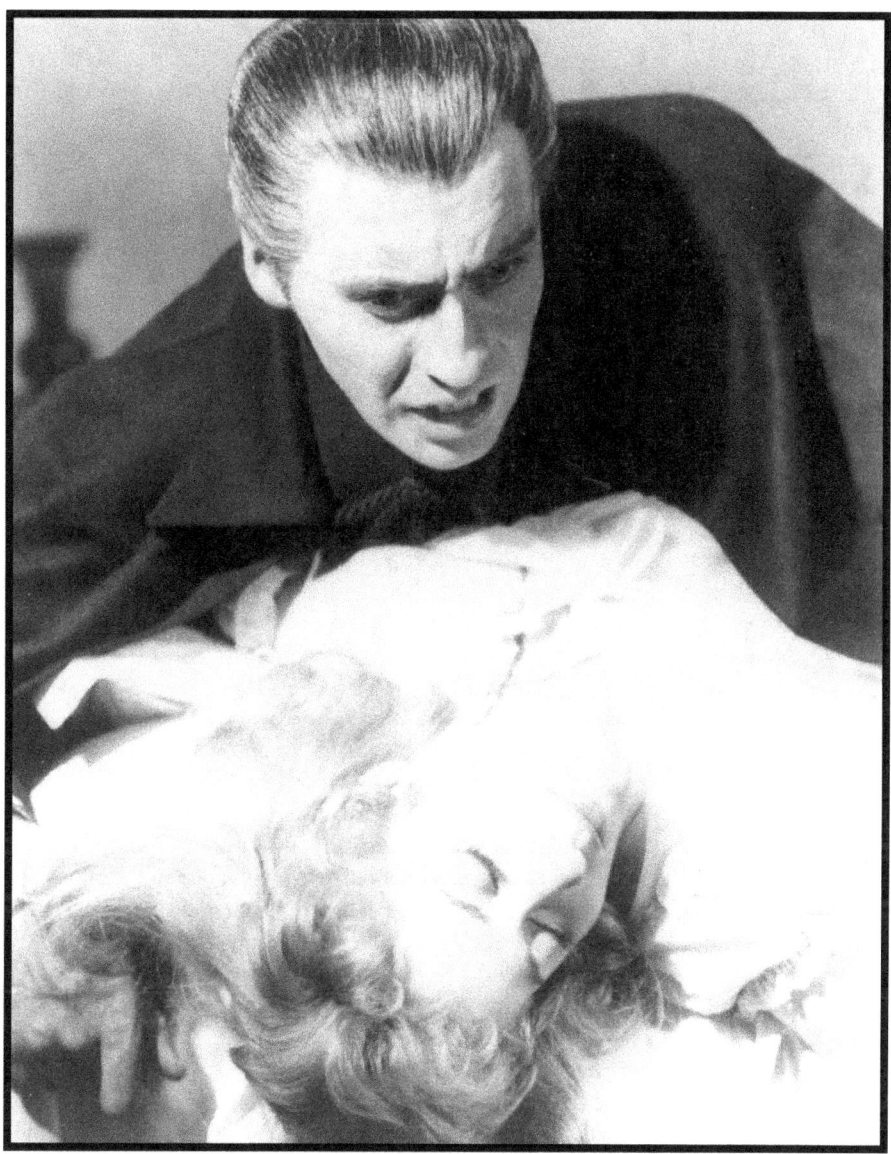

One of the classic studio photographs promoting *Horror of Dracula* emphasizes the erotic appeal of the vampire.

of being released during a period in which Dracula had achieved respectability and was no longer considered exploitation. It succeeded commercially because it was the wrong film at the right time.

Regardless of commercial success, Terence Fisher's *Horror of Dracula* is a far superior film. Peter Cushing and Christopher Lee remain, respectively, the definitive Van Helsing and Count Dracula. The movie may not be on any Top Grossing Films chart, like so many inferior horror movies, but it is a genuine film classic. With a minimal expense account and armed only with talent and creativity, Fisher showed celebrated directors how to make a horror movie, and not just once. Three years after *Horror of*

Dracula, Fisher would again display his expertise with the best werewolf movie ever made.

Following the success of their Frankenstein and Dracula movies, Hammer Films reigned supreme as the world's major producer of horror movies. The studio also made adventure films and psychological thrillers, but Hammer remained noted for their horror movies. In 1959, Terence Fisher directed Peter Cushing and Christopher Lee in sterling remakes of *The Mummy* and *The Hound of the Baskervilles*, with Cushing in the latter film again bringing his inimitable talents to a familiar role and achieving distinction. In 1960, Fisher also directed Cushing and Lee in a version of Robert Louis Stevenson's *Dr. Jekyll and Mr. Hyde* entitled *The Two Faces of Dr. Jekyll*. While these films are worth seeing, none of them achieve classic stature. However, it was in 1961 that the elements that created a true Hammer classic came together again. The movie was Hammer's only movie about a superstition that rivals the vampire for its ability to terrify generations over the centuries in all parts of the world. This is the capability of a human being to change into a ferocious animal. In some countries, the animal differs, but it is the transformation into a wolf that is most prevalent.

Lacking a literary counterpart that has captured the imagination the way that Dracula and Frankenstein have, the werewolf has been portrayed on the screen numerous times. The first major werewolf movie was Universal's *The Werewolf of London*, released in 1935. This is an interesting but not altogether satisfying film with only a few moments of genuine terror. More successful was Universal's *The Wolf Man*, released in 1941, with Lon Chaney, Jr. as the hapless hero who is bitten by a werewolf and then becomes one himself. The movie benefits from an intelligent script, a fine cast, stylish direction and atmospheric sets. Justifiably popular, this movie set the standard for most of the werewolf movies that followed. Chaney reprised his role in four more films of decreasing quality over the next decade, ultimately leading to the monster rallies where he met Frankenstein and Dracula and eventually, just like his fellow Universal monsters, ending his character's career in an undignified manner by meeting Abbott and Costello.

By the mid-1950s, werewolves on screen were perhaps at an all-time nadir with such films as the bottom-of-the-bill quickie, *The Werewolf* in 1956, and the adolescent exploitation with the infamous title, *I Was a Teenage Werewolf*, in 1957. Four years later, however, the werewolf would be the subject of a true horror classic.

In 1933, Guy Endore's novel *The Werewolf of Paris* was published and caused quite a sensation due to its graphic brutality. Narrated by the foster uncle of the main character, the novel begins in the early 19th century with a feud between two families who occupy neighboring castles in France. When a young member of the Pitamont family disguises himself as a monk and kills two members of the Pitavel family, he is captured and imprisoned in a pit for half a century, during which he is reduced to insanity. Upon his release, he is more animal than man and the Pitamont blood will forever be infected. In the guise of a priest, a deranged Pitamont rapes a young servant girl who subsequently gives birth to a son named Bertrand on Christmas day. As a child, Bertrand Caillet is afflicted with a strange hunger that can only be satisfied through the killing of animals. After being wounded by a bullet that has been blessed, Bertrand is locked in his room by his uncle, who suspects Bertrand's true nature and feeds him raw meat to satisfy his cravings.

Entering young manhood, Bertrand's unnatural instincts are aroused again by a visit to a prostitute and he is whipped into submission by his uncle. However, the cruelty of the punishment lowers Bertrand's resistance to his unnatural cravings. He runs away and experiences his first full transformation into a werewolf, in which form he savagely kills his best friend. He escapes to Paris where he joins the military during the Siege and Commune of 1870-71 while his uncle pursues him. Famine and war are pervasive in the city and Bertrand is able to conceal his depraved deeds amid the carnage that surrounds him. Haunted by his uncontrollable desires, he pillages graveyards to avoid killing. While brooding over his fate, Bertrand falls in love with Sophie, the daughter of a wealthy banker, who has a strange attraction to perversion and death which draws her to the moody soldier. Bertrand and Sophie engage in a morbid relationship that prevents Bertrand from killing again, not only because she loves him but because she allows him to inflict small cuts upon her body and feed off her to satisfy his desires. Eventually, this is not enough for Bertrand, who leaves Sophie's side one night and attacks a soldier who overpowers him. Court-martialed for his bestial attack, Bertrand

is committed to an asylum where he is cruelly treated until he escapes and falls to his death. Upon exhumation of his grave several years later, the bones of a wolf are all that remain.

The Werewolf of Paris was a best-seller and brought Endore to Hollywood. In the mid-1930s, he co-wrote the screenplays for three horror movies, *The Mark of the Vampire*, *Devil Doll* and *Mad Love*. During the course of his career, he received acclaim from literary critics for his historical novels but he never wrote another horror novel. Though *The Werewolf of Paris* is exceedingly well-written, it was out of print within a few years. It did not achieve the status of a horror classic, possibly because Endore transfers his emphasis midway through the novel from Bertrand's individual horrors to the mass horrors of war, injustice and poverty. The author was obviously intent on contrasting the deliberate savagery of humans on a mass scale to the uncontrollable savagery of one man. Compared to the hundreds of thousands of people being massacred through politics and war, the handful of crimes committed by Bertrand seem almost insignificant. Such a message is provocative but, within the context of the novel, it interferes with the narrative drive of the main story. In the classic novels by Bram Stoker and Mary Shelley, the monster remains the major threat and focus of attention until his destruction, and those novels also contain cogent social messages. Endore reduces his monster to a supporting character and this prevents Bertrand's werewolf from attaining the literary immortality of Dracula or Frankenstein.

Hammer's film version of Endore's novel is scripted by John Elder, a pseudonym for Anthony Hinds, and eliminates this problem with the protagonist remaining the focus of the film. Elder's superbly constructed script incorporates many other changes, including the setting, and departs radically from the novel for the second half. The setting of the movie is not France but Spain, since the studio could save expenses by utilizing sets from an unfilmed project about the Spanish Inquisition. However, the spirit of the novel and its characters, though necessarily condensed and modified, is translated to the screen with fidelity. Indeed, many scenes and lines of dialogue are taken directly from the novel, particularly for the first half of the film. The scope of the movie, in view of Hammer's customary modest budget, is not as ambitious as that of the novel. Bigotry and ignorance replace war and injustice as societal villains, while the moral decadence of an aristocratic feudal system remains intact.

Elder changes the names of all of the characters and makes them more sympathetic than their counterparts in the novel. Leon's foster parents, Don Alfredo Corledo and his servant Teresa, have an emotionally closer relationship than Bertrand and his uncle.

A beggar (Richard Wordsworth) becomes sport for the decadent nobles in *The Curse of the Werewolf*.

Leon's mother is a far more sensitive character than Bertrand's mother. Christina, Leon's love interest, inspires compassion and warmth while the cruel Sophie invites indifference and contempt. Most of all, however, it is the protagonist who emerges as a truly tragic character in the film. Unlike Bertrand, whose actions eventually indicate a perverted delight in his cravings, Leon desperately and repeatedly fights the evil within him and truly wants to destroy his bestial side. Leon's fate is ultimately far more poignant for himself and for those who love him.

The Curse of the Werewolf begins in a small village in Spain which is ruled by the sadistic Marques Siniestro, whose castle dominates the countryside. In search of food, a beggar unintentionally interrupts the marriage of the Marques and soon becomes sport for the wealthy wedding guests. Imprisoned in the dungeon for a chance remark, the beggar is reduced to savagery, his only friend seemingly the young mute daughter of the jailer. Years later, the daughter has become a young woman and is a servant to the aged Marques. After rejecting the advances of her master, the servant girl is thrown into the dungeon with the beggar. The animalistic beggar rapes the servant who, subsequently kills the Marques and attempts suicide. She is rescued by a kindly nobleman, Don Alfredo who takes her home to his servant Teresa. The servant dies giving birth, to her son Leon on Christmas day. Don Alfredo and Teresa raise Leon, but the boy's childhood is filled with nightmares and strange visions that he does not understand. After several animals are butchered, Leon is frightened when he awakens with a silver bullet in his leg. Don Alfredo, aware that the town watchman has shot at a wolf, deduces Leon's condition and locks him in a room to contain his bestial nature. Advised by the local priest that being loved will enable Leon to conquer his bestial side, Don Alfredo and Teresa vow to love Leon as their son. As a result of this love, the spirit of the beast within Leon is suppressed.

Years later, Leon leaves his happy home to make his way in the world, the nightmares of his childhood now forgotten. Obtaining employment in a vineyard, Leon falls in love with Christina, the manager's daughter. Christina also loves Leon but her father has promised her to the owner's son. Frustrated and separated from Christina, Leon is persuaded by another worker to visit a local tavern where he is lured by a prostitute to her room. But years before the priest had warned Don Alfredo that whatever weakens the goodness in Leon's soul will strengthen the spirit of the wolf that resides within him, particularly during the cycle of the full moon. And now the debauchery surrounding Leon combined with separation from those who love him and a full moon above reawakens the long-dormant desires within him. He struggles to resist the inexplicable cravings but is powerless against the forces of evil. The next day the prostitute's mangled body is found along with the bodies of two other people, including Leon's co-worker.

Exhausted and confused, Leon returns home and learns the truth about his condition from Don Alfredo and Teresa. Shocked beyond belief, Leon is told by the priest that he will have to be kept in chains for the rest of his life to keep him from killing again. Leon cannot bear such a fate and runs away from the distraught Don Alfredo and Teresa. Crying miserably, he stumbles across the countryside until he returns to town to be questioned by the police and temporarily released. But that night in his room, he feels the urges once again returning and cries out in agony, causing Christina to come from across the courtyard into his room. Terrified that he will harm her, Leon loses consciousness. The next morning, he awakens in Christina's arms and learns that her love was strong enough to defeat the spirit of the wolf. Overjoyed with relief, Leon asks Christina to marry him and she agrees but, before they can elope, the police arrive and arrest him. Don Alfredo learns of Leon's arrest and pleads with the mayor for his release into the priest's care, but the mayor will not listen to either Don Alfredo or the priest. That night, the full moon rises again and Leon, away from Christina, changes into a werewolf. After killing a drunken prisoner, Leon escapes and terrorizes the town as the panic-stricken citizens form into a mob to hunt him down. Knowing what he must do, Don Alfredo tracks Leon and mercifully kills him with a silver bullet.

The Curse of the Werewolf is unique in that it relates the complete story of a lycanthrope. It begins with incidents that will have a direct relation to his birth and ends with his death. Like *Horror of Dracula*, it is a story of good versus evil, but in this film the battle is waged within a person for his soul. It is a more emotional film as well as a more pessimistic one. The actual villain of the story is not the werewolf but the Marques, whose face will eventually reflect his many sins. One of the tragic aspects of the film is that the harm inflicted upon so many innocent people by the Marques will affect countless others and will eventually destroy Leon, who is not even born until after the Marques dies. Conceived in violence, Leon is doomed from birth, as evident from the circumstances of his baptism as well as those of his parentage. His mother was doomed because of her virtue. His father was doomed because of his poverty.

Oliver Reed and Yvonne Romain pose for a publicity photograph for *The Curse of the Werewolf*.

Leon's foster parents and Christina desperately try to destroy his curse with love, but it is to no avail, for their love is not powerful enough to surmount the decadence of his society. Christianity is once again the enemy of evil, the only force that can destroy the spirit of the beast, but it does not seem as omnipotent in this film. Just as Dracula is destroyed by a symbol of the cross that also saves Mina, Leon's bestial side is destroyed by a bullet that has been blessed but it also kills Leon. It is significant that, after Leon dies, he does not change back into human form as so many other cinematic werewolves

have done. No release and no salvation for Leon exist. The spirit of evil within him has been destroyed but not until after it has consumed him, leaving his foster parents grief-stricken and Christina devastated.

The Curse of the Werewolf is as much a love story as it is a horror film. Once again, Terence Fisher's taut, economic direction gives the film a mesmerizing rhythm due to his impeccable sense of dramatic timing, which steadily and assuredly builds momentum to the heartrending finale. Fisher's unconventional use of glossy color textures and his striking visual sense create a mystifying atmosphere throughout the film. Each scene indicates deliberate compositional style and preparation which adds in subtle ways to the content of the story. It is a rare horror film that achieves such poignancy and affects the emotions so deeply. This is obviously Fisher's intent, as evident from the extreme close-up of the werewolf's eyes which accompany the main titles. They are the blood-soaked eyes of a murderous beast, yet tears gradually appear and flow freely as though to reflect the trapped soul within trying desperately to break free. This shot alone sets the tone for one of the saddest depictions of good trapped within evil that has ever appeared on the motion picture screen.

Oliver Reed is superb as Leon. This was his first starring role and it is an extremely sensitive and powerful portrayal which allows him to completely capture the emotional turmoil of a man struggling desperately to resist the overpowering forces within him. In the scene with the prostitute, the emotions of increasing confusion and suffering he displays are so agonizingly commanding that something evil and potent seems to be visibly forcing its way to the surface. Once he is aware of his nature and bloodlust, his performance elicits an enormous amount of sympathy, not only because of his plight, but because his actions have already doomed him. Through his agonizing expressions, he distinctly conveys the impression that he is waging a battle for his life with his own nature. However, as the film progresses, the torment he displays becomes increasingly unbearable not only because of the inner pain he displays but because his expression clearly suggests that he is losing the battle. And most impressively, in the final scenes in which the werewolf is revealed, Reed fully captures the tragedy of his character. Even as he is about to pounce upon the father that he loves, the barely recognizable Reed is able to suggest through his tear-filled eyes that beneath the animalistic ferocity and murderous bloodlust is an innocent and tortured soul desperately begging for the release of death. It is a truly memorable performance.

Clifford Evans is also excellent as Don Alfredo, giving a finely textured performance by underplaying his scenes with quiet strength and resolve. Beneath the exterior that lacks overt emotion, Evans conveys through warmth in his voice and gentle expressions his love for Leon and even for Teresa. Without the credibility of this emotion, the

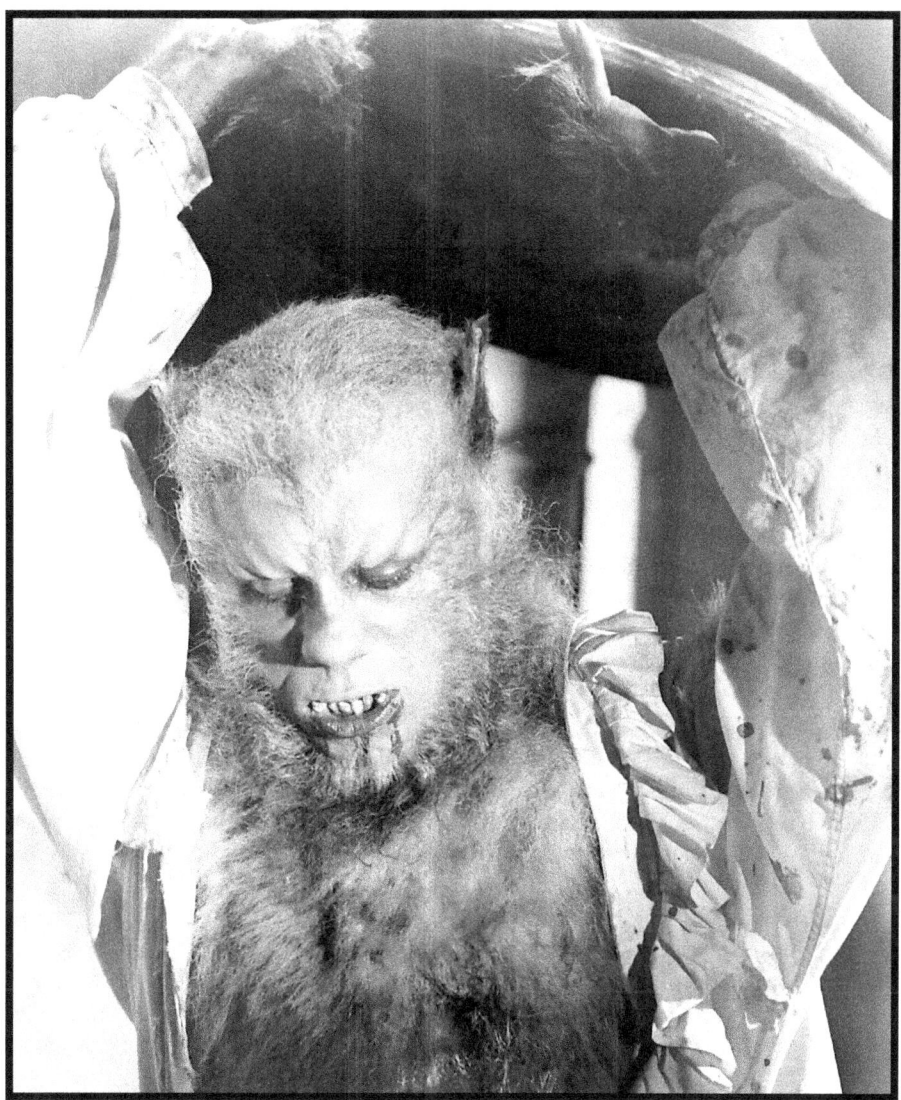

Oliver Reed is superb as Leon the tortured werewolf in *The Curse of the Werewolf*.

tragedy of the story would not be as effective as it is. As Leon's unfortunate mother, Yvonne Romain doesn't have a single line of dialogue but her expressions of fear as she is brutalized and hatred as she finds vengeance speak volumes. Catherine Feller as Christina and Hira Talfrey as Teresa both give touching portrayals, with the final shot of the film in which they cling to one another in sorrow conveying their loss and pain. Richard Wordsworth also makes a distinct impression as the beggar. Worthy of special mention is Anthony Dawson, who is memorable as the despicable Marques, his voice and expressions as well as his arrogant manner exuding aristocratic decadence and evil.

    The production qualities are flawless. The period details are astonishing for a low-budget movie. All of the interiors, from the castle and its superficial elegance befitting aristocratic decadence to the genuine warmth of Don Alfredo's home, look not only authentic but are filled with exquisite period detail. The make-up for the werewolf is horrifying and frightening but still looks like Reed, thus affecting audiences subconsciously. Equally laudable is Benjamin Frankel's audacious score, which is unique because it is atonal and deliberately lacks harmony, thus perfectly complementing the lurid images on the screen.

Upon its release, *The Curse of the Werewolf* received mixed reviews, including many severely negative ones. Despite its quality, it failed at the box office and did not even earn the minimum amount of $1 million that would qualify its placement on *Variety*'s annual list.

The commercial failure of the movie can perhaps in part be attributed to the studio's improper handling of it. In the United States, it was released by Universal-International as the top half of a double bill with one of Hammer's lesser productions, *Shadow of the Cat*. Most advertisements showed either a close-up of the werewolf's face or a medium shot of the werewolf carrying a woman's body, the latter shot never occurring in the movie. Across the posters were the words: "His beast-blood demanded he kill, kill, kill!" The type of audience responding to such lurid taglines probably couldn't appreciate the finer qualities of the movie and discerning filmgoers were turned off by such exploitation. And in 1961, horror was still simply not an acceptable genre. As a result, the movie didn't last long in theaters and its financial disappointment halted any plans Hammer may have had for additional werewolf films.

The superiority of *The Curse of the Werewolf* is more evident when compared to expensive horror movies that were produced in subsequent decades. By the 1980s, the major studios were prepared to lavish huge budgets on technically advanced special effects for movies about werewolves. *The Howling* (1980) features credible special effects but little else. The makers of this film display a condescending attitude toward the genre even though they try to disguise it as an homage with its references to past horror films, including a character named Terry Fisher. *An American Werewolf in London* (1981) tries to duplicate the Hammer look in a modern setting but also tries to be modish for the young hip audience. It fails on both counts. In both of these movies, the transformations of the main characters into werewolves are more realistic, due to advanced special effect techniques, but the films revolve around the effects instead of an intelligent story. Furthermore, the werewolves may look convincing but they bear no resemblance to the actors from whom they were supposedly transformed. This decreases audience involvement and focuses attention again on the effects as the reason for the movies.

The 1990s featured still more unsuccessful attempts to create a genuine horror movie. *Wolf* (1994) is another big-budgeted movie with a big-name director, Mike Nichols, and a big-name star, Jack Nicholson. In this pretentious film, the werewolf theme is secondary to the theme of cutthroat tactics of the publishing business. This indicates the contemptuous attitude of the filmmakers toward horror. But all Nichols proves is that he can be as pompous as Coppola. Except for the opening scene, little tension or atmosphere is generated and Nicholson overacts alarmingly to compensate for the hollow script and the increasingly flat direction. Even worse is *An American Werewolf in Paris* (1997), which tries to attract the audience of the similarly titled movie of the previous decade with its emphasis on gruesome bloodletting. Once again, except for the gore, the film has nothing else to offer discriminating audiences.

However, like the expensive Dracula and Frankenstein movies, most of these big-budget werewolf movies enjoyed varying degrees of commercial success denied *The Curse of the Werewolf.* They were released when adults and serious filmgoers were no longer ashamed to see horror films. They were publicized not as exploitation films but as serious films made by skillful filmmakers for intelligent adult audiences. They were reviewed by critics as worthy fare, quite unlike the patronizing attitude lavished upon the Hammer film. However, *The Curse of the Werewolf* is far superior to such films. It continues to be denied such recognition, except by genre fans, because of the condescending attitude of a large percentage of critics and filmgoers who consider any horror film made prior to the genre's legitimacy as quaint and unworthy of serious discussion. And in an era in which commercial success is the determining factor of a film's merits, the movie's failure at the box office consigns it even further to the bin of forgotten films. Like *Horror of Dracula*, it was a film released at the wrong time.

The final factor in assessing a movie's merits is the movie itself. And thanks to home video and the few repertory theaters that are still in existence, the movie's fans seem to be steadily increasing. In 2004, the American Cinematheque presented a new print of the movie as part of its *5th Annual Festival of Fantasy, Horror and Science Fiction Films* at the Egyptian Theater in Los Angeles. Generally unknown to many audience members, the movie retained its ability to entertain, terrify and ultimately entice unexpected emotional responses from the audience. Indeed, the movie's finale was greeted with applause.

Unfortunately, Terence Fisher was not alive to see such acclaim and approval. He died at the age of 76 in 1980. He is now recognized within England as a major British film director but, because of the genre in which he worked, he is still not given the high acclaim bestowed upon more esteemed colleagues. However, his films will always be available as testament to his artistry.

Hammer Films remained a vibrant company throughout the 1960s and continued to produce many quality movies, all of which exhibit their identifiable style. Most of these are horror movies, including such fine entries as *Kiss of the Vampire* (1963) and *The Reptile* (1965). Terence Fisher continued to display his expertise with *The Gorgon* (1964) and *The Devil Rides Out* (1967), along with his Frankenstein films. Hammer also concluded its Quatermass trilogy with its notable *Quatermass and the Pit* (USA title: *Five Million Years to Earth*) in 1967, a superior science fiction movie which again belies its modest cost.

By the late 1960s, Hammer started to decline. The formerly innovative and influential studio could not keep pace with changes in the film industry which, ironically, were in part initiated by its own product. As Hollywood realized that huge profits could be made by genre films and flooded the market with inferior product filled with mindless violence and gratuitous sex, Hammer just couldn't compete. In a misguided attempt to keep up, Hammer increased the amount of graphic gore in its films until such scenes, which formerly had been relatively mild and carefully integrated within plot requirements, no longer seemed justified. More regrettably, the studio replaced discreet eroticism with nudity and sex scenes which were equally unjustified. And to attract younger audiences, their films included youth-oriented themes, which alienated their loyal fans. Most important, the members of the unique Hammer team, the talented artisans who had contributed immeasurably to the company's success, began to drift away. By the early 1970s, enormous budgets lavished on horror movies by the major studios drove the final nail into Hammer's coffin.

Because the current climate is favorable to horror movies and since several major directors have expressed their admiration for Hammer films, various attempts occurred over the years to revive the company. Periodic announcements to that effect have been reported. However, without the special team of artists that made Hammer Film Productions special, the attempts are doomed to failure. Hammer was more than just a name. It was the vision of talented and creative people who joined together to make something distinctive, something uniquely identifiable and, above all, great movies. That Hammer can never be revived. The name may resurface in some shape or form but it will not be the same.

However, Hammer Film Productions left a legacy of many good movies, several excellent ones and two certified classics.

Horror of Dracula (aka *Dracula*) [Universal-International/1958]
CREDITS: Executive Producer: Michael Carreras; Producer: Anthony Hinds; Director: Terence Fisher; Screenplay: Jimmy Sangster, based upon the novel, "Dracula" by Bram Stoker; Cinematographer: Jack Asher; Editors: James Needs, Bill Lenny; Production Design: Bernard Robinson; Make-up: Phil Leakey; Music: James Bernard; Associate Producer: Anthony Nelson Keys
CAST: Peter Cushing (Dr. Van Helsing); Christopher Lee (Count Dracula); Michael Gough (Arthur Holmwood); Melissa Stribling (Mina Holmwood); Carol Marsh (Lucy Holmwood); John Van Eyssen (Jonathan Harker); Valerie Gaunt (Vampire Woman); Olga Dickie (Gerda); Miles Malleson (Marx); Charles Lloyd Pack (Dr. Seward)

The Curse of the Werewolf [Universal-International/1961]
CREDITS: Executive Producer: Michael Carreras; Producer: Anthony Hinds; Director: Terence Fisher; Screenplay: John Elder, based on the novel "The Werewolf of Paris" by Guy Endore; Cinematographer: Arthur Grant; Editor: Alfred Cox; Production Designer: Bernard Robinson; Make-up: Roy Ashton; Music: Benjamin Frankel; Associate Producer: Anthony Nelson Keys
CAST: Clifford Evans (Don Alfredo); Oliver Reed (Leon); Yvonne Romain (Servant Girl); Catherine Feller (Christina); Anthony Dawson (The Marques Siniestro); Josephine Llewellyn (The Marquesa); Richard Wordsworth (The Beggar); Hira Talfrey (Teresa); Justin Waters (Young Leon); John Gabriel (The Priest); Warren Mitchell (Pepe); Anne Blake (Rosa); George Woodbridge (Dominique); Michael Ripper (Old Soaker)

Afterword

In 1996, Gordon Scott was one of the celebrity guests at the Hollywood Collectors Show in Secaucus, New Jersey. Looking robust and quite younger than his 69 years, Scott proved to be an extremely modest and unassuming gentleman. While he expressed justified pride in *Tarzan's Greatest Adventure*, he gave credit for the success of the film to everyone but himself, including the producers, the director and his co-stars. He spoke very highly of Sy Weintraub and Harvey Hayutin for creating the impetus that resulted in the movie and its companion, *Tarzan the Magnificent*. He also praised the supporting actors of both films for being an integral part of their success, lavishing praise on Anthony Quayle, Sean Connery and Jock Mahoney, among others. Not once during the course of his many conversations with fans did he assume any credit for himself.

Unfortunately, neither the movies nor Scott have received the acclaim or renown they deserve, though their fans have increased in recent years thanks to cable television. As of this date, neither *Tarzan's Greatest Adventure* nor *Tarzan the Magnificent* has been released on home video. Undoubtedly, *Tarzan's Greatest Adventure* warrants a special two-disc presentation of the movie accompanied by interviews with surviving participants and knowledgeable critics. John Guillermin would hopefully be agreeable to supply invaluable information on the making of the movie. Gordon Scott would prob-

Gordon Scott chats with author Nicholas Anez.

ably be more than willing to provide commentary which would certainly be interesting, considering the many anecdotes he related at Secaucus. Quite possibly, Sean Connery would be willing to add comments, especially since in 2005 he graciously agreed to do the same for a DVD release of *Darby O'Gill and the Little People*.

Warlock is another movie deserving of such treatment. Once again, thanks to cable television, this movie has also been receiving overdue recognition but primarily from fans of the genre. No doubt *Warlock* is a far superior movie to *Unforgiven* or *Dances with Wolves*, both of which were the recipients of numerous awards, or critically acclaimed movies like *Little Big Man* and other social commentaries masquerading as movies. *Warlock* resonates with far more intelligence and sophistication than all of those anti-Westerns combined, but it is a traditional Western, despite its deep psychological and emotional undertones. As a result, it remains relatively unknown, which is regrettable in view of the praise lavished on so many unworthy movies.

For instance, another "Western" held in high esteem is *The Good, the Bad and the Ugly*. An interesting incident occurred during the showing of this movie during its premiere Boston engagement. One scene has the protagonist, played by Clint Eastwood, riding in civilian clothing into a Civil War encampment in the midst of a campaign and being greeted by the commanding officer like he was dropping in for tea. Behind me in the audience, I heard a woman say, "I can't take any more of this," and she proceeded to leave the theater. In the lobby, she introduced herself as an American History professor at a local university and explained that if any civilian ever rode into a Civil War military camp, he would have been immediately shot as a spy, no questions asked.

That was only one of the many complaints she had about the movie, both from a historical as well as cinematic perspective. Yet this absurd movie was recently released on a special two-disc edition DVD with added commentaries and documentaries while *Warlock* had to suffice with just a single disc presentation of the movie, the only supplement being the trailer. Some good news exists for fans of the movie. Though a soundtrack of the Leigh Harline score was not issued at the time of the film's release, it finally became available to the public 46 years later. In December 2005, Intrada released a CD of the soundtrack.

As *On Her Majesty's Secret Service* gradually builds fans, George Lazenby becomes more appreciated. In June 2005, *Bondstars.com* hosted an event at Pinewood Studios entitled "James Bond: A Celebration + An Evening with George Lazenby," which was also attended by numerous other personnel from the series. It was reported on the *Bondstars* website by Gareth Owen that both Lazenby and *On Her Majesty's Secret Service*, which he introduced, were greeted with "rapturous applause and a standing ovation." He was equally popular at the Hollywood Collectors Show in Los Angeles in August 2005, where he appeared along with other veterans of Bond movies and proved to be as congenial and charming as his 007 had been 36 years before.

George Lazenby

No doubt exists in my mind that Lazenby made a far more lasting impression as James Bond in only one movie than Pierce Brosnan did in four movies. But while Lazenby's film was the right film at the wrong time, the Brosnan films were designed expressly to be the right film at the right time. Their popularity was due not to the name of James Bond but to the fact that they followed the currently fashionable trends of other overblown action spectacles. Lazenby was actually playing Bond, while Brosnan's character was interchangeable with other contemporary heroes. Thus, with the Bond series currently in a state of uncertainty (as far as true 007 fans are concerned), Lazenby's fame and his single Bond movie will almost certainly continue to increase in popularity and acclaim.

Incidentally, *On Her Majesty's Secret Service* also received some belated attention in 1994 in England when the theme song, "We Have All the Time in the World," as sung by Louis Armstrong, was used during a commercial for Guinness beer. Popular demand prompted the rerelease of the song which became a big hit, reaching Number 3 on the U.K. charts. In 2003, Capitol rereleased the soundtrack of John Barry's ultimate Bond score for the movie with the addition of 10 previously unreleased tracks, but they were regrettably not interpolated chronologically into the score.

Horror of Dracula and *The Curse of the Werewolf*, appreciated primarily by genre fans, will hopefully expand beyond that core audience. The aforementioned presentation by American Cinematheque in 2004 of the latter film is a significant step in expanding renown for the Hammer team. While the enormously budgeted horror movies of later decades received critical acclaim, the reasons for the deficiency of such movies are now apparent. When Francis Coppola made his version of *Dracula*, he included all of the ingredients necessary to bleed as much money as possible out of the lucrative teenage market. When Terence Fisher made his version, he set out to make a *good* movie.

As the DVD market continues to grow, many more of the films discussed in this book hopefully will become available. While the best way to see such films is in a theater, this is becoming increasingly difficult. A regrettable consequence of the home video explosion was the near-extinction of revival theaters. In past years, Boston had several such theaters, but they are all gone. Even the Brattle Theater only shows older movies infrequently. Enough purists who want to see movies the way they are meant to be seen simply do not exist. In New York City, The Film Forum still thankfully endures. In the Los Angeles area the Egyptian Theater and in Hollywood The New Beverly Cinema prosper, as does the Aero Theater in Santa Monica. Hopefully, some of the unappreciated movies discussed in this book will someday play in these theaters and other surviving revival houses.

It is partially satisfying that directors such as John Sturges, Edward Dmytryk, J. King Vidor and Henry King have received acclaim for films other than the ones discussed in this book. But many other directors such as John Guillermin, Jack Arnold, Terence Fisher and Peter Hunt remain generally unknown for their achievements. This lack of recognition, of course, also applies to the actors, writers, composers and other personnel who contributed so much to the quality of these films. It is hoped that time will address this injustice.

The talents responsible for all of the movies that were discussed in this book, many of whom have long since left us, would no doubt appreciate the fact that their movies are still being enjoyed. These movies were primarily made to entertain and please audiences, to make people laugh, cry, and even think, but most of all, to move them emotionally for years to come.

In that respect, they succeeded.

INDEX

Abbott (Bud) and Costello (Lou) 254, 269
Across the Wide Missouri 186,188
Act of Love 221
Action of the Tiger 68
Adams, Ken 69, 72, 89
Adams, Maud 105
Adams, Ramon F. 131
Adobe Walls (novel) 189, 190
Adventures of Tarzan, The 16
"After the O.K. Corral" (TV) 157
Albert, Eddie 204
Aldrich, Robert 190, 204
Alias Jesse James 151
Alias Smith and Jones (TV) 157
All the King's Men 223
Allen, Rex 198
Allen, Woody 81
All-Story (magazine) 12, 13
"All Time High" 106
Along the Great Divide 191
Alpert, Hollis 73, 91
Amateau, Rod 166
Ambler, Buster 43
Ambush 186
American Cinematographer (magazine) 20, 23
American Cinematheque (cultural organization dedicated to film) 277, 281
American Werewolf in London, An 276
American Werewolf in Paris, An 276
Amis, Kingsley 83
"And the Moon Grew Brighter and Brighter" (song) 193
Anderson, John 146, 194
Andersonville (novel) 221
And Die in the West (book) 132
Andress, Ursula 68, 120
Andrews, Dana 227, 246
Andrews, David 177
Anhalt, Edward 157, 160
Another Time, Another Place 34, 65
Apache 190
Appointment with Destiny (TV) 165
Apted, Michael 117
Aquanetta 26
Archer, Eugene 46
Arizona Historical Review (magazine)129
Arizonian, The 137, 138, 139
Armstrong, Louis 90

Arness, James 151, 203, 231, 232, 245
Arnold, David 116
Arnold, Jack 243, 245 281
Around the World in 80 Days 202
Arrowhead 188-190, 211, 231
Arruza, Carlos 236
Ashby, Linden 177
Asphalt Jungle, The (novel) 135, 191
Astonished Heart, The 250
At Gunpoint 239
Athanas, Verne 200, 201
Atwater, Barry 144
Auger, Claudine 78, 79, 107
Aurthur, Robert Alan 152, 155
Autry, Gene 44, 184, 216, 217

Bach, Barbara 101
Backlash 198-200, 202, 212
Bad Day at Black Rock 191, 201
Badham, John 264
Badlanders, The 191
Badman's Country 150
Balderson, John 253, 263
Bancroft, Anne 197
Barabas, Gabor 231
Barabas, Suzanne 231
Barker, Lex 29, 30, 31, 32
Barra, Allen 134, 171
Barrow, Clyde 93
Barry, Gene 150, 167
Barry, John 69, 72, 76, 79, 85, 89, 90, 96, 98, 102, 104, 106, 111, 116, 281
Bart, Lionel 72
Bartholomew, Ed 131
Basinger, Kim 107
Bassett, Charlie 148
Bassey, Shirley 76, 79, 96
Batman 113
Bat Masterson (TV) 147
Battle of Britain, The 120
Beatles, the 99
Beauchamp, D.D. 192, 193
Beery, Noah 239
Behan, Johnny 126, 129, 132, 133, 146, 158, 159, 163, 164, 168, 171, 173,, 176, 177
Behlmer, Rudy 20, 23
Belford, Barbara 252
Bell, Bob Boze 133

282   Celluloid Adventures

Bell, Rex 139
Bellboy, The 46, 47
Bend of the River 188, 191, 192
Ben-Hur 42, 207
Benson, Raymond 63, 83
Berkeley, Martin 220
Bernard, James 260
Berry, Halle 118
Best American Short Stories, The: 1953 (book) 229
Best of James Bond 30th Anniversay Limited Edition, The (cd) 69, 79
Best Years of Our Lives, The 221, 227
Bezzerides, A.I. 207
Bianchi, Daniela 72
Biberman, Abner 241, 245
Beihn, Michael 171
Big Clock, The 66
Big Country, The 204, 206
Big Sky, The 188
Bigger Than Life 66
Billy the Kid 186
Binder, Maurice 69
Bissell, Whit 244
Black Dakotas, The 227
Black, Don 79, 96
Blackman, Honor 75, 101
Blaylock, Celia Ann (Mattie) 126, 168, 173, 177
Blair, Betsy 234
Bliss, Caroline 111, 113
Blob, The 261
Blood of Dracula 261
"Blood Son" (story) 262
Blue Book (magazine) 13
Blue Max, The 59
Boetticher, Budd 234, 235, 236, 237, 238, 239, 244
Bond, Samantha 115, 116
Bond, Ward 142, 232, 233, 234, 245
Bondstars.com (website) 280
Bonnie and Clyde 93
Boone, Richard 193, 194, 235
Boothe, Powers 171
Bouquet, Carole 104
Boxlietner, Bruce 166
Boyd, Stephen 206
Boyd, William 184
Boyer, Glenn 131, 165
Brady, Clark 13
Bram Stoker (book) 252
Bram Stoker's Dracula 10, 265-267, 281

Branded 188
Brandenauer, Klaus Maria 107
Brando, Marlon 188
Brandon, Henry 138
Bravados, The 10, 204-206, 213
Bravados, The (novel) 204-205
Bray, Robert 144
Breakenridge, William (Billy) 129,130, 133, 172
Breck, Peter 156
Brennan, Frederick Hazlitt 147
Brennan, Walter 142, 201, 217, 245
Brent, Eve 32
Bricusse, Leslie 76, 79, 85, 89
Bridge at Remagen, The 59
Bridges, Lloyd 145, 219, 246
Brigham Young 187
Bright Promise (TV) 246
Brinkley, Charles 134
Brix, Herman 21, 23
Broccoli, Albert R. 64, 68, 77, 81, 83, 85, 94, 100, 102, 104, 110, 113
Broccoli, Barbara 113
Brocius, Curly Bill 126, 133, 139, 145, 158, 167, 169, 171, 174, 176
Brode, Douglas 59
Broder, Jack 223
Broken Arrow 185, 186, 188, 190, 206
Broken Lance 190, 191
Bronson, Charles 112, 191
Brooks, Mel 266
Brooks, Richard 186, 208
Brosnan, John 63
Brosnan, Pierce 113, 115, 116, 118, 281
Broughton, Bruce 171
Brown, Clara 127, 133
Brown, Harry Joe 235
Brown, Johnny Mack 137, 139
Brown, Robert 195, 109, 111, 113
Brown, Vanessa 29
Browning, Tod 254
Brynner, Yul 208
Buchanan Edgar 139, 145, 186, 187
Buchanan Rides Alone 236
Buffalo Bill 227
Buffalo Bill, Hero of the Far West 59
Bullfighter and the Lady, The 221, 235
Burne Hogarth's The Golden Age of Tarzan (book) 51
Burnett, W.R. 135, 139, 189, 191
Burns, Walter Noble 129, 130, 139
Burroughs Cyclopaedia, The (book) 13

Burroughs, Edgar Rice 12, 13, 15, 16, 17, 18, 19, 20, 21, 29, 33, 48, 50, 51, 52, 54, 55, 58, 63
Burs Under the Saddle (book) 131
Burton, Richard 81
Bwana Devil 221, 223

Cagney, James 194, 195
Caine, Michael 81
Caine Mutiny, The 191
Calhern, Louis 186
Calhoun, Rory 143, 144, 165
Callaway Went Thataway 207
Calling Wild Bill Elliot 217
Cameron, Earl 45
Camfield, Bill 157
Campbell, Martin 115
Campbell, R. Wright 241
Campbell, William 193, 199
Canyon Passage 227
Captain Sinbad 70
"Captives, The" (story) 237
Capture of Tarzan, The 21, 22, 23
Carder, Charles 237
Carey, Carey 136
Carey, Harry Jr. 232
Carey, Macdonald 222, 224, 246
Carlisle, Robert 117
Carmen Jones 225
Carmilla (book) 253
Carpetbaggers, The 173
Carradine, John 44-45, 254
Carrera, Barbara 107
Carreras, Enrique 249
Carreras, Michael 250
Carroll, John 239
Casablanca 246
Casino Royale (1967) 81, 82, 83, 85, 120
Casino Royale (2006) 119
Casino Royale (novel) 63, 64, 81, 82, 120
Casino Royale (TV) 64, 82
Cassell, Wally 219
Cassidy, Butch 150
Castle, Don 149
Castle, William 144
Caviezel, James 177
Celi, Adolfo 79, 107
Chandler, Jeff 206, 207
Chandler, Raymond 62
Chaney, Lon 249
Chaney, Lon Jr. 268, 269
Chapman, James 63

Chase, Borden 192, 193, 198, 199, 200
Cheyenne Autumn 156, 157
Chief Crazy Horse 198
Chiles, Lois 102
Churney, Richard 225
Cinerama Holiday 198
Citizen Kane 232
Clairborne, Billy 125, 174
Clanton, Billy 125, 126, 132, 142, 148, 149, 150, 159
Clanton, Ike 127, 133, 144, 151, 161, 168, 170, 174, 176, 217
Clanton, Newton (Old Man) 140, 142, 171, 175
Clark, Harvey 137
Clarke, Gary 193
Cleese, John 117, 118
Clements, Manny 176
Clift, Montgomery 81
Climax Mystery Theater (TV) 64
Clum, John 127, 129, 130, 132, 148, 161, 166, 176
Coburn, James 81
Cockrell, Gary 45
Cody, Buffalo Bill 150
Cohn, Harry 227
Collins, Joan 206
Colonel Bogey 250
Colonel Sun 83
Colorado Territory 227
Comanche Station 236
Connery, Sean 34, 38, 65, 66, 67, 68, 69, 70, 72, 73, 75, 76, 78, 79, 81, 83, 85, 86, 90, 92, 93, 95, 97, 106, 107, 108, 113, 115, 118, 121, 122, 279, 280
Conrad, William 203
Conti, Bill 104
Converse, Frank 161
Conway, Pat 150
Coolidge, Rita 106
Coon, Gene 243
Cooper, Gary 186, 188, 190, 204, 206
Coppola, Francis ford 265, 266, 276, 281
Cosmatos, George 168
Costner, Kevin 167, 176, 177, 210
Cotton, Joseph 59, 232, 233, 234, 235, 244, 245, 246
Couffer, Jack 229
Count Dracula (1970) 261
Count Dracula (TV) 263
Cowboy 204
Cowboys, The 210

Cowling, Bruce 144
Coy, Walter 155
Crabbe, Buster 19, 150
Craig, Daniel 119
Craig, James 139
Crain, Jeanne 193
Crawford, Joan 190
Creature from the Black Lagoon 243
Creeping Unknown, The 250
Cronin, Lee 163
Cronkite, Walter 144
Crosby, Kim 54
Crowther, Bosley 69, 73, 75, 76, 80, 142, 156, 160
Crutchfield, Les 34
Cruz, Florentino 159
Curse of Frankenstein, The 251, 255
Curse of the Werewolf, The 9, 10, 249, 270-276, 277, 278, 281
Curtis, Dan 263
Curtis, Ken and the Pioneers 225
Curtis, Tony 54, 241
Curtiz, Michael 186
Cushing, Peter 251, 255, 258, 259, 261, 265, 266, 267, 268

Daddy Long Legs 34
Dahl, Roald 84
Dake, Cawley 172
Dakota Lil 200
Dalton, Timothy 109, 110, 111, 113
Dances with Wolves 167, 210, 280
Darby O'Gill and the Little People 34, 66, 280
Dark Shadows (TV) 263
Darnell, Linda 142
Davenport, Nigel 263
Daves, Delmer 10, 185, 188, 190, 191, 198, 202, 204, 206, 209
Davi, Robert 113
David and Bathsheba 188
David, Hal 90
Davis, Jim 157, 217, 219
Dawn at Socorro 144
Dawson, Anthony 68, 275
Day, Robert 42, 43, 48, 49, 59, 60
Days of My Life, The 222
Days of Our Lives, The (TV) 246
Deane, Hamilton 253, 263
Death of a Salesman 228
Death on the Nile 59
Death Valley Days (TV) 157

Death Wish 112
Decision at Sundown 10, 236-239, 248
Decision at Sundown (novel) 237-238
Dee, Sandra 242
Deger, Larry 176 148
Dehn, Paul 75
Deighton, Len 110
Delaney, Dana 170
DeMunn, Jeffrey 166
Dench, Judi 115, 116, 118
Deno, Lottie 148
Denver and the Rio Grande 200
Derek, Bo 52
Derek, John 195
Destry Rides Again 138
Devil Doll 270
Devil Rides Out, The 277
Devil's Disciple, The 75
Devil's Doorway 185-186, 211
Diamonds are Forever 95-97, 118
"Diamonds Are Forever" (song) 96
Diane 97
Dickinson, Angie 232
Die Another Day 117-118
Die Hard 116
Dinehart, Alan 146
Disney, Walt 34, 57, 66, 73, 245
Disney's Legend of Tarzan (TV) 57
Distant Drums 186
Dix, Richard 137, 140
Dmytryk, Edward 152, 155, 156, 190, 206, 230, 281
"Do You Know Christmas Trees Are Born?" (song) 89-90
Doc 164-165, 209
Dodge City 139
Dodge, Fred 131, 132
Don't Go Near the Water 231
Donovan, King 219
Don't Give Up the Ship 39, 42
Dor, Karen 85
Double Indemnity 239
Doucette, John 221
Douglas, Gordon 186, 204
Douglas, Kirk 147, 148, 149, 191, 193, 202, 206, 208, 221
Dowling, Doris 231
Downs, Cathy 142
Dr. Jekyll and Mr. Hyde 268
Dr. No 64-70, 123
Dr. No (novel) 72
Dracula (1931) 249, 254

Dracula (1979) 264-265
Dracula (novel) 251, 252, 253, 259
Dracula (play) 253-254, 263
Dracula, Prince of Darkness 261
Dracula's Daughter 254
Drake, Charles 244
Drake, Tom 155
Drango 206
Draper, Rusty 198
Dru, Joanne 224, 242
Drum Beat 190-191, 211
Dubbs, Rowdy 176
"Duel at Shiloh" (TV) 193
Duel in the Sun 191, 204, 232
Duel of the Titans 59
Duggan, Andrew 239
Dunbar, Dorothy 16
Dwan, Alan 138

Earp, Allie 131
Earp Brothers of Tombstone, The 131
Earp, James 140, 141, 142, 144, 145, 148, 173
Earp, Josephine Marcus 126, 129, 131, 132, 165, 166, 168, 169, 170, 171, 173, 175
Earp, Morgan 125, 127, 128, 132, 139, 142, 144, 145, 146, 148, 158, 161, 168, 169, 170, 172, 173, 174, 179
Earp, Virgil 125, 127, 128, 131, 132, 139, 146, 148, 158, 161, 168, 169, 170, 172, 173, 174, 179
Earp, Warren 129, 173, 174
Earp, Wyatt 9, 125-180
Eastwood, Clint 10, 208, 209, 210, 280
Eaton, Shirley 75
Edgar Rice Burroughs: Master of Adventure (book) 13
Edgar Rice Burroughs: The Man Who Created Tarzan (book) 15
Edge of Fury 230
Edward, Alan 137
Edwards, Blake 166, 241
El Dorado 208
"Elaine" (song) 221
Elam, Jack 187
Elder, John 270
Ellery Queen's Mystery Magazine (magazine) 229
Elliot, Allison 177
Elliot, Denholm 262
Elliot, Sam 170
Elliot, William 138, 216, 245

Ellis, Antony 203
Ely, Ron 50, 55
Emory, Richard 219
Endore, Guy 269, 270
Engel, Samuel G. 140
Erickson, John 150
Escape from Fort Bravo 188
Essoe, Gabe 13
Evans, Clifford 274
Evans, Joan 244
Evil Under the Sun 120
Exorcist, The 265
Eyles, Allen 13

5th Annual Festival of Fantasy, Horror and Science Fiction Films, The 277
Fabrique, Dr. 145
Fabulous Fantasy Films, The (book) 59
Far Country, The 191, 195, 229
Farmer, Philip Jose 51, 63
Farrow, John 188, 223
Fattig, Timothy 134
Feirstein, Bruce 115, 116, 117
Feldman, Charles K. 64, 81
Feller, Catherine 275
Fenton, Frank 207
Ferzetti, Gabrielle 90
Filming of the West, The (book) 130
Fimmel, Travis 57
Fine Madness, A 106
Finlay, Frank 263
First Knight 121
First Man into Space 43
Fisher, Kate 128, 149, 169, 170, 172, 176, 177
Fisher, Terence 250, 255, 257, 259, 261, 268, 274, 277, 281
Fistful of Dollars, A 208
Five Million Years to Earth 277
Flash Gordon 106
Fleming, Ian 48, 62, 66, 67, 77, 78, 81, 83, 86, 89, 94, 95, 96, 98, 100, 102, 106, 110, 112, 113, 115, 119
Flipper 70
Florey, Med 156
Fluharty, Vernon 237
Fly, The 261
Fonda, Henry 141, 152, 155, 184, 202, 206
For a Few Dollars More 208
For Your Eyes Only 102-104, 105, 106, 118
For Your Eyes Only (story) 102
Ford, Glenn 198, 202, 204

Ford, John 10, 44, 140, 141, 156, 179, 184, 185, 197, 198, 208, 231, 232
Ford, Wallace 155
Fort Apache 184
Fort Ti 225
Forty Guns 149-150
Foster, Hal 17, 51
Foster, Preston 137
Four Eyes and Six Guns (TV) 167
Four Faces West 227
Four Sided Triangle 250
Fowley, Douglas 146
Fox, James 108
Franciosa, Anthony 194
Francis Goes to the Races 188
Franco, Jess 262
Frank, Melvin 207
Frankel, Benjamin
Frankenstein 249, 250, 254
Frankenstein (novel) 250, 251
Frankenstein: The True Story (TV) 263
Franz, Arthur 230, 246
Fraser, George MacDonald 106
Frazee, Steve 229
French, Valerie 239
Freund, Karl 254
Friedhofer, Hugo 206
Frobe, Gert 75
"From a View to a Kill" (story) 108
From Alamo to El Dorado (cd) 147
From Hell to Texas 204
From Here to Eternity 227
From Russia with Love 9, 70-73, 89, 102, 123
From Russia with Love (novel) 64, 72
"From Russia with Love" (song) 72
Frontier Marshal 136, 137, 138, 139, 143
Frye, Dwight 254
Fuller, Samuel 150
Funeral in Berlin 120
Furies, The 185
Fury, David 14

Gabel, Scilla 34, 38
Gable, Clark 34, 185, 204
Gallagher, Tag 130
Gambler Returns, The Luck of the Draw, The (TV) 167
Gamley, Douglas 37
Garden of Evil 190
Gardner, Jack 134
Gardner, John 83
Gardner, Maurice 46

Garfield, Brian 130
Garmes, Lee 223, 224
Garner, Don 142
Garner, James 160, 161, 166
Garrett, Pat 150
Gates, Larry 161
Gatto, Steve 133
Gazzara, Ben 234
Geer, Will 143
Geisha Boy, The 261
George, George W. 233
Gidget 156
Gidget Meets Dracula 265
Gilbert, Lewis 84, 101
Gilded Rooster, The (novel) 195-196
Giler, Berne 34, 42, 48
Gill, Brendan 76
Gillman, Sam 163
Gish, Anabeth 177
Glen, John 104, 105, 106, 109, 110
Going, Joanna 177
Gold 121
Goldeneye 113-115
Goldfinger 9, 73-77, 79, 80, 95, 99, 118, 120, 123
"Goldfinger" (song) 76
Goldsmith, Jerry 161-162
Gomberg, Sy 242
Good, the Bad, the Ugly, The 209, 280
Gordon, Dan 175
Gordon, Leo 179, 207
Gough, Michael 259
Graves, Peter 145, 221
Gray, Charles 85, 96
Great Adventures of Wild Bill Hickock, The 217
Greatest Show on Earth, The 188
Greene, Lorne 165
Green Man, The 43
Greengage Summer, The 84
Greystoke: The Legend of Tarzan, Lord of the Apes 52-54, 56, 59
Griffith, Gordon 15
Griffith, James 144
Gruber, Frank 140, 199, 200
Guillermin, John 34, 36, 43, 48, 59, 281
Gun Belt 143, 144
Gun Crazy 233
Gun for a Coward 239-241, 244, 248
Gun Fury 223
Gun the Man Down 231-232, 245, 247
Gunfight at O.K. Corral (cd) 225

Gunfight at the O.K. Corral 9, 147-149, 157, 172, 181, 202
Gunfighter, The 185, 204
Gunfighter Ballads and Trail Songs (LP) 193
Gunmen of the Rio Grande 157
Gunsmoke: A Complete History (book) 231
Gunsmoke (TV) 147, 171, 190, 203, 231, 232, 245
Guys and Dolls 198

Hadley, Reed 219
Hall, Conrad 229
Hall, Oakley 151
Halliday Brand, The 233-234, 245 247
Hamill, Pete 164
Hamilton, Guy 74, 95, 98, 99, 120, 121
Hamlet 34, 265
Hamlisch, Marvin 101
Hammer, Will 249
Hanging Tree, The 156, 206
Hannah Lee 10, 221-225, 246, 247
"Hannah Lee" (song) 225
Hardy, Phil 156
Harline, Leigh 155, 280
Harmon, Mark 177
Hart, Dorothy 30
Hart, James V. 266
Hart, William S. 134, 135, 166, 184
Harvey, Laurence 81
Harwood, Johanna 67, 72
Hathaway, Henry 187, 190, 204, 208
Haunted Strangler, The 43
Hawaii 5-0 (TV) 121
Hawks, Howard 10, 184, 188, 208, 231
Hayes, Ron 147
Hayutin, Harvey 34, 35, 38, 40, 47, 58, 60, 279
Hayward, Susan 187
Healey, Myron 146, 231
Heaven's Gate 10
Heflin, Van 46, 188, 202
Hellcats of the Navy 239
Helldorado (book) 129, 130
Hellgate 231
Hellman, Sam 138, 140, 143
Henry, Mike 48, 49, 50, 51
Henry V 34
Henry, Will 163
Hersholt, Jean 195
Heston, Charlton 188, 190, 204
Hickey, Michael 132
High Noon 188, 210

High Sierra 135
Hill, The 121
Hinds, Anthony 250, 270
Hinds, William 249
Hitchcock, Alfred 34, 87, 227, 232, 253
Hogarth, Burne 51
Holden, William 81, 188, 206, 208
Holliday, John H. "Doc" 125, 127, 128, 130, 132, 133, 135, 137, 138, 139, 141, 143, 144,
145, 146, 147, 148, 150, 156, 157, 158, 159, 161, 164, 168, 169, 170, 171, 172, 173, 174, 176, 177, 197
Holliday, Melanie 128
Holt, Tim 220
Holtsmark, Erling 13
Hondo 188, 189, 223
Hooker, Henry 172
Hope, Bob 72, 150
Hopkins, Anthony 259, 266
Hopkins, John 78
Hopper, Dennis 149
Horn, Tom 222
Horror of Dracula 9, 10, 249, 255-261, 267, 268, 272, 277, 278, 281
Horse Soldiers, The 156, 206, 207
Hotel (TV) 121
Hound of the Baskervilles, The 268
Hour of the Gun 9, 157-162, 180, 181-182
House of Dracula 254
House of Frankenstein 254
House on Haunted Hill 156
Howard, James Newton 178
Howling, The 276
How the West Was Won 70
Hudson, John 149
Hudson, Rock 223, 244
Huggins, Roy 226
Hughes, Howard 143
Hughes, Russell 196
Hunt, Peter 66, 72, 75, 79, 88, 89, 91, 93, 94, 120, 281
Hunter, Jeffrey 202, 240, 244
Huston, John 136, 186
Huston, Virginia 30
Huston, Walter 136, 143, 144, 165

I Am Legend (book) 262
I Married Wyatt Earp (book) 131
I Married Wyatt Earp (TV) 165
I Was a Teenage Werewolf 269

Ian Fleming: The Man Behind James Bond (book) 63
Ihnat, Steve 161
Illustrated Life and Times of Wyatt Earp, The (book) 133
In Early Arizona 138
"In the Performance of Duty" (TV) 171
Inchon 120
Incredible Shrinking Man, The 243
Indian Charley 159, 176
Indian Fighter, The 202
Indiana Jones (and the Last Crusade) 113
Inspector Calls, An 74
Invaders from Mars 230
Invasion of the Body Snatchers 229
Inventing Wyatt Earp (book) 134
Ireland, John 142, 149, 219, 222, 223, 224, 244, 246
"It All Happened in Tombstone" (article) 129
It Came from Outer Space 243
It's a Hell of a Life But Not a Bad Living (book) 155

James Bond: A Celebration + An Evening with George Lazenby (convention) 280
James Bond Bedside Companion, The (book) 63
James Bond Dossier, The (book) 63
James Bond Films, The (book) 63
James Bond: The Authorized Biography of 007 (book) 63
"James Bond Theme, The" 69
James, Henry 156
James, Tim 165
Jarre, Kevin 171, 172
Jayhawkers, The 206-208, 213
Jeffries, Lionel 45
Jennie Lees Ha una Nuova Pistola 157
Jesse James 138, 184, 187, 204
Jesse James vs. the Daltons 225
Jesse James' Women 192
Jewel of the Seven Stars (book) 252
Joe Butterfly 241
John Ford: The Man and His Films (book) 130
Johnny Guitar 190, 196
Johnson, Lynn-Holly 104
Jones, Bob 37, 43
Jones, Buck 177, 220
Jones, Grace 109
Jones, Ken 43
Jones, Stan 225

Jones, Tom 79
Jory, Victor 139
Jourdan, Louis 105, 263
Joyce, Brenda 26, 29
Jubal 198
Jungle Book 223
Jungle Book (novel) 12
Jungle Tales of Tarzan (story collection) 17
Jungle Tales of Tarzan (Hogarth book) 51
Jurado, Katy 190
Jurgens, Curt 101
"Justice at the O.K. Corral" (TV) 179

Kamen, Michael 113
Kansan, The 140
Kantor, MacKinlay 221, 222, 233
Karloff, Boris 250, 251
Kasdan, Lawrence 175, 177
Kauffman, Stanley 69, 72, 76
Kazan, Elia 188, 227
Keach, Stacy 164
Keith, Brian 190, 193
Kelley, DeForest 144, 149, 155, 163
Kelley, Jim "Dog" 145, 147
Kennedy, Arthur 156
Kennedy, Burt 231, 232, 234, 235, 245
Kennedy, Douglas 221
Kennedy, John F. 64, 93
Kennedy, Robert 92
Kerr, Deborah 81
Kershner, Irvin 106
Kid for Two Farthings, A 34
Killer is Loose, The 235
Kilmer, Val 170
King and Four Queens, The 34
King, Henry 184, 185, 204, 206, 281
King Kong (1933) 31
King Kong (1976) 59, 106
King Solomon's Mines 42, 186
Kings of the Jungle (book) 14
Kinski, Klaus 262, 265
Kingston, Natalie 17
Kipling, Rudyard 12
Kismet 229
Kiss of the Vampire 277
Kit Carson 227
Kitzmiller, John
Kneale, Nigel 250
Knott, Charles 37
Kojak (TV) 121
Korda, Alexander 223
Kotto, Yaphet

Ladd, Alan 188, 190, 191
Ladengast, Walter 265
Laine, Frankie 149, 172, 193
Lair of the White Worm, The (book) 252
Lake, Caroline 131
Lake, Stuart 129, 130, 136, 138, 139, 143, 144, 145
Lambert, Christopher 52, 53, 54
Lancaster, Burt 147, 148, 190, 202, 208
Lang, Charles Jr. 235, 237
Lang, Fritz 188
Lang, Stephen 170
Lange, Arthur 221
Langella, Frank 263, 264, 265
Lara, Joe 54, 55
Larsen, Keith 145, 221
Larsen, Wolf 55
Last Frontier, The 195-198, 205, 212
"The Last Frontier" (song) 198
Last Hunt, The 198
Last Man on Earth, The 262
Last Train from Gun Hill 156, 206
Last Wagon, The 198
Laura 227
Law and Jake Wade, The 204
Law and Order (1932) 135-136, 142, 143, 180, 181
Law and Order (1940) 139
Law and Order (1953) 135, 143
Law for Tombstone 137
Lawless Street, A 235
Lawrence of Arabia 70
Lazenby, George 77, 85, 87, 90, 91, 93, 94, 97, 100, 121, 122, 280, 281
LeCarre, John 110
Lee, Bernard 68. 72, 75, 90, 99, 101, 102, 104, 105
Lee, Christopher 100, 251, 255, 259, 261, 262, 267, 268
LeFanu, Sheridan 252
"Legend of Wyatt Earp, The" (song) 147
Legrand, Michel 108
Lenya, Lotte 72
Leonard, Elmore 237
Leone, Sergio 208, 209
Lesser, Sol 19, 23, 25, 29, 30, 32, 33, 50
Lethal Weapon 112
Lethal Weapon 2 113
Levino, Albert 139
Lewis, Jerry 39, 40, 46, 219, 261
Lewis, Joseph H. 233, 235, 245
Lewton, Val 249

Library Journal (periodical) 199
License to Kill 111-113, 118, 119
License to Thrill (book) 63
Life and Legend of Wyatt Earp, The (TV) 145-147
Life of Ian Fleming, The (book) 63
Lincoln, Abraham 130
Lincoln, Elmo 14, 15, 16, 19, 25, 29
Lindfors, Viveca 195, 234
Lindley, Bert 134
Linford, Dee 192
Little Big Horn 218-219, 223, 231, 246
Little Big Man 209, 280
Little Caesar 135
Live and Let Die 97-99, 118
Live and Let Die (novel) 112
"Live and Let Die" (song) 98-99
Living Daylights, The 109-111
Living Daylights, The (story) 110
Llwewlyn, Desmond 72, 75, 90, 101, 104, 106, 109, 115, 116, 117
Lodger, The 253
Lom, Herbert 262
London, Dirk 146
London Sunday Times (newspaper) 33
London Times (newspaper) 48
Lonely Are the Brave 208
Long Haul, The 239
Longest Day, The 70
Lonsdale, Michel 192
Lord, Jack 66, 68
Lorraine, Louise 16
Los Angeles Times, The (newspaper) 41
Lost Films of the Fifties, The (book) 59
Love Me Tender 202
Lowell, Carey 113
Lubet, Steven 133
Lue, William 225
Lugosi, Bela 253, 254
Lupoff, Richard 13
Lust for Life 34
Lusty Men, The 194

Ma and Pa Kettle 188
Macabre 261
Macdonald, Ross 62
MacDowell, Andie 53
MacGinnis, Niall 34, 38, 40
MacKenzie, Joyce 31
MacMurray, Fred 223, 239, 240, 241, 245
Macnee, Patrick 109
Macready, George 30

Mad Love 270
Madison, Guy 157, 197
Madonna 117
Magnificent Ambersons, The 232
Magnificent Matador, The 235
Magnificent Obsession 34
Magnficent Seven, The 208
Mahoney, Jock 44, 47, 48, 50, 51, 59, 279
Maibaum, Richard 66, 67, 72, 75, 78, 86, 88, 89, 94, 95, 98, 99, 101, 102, 106, 108, 109, 111, 113, 121
Malone, Dorothy 155
Man Called Gannon, A 194
Man from Laramie, The 191, 195, 196, 198
Man in the Iron Mask, The 250
Man in the Vault, The 231
Man of the West 204
Man Who Could Cheat Death, The 39
Man Who Haunted Himself, The 97
Man Who Shot Liberty Valance, The 208
Man With the Golden Gun, The 99-100
Man With the Golden Gun, The (novel) 83
Man Without a Star 10, 191-194, 198, 211-212
Man Without a Star (novel) 192-193
"Man Without a Star" (song) 193
Mankiewicz, Tom 96, 98, 99
Mann, Anthony 10, 143, 185, 186, 188, 191, 195, 197, 200, 202, 204, 209, 229
Marceau, Sophie 117
Marcellino, Muzzy 202
March, Jane 55
Marciano, Rocky 223
Mark of the Vampire 270
Markey, Enid 14
Markham, Monte 161
Markham, Robert 83
Marks, A. 92
Marks, Paula Mitchell 132
Marlowe, Hugh 187
Marnie 73
Marsh, Carol 259
Marshal of Mesa City 138
Martin, Dean 81, 206, 219
Martin, Don 228
Martin, George 98, 100
Marvin, Lee 208
Mary Poppins 77
Mary Shelley's Frankenstein 266
Masden, Michael 177
Masterson, Jim 145

Masterson of Kansas 144
Masterson, William B."Bat" 127, 128, 130, 131, 135, 144, 145, 147, 148, 149, 150, 167
Mather, Berkeley 67
Matheson, Richard 262, 263
Matinee Theater (TV) 254
Mature, Victor 141, 142, 197, 198, 239
Maurey, Nicole 207
Maverick (TV) 156
Maxwell, Lois 68, 72, 75, 90, 99, 101, 102, 104, 105, 109
Mayo, Virginia 202
McCarthy, Kevin 229
McCartney, Paul 99, 100
McCowen, Alec
McDowell, Andie 52
McGann, William 139
McGowan, Dorrell 217
McGowan, Stuart 217
McGraw, Charles 220, 245
McIntire, John 199, 229, 245
McLaglen, Andrew 231, 232, 245
McLaurey, Frank 125, 126, 132, 176
McLaurey, Tom 125, 126, 168, 176
McClory, Kevin 64, 66, 77, 78, 103, 106, 108, 119, 120
McMasters, Sherm 161
McNeile, H.C. 62
McRae, Joel 144, 145, 151, 208, 227, 228, 244, 245
Meadow, Herb 228
Meagher, Mike 176
Megowan, Don 232
Melville, Sam 161
Menzies, William Cameron 230
Merrill, Frank 16, 17
Metford, George 254
Meyer, Emile 232
Michaels, Dolores 155
Middleton, Robert 202
Milestone, Lewis 227
Miller, David 208
Miller, Dennis 41, 59
Miller, Winston, 140
Millican, James 143, 144
Milner, Martin 149
Miner, Allen H. 204
Minnelli, Vincent 34
Mirror Crack'd, The 120
Misadventures of Merlin Jones, The 73
Missouri Breaks, The 209

Good Movies; Bad Timing   **291**

Mister Cory 241
Mister Roberts 198
Mitchell, Cameron 143, 165
Mitchell, Guy 225
Mitchum, Robert 164, 171, 190, 194, 208
Mix, Tom 134, 166, 184
Mohr, Gerald 150
Monroe, Matt 72
Montgomery, George 143, 144, 150, 151
Moonlighter, The 223
Moonraker 101-102, 104, 105, 118
Moore, Roger 97, 98, 99, 100, 101, 102, 104, 105, 106, 107, 108, 111, 115, 120, 121
Morgan, Harry 217
Morris, Glenn 23
"Mr. Kiss-Kiss Bang-Bang" (theme) 79
Mulock, Al 34, 38, 45
Mummy, The (1932) 249
Mummy, The (1959) 268
Murder in Tombstone: The Forgotten Trial of Wyatt Earp (book) 133
Murnau, F.W. 253, 265
Murphy, Audie 186, 241, 242, 244, 245
Murray, Don 204
"My Brother Down There" (story) 229
My Darling Clementine 9, 140-143, 149, 155, 180, 181,184, 197, 217, 223
My Outlaw Brother 221

Naked Spur, The 188, 201
Narrow Margin 220
Nebraskan, The 225
Nelson, Barry 64
Nelson, Ralph 209
Never Say Never Again 106-108, 109
"Never Say Never Again" (song) 108
New Adventures of Tarzan, The 21, 60
New Republic, The (magazine) 69, 72, 76
New Story 13
New York Times, The (newspaper) 40, 46, 69, 72, 76, 80, 91, 92, 136, 142, 156, 160
New Yorker, The (magazine) 76
Newley, Anthony 76
Newman, Alfred 206
Newman, Emil 221
Newman, Lionel 202, 206
Newman, Martin 193
Newman, Paul 81
Newsweek (magazine) 69, 76, 80, 91, 156
Nichols, Dudley 187
Nichols, Mike 276
Nicholson, Jack 276

Night Passage 200
Nina 90
Niven, David 81
No Name On the Bullet 10, 242-244, 248
"Nobody Does It Better" (song) 101
Norman, Monte 68, 69
North, Edmund 201
Northwest Passage 191
Nosferatu 353
Nosferatu the Vampire 265

O'Brian, Hugh 146, 167, 172, 178, 219
O'Brien, George 136, 138
O'Connell, Arthur 202
Octopussy 104-106, 108, 109, 118
Octopussy (story) 106
Offense, The 121
O'Hara, Catherine 177
O'Keefe, Miles 52
O.K. Corral Inquest, The (book) 133
Oldman, Gary 265
Olivier, Laurence 34, 259, 265, 266
Omega Man, The 262
On Her Majesty's Secret Service 9, 85-94, 102, 103, 104, 113, 118, 120, 121, 122, 123-124, 280, 281
On Her Majesty's Secret Service (novel) 83
Once Upon a Time in the West 209
Only the Valiant 186, 204
Open Range 210
O'Rourke, Frank 204
Osmond, Marie 166
O'Sullivan, Maureen 18, 19, 20, 21, 23, 24, 25, 29
Out of the Past 227
Outcast of the Islands 34
Outlaw, The 143
Outlaw Territory 225, 247
Outlaws is Coming, The 157
Owen, Gareth 280
Ox-Bow Incident, The 184, 227

Pacula, Joanna 170
Padilla, Manuel 48, 49, 50
Palance, Jack 188, 190, 262, 263
Pale Rider 210
Paluzzi, Luciana 79, 107
Paradise (TV) 167
Paratrooper 68
Parker, Bonnie 93
Parker, Fess 206, 207
Parsons, George 127, 132, 166

Paxton, Bill 170
Peace Marshal (novel) 140
Peck, Gregory 185, 186, 204, 206
Peckinpah, Sam 93, 208, 209
Penn, Arthur 93, 209
Perkins, Anthony 202
Perry, Frank 164, 209
Persuaders, The (TV) 120
Petracca, Joseph 201, 207
Phenix City Story, The 229
Pierce, James 16, 19, 50
Pillow Talk 42, 208
Pleasance, Donald 85
Polidori, John 252
Pollar, Gene 15
Pony Soldier 188
Porges, Irwin 15
Portrait of Jennie 232
Powder River 143, 144, 165
Power, Tyrone 184, 187
Preminger, Otto 225, 227
Presley, Elvis 202
Preston, Robert 197
"Property of a Lady, The" (story) 106
Proud Ones, The 200-202, 212
Proud Ones, The (novel) 200-201
Pryce, Jonathan 116
Pulp Jungle, The (book) 199
Pursued 184
Purvis, Neal 117, 118
Pyle, Denver 231

Quaid, Dennis 176
Quatermass and the Pit 277
Quatermass Experiment, The 250
Quayle, Anthony 34, 37, 40, 43, 279
Quiet American, The 241
Quinn, Anthony 152, 155, 203, 206
Quo Vadis 188

Rage at Dawn 200
Ramona 204
Ramrod 227
Rancho Notorious 188
Range Rider (TV) 43
Raiders of Fortune 239
Ransom 66
Ratoff, Gregory 64
Rawhide 187-188, 211
Rawhide (TV) 245, 246
Ray, Nicholas 190, 194, 195, 202
Reagan, Ronald 143

Real McCoys, The 245
Real West, The 179
Real Wyatt Earp: A Documentary Biography, The 133
Red Badge of Courage, The 186
Red River 184, 192, 223
Red Sun 120
Reed, Carol 34, 232
Reed, Donna 199, 227
Reed, Oliver 274, 276
Reed, Tom 136
Reed, Walter 221
Reeves, Keanu 265
Reeves, Richard 231
Reeves, Steve 59
Remo Williams: The Adventure Begins 120
Renoir, Jean 227
Reptile, The 277
Requiem for a Heavyweight (TV) 68
Return of Dracula, The 261
Return of Tarzan, The (novel) 15
Return of the Man from U.N.C.L.E., The 121
Return of the Texan, The 190
Revenge of Tarzan, The 15, 16, 60
Rich Man, Poor Man (TV) 122
Richards, Denise 116
Richards, Paul 221
Richter, W.D. 264
Ride Back, The 203-204, 212
Ride Back, The (radio) 203
Ride Lonesome 236
Ride the High Country 208, 244
Rigg, Diana 90
Ringo, Johnny 126, 133, 139, 148, 149, 151, 163, 164, 167, 169, 170, 171, 172, 176
Rio Bravo 156, 206, 207, 210
Rio Bravo and Other Movie and TV Theme Songs (cd) 193
Rio Grande 185
"Risico" (story) 102
Ritter, Tex 198
Robards, Jason 161
Roberts, Richard 195
Roberts, Tanya 109
Robin and Marian 121
Rock-a-Bye Baby 261
Rocketship X-M 218
Rogers, Roy 184, 216, 217
Roland, Gilbert 242
Romain, Yvonne 275
Romance of Tarzan, The 14, 15
Romero, Cesar 138

Ron (*Variety* reviewer) 40
Rosemary's Baby 265
Rossellini, Isabella 177
Rovin, Jeff
Roymer, James 252
Rubin, Steven Jay
Rule, Bert 37, 43
Rule, Janice 240
Run for Cover 194-195, 212
Running Target 229-231, 247
Russell, Kurt 170
Ryan, Robert 161, 201, 202, 208
Rydell, Mark 210
Ryder, Winona 265

Safari 66
Saint, The (TV) 97
Saint Jack 121
Saint Johnson (novel) 135, 137
Sakata, Harold 75
Salem, Pamela 108
Salmi, Albert 206
Saltzman, Harry 64, 77, 81, 83, 85, 94, 100
Samson and Delilah 186
San Diego Union, The (newspaper) 127
Sarrazin, Michael 194
Saturday Review, The (magazine)73, 91
Savalas, Telly 90, 94, 121
Saville, Philip 263
Scaife, Ted 34, 37, 43
Scheuer, Philip K. 41
Schramm, Karla 15
Schwartzman, Jack 106
Scott, Gordon 31, 32, 34, 36, 38, 40, 43, 44, 46, 47, 48, 49, 50, 51, 54, 59, 279
Scott, John 53
Scott, Randolph 138, 208, 223, 234, 235, 237, 238, 239, 244
Sea Hunt (TV) 246
Searchers, The 184, 185, 198, 202, 209, 210, 240
Searle, Kamuela 15
Segal, George 81
Selander, Lesley 220, 235, 244
Sellers, Peter 81
Selznick, David O. 191, 232
Semple, Lorenzo Jr. 106
Serling, Rod 68
Serra, Eric 115
Seven Men from Now 231, 234, 235
Seventh Cavalry 235
Seymour, Jane 99

Shadow of a Doubt 232
Shadow of the Cat 276
Shaggy Dog, The 208
Shane 185, 188, 191, 210
Shane, Sara 34, 36, 38
Shanghai Express 223
Shanssey, John 176
Sharkey-Fitzsimmons Fight 128
Shaw, Robert 72, 106
She 59
She Wore a Yellow Ribbon 184
Sheena 59
Sheffield, Johnny 24, 25, 26, 33
Shelley, Mary 250, 251, 263, 266, 270
Sher, Jack 242
Sheriff del O.K. Corral, El 157
Sherman, Harry 140
Sheybal, Vladek 72
Shootist, The 210
Shout at the Devil 121
Show Them No Mercy 187
Showdown, The 216-218, 245, 246
"Showdown at the O.K. Corral" (TV) 165
Shreck, Max 253, 265
Sieber, Al 189
Siegel, Don 210, 229
Silva, Henry 206, 207
Silva Lee A. 134
Simmons, Richard Alan 220, 226
Sims, Ray 43
Sinatra, Frank 81
Sinatra, Nancy 85
Since You Went Away 232
Slavin, George 233
Smith, John 145
Snelling, O.F. 63
Sniper, The 230
So Long at the Fair 250
Soble, Ron 163
Soldier Blue 209
Some Like It Hot 42, 208
Son of Belle Starr 192
Son of Dracula 254, 255, 264
Son of Tarzan, The 15, 16, 17, 19
Sorensen, Ricky 32
Sound and the Fury, The 9
Sound of Fury, The 219
Sound of Music, The 80
South Pacific 206, 261
Spaceways 250
"Spectre of the Gun" (TV) 162
Spence, Pete 161, 176

Spicer, Wells 127, 132, 176
Spillane, Mickey 62
Spottiswoode, Roger 116
Spy Who Loved Me, The 100-101, 105, 118
Spy Who Loved Me, The (novel) 100
St. John, Betta 45
St. John, Jill 96
Stack, Robert 221, 245
Stafford, Dan 157
Stagecoach 138, 184
Stamp, Terence 264
Stanwyck, Barbara 150, 185
Star Trek (TV) 162
Stars in My Crown 227
Steele, Karen 239
Stehl, Edgar 244
Stephens, Harvey 140
Steppat, Ilse 90
Stevens, Charles 140
Stevens, George 188, 227
Stevens, Warren 244
Stevenson, Robert Louis 268
Stewart, Alexandra 45
Stewart, James 143, 156, 185, 188, 191, 208
Stillwell, Frank 159, 174, 176
Stockwell, Dean 240
Stoker, Bram 251, 252, 253, 254, 255, 256, 259, 261, 262, 263, 264, 265, 266, 270
Stony Burke (TV) 66
Strange One, The 234
Stranger On Horseback 227-229, 245, 247
Stranger Wore a Gun, The 223
Streetfight in Tombstone, Near the O.K. Corral (book) 133
Streetfight Trilogy (books) 132
Stribling, Melissa 259
Stringer, Michael 37
Sturges, John 10, 147, 149, 157, 160, 188, 191, 198, 199, 200, 202, 204, 206, 209, 281
Sturges, Preston 227
Sullivan, Barry 150
Sundance Kid, The 150
Sunrise 253
Sunset 166-167
Sutherland, Urilla 126, 173, 174, 176, 177, 178
Sweet Ride, The 96

3 Godfathers 184
3:10 to Yuma 202
Tabler, Dempsey P. 15
Talfrey, Hira 275
Taliaferro, John 15
Tall Man Riding 235
Tall Men, The 191, 198
Tall T, The 235, 236, 237, 239
Tamahori, Lee
Tartars, The 244
Tarzan (comic book) 28, 29, 51
Tarzan (Disney) 56-57
Tarzan (newspaper comic strip) 17, 33
Tarzan (radio series) 19
Tarzan (TV, 1966) 50-51
Tarzan (TV, 1991) 55
Tarzan (TV, 2003) 57
Tarzan Alive (book) 51
Tarzan and His Mate 9, 20, 41
Tarzan and Jane 57
"Tarzan and MGM: the Rest of the Story" (article) 23
Tarzan and the Amazons 26, 27, 31
Tarzan and the Foreign Legion (novel) 50
Tarzan and the Great River 49
Tarzan and the Golden Lion 16
Tarzan and the Green Goddess 22
Tarzan and the Huntress 26-27
Tarzan and the Jewels of Opar (novel) 17
Tarzan and the Jungle Boy 49
Tarzan and the Jungle Queen 29
Tarzan and the Leopard Woman 26, 31
Tarzan and the Lost City 55, 56
Tarzan and the Lost Safari 32, 45
Tarzan and the Mermaids 27-28
Tarzan and the She-Devil 31
Tarzan and the Slave Girl 29
Tarzan and the Valley of Gold 48-49
Tarzan and Tradition: Classical Myths in Popular Society (book) 13
Tarzan Escapes 22, 23
Tarzan Finds a Son! 23, 24
Tarzan Forever (book) 15
Tarzan Goes to India 47
"Tarzan: Hollywood's Greatest Jungle Hero" (article) 20
Tarzan II 57
Tarzan in Manhattan (TV) 54
Tarzan Lord of the Jungle (TV) 51
Tarzan My Father (book) 28
Tarzan Novels of Edgar Rice Burroughs, The (book) 13
Tarzan of the Apes 14, 15, 60
Tarzan of the Apes (novel) 12, 51, 52, 56
Tarzan of the Movies (book) 13
Tarzan the Ape Man (1932) 9, 18, 35

Tarzan the Ape Man (1959) 41-42
Tarzan the Ape Man (1981) 51
Tarzan: The Epic Adventures (TV) 55
Tarzan the Fearless 19
Tarzan the Magnificent 42-47, 58, 59, 60, 279
Tarzan the Mighty 16
Tarzan the Terrible (novel) 16
Tarzan the Tiger 17
Tarzan the Untamed (novel) 24
Tarzan Triumphant (novel) 19
Tarzan Triumphs 25
Tarzan's Desert Mystery 25
Tarzan's Fight for Life 32
Tarzan's Greatest Adventure 8, 35-42, 45, 54, 58, 59, 60, 66, 279
Tarzan's Hidden Jungle 32
Tarzan's Magic Fountain 29
Tarzan's New York Adventure 24, 26
Tarzan's Peril 29
Tarzan's Revenge 23
Tarzan's Savage Fury 30
Tarzan's Secret Treasure 24
Tarzan's Three Challenges 47
Taylor, Joan 227
Taylor, Kent 139
Taylor, Robert 186, 187, 188, 198, 204
Tefertiller, Casey 133, 134, 167, 171
Ten Commandments, The 202
Tenney, John 171
Texas Rangers, The 239
That's My Boy 219
Them! 231
Thing That Couldn't Die, The 261
Thing, The 231
This Earth is Mine 244
Thompson, Howard 40
Three Hours to Kill 225-229, 235, 247
Three Stooges, The 157, 223
Thunderball 77-80, 85, 92, 103, 106, 108, 118, 120, 123 117
Thunderball (novel) 64, 67
"Thunderball" (song) 79
"Thunderball" (story) 64
Tilgham, Bill 147
Time (Magazine) 69, 80
Time for Dying, A 244
Tin Star, The 202
Tingwell, Charles 45
Tiomkin, Dimitri 149
To Hell and Back 241
Tobey, Kenneth 149
Tolan, Michael 161

Tomahawk 188
Tombstone 9, 167-172, 175, 178, 179, 180, 182, 210
Tombstone: An Iliad of the Southwest 129, 139
Tombstone Territory (TV) 150
Tombstone, the Town Too Tough to Die 139, 149
Tomorrow Never Dies 115-116
Topol 104
Toughest Gun in Tombstone, The 151
Tourneur, Jacques 227, 228, 245
Towering Inferno, The 59
Track of the Cat 190
Tracy, Spencer 190, 191
Trail of the Lonesome Pine, The 239
Tramplers, The 59
Trevor, Claire
Trosper, Guy 186
True Grit 156, 208
True Story of Jesse James, The 202, 240
Truth About Wyatt Earp, The 133
Tube (*Variety* reviewer) 46
Turner, Alford E. 133
Tusca, Jon 130
Two Faces of Dr. Jekyll, The 268

Ullery, David 13
Ullman, Daniel 144
Under Ten Flags 46, 47
Unforgiven 210, 280
Unforgiven, The 244, 245
Untamed Frontier 234
Untouchables, The (TV) 245
Uris, Leon 147
USA Today 118

Valachi Papers, The 120
Van Cleef, Lee 206
Van Dien, Casper 55
Van Eyssen, John 259
Van Fleet, Jo 149
Van Helsing 266
Van Sloane, Edward 254
Variety (trade newspaper) 10, 40, 42, 46, 47, 70, 73, 77, 80, 119, 156, 186, 187, 198, 206, 207, 261, 276
Varney the Vampire 252
Vera Cruz 190, 191
"Very Deadly Game, A" (TV) 121
Vidor, King 191, 192, 204, 281
View to a Kill, A 108-109

Villarias, Carlos
Vincent, Jan Michael 54
Virginian, The (TV) 193, 245
Viva Zapata 188
Vlad Tepes (Vlad Dracula, Prince Dracula) 252, 253, 263, 266
Von Ronkle, Alford 222
Von Sydow, Max 107
Vowell, David 165

Wade, Robert 117, 118
Wagon Train (TV) 245
Wagonmaster 185, 231
Wagner, Robert 202
Wait Until Dark 120
Walcott, Joe 223
Walken, Christopher 109
Walsh, Raoul 184, 186, 191
Wandering Star and Other Movie and TV Songs (cd) 225
Ward, Fred 167
Warhead 119
Warhead 2000 119
Warlock 9, 152-156, 180, 181, 206, 211, 280
Warlock (novel) 151-152
War Paint 219-221, 245, 246
Warren, Charles, Marquis 188, 190, 218, 219, 231, 245
Warwick, Dionne 79
Waters, Frank 131
Wayne, John 156, 167, 184, 185, 188, 198, 206, 208, 210, 215, 216, 231, 232, 234, 235
"We Have All the Time in the World" (song) 90, 281
Webb, Robert D. 202
Weiler, A.H. 91
Weinstein, Marvin 230, 231
Weintraub, Sy 33, 35, 38, 40, 41, 42, 47, 48, 50, 51, 58, 59, 279
Weissmuller, Johnny 18, 19, 20, 21, 23, 24, 25, 28, 29, 32, 33, 41, 48, 50, 56
Weissmuller, Johnny Jr. 28
Wellman, William 184, 186, 188, 190, 204, 227
Werewolf, The 269
Werewolf of London, The 268
Werewolf of Paris, The (novel) 269-270
Werker, Alfred 226
Werschkull, Gordon 31 (see Scott, Gordon)
Westbound 236
Western, The (book, Eyles) 130
Western, The (book, Hardy) 156
Westerner, The 184, 227
Western Films: A Complete Guide (book) 130
Whale, James 250, 251, 254
Where the Sidewalk Ends 227
"Which Way to the O.K. Corral?" (TV) 165
Whispering Smith 245
White Christmas 191
White, Fred 172
Whittingham, Jack 64, 66, 77, 78, 106, 119
Who Rides with Wyatt (novel) 163
Wichita 144-145
Wichita Town (TV) 151, 245
Wicked Water (novel) 221-222
Widmark, Richard 152, 155, 198, 199, 200, 204, 206
Wild and the Innocent, The 241-242, 244
Wild Bill Hickock 134
Wild Bunch, The 93, 156, 209
Wild West Days 137
Wilder, Billy 245
Wilke, Robert 221, 232
Williams, Bill 234
Williams, Jobeth 177
Williams, Roger 29
Willis, Bruce 166
Wilson, Michael G. 102, 108, 109, 111, 113, 117
Winchester '73 143, 185, 192
Windsor, Marie 217, 219
Wings of Eagles, The 232
Winningham, Mare 177
Wolf 10, 276
Wolf Man, The 249, 268, 269
Wood, Christopher 101
Wordsworth, Richard 275
World in My Corner, The 241
World is Not Enough, The 116
Wrong Man, The 34
Wyatt Earp 9, 172-178, 179, 180, 182, 210
Wyatt Earp: A Biography of the Legend – Volume One, The Cowtown Years 134
Wyatt Earp: A Biography of the Western Lawman 133
Wyatt Earp Birthplace Historic House Museum 180
Wyatt Earp, Frontier Marshal (book) 129
Wyatt Earp: Return to Tombstone (TV) 78
Wyatt Earp: The Biography (book) 134
Wyatt Earp: The Life Behind the Legend (book) 133
Wyatt Earp: The Man and the Myth (book) 131

Wyatt Earp: The Untold Story (book) 131
Wyler, William 184, 204, 227

Yancey Derringer (TV) 43
Yates, Herbert J. 216
Yellow Sky 204
Yeoh, Michelle 116
Yordan, Philip 196, 205
You Are There (TV) 144
You Only Live Twice 83-85, 88, 89, 92, 96, 101, 118
You Only Live Twice (novel) 83, 94
"You Only Live Twice" (song) 85
Young Billy Young 163-164
Young Indiana Jones and the Hollywood Follies (TV) 179
Young, Terence 68, 72, 78, 79, 120
Yulin Harris 164

Zerbe, Anthony 113

If you enjoyed this book,
call or write for a free catalog
**Midnight
Marquee Press
9721 Britinay Lane
Baltimore, MD 21234**

410-665-1198
www.midmar.com

www.ingramcontent.com/pod-product-compliance
Lightning Source LLC
Chambersburg PA
CBHW071222080526
44587CB00013BA/1463